# RUSSIAN ROOTS

## MARINA BRIERLEY

# Acknowledgements – images

| Page | |
|---|---|
| 5 | *www.shilov.unicorn.ru* |
| 9 | *Victoria and Albert Museum* |
| 10 | *I.A. Bilibin; courtesy of Aurora Art publishers (St. Petersburg)* |
| 11 | *www.logoi.com* |
| 13 | *Dimitry Moor, 1919* |
| 19 | *Museum of Political History category of allposters.com* |
| 22 | *BBC Hulton Picture library* |
| 24, 25 | *The Mansell Collection* |
| 26 | *Paul Popper Ltd.* |
| 27 | *Hulton-Deutsch Collection* |
| 33 | *Society for Cultural Relations with the USSR* |
| | |
| 41 | *David King Collection* |
| 44 (top) | *BBC Hulton Picture library* |
| 44 (bottom) | *Hulton Deutsch Collection* |
| 52 | *Paul Popper Ltd.* |
| 53 | *David King Collection* |
| 56 | *Alexander Chunosov/Network* |
| | |
| 87 | *The Mansell Collection* |
| 108 | *BBC Hulton Picture Library* |
| 110 | *John Hillelson Agency* |
| | |
| 119 | *Blinoff, http://streetsofshanghai.pbworks.com/The-White-Russians* |
| | |
| 226 | *Musee Royal de l'Armee et d'Histoire Militaire, Brussels* |

*Remaining images are mostly from private family collections.*
*Every effort has been made to contact copyright holders. The publisher apologises to anyone whose rights have been overlooked and will be happy to correct any errors or omissions.*

ISBN: 978-0-9561588-0-2

Further copies can be obtained from: www.hollybooks.co.uk
Contact: enquiries@hollybooks.co.uk (comments welcome).

# Dedications

To my father John,
with love and gratitude for the past.

To my husband Ken,
with love and joy in the present.

To our sons Daniel and Stefan,
with love and hope for the future.

In memory of Julie my mother and Nina,
two Russian born sisters whose graves
lie on opposite sides of the world.

# Introduction.

This family history was primarily written for the descendants of Russian émigrés, wherever in the world they may be. It is especially relevant for those who may bear Russian names but are only dimly aware of their unique and fascinating heritage. For them, and indeed anyone with an interest in history and humanity, I offer the stories of my parents' families - the Shliapnikoffs and the Shalavins. One an ambitious, middle class family of traders and business people, the other of proud peasant stock, solid people of the land. Other families are also featured, albeit briefly, as the fate of our families was typical of the thousands who left their beloved Russia, fleeing Communism in the 1930's across remote borders and into the Manchurian wilderness.

In describing the experiences of these families, I have drawn upon the memories of surviving relatives and friends, and the stories that their parents passed down to them. It is now 79 years since our extended family escaped the former Soviet Union, but the reasons they did so remain as an enduring legacy to the folly of taking liberty for granted.

Our forebears made a political decision when they turned their backs on their homeland. The society in which they were living, nay existing, had become so unbearable that they chose to risk death to leave it. That generation understood and valued personal freedom and how entwined it is with economic freedom - the freedom to buy and sell, for profit and mutual benefit. It is my intention to reclaim the spirit of enterprise that my great grandparents and grandparents recognised and upheld in their lives. To celebrate their achievements as worthy exemplars of a system of life based on hard work, responsibility, independence and economic liberty. That is, the freedom to succeed or to fail based entirely on merit, effort and knowledge of the market. Knowledge that they *had* to learn in order to survive, whether it be the villages of Manchuria or the streets of Shanghai.

For a short period of 20 odd years, from 1930 to about 1950 my forebears were stateless people, living as illegal migrants in an unstable country torn by civil war, crime and invasion. China at that time was no paradise for these intrepid families, but it was birthplace and home for a generation of Russians, so a brief history is included for those who wish to understand the context of our family's lives. For this reason also the first two chapters are devoted exclusively to Russian history. No prior knowledge is assumed and it is hoped the reader will seek further enlightenment from my references.

I have attempted to paint a personal portrait of at least a few of the individuals in this story who I am privileged to have as members of my immediate and extended family. But for every one of them there are many more unsung heroes, who faced similar difficulties and overcame them to enjoy free lives as successful citizens of their new communities, whether that be in Australia, America or Argentina. In N.S.W. alone there are hundreds of thousands of Russian Australians, the vast majority of whom fled the Soviet Union via China. Since I am one of their descendants, born and brought up in Australia, I shall be focusing on the experiences of Russian Australians, though our relatives are scattered far and wide throughout the world.

Our story is a compelling one that may inspire a teenage Alexandra or Nicholas to question their origins. I hope they will appreciate the terrible price the Russian people paid for their leaders' experiments with a fundamentally flawed social system and to recognise the liberating power and glory of a free society. If moreover, they have become completely integrated into their host culture, I hope they will be moved to take a fresh look at the rich cultural heritage that is their birthright. Should they grapple with the language, marvel at the music, cry with the literature and laugh at the proverbs; in short, discover their Russian souls, then my efforts will not have been in vain.

# Acknowledgements

I am indebted to many people who kindly offered their memories and experiences to make this family history possible. My dear father, who gave every encouragement, sending magazine and book extracts, news articles, numerous letters, proverbs and constant love, despite being over 13,000 miles away. We are never apart though we live in different hemispheres.

Thanks also to my aunt Olga in the USA who cheered me with her kind words and encouragement when my motivation was flagging. Her memories too, were invaluable. I am also grateful to my aunt Galina in Sydney, who handed over her own precious memoirs, full of fascinating details. To my sister Helen, who gave valuable administrative help, many photographs and recalled precious stories of family life both in China and Australia. To my aunt Vera, for her support and useful anecdotes, as too cousin Tania in California. I must also thank my relatives in St. Petersburg, dear aunt Lara and cousins Irina and Anna, who opened up their homes and hearts to me and gave me a fleeting insight into their lives.

Grateful recognition is also due to Russian friends who generously gave their assistance and memories. In Moscow, Andrei and Olga who, through their successful lives, demonstrate hope for the future of this troubled nation. In Sydney, members of the Russian Historical Association, Irene Kounitsky in particular, to whom I am indebted for interesting notes about Shanghai and Tubabao. Eugene Konashenko, who sent useful details and dear Olga Pronin, for both information and subtle advice. In England, kind friends have helped by translating parts of my book for the benefit of relatives and I must thank dear Irene Chilton, Gulshat Uyukbayeva and Allya and Anton Grizenko.

Professional historians and authors that I have borrowed from are acknowledged in my references. Any misinterpretations of their works are entirely my fault and judgements made are exclusively mine. For meticulous proofreading and kind thoughts, I must thank the congenial Trevor Windsor. Thanks also to my long suffering sons for their constructive comments.

But my greatest debt is to my aunt by birth, Nina from the former USSR, who gave over a full week in the final months of her life, as it transpired, to relate her poignant story. It could so easily have been a tragedy but her strength, optimism and joy of life sustained her through her many challenges until the very end. She recalled as many of the 75 years of her wondrous life as she could remember, including many stories about our relatives. My debt to her is beyond words.

Final thanks, the enormity of which cannot be measured, must go to my husband, who made the production of this book possible. Not only was he responsible for all the graphics and technical wizardry but he was also my sternest critic and organiser. That so much remains haphazard is due entirely to me. Thank you Ken.

# Contents

# Chapter 1

# Setting the scene,
# a brief history of Russia.

**На Бога надейся, а сам не плошай.**

*Trust in God but rely on yourself.*

# Early years (c. 900 ~ 1800) - birth of a nation.

This is the story of my forefathers' flight from tyranny and a family history that spans over one hundred years, witnessing some of the most cataclysmic events of the 20th century. The Great War, revolutions, the rise of China, World War II and the mass exodus of displaced peoples that followed it, Cold War and the threat of nuclear Armageddon were all events that profoundly shaped our family's destiny. Inextricably linked to these events is the history of one nation, Russia, known as the USSR for much of that fateful century. Its rise would drive my family from their homeland; its fall would see happy reunions and heartache. To understand this enigmatic country it is useful to go back another thousand years to its birth as a Christian country. For our ancestors in common with most Russians were deeply religious, their faith sustaining them through the trials and sufferings of their motherland's turbulent history.

The story of Russia is often considered to begin with the conversion of the lands of *Rus* to Christianity, a process which began in the ninth century. The population at that time comprised various Slavic peoples who joined with the Russes, a Scandinavian tribe similar to the Vikings. The area they controlled lay west of the Ural Mountains and centred around the great rivers that flowed from the Baltic to the Black Sea. A small area compared to the great continent which would eventually bear their name. Two branches of Christianity had developed after the decline of the Roman Empire. One based in Rome, the Catholic faith, and the other, Orthodoxy, in the ancient city of Byzantium. Later it would be renamed Constantinople to honour the Roman Emperor Constantine, who converted to Christianity in the 4th century. Today, it is known as Istanbul in Turkey.

In 855 two missionary monks, Cyril and Methodius, were sent by the Patriarch of the Orthodox Church in Byzantium to Rus to convert the 'heathen' from their pagan beliefs. They must have had some successes as Christian settlements developed around the medieval city of Kiev in the Ukraine, which at the time was the capital of the Rus state. The monk Cyril is also remembered as the person who devised one alphabet for the different Slavic languages, the Cyrillic alphabet, and translated the Bible to Slavonic. The monks' groundwork eventually bore fruit when the Russian ruler of Kiev, Vladimir I, officially adopted the Christian faith for his state in 988 AD. Legend has it that Vladimir was ready to renounce paganism under pressure from surrounding monotheistic states and sent out envoys to investigate four major faiths: Judaism, Islam,

Catholicism and Orthodoxy. Islam was briefly considered. Vladimir, a prolific womaniser, may have liked the idea of 72 women in Paradise for each man, but giving up wine was too much. *'Drinking is the joy of the Russes. We cannot exist without that pleasure'*. Nor was he impressed by the rituals of the other two religions. But the ceremony and beauty of the Orthodox services overwhelmed the envoys. *'We knew not whether we were in heaven or on earth. For on earth there is no such splendour or such beauty, and we are at a loss to describe it.'* [1] Vladimir agreed with them, Orthodoxy became the official faith and in time the Russian people too were captivated by the majestic and glorious splendour of the Byzantine services. The legacy of the rich Byzantine culture is evident in the onion-domed churches of Russia, the glorious artistry of the frescoes on their walls, the unique and ornate icons and the hauntingly beautiful sung liturgy. 1988 saw the celebration of 1,000 years of Christianity in Russia and the medieval cities of Kiev, Suzdal and Vladimir, with their stunning churches, remain centres of pilgrimage not only for the devout but for all lovers of beauty.

*Orthodox cathedral, Sergiev Posad.*

From the 13th to the 15th centuries, the Mongolian Tartars led by Batu Khan, grandson of the fearsome Genghis, invaded and took control of Russia. The invasion must have been a terrifying experience for the defenceless people as the Tartar hordes thundered in on unfamiliar horses, brutally plundering and destroying the land and its people. Those that survived were treated with great cruelty. It is believed that a favoured treatment for prisoners was to tie them to planks of wood upon which the Mongols feasted, while their tormented victims in all likelihood starved. Such experiences had a profound impact on the Russian character, leading to a deep rooted fear of invasion and a perennial suspicion of foreigners. Russia was liberated from the Tartars by Ivan The Great, who consolidated Russia's power and independence from the invaders. It was he who first took the title of *Tsar*, derived from Caesar, meaning Emperor and implying supreme worldly and spiritual power. The Russian people, particularly the peasants, would grow to revere this god-like figure that had absolute control over them.

The 16th century was known as the *time of troubles*, a chaotic period of unrest characterised by conflict and challenges to the throne, the most famous challenger being the *pretender* Tsar, Boris Godunov. It ended in 1613 with the establishment of the Romanov dynasty by its first ruler Michael. Political stability at the top levels of society was temporarily attained, but for the majority of Russian people, 90% of them landless peasants, there was no reprieve from their sufferings. They continued to lead a precarious life of backbreaking labour on the land, chained to their lords under a medieval feudal system that afforded them no rights and virtually reduced them to the status of slaves. From time to time the desperate people revolted, inspired by the Cossacks, free peasant warriors. But even a potentially successful rebellion led by Stenka Razin, immortalised in song, was crushed when he was betrayed, captured and executed. He had promised the peasants their freedom and 7-10,000 men seized land from their rich owners which they plundered and burned, but the Cossacks were too excessive, too brutal and eventually alienated even their own supporters.[2] The nightmare of poverty and oppression continued for the majority of people, only the fortunate few lucky enough to have been born into the aristocracy or landed gentry were spared.

As most Russians were peasants it is they who encapsulated the traditional image of Russia – devout, to the point of superstition, emotional in private, passive in public, accepting of their harsh lot in life and illiterate – for when was there time and money for books? '*Only God and the Tsar knows*' was a typical refrain on life's mysteries. 'Только Бог и Цар знает'. Uttered through the ages, from generation to generation, it was a saying I often heard from my grandmother's lips. Just one of many phrases born on the Russian steppes that have been exported around the world.

At the end of the 17th century, Peter took the throne and attempted to modernise Russia. He was influenced by Western ideals, gleaned from his Scottish and Swiss tutors, and forged links with England, Holland and Germany. Out of the marshes and inhospitable terrain of the Baltic Sea coast he established the new capital of St. Petersburg. This was to be a Western city, Russia's window to the West. Italian architects were employed to create a wonderful new city of canals, the *Venice* of Russia. Baroque palaces, churches, bridges and statues were erected to show the world that Russia was no longer medieval and backward looking, but a modern, industrious nation. At this stage this was very much an illusion, which Peter reinforced by ordering his noblemen to wear fashionable Western clothes and to shave off their traditional beards. He even personally cut-off the beards of several disgruntled noblemen and levied an annual beard tax on all but peasants and priests. Peter may have had a vision of the future but his methods were still those of a tyrant. Nonetheless, some reforms were beneficial. Ability rather than birth and bribery determined promotion to positions of authority. He also encouraged the growth of a merchant class, recognising that prosperity could not come without the freedom to trade. He even improved the status of women. No longer confined to separate quarters, *terems*, with their servants, as in the eastern model, they were now free to attend state functions and even wear revealing French style dresses, rather than the traditional pinafore (*sarafan*). He encouraged industry, education and reform at every level of society. But it is perhaps for the creation of an army and a navy and his significant military victories that he is best remembered. The navy in particular, having gained maritime knowledge by travelling *incognito* to England and Holland to study ship-building techniques first hand. Peter should also be remembered for his

*Peter the Great, artist's impression.*

extraordinary personal qualities, ambition, patriotism, eminent practicality, ruthlessness and unwillingness to compromise. At seven feet tall he was a giant in stature as well as vision. Did he succeed in modernising Russia? Perhaps the best that can be said is that the process was begun, but forcibly imposing reform from 'above' alienated many people, particularly his most devout Christian subjects.

One far reaching development of the 17th century was the division of the Orthodox Church. Archbishop Nikon, the Patriarch of Moscow, tried to introduce reform to bring the church more in line with Western Christianity. For example, services were to be simplified and shortened and certain rituals such as blessing oneself with the sign of the cross was altered from using two fingers to three. Traditional Russians were horrified with this enforced attempt to tamper with their beloved faith. Peter upheld the reforms and extended them further by insisting that the calendar also be changed to the Western one. He encountered determined resistance. The 'Old Believers' maintained that the calendar began with the Biblical account of creation, when Adam was tempted by Eve. The year *must* have begun in September when apples are ripe, otherwise how could the serpent have tempted Eve? '*What fruit could the serpent have found, on the bare boughs of January, to bring about the fall of man?*' [3]. But it was not a joke, from such arguments they deduced that the Tsar was the Antichrist and they were prepared to resist to the death. They fled into the forests to escape persecution, thus breaking their feudal ties. In time their courageous defiance was seen not only as opposition to church reforms but to serfdom in general, Moscow rule and enforced Westernisation. When, in the 17th century, the Tsar's police went after them, thousands, seeing suicide as the only alternative to submitting to the Antichrist, locked themselves in their churches, set them alight and died for their faith. This act of martyrdom was to inspire the faith of generations of Orthodox Christians.

The church became irrevocably split but by no means weakened because of it. The two strands of Orthodoxy continued to flourish, with 'Old Believers' refusing to succumb to Tsar or State imposed revision of their precious faith. The theological arguments may have long since been forgotten but the blood of the martyrs encouraged their descendants to remain true to their beliefs. The situation may be likened to the persecution of the Pilgrim Fathers, also in the late 17th century, which led to the settlement of America. They too only wanted to be free to practice their faith as they understood it. Incidentally, both groups shared a deeply held Puritan ethic.

After Peter the Great the next most significant monarch to emerge was Catherine, who reigned in the late 18<sup>th</sup> century. She liked to consider herself a product of the Enlightenment and the Age of Reason that saw the birth of scientific enquiry and upheld logic and rationality as the means to discover truth, rather than faith. Ideas that were taken far more seriously in the West than they were in Russia. Nonetheless, she remained a despot, a ruler who accepted no limits to her arbitrary power and therefore held the power of life and death over her subjects. However, she attempted some administrative reforms to improve agricultural conditions, which appeared liberal in spirit if not in practice. She also encouraged a brilliant Court life which had much in common with other European societies. Following French examples, as all Europe did at the time, she promoted fine art, glittering fashions, actors, dancers and even manners - the art of etiquette which French aristocracy had perfected to the most sophisticated level. German teachers also came to the Russian court and encouraged the rise of a Western, liberal movement that sought more freedom for the individual against oppressive authority. Sadly for the Russian people it was a fledgling movement that was to have little effect.

Seeds of rebellion were sown nonetheless and contributed to the steady rise of discontent with the archaic Russian government. In the 18<sup>th</sup> century it would be the Cossacks who attempted a revolution, fired by their hatred with the conditions of the military service they were obliged to perform by the State. The institution of Serfdom showed no signs of abating and the Cossack revolt was strengthened by the support of the peasantry who were promised emancipation and religious freedom, especially for the Old Believers. An army of 15,000 led by Pugachev, who claimed to be Peter III, not dead at all, seized Kazan and threatened Moscow. However, while he was an able soldier, Pugachev could not unite the varying groups of unhappy subjects and was duly betrayed by personal enemies, caught and executed. Another revolt brutally suppressed. In response to such threats Catherine became even more despotic. She despised the French revolution and refused to recognise the independence of the United States, won through a vicious war with Britain in the American War of Independence and crowned by the Declaration of Human Rights. This document asserted proudly in 1789, *'We hold these truths to be self-evident, that all men are created equal, that they are endowed by their Creator with certain unalienable Rights, that among these are Life, Liberty, and the Pursuit of Happiness.'*

Such glorious ideals resonated throughout the following century, inspiring liberal movements in Britain, America and Europe. Recognition of these fundamental rights provides the moral foundation that underpins this family saga. Note that they are life, liberty and the *pursuit* of happiness, for each individual's notion of what is required to attain happiness is very different. Every man can decide for himself.

У каждого человека своя голова на плечах.

## Towards the 20th century, modern Russia emerging.

Admiration for all things French did not save Russia from an attempted invasion by Napoleon's forces in the early 19th century. While his armies gained stupendous victories across mainland Europe, the vast steppes of Russia were to prove impossible to conquer. Napoleon's victorious forces charged optimistically and foolishly into the heartland of Russia where they did not anticipate that the harsh winter could be so cruel. The Russian peasants retreated before the plundering armies, but pursued a 'scorched earth' policy. They burned all their crops behind them so as not to leave the French any food to replenish their overstretched supply lines. Starving and frozen by the bitter Russian winters, when temperatures dropped as low as -30$^C$, the soldiers were reduced to eating their horses. Some even disembowelled them and crawled inside the still warm

carcasses in order to find shelter from the unendurable cold. Russians were jubilant over their eventual victory but the cost had been high upon the native population. Once again, invading, marauding armies had shaken the peasant to his innermost being. Now they feared the west as well as the east and their tendency to mistrust foreigners seemed to be vindicated.

*Artist's impression of Napoleon's army retreating from a burning Moscow.*

During the 19th century the Russian population continued to grow and the first attempts at industrialisation appeared towards the end of the century. However, the vast majority of the people continued to work as landless labourers, dependent upon their landlords for the privilege of working his land. Increasingly, voices from the fledgling middle classes and thoughtful gentry made themselves heard and tried to encourage the monarchy to make reforms along Western lines. They challenged the very basis of

Tsarist rule, its autocracy, strong nationalism and the support of the Orthodox Church. Instead, they wished to bring in a system that was more akin to the European liberal models. Finally, these challenges seemed to bear fruit, when Alexander II was persuaded to emancipate the serfs in 1861. This freeing of the peasants from their feudal ties was long overdue and throughout the country the landlords read out the

*Meeting of Russian peasant elders, members of the mir.*

proclamations to incredulous and joyous peasants. However, their joy was short lived. The peasants found they could not afford to buy their own farms and instead had to pay for them in annual instalments. 49 such payments were required to pay off their land, by which time most peasants were dead. In the meantime, the village councils – *mirs*, continued to make the decisions on behalf of the peasants in the village. They were no more independent and free than they had been in the past and emancipation was perceived as a cruel hoax.

Political agitation increased. Various populist movements arose which often used terror as a means of bringing down the hated autocratic rule of the Tsar and especially the nobility. Assassination was a favourite tool of the rebels and the Tsar who had supposedly freed the peasants, Alexander, was himself assassinated 20 years later. Killed by a young student with a bomb thrown at his carriage, he bled to death watched by his son and successor, Alexander and his young grandson, Nicholas, who would be the last Tsar of all Russia. Sadly, for their subjects, both the new Tsars would draw the false conclusion that liberal reforms had led to the death of their predecessor and would clamp down on any such reforms in future. Look where modernisation had led their beloved father and grandfather! Ironically, Alexander II had drawn up plans for a Parliament the day before he was blown up. The first thing his son did as the new Tsar, was to tear up the plans. Both Alexander III and Nicholas II used the secret police, the Okhrana, to ruthlessly stamp out all opposition, hunting down rebels and executing or exiling them to the wastes of Siberia.

The literature of the period reflected to some extent, the turbulent nature of the time as well as the intellectuals' despair at the slow progress of their country. It is perhaps no accident that the cultural framework for the great literary flowering of the century was laid down at this time. Alexander Pushkin, arguably Russia's greatest poet was born in the last year of the 18th century and his bold and experimental use of the language was to set the standard for future writers. Later literary greats included the satirists Gogol and Turgeniev, whose skilled characterisation criticised serfdom. Dostoevsky, brilliant at psychological profiling though inherently pessimistic, depicted a dark and malevolent view of human nature. The rather more accessible Lermontov in 'A hero of our time' wrote of the lost soul who, though a member of the privileged class, had no purpose in life and was doomed to inaction. Leo Tolstoy, the noble born novelist, gave up his wealth to live as a peasant, believing the simpler lifestyle was somehow more virtuous. Their works reflect deep traits in the Russian psyche – nationalism and mysticism, a desire for security and stability, yet riven with conflict and despair.

Love of country and depth of feeling for one's art was also evident in the great musical flowering of that period, establishing Russian composition as amongst the finest in the world. Tchaikovsky's glorious music particularly, was renowned for its brilliant orchestration, its melody as well as his nationalist sentiments. The overtly political 1812 Overture for

*Image of the Firebird, a traditional folk story.*

example, glorified the defeat over Napoleon, with the music of the Russian national anthem triumphing over the strains of the Marseillaise, the emotional finale of thundering cannon enhanced by the spectacular addition of fireworks. Rimsky-Korsakov was immortalised for his hauntingly beautiful oriental 'Scheherazade', though the lesser known 'Golden cockerel', a satire on despotic rule was banned by the Tsar's censors. His protégé, Stravinsky, composing in the 20th century, as a French and then American émigré, was best known for the 'Firebird'; a musical piece based on Russian folklore. Mussorgsky gave us

'Night on Bare Mountain' which is universally acclaimed and regularly performed as is his 'Pictures at an Exhibition'. Composing somewhat later, a self imposed exile from his native land, Rachmaninov too brought rapture to the world through his glorious compositions. Is there anything so sublime as his 'Vespers'? The world of classical music and Russian culture in general, is forever indebted to these giants of their art.

Literature and music went some way towards expressing the passionate and deeply ambivalent Russian character, but could do little to alleviate the fundamental weaknesses of the country. The Tsar who was to take Imperial Russia into the 20th century inherited a very shaky and unstable Empire in 1894, fraught with domestic and international problems. Nicholas Romanov had not wanted the throne knowing that he was ill suited to the position and reluctant to take on the responsibility. *'What is going to happen to me, to all Russia? I am not ready to be the Tsar. I never wanted to become one.'* [4] Yet a year later encouraged by his wife, he became as committed to autocracy as Catherine had been. So, at the dawn of a new century when most Western nations had long since established parliamentary rule, the leader of the most populous nation in Europe still ruled by divine right, crowned by God and answerable to no one.

Imperial Russia at the turn of the 20th century was a nation of about 125 million people, only 55 million of them 'true' Russians, descendents of the Rus tribes, the remainder were made up of numerous and very different ethnic and religious groups. The most populous were the Ukrainians (little Russians) who accounted for about 22 million, but there were also Armenians, Byelorussians, Estonians, Finns, Georgians, Germans, Iranians, Kirghiz, Latvians, Mongols, Poles, Romanians and others. Some groups had been conquered, others had been acquired by the natural movement of peoples. Many had integrated peacefully into the larger state but some, for whom the Russian language was a foreign tongue, harboured deep nationalist feelings and yearned for independence.

*The Romanov family - Tsar Nicholas, Tsarina Alexandra and their children.*

Ruling such a vast continent, where it is morning in the far east and dusk in the west, posed numerous difficulties. Much of the land was, and still is, unsuitable for farming. The *tundra* of the Arctic Circle is virtually barren but even in the *taiga*, which stretches 1,000 kilometres south of the Arctic, the land is cold and covered in pine forests. Only in the southwest is farming possible and by 1900 only 5% of Russian land was cultivated. Such was the Empire that Nicholas II inherited, a formidable challenge to the most experienced and accomplished ruler, but for the gentle and sensitive Tsar it was to prove far too daunting.

By the end of the 19th century several distinct opposition groups had emerged to challenge the Tsar's autocratic rule. The largest were the Socialist Revolutionaries, a disparate group that consisted of peaceful reformers as well as radical fighting groups who used assassination as a political tool. However, they shared the common aim to take land from the Church and nobles and give it to the mirs on behalf of the peasants. Unsurprisingly, peasants who had fallen behind on their redemption payments supported this group. Then there were the Constitutional Democrats, many of them Liberals, who wanted the Tsar to share his power with an elected Parliament along British lines. It was these Liberal groups often supported by industrialists and landowners who offered the most hope for peaceful, lasting reform. But the peasants and workers were suspicious of their motives and they could not gain the trust of the very people they were trying to help. The violence and disorder of peasant and worker unrest frightened many liberals and so regrettably a mutually beneficial relationship could not be forged.

The group that would ultimately have the greatest influence on Russia was the Social Democrat Party. Formed in 1898, the party followed the teachings of the German thinker, Karl Marx who predicted that all industrial societies would inevitably lead to a Communist state. This theory would have a cataclysmic impact not only upon Russia, but ultimately the world. Since at its peak in the 1980's half of the world's population was living under some form of Communist regime[5], it is worth examining his doctrine. The following summary of Marxism is a brief, simplified version adapted from several sources listed in my references, intended for those who are unfamiliar with the theory.

## Marxism and its impact.

Karl Marx was born in Germany in 1818 but spent most of his life in England, leading a comparatively comfortable middle class lifestyle in London where he frequented the Reading Room of the British museum.

He and his companion Engels expressed their theory of society in 'The Communist Manifesto', written in 1848. They wrote that *The history of all hitherto existing society is the history of class struggles'*. According to this view all societies passed through a series of stages, reached by successive revolutions, until the last stage of perfect Communism was reached and there would be no need for further struggle.

Very broadly outlined, the process envisaged was thus. In early societies, organisation was primitive, there were no classes, no ownership of land and everyone was equal. As societies developed, a feudal system emerged. In this system, which was characteristic of medieval Europe but by no means exclusive to it, a minority of aristocrats owned land but the vast majority of people were peasants. That is, poor farmers who toiled the land but had no title to it nor to the fruits of their labour, receiving only subsistence from their landlords. Peasants were oppressed, often abetted by religions which taught them to accept their lot in life in exchange for reward in the after life. Consequently they lived short, brutal lives of hard labour. At this point there were basically just two classes, the oppressing rich minority, who gained their position through birth and the oppressed poor majority. At this very superficial level, Marx was generally accurate. Very broadly speaking, feudalism was the dominant social system in England until about the 15th century, in Western Europe until about the 18th century, in Russia until the 19th and in China until the 20th century. Eventually, as a result of industrialisation, a third class appeared – factory owners and business people, who displaced the ruling aristocracy. This was the start of the Bourgeois revolution and this transition of power could take place relatively peacefully. 'Bourgeoisie' was a French term that Marx adopted to refer to this new ruling class of capitalists. In this next

*"Workers (proletarians) of the world unite" proclaims the banner, the slogan taken from 'The Communist manifesto' by Marx and Engels. The emblem of a hammer and plough in the red star at the centre will later be replaced by the familiar hammer and sickle. The hammer representing the worker and the sickle, the peasant.*

13

vitally important phase of his theory, the now dominant ruling class of bourgeois capitalists grew richer and richer by exploiting the working classes. Former peasants, who had moved into factory work necessary for industrialised societies, were no better off he claimed and in fact were getting poorer and poorer. Marx and Engels studying British society in the 19th century believed that the hard labour conditions of many English workers vindicated their theory. From that scenario they predicted that the conditions of the workers, whom they called the *Proletariat* – those who owned nothing but their children, would become so unbearable that eventually they would rise up and revolt in a bloody Proletarian revolution.

This revolution would herald the next stage of Marxist theory – the Dictatorship of the Proletariat. Since the former oppressors, the monarchs, nobility, church members and the bourgeoisie, would hardly give up their riches without a fight, this period would require their brutal suppression. The apparatus of the State - police, courts and civil service, now working on behalf of the proletariat, would be required to stamp out all opposition. All land, industry – factories, mines, raw materials and machinery would be taken over by the State so that everyone could share equally in the wealth produced. This sharing of wealth constituted a Socialist society in which there would be no more class differences. In such a Socialist society people would learn to work together for the good of the community as a whole and not just selfishly for themselves. As opposition also decreased then there would be no more need for a state at all as everyone would willingly share the fruits of their labour according to the general principle *'From each according to his ability, to each according to his need.'* Every nation would follow this basic succession of stages until the whole world had gone through the revolutionary process. Then the flower of an ideal Communist society would blossom and all would live in harmony – a 'brotherhood of man'. Such is the theory in a nutshell. To call it a philosophy is to undermine that noble pursuit of wisdom and knowledge.

One criticism of Marxist theory is that he offers no explanation as to *why* the feudal system would be replaced by industrial societies and the emergence of a third class, only that it does – inevitably, as part of the predetermined historical process. Thus there is no reason why it happens in some nations before others and in some, not at all. Just as Marx used the example of Britain because it was the first industrial nation, we too, can learn valuable lessons from that nation, yet draw significantly different conclusions from Marx.[6]

Whilst the workers who flocked to the English factories did, by modern, affluent, Western standards, lead harsh, regimented lives in poor conditions it must be remembered that it was still an improvement to their lives in agriculture. After all, nobody was forcing them to leave the land to work in cities, they did so of their own volition for the higher incomes offered by industry. Comparatively better food, housing and improved child mortality rates are evident in the massive population explosion of that period. Between 1801 and 1831 the population of Great Britain grew from 11 million to 16+ million.[7] By 1900 it had nearly quadrupled to 40 million. Tragically, increased social affluence spawned a group of middle class intellectuals who, not understanding the source of wealth but nonetheless living off its profits, spent their time postulating theories which would contribute to the destruction of this wealth. Marx, living in Victorian England was just such a man.

Marx and his lifelong friend Friedrich Engels developed the notion of Communism, which would have such far reaching effects in the following century. Engels' father, who owned a cotton mill in Manchester, had sent 22 year old Friedrich there to ensure he gained some worthwhile employment. No doubt the senior Engels saw there was a good profit to be made in the burgeoning cotton mills of Lancashire. Sadly, for the world at large, the son rejected his father's capitalist principles, though not his income. Moreover, it is well documented that Marx and his entire family also lived off the Engels' income for much of the 40 odd years he lived in England, having been exiled from Germany, France and Belgium for subversive activity. Ironically it was the liberal authorities of 'capitalist' Britain, admirably upholding freedom of expression, however unpalatable, that gave them refuge. Short of money, Engels was even obliged to return to Germany for a while to work for his father, but continued to send money to Marx, in £1 postal orders and £5 notes.[8]

Marx and Engels came to the conclusion that conditions in England, as a now advanced 'capitalist' economy (in *their* view, it was in fact only partially capitalist) would oppress its workers more and more until they would rise up in a proletarian revolution and seize the factories for themselves. It was not to be. The workers in England did not get poorer – they got richer. And those for whom the pace of improvement was too slow formed a Labour party to work for a Socialist society through peaceful, parliamentary means. There was little chance of a Proletarian revolution in England, despite the fears of many conservatives. Moreover, by the time of Marx's death in 1883, America was fast emerging as a capitalist society, set to overtake its mother country. After all, England had exported its ideals of liberty, which the Americans established as the foundation of their society. Here too, there was no sign of the Proletarian revolution that would inexorably follow the triumph of the bourgeois capitalist revolution. So, reality proved Marx wrong comparatively quickly but that did not stop other revolutionaries adopting Marxist theory in pursuit of their own ambitions, namely Lenin and Mao. In both of their respective countries, Russia and China, they did indeed demonstrate that the Dictatorship of the Proletariat would be truly brutal and bloodthirsty, surely beyond even the wildest imaginings of their mentor, Marx.

Finally, not one single nation that attempted to implement Marxist theory during what became known as 'the people's century' ever emerged from the tyrannical dictatorship stage, to progress to the Communist 'nirvana'.

## Russian Bolshevism.

The theories of Marx were translated into Russian by George Plekhanov, founder of the Russian Social Democratic Labour Party in 1898, who came to be known as 'the father of Russian Marxism'. In keeping with Marxist doctrine, Plekhanov and his followers believed that the rapid industrialisation of the late 19th century in Russia would produce a huge, angry proletariat that would eventually revolt and destroy the oppressing bourgeois class, ushering in an egalitarian socialist society. Interestingly enough, Marx himself had not believed that it would be possible in a nation such as Russia, since the majority of the population was still engaged in agriculture and the capitalists as a class were still comparatively small. Nonetheless, the members of the RSDLP adopted his teachings and proceeded to discuss how best to revolutionise the nation. It soon became apparent that its members had differing views on how the ideal communist state would come about and in a crucial meeting of the party in 1903, held in London to avoid the Tsar's secret police, the RSDLP split into two factions. The group with the largest following amongst these delegates became known as the Bolsheviks (Bolshoi meaning large) and the other faction became the Mensheviks, or the 'smaller' party. In a wonderful example of Victorian 'spin' both names were in fact misnomers given that the Menshevik party represented a much larger core of followers amongst Russian revolutionaries in general. So, how did their views differ?

The Mensheviks, led by Julius Martov, believed that it was necessary to wait until the proletariat, the industrial working classes, became large enough and oppressed enough to spontaneously rise up against their oppressors. After all, Marx had predicted that this would happen automatically when the conditions were ripe. In the meantime they need do nothing more than simply attract as many members as possible and co-operate with other political parties, the Socialist Revolutionaries and even the Liberals, to bring about the conditions that would make a mass uprising feasible. After all, a bourgeois revolution had to take place first and since most Russians were still leading essentially feudal lives the capitalist class was still in its infancy. Strictly speaking, the Mensheviks were more consistent with actual Marxist doctrine.

The Bolsheviks were led by Vladimir Ilich Ulanov, better known as Lenin, the name he took when hiding from the secret police. Lenin believed that the party should consist of a small number of committed activists, who would lead the revolution on behalf of the proletariat. A mass following was both unnecessary and indeed counterproductive, as they would spend valuable time arguing amongst themselves. Thus there would be no co-operation with other parties, even the Mensheviks, and the Bolsheviks alone would act as the 'vanguard of the revolution'. As this much smaller number of revolutionaries would take the initiative and seize control, for the benefit of the oppressed so he said, there would be no need to wait for a bourgeois revolution to take place first. Again and again, Lenin would prove adept at modifying Marxist theory to suit the circumstances of the time. A supreme pragmatist, he was a master at taking opportunities, never allowing mere ideology to influence his decisions.

*A Bolshevik poster showing Lenin 'sweeping away' the old bourgeoisie, the capitalists, nobility and churchmen.*

## The country in turmoil.

At the dawn of the 20th century Russian cities had seen massive economic changes. Moscow and St. Petersburg in particular, had undergone huge growth as rapid recent industrialisation had seen the growth of factories and the transfer of hundreds of thousands of peasants from the villages to the cities. Since 1880 the population of St. Petersburg alone had increased from just under a million to almost a million and a half in the relatively short space of 20 years. Much of this population increase consisted of single young men who were housed in crowded dormitories with poor living conditions. Low pay and long hours, 14 or more hours a day were common place. Nevertheless, it must have offered some improvement to a harsh life on the farms, for there was no shortage of willing peasants seeking such work. Ironically, housing labourers together had the unexpected result of creating a climate of increased industrial action because the labourers were in a position to easily arrange strikes. However, the government, which had a vested interest in fast industrialisation, reacted brutally to such militant action. Striking was considered illegal and the army, often the dreaded Cossacks, were called out to put down any such action with cruel ferocity. Riflemen or mounted cavalry with swords attacked and mowed down demonstrators with sickening regularity. In 1902 there were 365 such attacks by the army in one year alone.[9] The government often *was* the employer as the state promoted industrialisation in response to the growing threat from Germany, and many industries were either wholly or partly state owned. Those that were not, were given special concessions by the government, which removed any incentive by those private employers to improve the conditions of their workforce. Little wonder then that some workers drew the conclusion, as did the Communists that both the authorities and all factory owners were united in their aim of keeping the workers oppressed.

Yet a fledgling private sector *was* developing, from smaller factory owners, shopkeepers, craftsmen and the professional classes who did not seek revolution but hoped for peaceful reform and a decrease in autocratic power by the Tsar. Such people aimed to introduce a Parliament, representative of the people, with whom the Tsar could share his power. One such merchant describes his father's life, *'We had no servant at home, nor did we eat from gold or silver dishes. The meal was substantial but we rarely had wine. My father did buy pictures and our house contained a number of good examples of work by Russian artists.'* [10] It would be very interesting to determine the prevalence of such petit bourgeois capitalists (as Marxists often disparagingly call them) and whether this group would have flourished into a healthy middle class had circumstances not intervened.

Russian industry was clearly flourishing in the late 19th century, through private enterprise as well as under the State's direction. Foreign investment was growing as European and even American firms forged trading links with Russia for their mutual benefit. 'Singer' sewing machines, the famous US company, were doing a roaring trade as were many others, making Russia one of the world's fastest growing economies before World War I. As in England a century earlier, cotton from the Southern American plantations fuelled the textile industry. Other factories churned out steel, cement and a variety of other products. Here also, as in England, were to be found genuine philanthropists. Kindly employers dedicated to the welfare of their workers. One such multi-millionaire was Yuri Maltsev, who had built up one of the largest industrial concerns in Russia, with several factories near Moscow, employing 20,000 workers. But Maltsev also built hospitals for his employees, schools for their children and even a church.[11] It was this man who was the prime benefactor of the Museum of Fine Arts in Moscow, inaugurated in 1912 by the Tsar, now the Pushkin Museum. Indeed, it was common practice for industrialists in Moscow to use some of their profits to fund the construction of churches.

*Singer advertising its sewing machines in Russia, in the 19th century.*
*Moscow even boasted a Singer manufacturing plant.*

At the dawn of the new century, conditions were undoubtedly harsh for the vast majority of Russia's workers and peasants, yet there were positive signs of growth and economic development. But in 1904-05 a series of unfortunate events were to take place with far reaching consequences. Firstly, a war between Japan and Russia over disputed territory in Korea and Manchuria. The Tsar himself welcomed a war as he hoped that an easy victory would increase his popularity and deflect attention away from domestic problems. It was not to be. Having underestimated the Eastern fleet, the Russian navy suffered a devastating and humiliating defeat. Far from improving the Tsar's situation the war exacerbated it. Food supplies to the cities dwindled and the diversion of raw materials to support the war effort led to the closure of factories, severely impacting the economy. Workers increasingly found themselves on the streets, jobless, hungry and angry.

Set against this tense climate 200,000 workers marched to the Tsar's Winter Palace in St. Petersburg in January, 1905 to petition the Emperor to make peace with Japan, improve working conditions and implement other reforms. It was intended to be a peaceful protest, led by priests carrying holy banners, and attended by families with women and children, many carrying portraits of the Tsar. He was still revered as their 'Little Father' and faith in his personal ability, if not holiness, was prevalent throughout the nation. The people proceeded with their march only to be met by mounted and armed troops, including the dreaded Cossacks. The result was a horrific bloodbath, troops indiscriminately fired on and hacked their way through the crowd. Old men, clutching their portraits of the Tsar, exclaimed with their last words, *'I may die, but*

*Soldiers firing on demonstrators in what came to be known as 'Bloody Sunday'.*

*I will see the Tsar'*. Estimates of the number of people killed vary from 500 to a thousand with many thousands more being injured. 'Bloody Sunday' as the massacre came to be called was to prove to be the beginning of a nation-wide revolution, though at this stage it did not directly threaten the monarchy.

As news of the tragedy spread, rioting and strikes broke out across the country. The Tsar's uncle, the Grand Duke Serge, was killed by a terrorist's bomb and in June, the crew of the battleship Potemkin mutinied, throwing their officers overboard and seizing control of the ship. Peasants in the countryside set fire to farms, butchered their landlords and destroyed their estates, cattle and crops. In October a General Strike began, closing down shops, offices, hospitals, factories, schools and even the Imperial Ballet. In the cities, a new form of unofficial authority emerged to create order from the chaos. These were the soviets – local councils, whose representatives or deputies were elected by the workers of the cities. Since their members came from the ranks of the workers themselves, the instructions issued by the soviets were obeyed when the formal authorities were not. The leader of the St. Petersburg Soviet was a charismatic speaker named Leon Davidovich Bronstein, better known as Trotsky. The Soviet took control of the strike, issuing instructions and even published its own newspaper, *Izvestia*. Mensheviks, the populist branch of Russian Marxists, encouraged the formation of soviets, though the general protests were spontaneous and not initiated by any particular party.

In view of the increased unrest, the Tsar was eventually forced to give way to the demands for a representative government. In October he issued the October Manifesto, which led to the formation of an elected Parliament or *Duma* as it is known, to help the Tsar run the country. It also gave the Russian people basic rights, such as free speech and the right to form political parties. Things appeared to be looking up.

In March 1906 elections for the Duma were held and a majority of anti-government candidates gained office, but less than two months later the Tsar issued his Fundamental Laws. They stated amongst other things, that *'To the Emperor of all the Russias, belongs supreme autocratic power'*. He could still dismiss the Duma whenever he wished, appoint and dismiss ministers and govern without consulting the Duma. With or without a Parliament, Russia was still far from being a democratic nation. However, the Tsar's position had been threatened and his special relationship with his subjects had been called into question. He may have survived this threat but long term survival of the monarchy would depend upon increased prosperity of the nation. In 1906 The Tsar appointed a new Prime Minister, Peter Stolypin, who took it upon himself to quash any potential revolts in the short term whilst implementing longer term reforms with the aim of making revolution appear less necessary and attractive. To this end he started by arresting thousands of terrorists, 21,000 of whom were exiled to Siberia and 1,008 executed by hanging.[12] The gallows came to be known as 'Stolypin's necktie'. Through sheer brute force, Stolypin succeeded in destroying the potential rebels. Amongst the executed was a young man whose early death was to make a huge impact on his 17 year old embittered brother Vladimir Ulanov, later to become known as Lenin.

Despite his use of draconian methods, Stolypin was shrewd enough to realise that brute force could not be used indefinitely and that far reaching agrarian reforms would be necessary to make Russia both peaceful and ultimately prosperous. Soon after becoming Prime Minister, Stolypin introduced measures, scrapping laws that had tied the peasants to the mir, the village councils that determined how much land each peasant family had and the crops they could grow. He hoped that hardworking,

*The 'sober and the strong', wealthier peasants and merchants.*

industrious peasants would buy up their neighbours' scattered strips of land to develop large, efficient farms. Surplus food would be sold to the cities for profit. Since they now had an incentive and the means to improve their farms, peasants could buy new machinery and introduce more productive methods of farming and varieties of crops. Stolypin pinned his hopes on the *sober and the strong,* who would grow prosperous from their farms and use their new found wealth to buy consumer goods which, in turn, would stimulate industrial production. Thus, the peasantry themselves would have a vested interest in their own land and its peaceful governance. The reforms worked and millions of peasants bought their own land and developed large efficient farms, becoming 'kulaks' in the process.

Never a flattering term, *kulak* means 'fist' in Russian and originally it referred to the village moneylenders, who, by dint of hard work had managed to accumulate a little capital. Now the term was extended to include all successful, productive farmers. By 1914, a quarter of all peasants had left the mir[13] and many were beginning to become prosperous as Stolypin had envisaged. Stolypin believed that it would take about 20 years for his reforms to come to fruition but barely five years into his programme he was assassinated, shot by a revolutionary whilst attending the Opera in 1911, in full view of the Tsar. Subsequent ministers did not have the same far reaching visions as Stolypin and reforms slowed. Nonetheless, in the years leading up to World War I a significant independent peasantry was clearly emerging.

## The Romanovs' personal tragedy.

Amid the turbulence and political instability that beset the beleaguered Tsar there arose an unexpected and sinister threat that was to destroy the credibility of his regime and strike at the innermost sanctum of his family.

Nicholas and Alexandra had been happily wed for many years and were totally devoted to each other; indeed their marriage was one of the most successful royal alliances of Queen Victoria's grandchildren. They were both related to the British monarchy, Nicholas through his mother, Dagmar, who was the sister of Edward's VIII's wife Alexandra, mother of George V, then King of England. Dagmar, a Danish princess was given the name Maria Fedorovna upon her marriage to the Tsar, Alexander III, according to Russian custom. Alexandra Romanova was the daughter of Princess Alice, the third of Victoria's nine children. Nicholas and Alexandra had four beautiful daughters and at last in 1904, Alexei, the long awaited heir to the Romanov dynasty was born. To their utter dismay, it was soon discovered that the boy suffered from the rare and incurable disease haemophilia, the 'curse of England' as it was known, carried through the female line of the British royal family. Alexei bled profusely at the slightest injury as a haemophiliac's blood does not clot. Little was known about the condition at the time and certainly there was no means of controlling it. To prevent the Romanov family appearing weak this terrifying affliction was kept secret from the Russian public and the poor child suffered agonisingly in private. Until, that was, Rasputin appeared.

If any one person could be held responsible for the downfall of the monarchy then Rasputin would be the main contender. A Siberian peasant, Gregory Efimovich had acquired a name for unsavoury behaviour. He was meant to be a holy man, a *starets*, a monk with healing powers, but he was also renowned for drinking and womanising and was even reputed to have raped a nun. Perhaps such actions were part of his belief that you could only communicate with God through sex, a view shared by others of the same religious sect. Many stories about him are likely to have been exaggerated and to give him his due, both his daughter, who later wrote his biography, and his long-suffering wife stood by him. Nonetheless, when he arrived in the city of St. Petersburg he exhibited a debauched style of living that disgusted its stalwart citizens; but there was no denying that he seemed to exert a peculiar influence amongst the fashionable ladies of the Imperial court. Perhaps he did indeed exert hypnotic powers with those piercing blue eyes or maybe his outrageous antics and uncouth manners offered a welcome contrast to dull, conventional court life. Certainly, many Russians traditionally revered holy men and the aristocracy were no exception.

Rasputin was soon brought to the attention of the Tsarina by two ladies of her retinue. Under normal circumstances the strait laced Tsarina

*Alexei being carried by a Cossack officer.*

would never have allowed such a man under her roof, but these were extraordinary times and they lived in constant fear that their dearly beloved son might be snatched away at any time. The slightest fall or scratch could provoke uncontrolled bleeding or, worse, internal bleeding that could prove fatal. Alexei was always fussed over and normal boyish games and activities, which the child undoubtedly craved, must have been a torment for his worried family. Even at age nine, photos show him carried as a babe in the burly arms of a huge Cossack soldier.

Deeply religious, both the Tsar and particularly the Tsarina, prayed every night for the safety of their only son. Their worse fears were confirmed one day, when a bout of continuous bleeding left Alexei exhausted and near death. In their desperation, they called upon the faith healer, Rasputin. He sat quietly praying by Alexei's bedside and in the morning it appeared as though the child had been miraculously cured. One possible explanation is that Rasputin had hypnotic qualities which could slow Alexei's blood flow. Whatever the reason, Nicholas and Alexandra were overjoyed and from that moment the 'mad monk' could do no wrong. Reports of his disreputable behaviour fell on deaf ears as the Tsar and Tsarina refused to listen so long as their son continued to be 'healed'. Outside the royal palace, Rasputin lived the life of a decadent rake, frequenting prostitutes, participating in orgies and, it was rumoured, seducing the respectable ladies of the court. Some people even accused the Tsarina of having an affair with him, though this was most unlikely because love letters between Nicholas and Alexandra, in their common language English, clearly reveal them to have been a devoted and loving couple.

The damage to the reputation of the royal family reached its peak after the death of Stolypin, who had refused to tolerate the wild-eyed monk at the Imperial court. Unchecked, Rasputin's influence over the royals steadily increased. He began to give political advice, particularly over the appointment of government ministers and the granting of government contracts to businessmen. Those who were friendly with Rasputin appeared to be treated much more favourably than those who were not.

Naturally, such corrupt favouritism did not go unnoticed by the public and the Romanov dynasty was plunged into further danger. There was talk of war in the air and anti-German feeling was beginning to run high. It was well known that Alexandra was originally German, born Alix, the daughter of Grand Duke Louis IV of Hesse and the Rhine. She had barely been tolerated from the beginning and what appeared to be her aloof and distant manner did not endear her to the Russians by whom she was increasingly hated, even accused of being a German spy. So unlike her mother-in-law, who whilst also foreign, had quickly adopted

*Rasputin, the 'mad monk' who contributed to the fall of the Romanovs.*

Russian ways and through her charm and warmth had won over the people. But Alexandra's influence on the Tsar, who many people still revered, was suspect and the fiasco with Rasputin was attributed to this evil, foreign queen. It was conveniently forgotten that she was also half English, through her mother, Princess Alice and that England was allied to Russia in the event of war.

In the final years before the outbreak of war in 1914, Russia lurched from crisis to crisis. There was an economic depression and deep unrest among the people, particularly in industry where the number of strikes rocketed. In 1913 the country celebrated the 300th anniversary of the founding of the Romanov dynasty but for the majority of the people there was little to celebrate. An enormous procession was staged displaying all the pomp and ceremony, for which the ruling family was renowned. Nicholas and Alexandra, dressed in imperial splendour, presented themselves to their subjects amidst all the glory that massed military might and the Orthodox Church could muster. The glittering spectacle was undoubtedly impressive and served to reinforce nationalist sentiment at this critical period in Russia's history.

Despite the tension and unrest in the country there was little hope among the revolutionary parties that they would achieve success at this time. Both the Bolsheviks and Mensheviks had put up candidates for the Duma elections in the hope of causing trouble for the Tsar and gaining publicity but the restrictive voting laws prevented them from being elected. Moreover, their appeal was limited to the industrial workers and it is doubtful that they would have gained an appreciable number of seats, as later events would confirm. Both Marxist parties remained disunited. Lenin despised the Mensheviks' efforts to gain mass support through democratic means and condemned them as being too soft. Martov, the leader of the Mensheviks, for his part, condemned the dictatorial methods of Lenin and his supporters and also for the unscrupulous means they had of obtaining funds. Incapable of earning money honestly and totally oblivious to morality the Bolsheviks resorted to bank robbery to fund their activities. Joseph Vissarionovich Djugashvili was a young Georgian communist only too keen to further the revolutionary cause through violence and theft. He helped coordinate these bank robberies and thus came to the attention of Lenin, under whom he would later reach the highest positions in the Bolshevik party. The world would come to know him as Stalin, the 'Man of Steel'.

*Stalin, in the pre-war years, as a bank robber for the Bolsheviks.*

## Impact of World War I.

The international situation continued to deteriorate. By 1907 Russia had joined France and England in a defensive alliance, which Germany would claim, had put a 'ring of steel' around them. Germany's close friendship with the ailing Austro-Hungarian empire had concerned Russia who had clear strategic interests in the lands known as the Balkans, through which she could gain access to the Mediterranean via the Black Sea. Moreover, Russia was the traditional supporter of the other Slav peoples of the area, sharing cultural and religious ties, particularly with Serbia whose independence from the former Turkish empire Russia had encouraged.

By 1914 the European nations had formed themselves into two huge power blocs or alliances, ostensibly for defensive reasons but thoroughly menacing all the same. When the heir to the Austro-Hungarian Empire was assassinated by a young Serb in the Bosnian city of Sarajevo in June, it proved to be the spark to set alight a great conflagration. At last Austria had the excuse it was seeking to crush the thorn Serbia once and for all.

But they were wary, knowing that Russia could and would not ignore this threat to its Balkan ambitions. Austria could not take on the Russian 'steamroller' without help. Would Germany come to their aid if necessary they enquired? Eager to show the world that Germany was now a force to be reckoned with Kaiser Wilhelm's response was an emphatic 'yes'. But even he did not envisage or arguably, desire a general war and warned his cousin 'Nicky' not to get involved. But already events were spiraling out of control of the three related monarchs, the British King being equally powerless. Nicholas considered the situation – would he ever have any influence in the strategic Black Sea area if he allowed Serbia to be engulfed by Austria? Surely they could not betray their fellow Slavs? Military strategy in this new industrial age demanded preparations well in advance of their use and if there was to be a war then the great armies would have to be ready. Nicholas issued the fateful command to mobilise in the last days of July and the steamroller of millions of soldiers swung into action, far sooner than the German strategists had expected. Germany declared war on Russia on the 1st of August and from that moment the die was cast for the future of the Russian people and their monarch. Thus were the great nations of Europe drawn one by one by their allies, into a cycle of destruction that would prove to be the greatest bloodbath the world had ever seen.

*The British and Russian royal families holidaying on the Isle of Wight. Edward VII is in the centre, on the left is his son, the future George V, who bears an uncanny resemblance to his cousin Nicolas, on the right.*

The flagging support for the Tsar was now forgotten by most people as they revelled in patriotic outbursts for the Motherland and the soldiers were keen to be blessed by the Tsar before they departed for battle. Even those who had to go without rifles or boots, clad only in their traditional fur shoes, appeared to hold no grudge. Anti-German feeling spread quickly and the capital city was renamed Petrograd, 'Peter's city', from the Russian word for city – *gorod* rather than the Germanic name 'Burgh'. Peter the Great who had built St. Petersburg had admired all things German, but his legacy was now roundly rejected.

The euphoria was short-lived. By Christmas, far from rejoicing in an easy victory the Russian armies had been massacred by the Germans. In just 5 months they had lost over a million men, taken prisoner, injured or killed. By 1915 the war was beginning to impact on the economy. If conditions were tough before the war they were now getting desperate. The 15 million military recruits deprived the factories of their labour and the farms of their workers. Before long, factories started to close and weeds grew on the fields. Russia's train system had been commandeered to transport the soldiers so it could no longer be used to transport vital food from the countryside to the towns and it was left to rot by the railway sidings. In 1913 there had been 22,000 wagons of grain reaching Moscow, by 1917 there were only 700. [14] Coal also could not be moved to the centres of industry, resulting in even more factory closures. Yet the population of both the major cities continued to grow as people fled to them ahead of the advancing Germans. As the swelling population of the cities competed for the ever decreasing food supply so inflation soared by 400% between 1914 and 1917. What little money was available could no longer pay for the meagre food remaining. On the war front, defeat followed defeat. By the end of the second year over three million men were dead, wounded or prisoners of war. Demoralised soldiers, tired of fighting futile battles were beginning to desert, often killing their officers in disgust and out of desperation. Not surprising when men were sent into battle without rifles and ordered to take weapons from the corpses around them.

The following month Nicholas decided to take personal command of the armed forces. No doubt he felt a leader's responsibility for the carnage his men endured and his motives were noble but it was a poor decision. He would now be personally blamed for the military defeats and, as he was now based in army headquarters, he was no longer in touch with developments in the capital where conditions had deteriorated even further. Alexandra was left in charge of the government and she in turn was increasingly dependent upon the charlatan, Rasputin. Together, they appointed and dismissed ministers according to how well they treated the egocentric monk. As a result, over the next 16 months, there were four different Prime Ministers, five Ministers of the Interior, four Agriculture ministers, three War ministers and two Ministers of Foreign Affairs.[15] It was said that Russia was ruled by a succession of donkeys and the Imperial court was justifiably mocked in European circles.

In desperation, a group of loyal nobles assassinated Rasputin, though not without some difficulty as he proved notoriously difficult to kill. However, huge amounts of poison, bullet wounds and finally being thrown into the frozen river eventually did the trick, though it was rumoured that when his body was found there was ice under his fingernails… He was undoubtedly a man of extraordinary constitution, though Russian mystics liked to believe in his supernatural powers. The nobleman Yusupov, who murdered him suggested this also in his memoirs, though it could be argued that he needed to demonise the monk in order to justify his murder. Yusupov, an effete and stupendously wealthy aristocrat, was known to have enjoyed dressing in women's clothes and some said,[16] he had once been rejected by Rasputin, who felt only disgust for homosexuals.

*Yusupov preparing to murder Rasputin (artistic impression).*

However, Rasputin's death could not save Russia. It was far too late. Starving, striking, desperate people were only momentarily elated by the news of the monk's death. The winter of 1916/17 saw temperatures plummet to -35$^C$, causing the boilers of vital railway engines to freeze and burst. With supplies of food and fuel dwindling Russia had reached rock bottom.

## The first Russian revolution.

By the end of February a quarter of a million workers were on strike in Petrograd. Angry and hungry labourers roamed the streets, holding meetings and trying to engage in processions but were persistently dispelled by the authorities. Eventually even loyal Cossacks refused to obey orders and they too, joined in the demonstrations against the Tsar. By this stage the Duma had long recognised the futility of the Tsar's position and pressed him to form a new government. An urgent telegram was despatched to inform him of the desperate straits of the city and to ask him to appoint a Prime Minister whom the people could trust. The reply? He dismissed the Duma. Further mutinies amongst the army regiments took place as soldiers shot their commanding officers. One unit after another sent to restore order defected to the rebels. Parliament saw no other option and so on the 27th of February (or 12 March according to the Gregorian calendar)[17] the Duma, the Russian Parliament, set up a 12 man Provisional Committee to take over the government.

On the same day, revolutionaries who also aimed to take over government functions established a soviet in Petrograd as had been done previously in 1905. This time the council consisted of former soldiers as well as workers. Events continued to move quickly. The next day Nicholas sent a telegram to the Duma stating that he *would* share power with them but the gesture was futile. President Rodzianko admitted it was too late and sure enough the following day army generals informed Nicholas they would no longer support him. The Tsar desperately tried to return to Petrograd from his army headquarters 300 miles away but the railway lines to the capital were blocked and he was forced to divert to Pskov, where revolutionaries stopped his train and demanded he abdicate. Realising that there was no way he could restore order without the support of the military Nicholas was forced to agree to their demands. On the 2nd of March, 1917 the supreme Emperor, Tsar of all the Russias voluntarily relinquished his throne. The country was now a Republic. Arguably this had not been the aim of the Progressives in the Duma. They had hoped for a constitutional monarchy with the Tsar sharing power with an elected assembly. Nicholas' insistence on sticking to the principle of autocracy, a view encouraged by his stubborn and blinkered wife, ultimately cost him very dearly indeed.

Thus did the first revolution of 1917 take place in February. There had been comparatively little bloodshed in the Tsar's overthrow, rather it could best be described as the collapse of a regime no one was prepared to defend. These events had been a spontaneous uprising from the desperate people, tired of food shortages, military defeats and crippling inflation. The monarchy had also alienated the growing numbers of middle classes and professional peoples who wanted a say in the running of their country. Crucially, the Army no longer wished to save the regime and so Nicholas found himself in a railway station signing the bill of abdication. This was not the revolution that would bring Communists to power, that would take place several months later.

Though there were many Social Revolutionaries and Mensheviks in the Petrograd Soviet and even a few in the Provisional Committee that took charge of the country, the leading Marxists were absent. Martov and Trotsky were abroad and Lenin was living in exile in Switzerland. All of them had been surprised by the sudden turn of events and the unexpected fall of the Tsar. Only a few weeks earlier, Lenin had gloomily told an audience of Swiss workers, that he doubted that *'he would live to see the coming Revolution.'*[18] The new Provisional Government, so called because it was only to run the country until proper elections could be held, was initially led by Prince Lvov, a Constitutional Democrat, whose Liberal party had previously dominated the Duma. Alexander Kerensky became the Minister of Justice. He was the leader of the Social Revolutionaries, whose agenda had always been land reform on behalf of the peasantry. Whilst they had committed many political assassinations in the past, their leader at this time was essentially a moderate man, and incidentally, son of Lenin's former school headmaster.

*The Winter Palace that was taken over by the Provisional Government.*

The Provisional Government's rule was challenged immediately by the alternative structure commanding the support of ordinary men, drawn as it was from their ranks. This was the 'Petrograd Soviet of Workers' and Soldiers' Deputies', a body which was quickly emulated by other soviets all over the country. Interestingly, both groups met in the Tauride Palace, in fact across the corridor from each other, and Kerensky took a leading role in both governments. For the moment these two groups were willing to co-operate with each other, though it quickly became apparent that the 2500 strong Soviet would have far more power. Its first action was to issue Order No. 1, which took control of all arms and equipment and abolished military titles. Since the soviets' orders were obeyed throughout the army and navy, their strength was confirmed. Removing officers' titles further undermined military discipline in an already demoralised army that was seeking only to end the bloody war with Germany.

Meanwhile Lenin, having overcome his initial shock at the turn of events, was keen to return to Russia from exile in Switzerland to lead a second proletarian revolution. Many Bolsheviks considered that the fall of the Tsar was only the first stage of the Marxist 'railway of history' because he was essentially replaced by a bourgeois government. It was time, in Lenin's view, for the workers to seize control but they would have to be led by a revolutionary forceful enough to take command on their behalf, namely himself. The problem was that he was 1,200 miles away and the land in between was held by Russia's enemies Germany and Austria. The Germans were quick to see the military advantage to be gained if Lenin were to stir up trouble for the Provisional Government, hopefully leading to Russia's withdrawal from the war. So they eagerly assisted Lenin to return to his country, like a *'bacillus to spread the plague of Bolshevism'*. They supplied him with a special armoured, sealed train and funds to help his cause. He returned via Sweden and Finland to a rapturous welcome by fellow Marxists at Finland railway station in Petrograd on the evening of April 16th, 1917, where he surprised them all by declaring that the Proletarian revolution should begin and they should work to overthrow the Provisional Government.

Despite considerable achievements in domestic reforms, including the introduction of universal suffrage and religious freedom, the Provisional Government had not addressed the most pressing concerns of the suffering Russian people. That is, the need for food, an end to the war and land distribution. Lenin was quick to capitalise on these desires and promoted his message of 'Peace, bread and land' both frequently and convincingly. He succeeded in recruiting many members of the soviets to the Bolshevik cause and by the summer of 1917 there were 240,000 members of the party, 91,000 in Moscow and Petrograd alone.[19] While these numbers may appear impressive remember that Russia had a population of about 160 million at that time and so the proportion of revolutionaries supporting Lenin was a mere 0.15%.

At the same time, in an attempt to lift morale and aid the allied war effort, Kerensky launched a new offensive against the Germans. Initial success could not be sustained however, and once again Russians forces suffered a dismal defeat at the cost of 60,000 troops killed. Many troops now deserted and returned to Petrograd to join in the street demonstrations demanding an end to war. Three days of rioting in July saw soldiers, workers and Bolsheviks roaming the streets shouting 'All power to the Soviets' but the revolutionaries were not yet strong enough to seize power. Kerensky still commanded loyal troops whom he ordered to fire on the 100,000 demonstrators to dispel them. Moreover, he was able quite accurately to discredit Lenin by calling him a traitor to Russia, even branding him a German agent for collaborating with the enemy. Once again, Lenin ran away to safety abroad, this time to Finland, travelling on forged documents and having shaved off his trademark goatee beard and hidden his bald forehead beneath a wig.

*Lenin in disguise on his false ID card.*

## 1917 - The Communists seize power.

More and more Bolsheviks were elected to the soviets, first in Petrograd, then Moscow and then in other large cities. Though some historians say that was '*because fewer members of the other parties chose to attend the soviets' endless meetings*'![20] Trotsky had returned to Russia in May but had been imprisoned in July after the abortive July revolt. In September the Bolsheviks received an expected boost to their cause when a certain General Kornilov, the new Commander in Chief of the army (a man described as having the *'heart of a lion and the brains of sheep'*) decided to stage his own coup and set himself up as military dictator. Kerensky, now the Prime Minister, did not have enough loyal troops to withstand this new threat and was forced to seek the help of the revolutionaries. Trotsky and other Communists were let out of prison and armed workers and soldiers, organised by the Bolsheviks defeated Kornilov's forces. And so the Red Guards were born (red – the traditional colour of revolutionaries), no longer considered to be German agents but 'heroes' and the saviours of Petrograd. Trotsky became President of the Petrograd Soviet and began to lay plans for the seizure of power. Then in October Lenin finally returned to Petrograd from his refuge in Finland, always at the most opportune time and when there was least risk to himself. Nonetheless, his dynamism, intellect and persuasive speaking ensured he soon took control. As leader of the Bolshevik party he persuaded other party members at a secret meeting that the time was right to take over the country. *'Hunger does not wait. The peasant uprising does not wait. The war does not wait.'* A Military Revolutionary Committee was established with Trotsky at its head, theoretically to defend the soviet, but really to plan a Bolshevik take-over in its name. By October of 1917 the Bolsheviks at last seemed to have a very real chance of succeeding.

As tactical coordinator of the uprising, Trotsky set up his headquarters in the Smolny Institute, an unused girls' school. It had been agreed by Lenin and his supporters that the take-over would take place on the 24/25th of October, the night before the All-Union Congress of Soviets (the body representing the nation's soviets) was due to take place. Lenin had not wished the delegates from around the country to actually debate the legitimacy of what he was doing, they may even have voted against it! Instead he intended to present them with *a fait accompli*, the deed already done. Kerensky suspected that an uprising was imminent but was powerless to prevent it. The army had already indicated they would support the Bolsheviks and the guards at the Peter and Paul Fortress, the royal armoury, had agreed to give their weapons to the revolutionaries.

On the 24th of October the second revolution began, when following Trotsky's meticulous planning, the soldiers of the Red Guards swung into action. First they seized the key strategic bridges over the canals of the city, preventing troop transport of reinforcements loyal to Kerensky; then the telegraph station was captured. The following morning they took control of government buildings, key railway stations and the power plant. Kerensky had slipped out that day to try to gather a supporting army but to no avail. The remaining members of the Provisional Government were ensconced in the Winter Palace, the magnificent city residence of the Tsar. It was said that Kerensky had even slept in the Tsar's bed. Only a Women's Battalion and army cadets, mere boys, guarded the seat of government at the time. Bolsheviks were already in control of the nearby naval base at Kronstadt whose ships had sailed up the river Neva, their guns trained on the city. The firing of blank shells from their flagship 'Aurora' upon the Winter Palace was to signal the onset of the Revolution.

Towards midnight of the 25th the Aurora fired and as it did so Red Guards 'stormed' the palace. There was no resistance. The women, boys and members of the Provisional Government surrendered without a fight and mercifully only a handful of people were killed. Thus did Russia succumb to Communist rule in the space of two nights. Years later Eisenstein, the famed Soviet filmmaker, would recreate the events of that fateful night in his film 'October', depicting the storming of the palace as a huge, violent affair with thousands of brave revolutionaries risking their lives to seize control of a well defended palace. He used live ammunition to make the film and it was said that more people were injured and more damage done to the palace then than during the revolution itself![21]

*The 'Aurora', the flagship of the Russian navy, whose sailors backed the Revolution of 1917. Four years later they would mutiny against the Bolshevik government and be massacred.*

Whilst these fateful events were taking place, the members of the All-Russian Congress of Soviets had been debating whether or not the Bolsheviks had acted correctly by initiating the revolution without their support, just as Lenin feared they would. The Mensheviks and many other members condemned the Bolsheviks' actions only to be roundly denounced by Trotsky to *'go where you belong, to the dustbin of History'*. Lenin need not have worried; when he finally emerged from hiding to address the Congress he was greeted with a standing ovation. The American journalist John Reed, who witnessed Lenin's announcement of the success of the revolution described him thus: *'A strange popular leader – a leader purely by virtue of his intellect; colourless, humourless, uncompromising and detached... but with the power of explaining profound ideas in simple terms... Now Lenin, gripping the edges of the reading-stand, let little winking eyes travel over the crowd as he stood there waiting, apparently oblivious to the long-rolling ovation, which lasted several minutes. When it finished, he said simply, "We shall now proceed to construct the Socialist order!"'* [22]

# Chapter 2

## The emergence of the Union of Soviet Socialist Republics.

**Цену вещи узнаешь, когда потеряешь.**

*The value of something is only appreciated after it is lost.*

# Russia under Lenin.

The new Council of Peoples' Commissars, or Sovnarkom as it was known, proceeded to introduce new legislation with dazzling speed. Within days of coming to power land was appropriated from landlords, nobles and the church, for distribution amongst the peasantry. In practice, the peasants had already begun the process themselves and initially at least it appeared that the Bolsheviks were happy to sanction their spontaneous land grabs. This was sheer duplicity on Lenin's part however, because private ownership could not be tolerated in a Communist state but 300 thousand Bolsheviks could hardly deprive a 120 million peasants of their promised land. Lenin would have to bide his time before taking it into State control as Marxist doctrine required. Sure enough, by February he had passed another decree stating that all land belonged to the State, though even then it could not yet be enforced. Some laws appear to have been genuinely popular; marriage and divorce became simpler but the most desired decree of all was peace with Germany. This however, would come at a huge price.

As a defeated nation Russia was in no position to negotiate favourable peace terms with her enemy. Though Trotsky, the new Commissar for Foreign Affairs ('Commissar' sounding more revolutionary than 'Minister'), tried to prolong the talks for as long as possible in the belief that German workers would also rise up and replace their 'imperialist' masters, following the Russian example. Then, it was hoped, they could negotiate more favourably, as one Workers' state to another. It was not to be. The German army went on the offensive again and this time Lenin had no choice but to accept even harsher terms. The subsequent Treaty of Brest-Litovsk, signed in the town of that name, took virtually a quarter of all territory that had previously been under Russian control. The Russian Empire lost not only 62 million people but also nearly three-quarters of its industrial resources such as iron and coal.[1] Russia would regain the Ukraine and Georgia in the following years but not the remaining states until after World War II, when the new state would reveal itself to be just as imperialist as its Tsarist predecessor.

On the domestic front, some of the new laws enacted had immediate and ominous effects. In line with Marxist logic the 'Dictatorship of the Proletariat' banned all non-Bolshevik newspapers, thus prohibiting freedom of expression, and all other non socialist parties. To prevent opposition a newly formed secret police was established, with far reaching powers to root out dissent, whether real or imagined. The dreaded Cheka, led by the sadistic Felix Dzerzhinsky, who proudly proclaimed, 'We stand for organised terror', was to be responsible for killing more than 250,000 in the seven years of Lenin's regime.[2] Those who like to believe that it was the future leader Stalin who corrupted the noble Communist experiment and that all would have been fine if only Lenin had lived longer should take heed of this fact.

The Provisional Government had promised the Russian people democratic elections in November 1917 and Lenin was not in a position yet to renege on this promise. The results clearly showed that the Bolsheviks were still far from being a majority party. The Socialist Revolutionaries, the traditional party of the peasantry, gained 370 of the 707 seats in the newly formed Constituent Assembly, the Parliament that was claimed to be truly representative of the Russian people. The Bolsheviks gained 175, making them the second largest group. Though the only liberal group, the Constitutional Democrats or Kadets, had already been banned and so were not allowed to take their seats. It was this assembly that was to draw up a new constitution, the rules by which Russia would be governed, but Lenin could hardly allow that when he had already passed so much legislation as leader of Sovnarkom, the 25-member body that he dominated.

The Constituent Assembly was eventually allowed to meet on the 5th of January, amidst an atmosphere of hostile tension and an aggressive display of weapons by Red Guards. Victor Chernov, the leader of the Socialist Revolutionaries, who strictly speaking, should have become the new Russian president, described the meeting. *'When we entered... we found that the corridors were full of armed guards. Every sentence of my speech was met with outcries, some spiteful, often supported by the brandishing of guns. Lenin demonstrated his contempt for the Assembly by lounging in his chair giving the impression of a man who was bored to death.'*[3]

This show of 'democracy' lasted for one day. The following day Bolshevik troops prevented anyone entering the Tauride palace and the Constituent Assembly was duly disbanded. For good measure two Kadets, liberals who had wanted to share power with the monarchy, were murdered. Chernov and the Socialist Revolutionaries instigated one final, vain protest at their treatment but armed Bolsheviks easily quashed them. So ended Russia's brief flirtation with democracy and the last free elections to be held in that country for 74 years. If the treatment of the Assembly does not seem outrageous, imagine the outcry there would be if, in say England, a minority party were to seize control of the army and then use them to prevent lawfully elected politicians from entering Westminster, then to abolish the Parliament the following day! This is the way the Bolsheviks took control of Russia, their regime born out of force and upheld by it for the next seventy odd years.

That same year the Bolsheviks changed their name to the All-Russian Communist Party and effectively ruled as a dictatorship from then on. The Socialist Revolutionaries and other suppressed parties would have to find other means of challenging the now dominant Communists, even if that meant war.

## Civil War, Communist victory and famine.

No sooner had the Bolsheviks established their rule, than they were immediately challenged by an unlikely alliance of the dispossessed. The frustrated members of the disbanded Constituent Assembly organised an army to confront the 'Reds'. They were joined by supporters of the Tsar, former landlords whose lands had been seized, nobles, churchmen (hostile to the godless Communists) and members of other banned parties, including liberals and democrats. Then there were 'capitalists', which would have encompassed a diverse group, from wealthy factory owners to small shopkeepers and independent craftspeople; in fact anyone who stood to lose by the enforced nationalisation of property and businesses. In addition, there was also a Czech Legion comprising 45,000 prisoners of war who were being shunted across Siberia to the port of Vladivostok where they would be shipped back to fight the Germans. These soldiers broke free, took over much of the Trans-Siberian railway and became a rallying force for enemies of the new government. Since Russia had withdrawn from the war early her allies were keen to see her rejoin the battle on the eastern front and sent arms and reinforcements to the 'Whites' as they came to be known, so called because it was the traditional colour of the Tsar. When WWI ended in 1918, England, France and Japan also sent troops to aid them, in part because they feared a Bolshevik victory would inspire Communist revolutions in their own countries. Following Germany's defeat these disparate groups came to be led by former Tsarist Generals horrified by what had happened to their country while they had been fighting for Imperial Russia. With so many groups supporting them, the White armies should have been a formidable fighting force. Yet after three bitter years of fighting and the loss of millions of lives they were to lose. Why was this so?

There were several reasons for the tragic defeat of the White army, but the most important was that it was never a unified fighting force under a single command. By its very nature, the White forces were fighting for very different aims. Some wished to see the return of the Tsar, others a democracy, some simply for a return of their land or property. It was further complicated by nationalist uprisings of minority groups such as Poles and Ukrainians who took advantage of the chaotic situation to advance their own aspirations for independence. Both Reds and Whites fought savagely for their cause, recruiting peasants by force into their armies. Whilst many of the peasants fighting for the Reds had little love for the Bolsheviks they feared that if the Whites won they would lose their newly acquired land. World history may have been so different if only they had seen through the Bolshevik propaganda and realised that they would not own their land anyway, since the Communists had already abolished private ownership.

Furthermore, the foreign help was a mixed blessing. Having just fought the most vicious and bloody war to date, allied troops simply wanted to return home rather than getting drawn into another country's domestic squabble. Some of the working class soldiers were even sympathetic to the communist cause and Bolshevik propaganda exploited this, dropping leaflets asking 'Why were they fighting fellow workers?' More worrying was the impact that their presence had on the Russian population who viewed foreign troops, however half-hearted, as invaders, alienating the people further from the Whites.

The White generals were to win significant individual victories and control of large areas of Russia, including most of Siberia. They threatened central Russia from all directions, forcing the seat of government to be moved to Moscow. But the inability of the White armies to mount a concerted and coordinated attack on several fronts at the same time enabled the Bolshevik forces to repel them one by one. When Admiral Kolchak was

*Communist cartoons showing the famed Generals, Denikin, Kolchak and Yudenich as dogs on leads controlled by Britain, France and the USA; powerful propaganda to a suffering people.*

eventually captured, the defiant White Russian officer requested permission to command his own execution. This brave and imperious man unflinchingly barked out the commands: '*Ready. Aim. Upon Admiral Kolchak of the Imperial Russian Navy – Fire!*'[4] Communist propaganda was particularly vicious toward him, as this poster shows.

*'Lands and factories for landlords and capitalists' says the sign over the regal figure, labelled Kolchak, implying he had Tsarist pretensions. The cart is pulled by a 'bourgeois' fat capitalist, a priest and a kulak, willingly supporting him. The hangman's rope, on the other hand, is for the workers and peasants.*

Trotsky's contribution to the Red army's victory should not be underestimated. This brilliant, ruthless and indefatigable man transformed the shabby and unwieldy Red army into an effective fighting force. How? Firstly, by introducing conscription for all men aged 18-40 then by summarily executing deserters, those reluctant to fight and even civilians harbouring deserters. This gave him the numbers of ordinary soldiers he needed but not the officers needed to lead the ill-disciplined and inexperienced men. His problem was that officers had traditionally been drawn from the nobility who were more likely to fight on the side of the Whites. To solve his difficulty Trotsky simply kidnapped the officers he needed and forced them to fight for him by holding their families hostage. To be doubly sure and to prevent sabotage each kidnapped officer was assigned a political commissar, a *Politruk*, whose job it was to ensure that any decisions made by the officer were in the interests of the Red army. In this way, Trotsky was able to recruit 22,000 officers.[5] The Cheka (secret police) were the apparatus of Trotsky's terror and during this period they grew both in number and ferocity. The Moscow headquarters of the Cheka was in Lubyanka Street, where in the basements of this dreaded building agents tortured prisoners for information. Long after the Civil War ended the premises continued to be used and feared by opponents of the Bolsheviks. Throughout the country Cheka units mercilessly beat, shot or hanged anyone who helped or fought for the Whites. Soon the very name 'Cheka' had become synonymous with Red Terror and evoked fear in everyone, Red or White.

On the other hand, Trotsky also used his considerable political and military skills to encourage the Red army. He commandeered a special train and used it to ferry him from one war zone to another, haranguing the troops, bringing supplies and ensuring the army was an effective and united force. The fact that the Reds only had to defend the smaller central industrial areas also contributed to their victory, whereas the Whites were scattered over huge areas. But terror was the key to Trotsky's success. One example demonstrates. When a company of soldiers tried to desert, like the Romans, he had one man in every ten shot – the company decimated. Some initiatives were sensible under the circumstances. Order No. 1 of the soviets', which had abolished military titles, was rescinded, after all officers had to be obeyed and respected in times of war. The Red Army also permitted promotion through ability and able soldiers in the ranks could now become officers, rare in Tsarist times. Morale played a part too in the Communist victory, as it does in any war. Some soldiers of the Red army believed they were fighting for the creation of a more just and equitable communist society. Poor, misguided souls. The Whites on the other hand, though many fought with equal zeal and conviction, seemed to be upholding a bankrupt and obsolete regime. The peasants for their part, caught in the middle of this horrific encounter, were under no such illusions. They hated both sides. Hence the need for propaganda such as this, appealing to peasant patriotism, on behalf of the Reds.

*Peasants urged to defend their land and freedom.*

The Reds ultimately won because they ensured that what little resources were available were diverted to the army. This *War Communism* would have a disastrous impact on the remaining civilian population, as peasants were forced to give up their food for the soldiers. Victory had come at an agonising cost. Ten million people are believed to have died in the Russian Civil War and over half of those from starvation.[6] How *did* this appalling situation come about?

In order to be certain of victory the Bolsheviks introduced draconian measures of control over its citizens. A Supreme Council of National Economy, *Vesenkha*, was introduced which prescribed what industrial

*Starving children in Samara, victims of War Communism.*

goods should be produced and how many. To that end all factories, with the exception of those employing less than 10 workers, were nationalised – taken over by the State. An 'iron' discipline was introduced whereby nobody was allowed to leave or change jobs and the penalty for striking or constant absenteeism was death. Private trading was officially banned. For the peasantry this was to have dire consequences. Previously if they had been fortunate enough to produce more food than they themselves needed they were free to sell the surplus and buy essential consumer goods. Now any surplus was forcibly taken by armed Cheka units instructed to use whatever means necessary. Many peasants resisted and thousands were shot. The natural reaction to such brutal theft was that peasants simply refused to grow more crops. What would be the point of working harder, when living on starvation rations, if it was going to be taken away regardless? So they sowed less grain and bred fewer animals. Meanwhile even money was officially discouraged by the State and a barter economy was introduced. Food was strictly rationed and Stalin (later) admitted, that *'the best times then... were when we could distribute to the workers of Leningrad and Moscow... one-eighth of a pound of black bread'.*[7] What were the worst times?

*Dead famine victims being carted away.*

As might be predicted, a horrific food shortage resulted in 1920, followed in the next year by indescribable famine. Estimates of the dead vary from five to seven million – who had the means or desire to count? But even the Communists' own newspaper, *Pravda*, admitted that 25 million Russians were living below subsistence level – the barest minimum required to survive.

Loyal supporters of the Tsar had yet another reason to condemn Lenin for in July, 1918 the royal family had been murdered by order of the Bolsheviks. After his abdication the Tsar and his family had initially been allowed to live in their palace at Tsarskoye Selo, the summer residence where the royals had spent many happy times together as a devoted and loving family.

*The Romanov family living as villagers.*

However, for their own safety they were moved to Tobolsk in Siberia, where the family lived as simple villagers. Just like any peasant, Nicholas had to fill in a form to receive bread rations. Under *'Occupation'* he wrote *'ex Emperor'*.

As the White armies approached they were moved yet again to Ekaterinburg in the Ural Mountains. It was feared that if the White forces liberated the royal family they would serve as a rallying point for the disparate groups of the White army and therefore make them harder to defeat in the civil war. To avoid this possibility, the Reds needed to destroy the Tsar. The conventional account of the killings claims that the local guards ordered Nicholas, his wife Alexandra, their children and the four loyal servants who had remained with them, into the basement of the house. There they were shot by Bolshevik guards. However, witness' accounts of the following events vary. Some said that their bodies were burnt, others that they dismembered and the parts thrown down a disused mine. Since the bodies remained undiscovered for most of the century a number of persistent rumours abounded. One being that only some of the royal family were killed whilst others managed to escape. In particular, many accounts suggested that the youngest daughter, Anastasia, had survived. [8]

# The New Economic Policy – Lenin's U-turn.

The Great Famine of 1920-21 was the direct result of Bolshevik policy initiated by Lenin, yet he did at least allow international relief to come to the aid of the Russians. So the Red Cross and other worthy charities, from countries with freer economies than Russia's, did their best to stem the tidal wave of hunger. (The following decade when the sorry story was repeated under Stalin's policies, no such aid would be forthcoming as that famine would be kept secret.) Communist propaganda blamed 'speculators' – greedy capitalists who hoarded grain then sold it at inflated prices. A 'black economy' did undoubtedly develop – food in short supply will always be worth more, no matter what the state decrees. Yet it was Party members and Red Guards who seemed to be able to obtain it, by whatever means. British eyewitnesses who managed to escape confirm this. *'It is a common occurrence when a horse falls down in the street for the people to cut off the flesh of the animal the moment it has breathed its last. Another way of getting food was by buying it at excessive prices from members of the Red Guard who are well fed.'* [9]

Despite the unforgivable and tragic consequences of War Communism, many party members actually welcomed it as a consistent application of their ideology. One can only assume they must have been inhuman monsters. Lenin, equally inhuman but no slave to ideology, or indeed principles of any kind, adapted Communist ideas in order to remain in control and to keep the country from disintegrating all together. For example, the factories had been nationalised or as the doctrine stated, brought under 'workers control'. The problem was that unskilled 'workers' per se do not usually know how to run factories as became patently obvious in the chaotic months following the revolution. So Lenin, much to the disgust of die-hard Bolsheviks, allowed 'bourgeois technical experts' – middle class managers, engineers and accountants to actually run the businesses. Such people may not have desired to work under such circumstances but it was probably better than being hounded down as enemy 'Whites' by Cheka agents. After all Dzerzhinsky had claimed to have executed 6,300 people in the first year of Cheka rule. Lenin's willingness to compromise, some said sacrifice, Marxist ideology showed his political acumen. He did after all, comment that, *'one man who knew how to run a railway, was worth twenty enthusiastic Bolsheviks.'* [10] How true.

Further events were to show Lenin that even more concessions would be required if the Bolsheviks were to stay in power and not be the victims of revolution themselves. For it was not the starving peasants that forced him to re-examine Communist doctrine, *their* plight had left him unmoved, but a revolt from his own loyal supporters, the sailors of Kronstadt naval base. These were the same men who had stood at the side of the Bolsheviks at the birth of the regime, whose flagship 'Aurora' signalled the start of the October revolution and who had until now been its most enthusiastic supporters. Trotsky had called them the 'heroes of the revolution'.

By March 1921 they were completely disillusioned with the results of that event. They had not removed one tyrannical regime for it to be simply replaced by another and rose up, 10,000 strong, to attack Petrograd. Their Manifesto revealed their sentiments. *'We joined the Communist Party to work for the good of the people... The worker instead of becoming the master of the factory, became a slave. He can neither work where he would like, nor can he reject work which is beyond his physical strength. Those who dare to say the truth are imprisoned to suffer in the torture cells of the Cheka or are shot...'* [11]

Once again Trotsky was to prove himself a ruthless and effective military leader. With Lenin's full backing Trotsky ordered the Red Army generals with 60,000 troops to surround and attack Kronstadt. First, they bombed the naval base then attacked the sailors' headquarters, often fighting in hand to hand combat. The revolt was viciously quashed and the remaining rebels were mopped up by the Cheka and shot. The Kronstadt heroes had been betrayed. Moreover it was not just at Kronstadt that the people were making their discontent known. Peasants in the countryside also rebelled, attacking and robbing grain convoys with some success for several weeks. And in the towns 77% of Russia's factory workers went on strike in spite of the death penalty for doing so, proof that Bolsheviks were hard and indifferent to the value of workers' lives. Even John Reed, the American Communist sympathiser who was present at the October revolution, stated, with what can only be described as relish, that he did not care about opponents being shot. *'To the wall with them! I say. I have learned one mighty expressive Russian word, rasstrellye – execute by shooting.'* [12] But they could not shoot all their opponents and it was clear that Lenin had to do something before these strikes spread throughout Russia and brought down his Bolshevik government.

War Communism was abandoned and the New Economic Policy *(NEP)* ushered in. What did this mean? Firstly, peasants could sell their surplus food again, for *profit*. The more food they grew, the more money they could earn. They would want to spend this money on manufactured goods so such goods had to be produced. The second feature of the NEP, that encouraged industry, allowed smaller factories - up to 20 workers, to be returned to their owners. Both these measures required a cash economy so the third element was to allow people to use money again. These simple economic freedoms, the essence of capitalism, would have a profound impact on the economy. The figures speak for themselves (rounded to whole numbers).[13]

|  | 1913 | 1922 | 1925 |
| --- | --- | --- | --- |
| Grain harvest (millions of tonnes) | 80 | 50 | 72 |
| Cattle (millions) | 59 | 46 | 62 |
| Pigs (millions) | 20 | 12 | 21 |
| Coal (millions of tonnes) | 29 | 10 | 18 |

Food production returned to its pre-war level and industrial output, though slower, eventually recovered as well. The New Economic Policy legalised the black economy which had handled 60% of all the food that reached Russia's towns. If the NEP had not been introduced one can only surmise that the Russian economy would have sunk to an agonising level

of poverty, making the Tsarist days seem like paradise by comparison. The only consolation being that it might have brought down the Bolshevik government as well. As it was, Lenin's willingness to employ capitalist measures saved his regime.

*Busy markets selling food and other wares after the introduction of the New Economic Policy.*

Committed Communists in his government were horrified at such blatant disregard for their doctrine, disregarding the recent horrors of obscene famine. Lenin's reply? *'Let the peasants have their little bit of capitalism, as long as we keep power. The Proletarian government is in no danger as long as it firmly holds transport and large-scale industry in its hands.'* [14] At other times he justified this step, declaring that *'by taking one step backwards they would later be able to take two steps forward towards communism.'* He was also shrewd enough to realise that domestic capitalism would be insufficient to raise productivity and that Russia would need to restore trading links with other countries in order to import the vital raw materials and resources necessary to rebuild her economy. Admirers of Lenin cite his 'flexibility' and astuteness and there was no doubt he possessed both of these qualities but he was also totally devoid of humanity.

Lenin did not live to see the full effects of his new state and its policies for he suffered a stroke in 1922, leaving him partially paralysed and died at the start of 1924, aged 53. The gunshot wounds he had suffered from a would-be assassin six years earlier and the stress of ruling virtually single handed had no doubt taken their toll. Supporters showed their reverence for his achievements by embalming his body and publicly displaying it in a glass case in a mausoleum in Moscow's Red Square, where it remains to this day. Lenin had no love of the Church believing religion to be, as Marx put it, the *'opiate of the masses'*, keeping them doped and servile to authority. Under Lenin's regime all church property was seized and its power as an institution broken. Many priests were jailed. However, Lenin had also realised that he could not simply declare war on religion as the Russian people were by and large devout Christians. So, in his typical flexible approach, he allowed some religious freedom, even to members of the Communist party. Personally, he would have scorned the Orthodox practice of embalming and displaying the bodies of holy men believed to be saints. How ironic that this would be the fate to befall him. For those who believe in an immortal soul, perhaps Lenin really is experiencing hell.

The city of St. Petersburg was renamed Leningrad in Lenin's honour and remained so for most of the twentieth century. He would probably have been horrified by such glorification for, to his credit, he was not vain and appeared not to seek personal aggrandisement. His crimes were not that he sought power for its own sake but that he was willing to use the Russian people to conduct a grotesque social experiment, an intellectual exercise as it were, disregarding the terrible human cost. He did not deserve the reverence in which he was held, and still is by some.

*Lenin embalmed in his eternal tomb.*

In 1924 Russia gained a new constitution and a new name, the Union of Soviet Socialist Republics commonly known as the Soviet Union. The USSR initially consisted of four republics, Russia, the Ukraine, Byelorussia and the Caucasus. While each republic had control over local issues, the new capital in Moscow retained control over industry, the armed forces and the secret police, the Cheka. Local commissars for those areas worked under instructions from Moscow. The constitution also laid down the basic 'rights' of the people, giving all adults the vote, with the exception of monks, lunatics and private traders![15] Though arguably the right to vote was of little consequence in a one party state. Even so, the system was skewed to give most weight to the votes of urban workers, who were more likely to support Communist policies than peasants. The concept of rights of course, was a travesty in a country founded upon the notion of collective good, the altar upon which individuals continued to be sacrificed.

## The power struggle and Stalin's rise.

There was no obvious successor to Lenin. Trotsky was probably the most able in many respects but he did not seek popularity amongst his peers and was regarded suspiciously by many in the party. Being Jewish certainly would not have helped his cause because many Russians, Communists included, harboured anti-Semitic feelings. Anti-Jewish pogroms had been encouraged under the Tsars to deflect discontent away from the authorities and Jewish regions were regularly ransacked and destroyed, particularly at Easter time.

Lenin had been aware of Stalin's ambition and recognised that, as General Secretary of the Party, he had amassed considerable power and had appointed his supporters to privileged positions. Lenin tried to warn the party of this danger, even stating his reservations clearly in a written testament to be made known after his death. Yet members of the Politburo, the seven man ruling body of the Communist party, decided not to publicise the testament, preferring to believe that they could work with Stalin. This was to prove a fatal mistake, not only for them personally but for the rest of the nation.

Following Lenin's death, the executive committee of the Communist Party, the *Politburo,* was divided on which direction to take the country. Those on the 'Right', led by Nikolai Bukharin and supported by Andrei Rykov and Mikhail Tomsky, thought they should continue with the New Economic Policy, which was clearly showing dividends. *'Enrich yourselves'* Bukharin had stated to the productive peasants, revealing an inherent capitalistic sympathy. It was apparent to him that only the profits earned by the *kulaks* (land owning peasants) would encourage them to produce more food; the desirable goal for them as individuals as well as for the nation. What was good for the kulaks would be good for Russia. For those on the 'Left' of the party, including Trotsky, Zinoviev and Kamenev, such ideas were anathema. They despised the very notion of private profits, considering them to be clearly contradictory to their Communist ideals. Stalin, on the other hand, would support whichever position would gain him power and proceeded to play one group off against the other.

Stalin initially pretended to support the 'Rightists', not through any love of the NEP it must be noted but purely to out manoeuvre his opponents on the Left. At the Party Congress in December of that year, the 'Leftists' were defeated and new Politburo members were elected, all of them Stalin's appointees. Having expelled his rivals from the Party, and in Trotsky's case, also from the country, he then turned on the remaining 'old' members of the Politburo, his former supporters. By then Stalin had loyal followers in the party and Bukharin, Rykov and Tomsky were powerless to defend themselves. By 1930 Stalin was in complete control.

So, Josef Stalin had eliminated all his opponents, both those party members who wished to follow Communist policies and those who wished to pursue the New Economic Policy. Stalin's old rival Trotsky had been exiled to Mexico, but even there he wasn't safe. Stalin's secret police infiltrated his heavily guarded house and buried an ice axe in his skull. Since this is how he treated his closest accomplices, one might reasonably expect him to show little mercy to the country at large, as indeed proved to be the case. His cruelty surpassed the expectations of even the most cynical and pessimistic.

So who was this man that was to dominate the Party and the nation? The son of a peasant from Tbilisi, Georgia, born Josef Djugashvili, he was a star pupil who won a scholarship to train for the priesthood. But he was expelled from the seminary for failure to attend the exams due to his increasing involvement in revolutionary activities. Assuming the pseudonym of 'Stalin', he had become a Social Democrat and when that Marxist party split in two, he supported the Bolshevik wing. Stalin soon showed himself adept at radical activities to further the Bolshevik cause. For example, we have seen how he gained notoriety in 1907 by leading a bank robbery in Tbilisi to obtain funds for their movement. He was often arrested in those early years and spent time in exile. In 1917 during the first revolution in February he had been in exile in Siberia and was only freed after that event. When Lenin came to power after the October revolution he appointed Stalin as *Peoples' Commissar for Nationalities*, Stalin himself being a member of a nationalist minority. However, he showed no empathy for his own country and had no qualms invading Georgia when they attempted to gain independence. He also held other key posts in the party administration, taking jobs which other people rejected. Slowly and insidiously he built up his power base. A 'grey man' or 'eminent mediocrity' as some saw him, he was not perceived as a threat until it was too late.

*A 'doctored' photo, produced after Lenin's death.*

Stalin had revealed his political ambition and cunning soon after Lenin's death by glorifying the dead leader and creating the illusion that he was Lenin's chosen successor, which was a blatant lie. Stalin arranged a massive funeral for Lenin with thousands of people lining the streets for the procession. Eyewitnesses described it as the funeral of a Tsar. Years later Stalin would have fake photographs published showing the two men side by side, constructing the myth that they had been close in life and that he was Lenin's heir.

Once in power Stalin used ruthless methods to achieve his twin goals of rapid industrialisation and collectivisation of agriculture. At the same time, in sad irony, the cult of Stalin was born. Under his explicit instructions and with the connivance of fawning henchmen, the nation was inundated with propaganda that he was the saviour of Russia. Stalin became their *'Shining Sun of Humanity'*, a *'Universal Genius'*, the *'Granite Bolshevik'*. His bust appeared on street corners and in shop windows, huge portraits of him adorned walls and buildings. Schools, hospitals, towns, rivers and lakes were named after him until the worship of his image approached religious fervour. So convincingly was this image portrayed that even in the 21st century I have met older Russians who refuse to hear ill of him.

Stalin believed that Russia must be modernised at breakneck speed if the advanced, capitalist countries were to be prevented from 'crushing' the new socialist state. To industrialise the country according to Communist principles, the State Planning Commission, *Gosplan,* was created to regulate every aspect of the nationalised economy. Its first 5 Year Plan, produced in 1928, detailed the development of industry, agriculture, railways, canals, trade, energy, housing, education and all public services. In each area, targets were set. Workers who failed to meet their targets were either executed or sent to labour camps in Siberia. After all, failure could be construed as sabotage and that was a treasonable offence. Illiterate peasants forced into the factories without training, knowledge of measurements or even basic safety, were often accused of sabotage when, through simple ignorance, they failed to meet Gosplan targets.

*Stalin with child.*
*Shortly afterwards the child's*
*father was killed on his orders.*

*A women's exercise club on parade,*
*paying tribute to Stalin.*

'Sabotage' had become such a problem by the 1930's that a special department of the NKVD, *Gulag,* had to be set up to administer the hundreds of newly created labour camps. The term *Gulag* is commonly used to refer to individual camps as well as the entire penal system. It is actually an abbreviation for The Chief Administration of Corrective Labour Camps and Colonies (Главное Управление Исправительно-Трудовых Лагерей и колоний) of the NKVD and an acronym from the three key words - ГУЛаг. The NKVD being the name of the Soviet security service at the time. The service was known as the *Cheka* from 1917, the *OGPU* from 1922, the *NKVD* from 1935 and, perhaps most famously, the *KGB* from 1954.

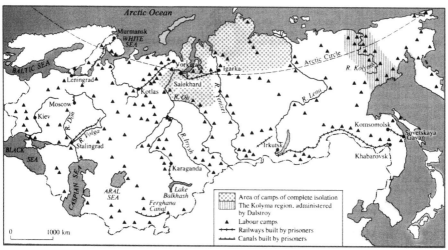

*Locations of the gulags – labour camps across Russia.*

Surrounded by watchtowers and barbed wire the camps stretched from the Black Sea in the West, right across Siberia to the Sea of Japan in the East. The harshest camps were undoubtedly those in the Arctic Circle where the ground was permanently frozen and had to be melted before it could be dug with bare hands. Newly arriving prisoners to these camps were horrified to discover tents surrounded by frozen corpses. Nobody had the energy to bury them, even if it were possible to dig through the permafrost, and so they provided additional insulation against the bitter Siberian winter.

Unfortunates sent to these labour camps were called *'zeks'*. At the start of the first 5 Year Gosplan plan there were about 30,000 zeks, by 1932 – two million, by 1937 – six million and by 1938 – eight million.[16] It is estimated that between 1936 and 1950 around 12 million zeks died in the camps. Their suffering and conditions have been well documented by the few survivors and the most comprehensive and moving account is provided by Alexander Solzhenitsyn.

It was not only 'saboteurs' or factory workers who did not meet their targets that were sent to the camps. Any dissident who dared to speak out against Stalin's regime or anyone who clung to outmoded ideas of individual effort for personal gain would be condemned as a 'reactionary'. Former nobles, officers, factory owners, landowners, shopkeepers and merchants perished in their hundreds of thousands. The fear of the secret police and their leader Beria, is reflected in the humour of the time: '*A flock of sheep was stopped by frontier guards at the Russo-Finnish border. "Why do you wish to leave Russia?" the guards asked them. "It's the NKVD," replied the terrified sheep. "Beria's ordered them to arrest all elephants." "But you aren't elephants!" the guards pointed out. "Yes," said the sheep, "But try telling that to the NKVD."*[17]

One might have expected that the farmers who produced the food upon which the industrial program depended, and who had at least tacitly supported Lenin when he had promised them their own land, would be spared such a fate. Not so. 100 million Russian people were peasants and the 5 Year Plan required that their agricultural output be increased dramatically to meet the demands of factory workers. Just as all industrial concerns were now State run so too would be all farms. They were to be 'collectivised' into huge farms. Peasants were forced to pool their land, resources, tools and animals. In return they would receive wages for their work. The peasant dream of owning their own small, individual farms, which Lenin and the Bolsheviks had tantalisingly and deceptively held out to them in order to win their support in the Civil War, was finally destroyed.

*Mass grave at Chelyabinsk. Excavated in 1989, it is estimated to contain the bodies of 80,000 victims of Stalin's secret police (NKVD). My relatives still live there.*

The peasants most likely to resist Collectivisation were those who were most successful. The five million or so who owned two or three horses, several cows and had a larger than average farm. These were the 'fat cats' of the farming world, the kulaks, who supposedly exploited their poorer counterparts. In December 1929, Stalin declared that he intended to *'liquidate the kulaks as a social class'*. Inaccurately branding them as a 'class' served the Marxist propaganda myth that destroying them would serve the interests of the 'proletariat', the working classes. Many of course, resisted this 'dekulakisation'. Some killed their own animals and burned their crops rather than hand their farms over to the State. One eyewitness described a peasant's response to enforced collectivisation. *'The woman... held a flaming sheaf of grain in her hands. Before anyone could reach her, she had tossed the burning sheaf onto the thatched roof of the house, which burst into flames instantaneously. "Infidels! Murderers!" The distraught woman was shrieking. "We worked all our lives for our house. You won't have it! The flames will have it!"'* [18]

Whole villages that resisted were bombed. About a third of all kulaks were deported to Siberia, another third to other regions and the remainder allowed to remain but given land of the worst kind. In the space of one year, Stalin and his police state had effectively destroyed the productive capacity of the nation's most successful farmers. One of the few British reporters who managed to observe the situation described the scene: *'On the one side, millions of starving peasants, their bodies often swollen from lack of food; on the other, soldier members of OGPU carrying out the instructions of the proletariat. They had gone over the country like a swarm of locusts and taken away everything edible; they had shot or exiled thousands of peasants, sometimes whole villages; they had reduced some of the most fertile land in the world to a melancholy desert.'* [19]

The placard reads
'We are truly happy'.

Over the course of the next two years between six to ten million people starved to death.[20] In November 1932, Stalin's wife, Nadia Alliluyeva, committed suicide after a bitter quarrel in which she accused her husband of being responsible for the famine, terror and misery wrought upon Russia. The famine itself was kept secret – Communist propaganda could not admit to failure on such a massive scale. Foreigners who visited Russia in the 1930's were shown model collective farms that appeared to be prosperous and happy. Nonetheless, word of the terror the secret police wrought on its cowed population prompted this French cartoon at the time.

Some very brave Russians even managed to joke about the situation as illustrated by the following extract: *'Stalin complained to a colleague that his office in the Kremlin was infested with mice and that traps and poison had failed to get rid of them. "No problem", the colleague replied. "Just declare that your office is a Collective Farm. Half the mice will run away and the other half will die of starvation."'* [21]

# Chapter 3

# Exodus from Russia.

## Каждый человек архитектор своего счастья.

*Every man is the architect of his own fortune.*

# Introducing the families.

Considerably more information is available from my mother's side of the family, there were also many more of them and so our story will begin with the *Shliapnikoffs* followed by my father's family, the *Shalavins*.

My maternal great-grandparents were Artemy and Praskovia Shliapnikoff. Artemy was born in 1873 in Kuznetsk, in central Russia, some 400 miles south-east of Moscow, near the large trading city of Samara. The family would later settle and start a business in this city, known then as Kuybishev. Artemy was the son of a merchant who traded in various goods, including furniture and household items such as ropes, brooms, brushes and the like. His brother Pavel had a business in the same street and to distinguish between the two Shliapnikoffs, the latter used the name Panin. What would Artemy's father's business have been like at the end of the 19th century? He may have had a warehouse of some kind, perhaps a gas lit shop. Horse and cart would have transported his goods, although the first cars had already been developed in Europe they were a long way off in Russia yet. A railway was beginning to be built across the great continent but that would have had little impact upon his local trade. Diversifying away from his father's furniture business, Artemy chose to trade in what the Russians believed to be an essential commodity, meat and its associated products. Russia's population was increasing rapidly and Artemy clearly saw the market potential for increased food production and distribution. It seems to have been a wise decision and the family became prosperous and upwardly mobile as a result.

Praskovia was born in 1880 and like many females of that generation married Artemy at a comparatively young age. By the time she was 19 years old she had already given birth to the first of their many offspring, my maternal grandmother Zinaida. By then Artemy was 26 years old and a solid member of Russia's burgeoning middle classes. Together with his brother they had built up a successful business. It is not clear just how large their concern was or whether it was mechanised sufficiently to be deemed a factory. Factory owner or not, as an employer, Artemy would have been considered a 'bourgeois' member of the oppressing 'capitalist' class by Marxist critics. Such critics often deny the existence of any class between the 'oppressors' and the 'oppressed' and yet Artemy, along with many others, belonged to neither group. The middle class was a growing phenomenon in late 19th century Russia and its existence evidence of the country's economic growth. Artemy lived a relatively comfortable lifestyle, supporting a wife and eleven children and employing a servant or nanny to look after them.

In 1917, the year of Russia's two revolutions, Artemy was 44, with eight surviving children, three teenagers – Zina, Alexei and Tatiana and five youngsters, Pelageya, Klavdia, Elena, Alexandra and Nikolai. Three others had died in infancy.

In November, 1917 the Shliapnikoff family viewed the events of that fateful year with alarm and trepidation. The Great War had surely impacted them as it had done all Russians, though in Kuznetsk they were far from the fighting front. The eldest of the eight siblings, Zina was just 18 at the time but mature enough to be fully aware of what was going on. Her younger brother, Alexei was 16 and thankfully, just that little bit too young to have been called up for the war effort. He had escaped the fighting but the family would not escape the consequences of the war nor the ensuing revolutions that first brought down the monarchy and then the Provisional Government. Business must have suffered considerably during the terrible years of hardship and inflation. A family of eight children, the youngest barely four, could not have escaped the privations of food shortages as well as the impact on their schooling and lives brought about by the mobilisation of farmers, teachers and factory workers. Lenin may even have been initially welcomed as the harbinger of peace, but at what cost they must have asked themselves if it meant surrendering to the German invader and the destruction of everything they held dear.

They would have heard of the Bolsheviks' intentions even in Kuznetsk. Artemy was likely to have been apprehensive and wary, what would it mean for his business? Would it be taken over by the new Marxist government, nationalised for the 'common good'? Were all companies to be controlled by the State or just the larger ones? Perhaps small concerns would be left alone.

Rumours and counter rumours abounded in the turbulent months following the revolution. The Bolsheviks were avowed atheists so what was to become of their beloved Church? The Shliapnikoffs along with millions of other Orthodox Christians considered the implications of a government no longer supported by the familiar institution. And most alarmingly of all, how would Russia fare without the bulwark of the monarchy? Would Lenin become the new Tsar? It was not a foolish question as subsequent events were to prove.

By 1930 the Shliapnikoff family of ten had grown considerably. Artemy and Praskovia's eldest daughter, Zina, had married into the Karetnikov family. They had also been merchants, though possibly

on a smaller scale. Zina's husband Nikolai traded in treats, such as sweets, raisins and peanuts. It is likely that the very ambitious Zina had higher aspirations for him but they were to remain unfulfilled for

*Zina and Nikolai.*

*Zina c. 1914.*

various reasons, not least the dislocations of war and revolution, which must have had a destructive impact on many families. They had two daughters, seven year old Nina and five year old Julia, my mother.

The eldest son, Alexei, had married Katya and they had three children: five year old son Georgi, three year old son Vladimir and two year old daughter Vera.

*Alexei and his wife Katya, c. 1928.*

The second daughter, Tanya, had married Peter Bakaldin and they had two children: five year old daughter Olga and three year old son Nikolai.

The third daughter, Polya, had married Volodya Pravosudov and they had three children: six year old son Konstantin, four year old son Dima and two year old daughter Vera.

*Volodya, Dima, Konstantin, Polya and Vera*
*c. 1929.*

*In her youth Polya was a renowned follower of fashion, even during the austere 1920's, as this early photograph demonstrates.*

*Polya and husband Volodya,c. 1925.*

The fourth daughter, Klavdia, had married Vassili Ryabtsev and they had two daughters: seven year old Larissa, born when Klavdia was only 16, and five year old Taissia. The girls are pictured below, with their proud parents, wearing traditional white ribbons in their hair.

*The pretty, sensitive face of the young Klavdia gazes out serenely from beneath her cloche hat as she poses with her earnest young husband.*

The fifth daughter, Elena, had married Ivan Cherviakoff and they had a four year old daughter, Galia.

The youngest daughter, Alexandra, then aged 17, had recently married Grigori Nikomin. The shy, attractive bride is pictured (right) wearing a fashionable *flapper* style dress, in her wedding photograph.

The youngest son, Nikolai, aged 16, was still single at that time.

The two older generations are shown in the impressive and poignant family portrait (overleaf), taken on the occasion of Alexandra's wedding in 1929. All eight of Artemy and Praskovia's offspring, and their respective spouses, are present. My aunt Nina surmised that the children, of whom she was one, must have been playing in a nearby room. Their elders probably thought it would be too difficult to keep so many youngsters still for them to be included. The family members appear solemn and serious, even the young and handsome teenager Nikolai portrays a sense of foreboding about their future. Perhaps they already had an inkling of the turmoil to come and wanted a record for posterity.

This precious photograph is the last of the Shliapnikoff family before they ventured forth to meet their various destinies and was to prove to be the last of Artemy and Praskovia with all their children.

*Shliapnikoff family portrait, 1929.*

**Key to Shliapnikoff Family Portrait, 1929.**

1 **Ivan and Elena**
   *(Vanya and Lena)*

   Иван и Елена
   *(Ваня и Лена)*

2 **Vassili and Klavdia**
   *(Vasya)*

   Василий и Клавдия
   *(Вася)*

3 **Pelageya and Vladimir**
   *(Polya and Volodya)*

   Пелагея и Владимир
   *(Поля и Володя)*

4 **Ekaterina and Alexei**
   *(Katya and Lyosha)*

   Екатерина и Алексей
   *(Катя и Лёша)*

5 **Tatiana and Peter**
   *(Tanya and Petya)*

   Татяна и Пётр
   *(Таня и Петя)*

6 **Nikolai and Zinaida**
   *(Kolya and Zina)*

   Николай и Зинаида
   *(Коля и Зина)*

7 **Grigori and Alexandra**
   *(Grisha and Shura)*

   Григорий и Александра
   *(Гриша и Шура)*

8 **Artemy and Praskovia**

   Артемий и Прасковия

9 **Nikolai**
   *(Kolya)*

   Николай
   *(Коля)*

# The flight of the Shliapnikoffs.

Somehow the family managed to eke out an existence during the turbulent 1920's. They may have greeted the death of Lenin with some relief but there was no respite from Bolshevik rule. Indeed, the emergence of Stalin as a new dictator must have confirmed all their worst fears and, in anticipation of more horrors to come, my family finally decided to leave the USSR. The departure of our extended family from the Soviet Union began in 1930, by which time Stalin had established his tyrannical rule over the country. The forcible removal of all opposition meant that thousands, and in time millions, of innocent people were arrested and sent to labour camps to die lingering deaths in the Siberian wastelands or to a frozen death in the gulags of the Arctic. Some may think that the luckiest were those who were summarily executed. One did not have to be politically active to suffer this fate, it was sufficient merely to belong to the bourgeois class. That alone was sufficient for a person to be condemned as a 'capitalist pig' and be doomed to destruction. It cannot be emphasised enough that one did not have to commit any crime in order to be arrested, but merely be a *reactionary*, someone who opposed the changes, whether a noble, church member or businessman.

One such victim was Artemy's brother, who the Communists had arrested and shot. How devastating must that have been for the family but worse was to come. Rumours reached Artemy that they would be coming for him next. The news would have been greeted with horror but no surprise under the circumstances. The Shliapnikoffs had been successful selling meat and the meat based products that Russians loved so much. They sold whole cows and oxen, as well as cuts of meat, to many Russian cities, including Moscow. Recent legislation in 1930 had declared private trade and the employment of labour for profit to be illegal.[1] As a wholesaler, a 'купец', who employed other workers, his business would be brought under 'workers' control'. Artemy faced the very real threat of at best being sent to the gulags, or shot as an enemy of the people. He was in a very dangerous situation. No longer young and with eight children, all but one of whom were married, the youngest being just 16, he had considerable responsibilities. At least one of the sons worked with him and many of the others were either directly or indirectly dependent upon the business. Of course there would also have been strong emotional bonds between the family members as well. Artemy gathered his wife and their offspring and spouses together. He told them that he could no longer live in his home country and would endeavour to leave it – who would join him? All but his two daughters Shura and Alexandra chose to risk their lives and follow him into exile and an uncertain future.

It is difficult to imagine just how terrifying the prospect of escaping from Stalin's Russia must have been, especially for those young parents who knew that they were not only risking their own lives but those of their children as well.

The family gathered their most valuable possessions – religious icons and the clothes that they could carry on their backs. Jewellery, especially gold, was hidden or sewn into their underclothes. They were going to need this to smooth their path, as the rouble would be of no value abroad. The women were undoubtedly unaware that twelve years earlier the Romanov princesses, the four daughters of the Tsar of Russia, had taken longer to die because the jewels sewn into their bodices had caused the bullets to ricochet off. All other possessions were sold or given away.

Slowly, the extended family made their way eastwards across the country towards the Chinese border, where they had heard it was possible to escape through the forest wilderness of Manchuria. There, along the remote Sino-Russian river border, the dreaded Soviet guards might be scarcer than in the well-guarded closed borders with Europe. The fleeing party consisted of Artemy and Praskovia, their two sons, four of their daughters, plus spouses and children. Six extended families, numbering twenty four desperate souls in all.

Ivan and Elena Cherviakoff fled Russia separately, for they had their own personal tribulations. Ivan's father Alexander was an Orthodox priest who had raised six children whilst practising his calling, as the Church expects, for family life is encouraged and marriage is obligatory. His son, Ivan was well educated and aspired to University but it was his misfortune to have been born in 1903. Thus his school leaving age coincided with the atheistic communist rule when offspring of religious leaders were clearly discriminated against. Initially banned from the University by the Bolsheviks, he eventually managed to attend one year before being ordered to leave. Nonetheless, a talented artist, he found work in the church, despite continual harassment, painting icons, and performing administrative tasks. He even succeeded in studying for a deacon's post and was ordained in 1927, a remarkable achievement in those turbulent years. But as church members they were constantly persecuted. One evening in 1930 a friend who had joined the Red Army informed him of a plot to blame Ivan for some vandalism. Clearly an excuse to arrest and presumably dispose of him, as friends testified years later to his daughter Galina. The family fled that very night with the two precious icons with which they had been blessed on their wedding day. With little more than a few clothes, jewellery and a small amount of money they began their long trek to China. Galina's grandfather Alexander who remained behind lived in constant fear until he was arrested in 1937, tried and sentenced to death. The family did not learn of his fate until 1989, his wife and children having had to live with his mysterious disappearance all that time, a tragically all too common story.

Both the Cherviakoffs and the Shliapnikoffs were (and some still are) Old Believers. In one respect, both families were the heirs to a tradition of pious rebellion, descendants of people who had died for their faith. It is interesting to consider whether some vestige of that rebellion, a defiant streak, gave them the strength to undertake such a perilous journey. Most Russians did not or could not flee. It seems that only the desperate, ambitious and independent fled. In both sets of families, the original émigré generation continued to practice the Old Believers' variant of Orthodoxy for much of the 20th century. For it was their faith that sustained them through their upheavals, a faith nurtured deep in the Russian birch forests some 300 years earlier.

The fleeing Shliapnikoffs moved from town to town by whatever means of transport they could find (train, boat, horse and cart and on foot, 'что шло', in fact anything that moved); sometimes travelling together but more often in smaller groups to avoid attracting attention. After several months they finally neared Vladivostock in the far eastern regions of Siberia, a journey of over 5,500 kilometres (3,420 miles) from Kuybishev (see map later in this chapter). That feat alone must have been terribly daunting in the dangerous, suspicion ridden atmosphere that was the Soviet Union of the 1930's but their greatest ordeals were yet to come. Most of the family settled temporarily around Ussurisk, a town on the Russian side of the border with Manchuria, China. Zina and her family lived together with Ivan and Elena Cherviakoff in Nikolsk. The two families shared a single room and the men folk made ends meet delivering goods by horse and cart, the children riding on the carts. Other family members arrived in due course and the adult members set about finding work whenever and wherever they could. The families were forced to live this precarious existence for several months whilst waiting to find the means and opportunity to leave the country illegally. Why illegally? By the 1930's the heavy hand of Stalinist dictatorship controlled the entire country and undoubtedly enormous numbers of people would have fled the country had it been permitted. This would have laid bare the myth of Soviet propaganda of a socialist paradise and exposed the tyranny for the whole world to see. Stalin could not risk the truth getting out so closed the borders and ordered armed guards to shoot those brave and desperate souls who tried to leave.

The long awaited opportunity to make their escape finally presented itself to the Shliapnikoffs. They gathered their belongings on their backs, including their treasured icons, took a horse and cart as far as they could into the thick forest before proceeding on foot to the banks of the river Amur that separated Russia from China. Here they split up for safety and also because the small boats that would carry them to freedom could only take a few at a time. They waited until the Soviet guards had completed their rounds of the area and then crept to the waiting boat. The border patrols had strict orders to shoot on sight and had the youngsters called out or the babies cried I may well not be here today to relate their tale. My grandmother told how the boat holding her and her two young daughters sprang a leak and began to sink. Deeply religious, they naturally turned to their faith in times of crises and prayed fervently for deliverance to the saints of the icons they carried with them. What could be more disastrous than to have travelled so far and to be so near safety, only to drown in the muddy waters of the Amur River? Few could swim and my mother's life long fear of water may well have stemmed from this terrifying experience. Their prayers were apparently answered and they arrived safely on the Chinese side where the doubtless equally frightened Chinese boatman was paid in the universal currency of gold.

Mother's cousin Olga, who was about five at the time, related the story of her family's difficult and frightening crossing, a story her mother Tanya had often related. Tanya and her two year old son Nikolai were the last people left on the Russian side. Little Olga must have gone on a separate boat with her father. Holding Nikolai in her arms Tanya stood by the tree so as not to cast a shadow and fed him sweets so he would not cry but then he became thirsty and asked for water. She said she seemed to be standing there forever waiting for the boat to return, an ordeal of considerable suspense and trauma, as anyone who has ever tried to keep a toddler quiet will appreciate. After what seemed an interminably long time, the boat finally arrived and carried her and Nikolai to safety.

Galina too, had her story of the crossing related by her mother. There was a limited number of crossing passages and only a restricted number could negotiate it safely at any one time without endangering the life of the guide and the other members of the party. When it was her parents' turn the guide could only take one more and neither wanted to go without the other but luckily a man in front gave up his place for them. The Cherviakoffs were forever grateful to Mr. Kosloff whom they met again in Shanghai many years later in happier circumstances.

Now they were all 'safely' in China but how safe? China was officially a Republic following the collapse of the Manchu dynasty, but in practice it was a country torn by strife and corruption, ruled by bloodthirsty warlords who thought nothing of summarily beheading their enemies or indeed anyone who broke their laws. European powers such as the British and the French had established areas of 'protection' in major international ports like Shanghai and Hong Kong but outside these ports naked force prevailed. The Nationalist party of Chiang Kai Shek had failed to unite the country and more and more people were falling for the persuasive ideology of Communism espoused by Mao Zedong. The nation was virtually in a state of civil war between these two groups. Last but not least, the aggressive Japanese were casting covetous eyes on the natural wealth and resources of the northern region of Manchuria. Was this really such a wonderful refuge for all those months of weary travelling? The exiles were in no doubt, despite the lawlessness and uncertainties, China was still infinitely preferable to the Russia they had been forced to abandon, offering them at least the possibility of carving out some sort of life for themselves.

Many more weeks of hard and dangerous trekking lay ahead of them before they would reach the city of Harbin. They knew a large Russian community was flourishing there and believed they could find shelter and more importantly, work. Moving from one small Chinese village to the next they experienced many hardships. One night they stayed at an inn and Tanya went to buy bread. The bakery was run by Russian immigrants who asked where she was staying. On learning about the inn the baker was horrified. The inn, it seemed, had a 'bad reputation' and the innkeeper was known to kidnap young women at night and sell them as concubines to rich Chinese. They could not verify the truth of this claim but stories such as this abounded and were perfectly plausible in the circumstances. Other tribulations followed which the comparatively affluent middle class people found daunting but simply had to take in their stride. In one village they slept on sleeping platforms with local peasants, all in a row, side by side and onboard ship they slept on deck, packed like sardines amongst poor travellers, from whom they became infested with fleas. Artemy and Praskovia must have been greatly relieved when at last they, their children and grandchildren arrived in the comparatively safe haven of Harbin, far removed from the horrors of their beloved homeland.

*The journey to freedom (overview)*

*...detailed map overleaf.*

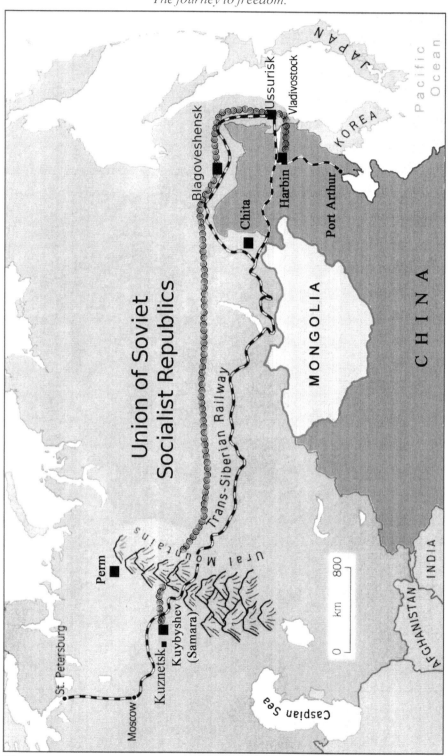

# The departure of the Shalavins.

The circumstances of my father's family's exodus from Russia were quite different, chiefly because they did not belong to the class of prosperous business people that had condemned the Shliapnikoffs. They were people of the land, some of the 80% of the Russian population who still worked in agriculture at the start of the century. But this proportion was dwindling fast as Stalin's industrialisation program and 5 Year plans ruthlessly conscripted peasants into the factories in an attempt to place the USSR among the industrial nations of the world. Accordingly, the 'bolshevisation' of industry, which had taken place under Lenin in the 20's, was extended to agriculture under Stalin in the 30's.

Under the policy of Collectivisation, it was presumed that modern, efficient farming methods could be introduced to increase productivity. The complete opposite happened. Farmers destroyed their animals and burned their crops rather than hand them over to the state. Millions of productive, successful peasants who resisted Collectivisation were banished to the labour camps. Yields plummeted and the horrific famine that resulted claimed the lives of over six million people. Stalin's decision to systematically destroy the kulaks, the most successful and productive farmers, directly impacted my paternal great grandparents, the Semenovs.

The Semenovs lived as independent farmers, quite possibly the beneficiaries of Stolypin's legacy that gave opportunities for peasants to throw off the shackles of the *mirs*. The patriarch of the family was Zinovey Nikonovich Semenov, his wife was Varvara Vasilevna Semenova, whose maiden name may have been Piankova. They had three daughters and a son. Their second daughter, Maria, was my grandmother and all our information about the family comes from her and her surviving son, Ivan, my father.

Formally known as Maria Zinovyevna, *Babushka* (Russian word for grandmother) was born in 1901 in Nikolaevka, near Blagoveshensk. Nikolaevka was a village in far eastern Siberia, near to the Amur River which runs between Russia and Manchuria, China. Judging by comments she made, Maria had a happy childhood in her village. Her parents worked hard on their land but they wanted for nothing in terms of basic necessities and even owned a few animals. She was proud of their independence and, despite their simple lives, she spoke wistfully of this last short lived golden period before the turmoil of war and revolution. Life in Nikolaevka was quite comfortable for the Semenovs. Although by no means prosperous they were certainly not destitute by the standards of the day. They owned their land rather than being tenant farmers and may have hired itinerant labour to help with the harvests as the better off farmers sometimes did. Maria claimed they had 'everything they needed for life'. Their lives were seeped in the old Russian traditions she was to keep alive throughout her many years of exile in very different cultures. The family were very proud and devout Old Believers, the faith that had remained true to the traditional Russian Orthodox Church since its split in the 17th century.

The oldest surviving photo of Maria is as a young girl clutching a basket of flowers, in the middle of a family portrait. Her father, Zinovey, the sturdy, man of the land gazes unflinchingly at the camera, undoubtedly proud that his hard work had made it possible to pay for this precious memento. Few peasants could afford such a privilege at that time. His son, in traditional gathered shirt and boots, is stern and handsome. The youngest daughter, Dunya, to whom Maria became very attached, perches precariously on her father's knee. It could not have been an easy life for their mother, but she looks stoic and capable. The year must have been about 1913, just before WW1 began and the tumultuous events that would destroy their way of life and the Russia they knew.

In another rare photograph, taken just before her marriage at the tender age of 16, Maria (back right) is pictured with her friends. The young girls in modest blouses and long skirts were probably wearing their 'Sunday best', for they were all avid churchgoers.

Maria was given away in marriage to a virtual stranger. Arranged marriages were not an official institution but parents commonly had a great deal of say in the process. I remember her describing the event rather stoically to me when I was about the same age as she was then. She said that at first she did not like

*Semenov family c. 1913 Blagoveshensk, Maria in centre with basket.*

Feodor but 'got used to him'. The marriage must have been reasonably happy though because she never uttered a bad word about him and trusted him sufficiently to slip across the river border into China with, sometime after the Russian revolution. Living on the border meant the couple were well placed to discover secret escape routes. The remaining members of her family were likely to have been branded 'kulaks' during Stalin's Collectivisation period in the 30's and may well have ended up in the Gulags or been victims of the famine. She never heard from any of them again. Her brother was reputed to have been killed by the Communists but the fate of her sisters and parents remains unknown. She particularly grieved for her younger sister Dunya, born when Maria was 12 and whom she 'mothered' until her own marriage.

Maria had left the comfort of her family for early wedlock, then her country when the Revolution, subsequent Civil War and famine destroyed all that she held dear. To add to her grief, her husband Feodor died shortly after their arrival in China, leaving her to fend for herself in a strange land. There were few hospitals or doctors in rural China and what little medicine was available was primitive. To become ill was a frightening experience and one simply had to try not to get sick. However, Feodor, for all their precautions, contacted typhoid and no-one was able to help him. He soon died, leaving Maria like a '*small blade of grass in a field*' былинка в поле. It must have been a harrowing time for the grief stricken young widow. But Maria was never one to succumb to life's tribulations; she had no choice but to carry on living and working as best she could. In time she found her way to one of the many settlements of Russians working on the Trans-Siberian railway, where she met Ivan Grigorievich Shalavin. Ivan had been working in Manchuria before the Revolution and wisely decided not to return to Russia afterwards. They met sometime around 1924-5 and married soon after.

Ivan Grigorievich was born around 1900 in Perm, a city in the Ural district of what was then Imperial Russia. Perm lies on the Western side of the impressive Ural mountain range that divides Western and Eastern Russia. My grandmother thought that he may have had two brothers and possibly sisters as well but she had no confirmed knowledge of them. Ivan left Perm to work on the main line of the Trans Siberian railway in Manchuria, China. We do not know exactly when he arrived in Manchuria but we do know that he travelled there officially because the line was controlled by the Russian authorities. Started by the Tsars in the 19th century, the railway was bitterly contested by the Red and White armies during the Civil war, control ultimately passing to the Reds following their victory in 1920. At any rate, Ivan Grigorievich was in

China after the Revolution and was employed by the Railway along with many other Russians. He had not escaped but had travelled there because employment opportunities were apparently better than in Perm.

As he had no family in Manchuria and Maria was a single young widow, theirs was presumably a love marriage and she certainly spoke fondly of her early days with this handsome young man, with whom she was to spend 15 years of her life. The marriage was not to last however and he and Maria parted company in 1940, she to seek better conditions for their two sons in Shanghai whilst he remained in Harbin. Maria later heard from mutual friends that he had died, aged just 45, in Harbin five years later, the same year that World War II ended.

One of life's survivors, Maria went on to marry twice more but it was this man's name she chose to have engraved on her tombstone, both in Russian and in English. Both their sons have had sons of their own so the Shalavin name looks set to endure in its new home in Australia but there has never been any contact with those who remained behind in their country of origin. We know that 'Shalavins' do still exist in Russia and a branch has been located in Alaska but it has not yet been established whether or not they are related to this mysterious, handsome young man who left his family in Perm to seek his fortune in China.

According to my father, *"the communists came, took everything and sent people to work on the kolhoze (collective farm). Now 70 plus years have passed and people are convinced that the system did not work, we hope that conditions will improve and there will be more freedom, the borders will open and then we will know the fate of our relatives, who suffered and who survived somehow."*

So what became of the rest of the Shalavins? We are still searching and would dearly love to know.

# Chapter 4

## China and life in Harbin.

## Охота пуще неволи

### *Free will is stronger than force*

# A brief background to China.

The vast nation of China has a long and at times illustrious history, from its birth as farming settlements over 5,000 years ago. They were the first people to invent gunpowder, paper, printing, clockwork, the compass, spectacles and the suspension bridge, often centuries before their western counterparts. They perfected and kept secret the art of fine silk making and superb porcelain. Indeed, we still use the term 'china' today to describe the finest crockery.

Various warring kingdoms had existed for about two millennia but the history of China as a unified nation can be traced back to the 3rd century BC when the young and ambitious King of Qin (pronounced 'chin') defeated rival kings and created a single nation under his control. He gave himself the title Shi Huangdi or First Supreme Emperor and gave the name of his kingdom to the country. A cruel, ruthless but cunningly clever despot, he is known, amongst other things, for consolidating and extending the Great Wall of China. Built to keep out the 'barbarians' from the north, this impressive edifice of some 4,100 kilometres is the longest man made construction in the world. But Shi Huangdi should better be remembered as a vicious leader who imposed extortionate taxes on his suffering people, practised slavery on a huge scale and mercilessly destroyed all opposition. A common interpretation indicates that he had 460 scholars buried alive and their books burnt for daring to question his rule. 'He who begins by burning books, ends by burning people' it was said prophetically of Hitler's regime. And so it was, both with Shi Huangdi and his 20th century spiritual successor, Mao Zedong.

The thousand generation dynasty Shi Huangdi intended to establish lasted a mere 11 years before his sudden death. Time enough however, to prepare for himself a tomb befitting an Emperor, guarded by an astonishing 8,000 life size clay warriors, each with its own unique face. Neither

*Part of the Great Wall of China.*

they nor the elaborate booby traps that were set prevented tomb raiders stealing the treasures buried with him and those of his wives who had failed to give him sons. Though the renowned and much visited Terracotta Army remains an enduring legacy of his power.

Shi Huangdi's brief rule was followed by a succession of dynasties of varying lengths, many of them ending in rebellion and the murder of the emperor. The Han dynasty lasted from the 3rd century BC to 220 AD, during which time the famous Silk Road was opened up to the west. Not so much a road as a series of tracks and passes between treacherous mountains. It stretched from China in the East, through the wilds of Mongolia, India, Afghanistan and the Middle East through to the Mediterranean. Intrepid merchants traded the coveted Chinese silk, gold and spices and in return Buddhist monks arrived to spread their religion throughout China. But it was the Tang dynasty of the 7th to 10th centuries that saw the 'Golden Age' of China. Poetry, painting and music flourished amongst the privileged gentry classes. Printing was invented, 500 years before the West, and the world's oldest printed book, the 'Diamond Sutra', was produced. The capital at that time Changan, was

the biggest city in the world with a population of over one million. The Emperor Tai Zong encouraged foreign trade and liberalised government policies, increasing China's wealth.

Further impressive advances were made during the subsequent Song dynasty but they could not prevent the Mongol hordes of Genghis Khan conquering north China in the 13th century. The Song dynasty ended when Kublai Khan declared himself to be the new Emperor in 1279.

*Tower of Buddhist Incense, Summer Palace, Beijing.*

The Polo brothers and their son Marco, had travelled to China in the 13th century. Marco Polo's book about his travels, written while he languished in a Genoese jail, had acquainted some Europeans with a tantalising insight into the nation. His tales of glorious cities dripping with gold, advanced technology, silk, fruit and spices sparked a fascination with the Orient throughout Europe. This fabled image reached its peak with stories of the great Kahn's court at Xanadu. News of his marble palaces and magnificent city showed the East to be exotic, wondrous and rich, compared to medieval Europe. But many disbelieved Polo and by and large east and west remained isolated and ignorant of one another.

China's isolation continued under the next dynasty when the Manchus invaded from Manchuria in the 17th century. The Manchus became the richest and most powerful people in China, though they had their own customs and often spoke a different language to the rest of the Chinese people. Yet such was their influence that wearing a pigtail amongst men, a sign of loyalty to the Manchus, became a national custom.

Fortunes of nations rise and fall and by the 19th century China had declined in relation to the progressing Western nations. The Manchu government had not encouraged communication and trade with the West and many Chinese were living in dire poverty. The ruling classes of government officials, the 'mandarins', spent half their lives in study to maintain their privileged positions, though their learning had little bearing on the modern world. An archaic class system perpetuated the stagnation of the country. The gentry were increasingly irrelevant, peasants continued to be oppressed and merchants were traditionally despised. Not surprisingly, business languished and corruption flourished. A vast terrain of inhospitable land, frequently flooded, made subsistence agriculture precarious for a population that had already reached 500 million by 1900.[1] In theory, peasants were meant to be regarded highly as they grew the food upon which all depended but in practice they were tied to the land and subject to the whims of feudal masters. Landlords were particularly despised as they

*Buddhist temple, Shanghai.*

appeared to live in relative luxury. Parents sold their children, husbands their wives and baby girls were abandoned when their parents could not afford their upkeep. Buddhism flourished, offering hope for a better after life.

It was against this backdrop that the first major incursions were made into Chinese territory by Western merchants and in due course by representatives of their nations. The expanding European states, in avid competition with each other, wished to open up trade with China. Chinese silk, tea, and porcelain were desirable commodities in the West but trade was far from free. The Chinese government sought to restrict it by limiting the import of goods to a small number of ports and imposing punitive taxes. These measures made the price of western goods artificially high, thereby curbing demand and adversely affecting trade with the West, Britain in particular. In response to the restricted legal trade, British traders sought a commodity the Chinese would buy - illegal opium. So the British East India Trading Company, having taken control of the opium growing regions of India, began smuggling the drug into China.

Over time many Chinese people became addicted to the substance and demand for it grew rapidly. In 1839 the Chinese government suspended all trade until the British merchants handed over their opium and signed a bond declaring, under penalty of death, that they would no longer trade in the drug. They refused. The entire British merchant population was held hostage and three million pounds of opium was taken and destroyed by the Chinese authorities in Canton. Britain viewed the destruction of the opium as the unlawful confiscation of private property and responded by sending a naval squadron from India, signalling the start of the first 'Opium War' of 1839 to 1842. China was no match for the militarily superior British navy and she suffered a crushing defeat that forced her to sue for peace. The resulting Treaty of Nanking compelled China to open up several ports to foreign trade, including Shanghai, and allow those ports to be defended by foreign troops. The island of Hong Kong was also ceded to Britain. The following year, British settlement began in Shanghai and the French, Germans, Japanese and eventually Americans quickly followed their example, the Americans' trading rights eventually merging with the British. The Chinese government's attempt to control trade had indeed cost it dearly. It had set out to prevent the legitimate import of foreign goods and ended up losing a war, being forced to sign a humiliating and costly treaty and indirectly creating a debilitating drug dependency amongst its citizens.

Many Chinese blamed the Manchu rulers for allowing China to be over-run by foreigners, who were perceived as 'barbarians' and 'foreign devils'. In 1850 a massive rebellion broke out against Manchu and foreign influence. The Taiping rebellion was supported by the Triads, a Buddhist secret society that aimed to overthrow the Manchu dynasty. The uprising continued for 14 years, during which time 600 cities were ruined and many thousands of people killed. The Manchus were only able to put down the rebellion with European help, which naturally made them even more unpopular.

*'Lion', Forbidden city, Beijing.*

Amid this bitter conflict, in 1856-60 a second war broke out between a joint Anglo-French force and Chinese rebels. Beijing, the capital city of China was attacked and the Summer Palace burned. Further treaties ensued, considered 'unequal' in the eyes of many Chinese, granting special privileges to foreigners as well as control of seaports. By the end of the 19th century there were 50 treaty ports open to trade and foreign residence and large areas of Chinese territory that were considered 'spheres of influence' by various European powers. Not all Chinese considered the foreign influence pernicious, as evidenced by the flood of refugees into the British controlled ports of Shanghai and Hong Kong. Clearly living under the protection of British law was considered more desirable than taking one's chances with the vicious warlords or corrupt Mandarins. The areas of foreign domination became very successful centres of entrepreneurial activity, from which many locals benefited. Contrast this with the unbearable dues imposed on Chinese peasants by their own government. In one province they were forced to pay: 'land tax, kettle tax, stocking tax, bedding tax, wheat bran tax, water-mill tax, copper tax, flour shop tax, extraordinary (!) tax', wealthy house tax and army mule tax'.[2] Chinese peasants were undoubtedly oppressed by their rulers for whom it was convenient to blame Westerners. Discontent with Manchu rule and, by association, foreign influence, grew. The latter encouraged by a cruel and ruthless Empress who actively promoted a hatred of foreigners.

86

# China at the start of the 20th century.

At the turn of the 20th century, nationalist forces in China rallied round a charismatic young doctor named Sun Yat Sen. Doctor Sun was emphatically not anti-western. A Christian, he had been educated in American schools in Hawaii and in a British college in Hong Kong. He recognised that for China to progress it would have to become a republic along Western lines, which would mean an end to the Manchu dynasty that was so opposed to change. Accordingly, he formed several secret societies with the specific aim of overthrowing the Manchus. Ten such attempts were made over the course of several years but by 1911 all had failed.

In 1908 the 73 year old Empress died and the 'Dragon Throne' passed to her two year old nephew Puyi who became Emperor, though the child's uncle was appointed Regent to rule in his place until he was old enough to assume control. For a while things settled down but discontent erupted again in 1911. As before, poor harvests leading to distress and famine amongst the peasants fuelled the uprising. Increasing government taxes also upset wealthier Chinese and one by one, the various provincial rebellions combined to form a full-scale revolution against the

*Emperor Puyi.*

Manchu state. The Manchus dispatched Yuan Shikai, the most competent General in China to suppress the rebels, which he did. However, recognising his unique and commanding position, Yuan Shikai took the opportunity to persuade the rebels to accept him as leader after the removal of the Manchus.

Meanwhile, Sun Yat Sen had been in America on a fund raising tour and when he returned he was elected President of the 'United Provinces of China', to popular acclaim by an assembly of the rebels. Yuan Shikai still commanded the military however, so to avoid civil war between their

respective supporters Dr Sun magnanimously stepped down. In 1912, the five year old Emperor Puyi, or rather his uncle the Regent on his behalf, relinquished the Imperial throne. China had become a Republic.

The problems of ruling China however, had by no means disappeared and in many ways had only become more apparent. Yuan Shikai was not really interested in democracy and instead decided to set up a new dynasty. But he could not avoid Japanese encroachment on Chinese lands and, much to the horror and dismay of the Chinese people, Yuan acceded to Japanese demands for territory in an attempt to avoid war. His actions cost him his popularity and with it his chance of becoming the new emperor. He died shortly after in 1916, ostensibly of a stroke though some said of a broken heart.

Following Shikai's death China again fell into disunity. Sun Yat Sen's party, the People's National party, known as the Guomindang or *GMD*, set up its government in Guangzhou (Canton) but its power was confined to the immediate region. Elsewhere the warlords ruled with varying degrees of efficacy and barbarity. Some prided themselves on the 'order and cleanliness' of their provinces. The following extract, related by a French journalist who interviewed Marshal Zhang Zuolin, the warlord of Manchuria in 1927, shows just how viciously such order was maintained.
*'The city, I must say, was well policed. I remember seeing two heads, still dripping with blood, swaying in a fisherman's net by the door of a theatre; two soldiers had been executed there for having disregarded the law that forbade them to enter without paying.'* [3]

During World War I China had fought on the side of the Western allies and the people had expected that the Paris Peace Conference would put an end to the 'unequal treaties' and return those German ports that had been seized by Japan to the Chinese. But when this did not happen a massive demonstration of 10,000 students was held in Beijing, followed by strikes, protests and boycotts of Japanese goods.

Against this background of unrest and discontent, a young librarian at Beijing University named Mao Zedong set up the Chinese Communist Party in 1921. Mao had been inspired by the victory of the Communists in Russia, in his own words, *"the gunfire of the Russian Revolution brought Marxism to China"*. Mao's party was initially very small, only 57 members in fact, so it was prudent to work with the GMD in the first instance to achieve their common goals. This was also the advice of the Russian Soviet leaders.

At the same time, Sun Yat Sen was reorganising his own party, based on the principles of freedom, democracy and the 'people's livelihood'. Dr. Sun could not possibly achieve his aim of a united China free from warlord control without foreign help and he appealed for assistance from Britain in the first instance. Since he was also seeking freedom from foreign interference it is perhaps unsurprising that they were suspicious and refused. Ironically, in the light of future developments, he then sought help from the USSR. They were more than happy to help the GMD develop along Russian Communist lines, with strict party discipline and total obedience to party decisions. Naturally they were expected to allow the Chinese Communist party into their ranks.

Sun Yat Sen died in 1925 and the leadership of the GMD then passed to his brother-in-law, Chiang Kaishek, who also became Commander-in-Chief of the new GMD army. With 500 trained officers leaving his military academy at Huangpu he could begin the enormous task of conquering and unifying China. Less idealistic and perhaps more pragmatic than Sun Yat Sen, he achieved considerable success in gaining the support of many provinces, through a combination of anti-warlord propaganda, combat where necessary and outright bribery. At times warlords were forced to surrender to him simply because their armies had mutinied and joined the GMD.

By the late 1920's the GMD, with the Communists, had conquered all of Southern China and extended their influence to much of the North. However, it was becoming clear that the alliance could not last much longer. In 1926, Mao told a GMD meeting that: *'In a very short time, several hundred million peasants will rise like a tornado... They will break through the chains that hold them and push forward along the road to freedom!'* [4]. Holding true to Marxist theory he believed that the peasants would successfully revolt and destroy the ruling land-owning classes. Many of the GMD members were themselves landlords and party funds often came from businessmen, particularly from Shanghai, so the GMD was increasingly seen as a 'capitalist' party. They had a lot to lose if the Communists should win. Chiang Kaishek came to the conclusion that they must crush the Communists. In 1927 he struck. There had been a Communist uprising in Shanghai, led by Zhou Enlai and a Soviet Council set up to run the city. Several days later, Chiang Kaishek's army arrived and brutally crushed the fledgling council and thousands of their supporters. Over the next five weeks, there were daily massacres in the streets of Shanghai, estimates vary from 5,000 to 15,000 gunned down in the streets, without trials or even questioning. Some reports claim that people could be killed just for wearing red clothes.[5] The International Settlement stood by and watched, some say even supplying rifles and ammunition. It was a similar story in other parts of the country; Chiang's men treated the Communists with equal severity, sending thousands of them fleeing for their lives. Mao and a small band of committed followers retreated to the countryside. Persecution of a group often has the opposite effect to that intended by the perpetrator and so it was with Mao's movement. It arose strengthened from the onslaught.

By 1928 Chiang Kaishek had defeated a number of warlords and allied with others to establish a new National Government, with himself as leader. However, he really only controlled the North. Other areas were still prey to gangs of bandits who, not content with destroying whole villages, existed by theft and kidnapping, ruthlessly enforced by vicious executions such as cutting in two at the waist. In the South, the area around the Jiangxi Soviet was still controlled by the Communists and their influence was spreading. One of the reasons for this local support was the Land Law of 1930, introduced by Mao to distribute land in the regions under his control amongst the peasants. It is ironic that, like Lenin before him, who also recognised the inherent desire for private land ownership, his support grew out of an entirely cynical and dishonest exploitation of the peasants' dreams. Dishonest, because neither Mao nor Lenin had ever intended to create a class of peasant freeholders. After all Marxist ideology did not support the concept of individual property rights. Another reason for the growth in support for the Red Army was the discipline the Communists imposed upon their soldiers when passing through villages and dealing with the peasants. Some examples: *'...Be courteous and polite to the people and help them when you can ...Return all borrowed articles ...Replace all damaged articles ...Be honest in all transaction with the peasants ...Pay for all articles purchased, and so on.'* [6] How interesting and tragic that those simple rules of courtesy and free exchange of goods and services for mutual benefit, that is, the basis of a market economy, should be the very means by which the peasants were won over to the Communist cause.

Chiang Kaishek on the other hand showed no such consideration for either peasants or Communists. He launched one extermination campaign after another in an effort to wipe out all traces of the Red Army and their supporters. As the Red Army was still comparatively weak militarily they could only fight back using hit and run tactics or deadly ambushes – guerrilla warfare. Years later the Vietnamese would adopt the same tactics against the Americans, having learnt from Mao's successes against a numerically superior and better equipped adversary. The strategy of luring the GMD forces into Communist held territories in order to ambush them risked the destruction of villages by the GMD as they sought to deny the communists a base. It is estimated that more than a million peasants were either killed or starved to death as a result of these tactics, for which Mao must also be held partly responsible. Of course, Communist propaganda made much of the inherent cruelty of the GMD forces and there is undeniable truth to this claim. Though perhaps some could also have questioned Mao's humanity and the price he was willing others to pay in order to defeat his enemies. The parallels with Russia and later, Vietnam are all too real.

While the Guomindang and the Communists were fighting for control of China, the Japanese were planning their own offensives. They already had some degree of influence in Manchuria, where they controlled many mines, railways, factories and ports. They even had a friendly agreement with the warlord in control, Zhang Zuolin. His rule weakened the central government's power in Beijing, which suited the Japanese. However, when Zhang had agreed to accept Chiang Kaishek as the new ruler, the Japanese felt threatened. Zhang and Chiang together could oppose Japanese domination of Manchuria and so two Japanese colonels blew up Zhang's private train - with him in it. The Japanese thought they could control the warlord's son, Zhang Xueliang, a luxury-loving gambler and a drug addict but they were to be proved wrong…

## The refugees in Harbin, Manchuria.

This was the state of the country which thousands of Russians risked their lives to reach and make their new home, convinced that however dangerous and uncertain their prospects in China, it would still be preferable to the totalitarian state they had left behind. It is not clear whether or not the Russian exiles were entirely aware of what they were letting themselves in for. They most certainly had not anticipated the eventual Communist take-over of the country but they were prepared to take their chances with 'normal' criminal banditry and violence. Despite the turmoil raging throughout the rest of the nation, the predominantly Russian settlement of Harbin in northern Manchuria appeared to be relatively calm and relations with the many Chinese who also lived there were amicable.

The history of Harbin and that of the Trans Siberian railway are intrinsically linked. As Russia is such a huge country the obvious solution to her transport problems in the 19th century lay with the railway, developed in England. By the 1850's the technology of steam trains had quickly spread to other developing countries and the Western parts of the USSR were soon covered by tracks. The vast hinterland had yet to be conquered but by the end of the century, the Trans Siberian railway line was pushing towards the border with China. It aimed for the port of Vladivostok on the Eastern coast and had reached the city of Chita. Chita would later become a prison town of labour camps, the furthest point on the Trans-Siberian railway where prisoners were sent.

The border with China at Chita veered north, following the course of the river Amur, leaving a huge piece of Chinese territory jutting into the Russian nation (seen on the map in the previous chapter). Cutting straight through the Chinese territory would save 300 miles, which obviously made sound economic sense. The region was an undeveloped wilderness at the time, though with a comparatively milder climate than the northern side of the river. Accordingly, the representatives of the Imperial Russian government contacted the Chinese court and requested permission to build the railway. Talks began in Peking in 1885 and in the following year, the Russian Minister of Finance – Sergei Witte, Prince Lobanoff and the Chinese representatives, signed a contract in Moscow. They agreed to build and utilise the railway for 80 years, after which it would automatically become Chinese property. China also had the option to buy it after thirty six years.[7]

In the summer of 1897 the first party of engineers arrived in Manchuria. They had no maps of the area but soon plans were drawn up and work began. Harbin was chosen as the railway hub as it was on the river Sungari, which flowed into the Amur. Building materials could arrive by ship from Russia using these rivers. Construction was interrupted by the Boxer rebellion in 1900 when nationalist Chinese, angered by the apparent exploitation of their country, attacked the foreigners. However, construction resumed when the rebellion was crushed and the town rapidly developed, to the advantage of both Russians and the many Chinese who found employment in the burgeoning metropolis.

Harbin flourished in the dawn of the new century and there was plenty of work in addition to the railway. The railway had stimulated the growth of an entire infrastructure – power stations, roads, hospitals, churches, bridges, tunnels, stations, much of this built by manual labour or with the aid of horses. All expenses were paid for in gold by the Imperial treasury.

In 1924 Soviet Russia took control of the railway. They declared to the Chinese government that the contract they had signed was void, as the Imperial Russian State no longer existed. According to one Russian émigré source, the Soviets then offered the Russian workers, most of whom had now settled in Harbin, the choice of Soviet or Chinese citizenship. This seemed to be an uncharacteristically tolerant gesture on the part of the new Soviet government and, if true, one can only surmise that in the wake of a bitter civil war, the new regime simply did not have the resources to forcibly return the expatriates.

The Soviets were nominally in control for only a few years. By 1932 the Japanese had occupied Manchuria and renamed the country Manzhouguo, meaning Manchu-land, placing the former Emperor of China – Puyi, back on the throne. Now aged 26 he had been living a luxurious and dissolute life since his forced abdication as a 5 year old child and doubtless welcomed the opportunity to regain at least some of his former status. Following his abdication he had led a life of splendid isolation in the Forbidden City at Beijing, received a British education at the hands of a formidable Public school tutor and married two beautiful young Chinese noblewomen.[8] However, it soon became clear that he was to be no more than a puppet ruler on behalf of his Japanese masters. In 1935 they bought the railway from the Soviets and all Soviet citizens were evacuated back to Russia but the stateless White Russians were allowed to remain in Harbin. Neither the Shalavins nor the Shliapnikoffs had any documentation to associate themselves with the USSR; they were truly citizens without a country. Mercifully, they were not dragged back, nor do they appear to have been unduly affected by the momentous changes in the leadership of their Chinese haven.

Harbin was clearly differentiated into 'Old Harbin', the original settlement founded by the first Russians with Imperial encouragement, and the new city, stimulated by the waves of Russians fleeing the Revolution, Civil War and the Soviet Union. The old city consisted of residential suburbs of roughly about 1,000 people, each with its own small Orthodox church, surrounding the larger city with its cathedral. The Russians and Chinese generally lived apart, their respective streets linked by trams. The houses were generally built by their owners, usually of wood but occasionally brick.

*Map of Harbin, 1938.*

The 1938 map of the city above, in Russian and Mandarin, shows many interesting features of both parts of the city. Firstly, a key in the bottom left hand corner shows aspects of the town as it was in 1898. The original settlement is in the lower right hand side. The main offices of the Far

Eastern Railway Company were located in the old town and linked to the Sungari River by a primitive road. Interestingly, along that road the map of 1938 shows the location of an 'English Exporting company'. On the banks of the river was a small fortress and wooded areas, at least one of which was still intact 40 years later. 'Forest Street' just below it seems to confirm this, no doubt a little oasis of green in what had become a busy industrial city. Other original features mentioned in the legend include a few named farmhouses, a large lake, 'upon which ducks swam' and a field of poppies, whose seeds in traditional cakes are much loved by Russians.

By the 1930's 'new' Harbin had become a relatively large city with a population of about a quarter of a million. Amongst other institutions it had a quality department store, the Churin, which was considered prestigious even by Shanghai's international standards. Russian craftsmen, particularly jewellers, who had worked there and would later move to Shanghai, would have impressive credentials to advertise. By that time the Russian community was firmly established in the bustling city that Harbin had become. There were bakers, butchers, chemists, shops of all kinds and schools, both vocational and grammar. There were even tertiary institutes that graduated doctors, dentists, teachers and engineers; a popular one being the 'Polytechnic'. By 1938 there were also numerous factories, an electric power station, a large railway depot naturally, many mechanics' workshops, a hospital township, airport and a hippodrome for horse racing. There was even a Japanese memorial located on the edge of the city. In the light of their treatment of the Chinese at this time it must have been a very sensitive construction. Clearly, the city had grown tremendously in the space of only 40 years.

Prior to the establishment of the Japanese regime, an interesting system of justice existed in Harbin. In the absence of any official Russian or Chinese governments, the two cultures devised their own systems of law which more or less harmonised with each another. For example, the Russians would have their own community court of elders and priests to settle disputes, whose authority was generally recognised. The Chinese had their own courts, often conducted in a kind of pidgin Russian (a combination of Chinese and Russian), which appears to suggest the Chinese also tried Russians. An anecdote from this time relates the story of a Chinese judge with a prisoner before him. He says that, according to Chinese law, this convicted criminal would be beheaded. According to Russian law, he would spend 25 years in a labour camp but *he* would simply fine him 25 roubles. If the story is true then the judge was

*Orthodox cathedral, Harbin.*

unusually forgiving. On the whole, Russians earned a reputation for being law-abiding citizens. Just as well, given that many men in Manchuria owned or had access to rifles or firearms of some description. Hunting was both a popular pastime and a necessary source of food – geese, ducks, wild goats, bears, elks, boars and even occasionally Siberian tigers. Firearms would also have been used to defend themselves against the ever present threat of bandits in a land where warlords and their gangs still controlled much of the country.

At the celebration of Christ's baptism, on the 19th of January, the Russians would build a huge cross of ice – three metres high, and hold a winter service outside. Some brave souls would make a large hole in the ice and plunge in for a swim to emulate the baptism. Interestingly enough, following the recent reopening of China to foreigners, the building of ice structures has seen something of a revival and become a tourist attraction. Once again, intrepid divers are taking the plunge.

Those Russian houses that had not been destroyed by the Chinese have been restored, including at least one of the Orthodox churches, and the city is once again assuming something of a Russian character. Elderly émigrés are returning to the city where they spent their youth and have reported the changes. The Russian Orthodox cemetery is now a park. My grandfather was buried there and my

*Ice cross, Harbin.*

father, ever the sentimental optimist, hopes that he has a tree to mark his resting place, where birds would come and sing to him in the spring.

## The Shalavins' experiences

In Manchuria, Maria Zinovyevna was living a harsh but satisfying life, rich in spirit and *joie de vivre*, if not material comfort. She had remarried, this time a match of her own choosing and believed she had at last found love with her young husband, Ivan Grigorievich. They had three children – Leonid, born about 1925, Ivan (my father), known as Vanya, born two years later and Anatoly, born in 1929. Two photographs of Ivan senior survive. The first one was presumably to commemorate the birth of their first son, showing Maria, Ivan and baby Leonid (Lyona). Sadly, the child died in infancy, aged one.

*Maria, Ivan Grigorievich and Leonard, c. 1925.*

The other (overleaf) is a group picture of a sociable picnic by the water's edge, with a large happy crowd enjoying the surroundings and warm weather. Many are in swimsuits and Ivan's tanned, handsome face stands out quite markedly. He had thick black hair, perfect olive skin and a swarthy almost Latin appearance. Both sons took after their father in appearance and it has been commented that my father looks more like a Spaniard than a Russian. The resemblance between Ivan and his second son, his namesake, in later years would be remarkable.

*A picnic in Manchuria. Ivan senior is on the right holding the infant, Vanya; c.1928.*

The photographs are very old and worn, Maria lovingly carried them around with her throughout all her years of exile, across three continents, China, Canada and finally, Australia.

This marriage, while lasting considerably longer than her first, was not particularly successful. She loved her young husband but despaired of his tendency to drink and his apparent inability to provide for his family. It was her strength and resilience that kept the family together and against all odds the boys enjoyed an idyllic childhood in the woods of Manchuria, until circumstances forced them to move to Southern China.

Maria was a wonderful, fervently dedicated mother who took all that life could throw at her and always bounced back with cheerful optimism, humour and a ready Russian proverb. She had a deep faith in God and all the trappings of the Orthodox religion, a faith that sustained her through years of hardship and exile. Little educated, except from the school of life, she was superstitious, devout and intensely moral, with a profound sense of honesty and integrity, traits which she passed on to my father. For most of her life she had to support herself through dogged hard work, as a housekeeper, cook and servant; indeed any work she could find amongst the Russian community.

Life in Harbin with Ivan Grigorievich however, was to prove a challenge. It must have been frustrating being married to a man who did not live up to her expectations, but she never spoke ill of him and remained loyal to his memory. At some time during the 1920's, Ivan stopped working for the Railway and went to work for the Fire Brigade in Harbin, the city where he had met Maria. She did not elaborate on the details of his employment, as he was not there for very long but such work raises all kinds of interesting questions, which alas, I never asked. Who ran the Fire Brigade? We can only assume it was a voluntary organisation drawn from the local Russian community. Did they collaborate with the local Chinese? How did people pay for this service? All we can surmise with some degree of certainty is that it was a privately run service as no effective state infrastructure existed in Manchuria at the time.

Ivan and Maria's eldest surviving son, Ivan Ivanovich (the suffix *ovich* meaning 'son of' – the patronymic being the formal mode of address) was born in Harbin on 5th March 1927. He spent his early toddler years there in the warm and secure company of his devoted parents. Like most Russian children he, and later his brother Anatoly (Tolya), began school at age seven, attending one of the many local Russian schools. Ivan, familiarly Vanya, enjoyed the experience, learning Russian, reading traditional folk tales from the Motherland and especially arithmetic, which he has always enjoyed. He still relishes mathematical challenges to this day,

*Vanya and Tolya c. 1931.*

taking pride in his excellent prowess. During those early years of the boys' education, the Japanese occupation was to have a notable impact on their schooling. Since not only did they learn their mother tongue but the children were also obliged to learn Japanese. Vanya particularly remembers being instructed to sing the Japanese national anthem, to Puyi, the Chinese Emperor of Manzhouguo. All schools had to pay lip service to their Japanese conquerors. How ironic that this feeble 'Emperor', who had relinquished all his power back in 1912, should now appear to be revered by his subjects, albeit under Japanese orders. No doubt it suited Japanese propaganda to pretend they were permitting some degree of self-rule to the Chinese. Most accounts seem to agree that the White Russians living under Japanese jurisdiction did not suffer unduly and were generally free to get on with their own lives, unlike the Chinese who were treated barbarically. After the declaration of general war this was to change to some extent when Russians were conscripted into the Japanese army.

*Village community in Manchuria, Maria is on the far left.*

After the Fire Brigade, Ivan acquired a horse, *Zhiganka* (Flame), and a large cart and worked as a deliveryman for a while. However, there was little work and Ivan found himself increasingly drawn to alcohol. Like many Russian men, trapped in circumstances seemingly beyond their control and with no better prospects in sight, vodka appeared to be the only salvation. Ever the resourceful and practical mother, Maria cajoled him to sell the horse and move to Veyshahe where there was said to be work on the branch line. Her husband agreed and they uprooted and travelled 120 miles to this remote railway station, where they hoped he could find some stable employment and be able to provide a secure home for their two sons. Working for a railway was probably more lucrative than the alternatives, though their lifestyle was still poor. So, Ivan and his family embarked on a new life in this remote outpost of the Chinese Eastern Railway, a spur off the great Trans Siberian, which owed its existence to the timber cutting industry. They lived in Veyshahe station in the far north of Manchuria for approximately four years, from 1936 to 1940. Russians managed the railroad and the Chinese supplied the manual labour but the real masters of the railway at that time were the occupying Japanese.

When the family moved to Veyshahe, the boys, to their delight, encountered a blissful lifestyle in the Manchurian forest wilderness that surrounded their new home. Vanya and Tolya spent three unforgettable years in the village and Vanya fondly remembers this heavenly interlude in the forests of Manchuria. Nature there was beautiful, he claims. We lived as though on a *dacha*, a summer resort, picking mushrooms, grapes, raspberries, as well as fishing and swimming in the crystal clear waters of the lakes and mountain rivers. They even learned to ride ponies. In winter, when temperatures would plummet to -30$^C$, they would toboggan on the snow or skate on the frozen lakes. *"We loved it all! It was the best time of our childhood lives,"* he reminisced enthusiastically. The natural surroundings were indeed stunning and teeming with wildlife. Vanya even came across a bear once. He recalls how he shouted with alarm and the bear and he promptly ran off in different directions! He also remembers how they used to hunt birds with slingshots and took pride in their skilled aim, until one day he brought down a lovely bird. As it lay dying, it looked up at him as if to say *"What have I done to you?"* Consumed with guilt, he never again killed birds in this fashion.

The boys took great delight in fishing expeditions. Vanya related how he and his brother would happily rise at 3 a.m., walk three miles on railway tracks, carefully stepping from sleeper to sleeper in the dark, to reach a favoured fishing spot before sunrise. Yet years later when told to rise before dawn for work or some other undesirable task he would groan with displeasure. Difficult tasks performed freely are far more productive than those performed under duress he claims. Охота пуще неволи. Voluntary effort is better than forced; surely a saying of universal truth.

Food was abundant in this veritable paradise. For while his parents had little income his resourceful mother could produce wonderful dishes from basic staples and the fruits of the forest. In time honoured tradition she would grow as many varieties of vegetables as the climate would sustain in the summer and then pickle or preserve them, along with the natural produce growing wild in the woods, for winter consumption. *Pelemeni*, meat filled dumplings, called *won ton* by the Chinese, were a particular favourite; although Russians, unlike the Chinese, do not normally serve them in soup. Maria would make them by the hundreds in cold weather. No freezer was needed to store them; they would simply be placed on a board outside until frozen then packed in bags and left to hang in the cold air. It was necessary to keep a keen eye on them however lest any stray animals be tempted to help themselves. Maria's self sufficiency meant they rarely needed to eat at the local Chinese cafes and food stalls. But there was one café by the railroad track that my father says they went to occasionally. He related the story of how one day he saw a stray dog that had wandered onto the tracks mown down by a passing train. No sooner had the train passed than the cook from the café dashed out to drag the hapless corpse back to his kitchen. What good luck for him. All meat is food – 'chow', when one is poor and in parts of China dogs were deliberately bred for food. The Shalavins however, did not eat there again.

Living in such a beautiful wilderness was indeed idyllic, providing one was healthy. An incident from Vanya's childhood, which he does not remember so favourably, was to have far reaching consequences. In 1937 when he was just ten Vanya had broken his shoulder falling out of a tree and had to go to the Russian hospital in Harbin. It took him 12 hours just to reach the station for the six-hour rail journey, an agonising time he recalls. Eventually, doctors reset his shoulder but not accurately. Seven years later it was X-rayed in Shanghai and found to be misaligned, but he did not want to have it broken and reset as there was no guarantee of success. He has lived with one undeveloped shoulder ever since but it has never prevented him from working hard physically and true to his serene nature he has never complained of his injury. Obtaining good medical care was a considerable challenge for the poorer Russians in China.

Sadly, the tranquil life would end when Vanya left for boarding school in Harbin, a year earlier than his brother. There were no secondary schools in the vicinity and the primary school the boys had attended was a single room school, catering for all the young local children. He gives few details of this period, except to say that he hated it. I can only surmise that this was no comfortable institution. His parents could not have afforded a decent private school, even if they had existed in Harbin. (Though Shanghai had its share of prestigious private colleges for privileged foreigners). His school, funded by Russian charities, would undoubtedly have been very Spartan and Vanya remembers it being run according to strict discipline. The year was 1939 when war in Europe began which may have added to the tension and deprivation. No wonder Vanya claimed to have left his country 'heaven' for 'hell'. At 13 he fell sick and nearly died. It is not clear exactly what he was suffering from, possibly pneumonia. He was gaunt and near death according to his mother, who was horrified by the condition she found him in when she was eventually notified to collect him and take him home. She nursed him back to health, no doubt with generous helpings of home grown food and the tender loving care that only a mother can give. Following his recovery he had to endure one more year of this hated school in Harbin. In 1940, for reasons unknown to him, his mother decided to undertake the considerable task of resettling in Shanghai. Perhaps she had been moved by the boys' unhappy experiences at the Harbin school, anticipated wartime problems or was simply exasperated with her husband. At any rate, their father stayed in Harbin and the teenage boys and their devoted mother relocated to Shanghai, where Vanya and Tolya were admitted to the Russian Commercial College as boarders and Maria found work as a live-in housekeeper to an ambitious and successful Russian family - the Shliapnikoffs.

## The Shliapnikoffs' experiences.

The story of the Shliapnikoffs' exodus from Russia continues with their eventual arrival in Harbin, the capital city of Manchuria. The city was overflowing with Russian immigrants. Many other people had made similarly dangerous journeys in recent years though Harbin had been a magnet for Russians ever since the construction of the Trans Siberian railway.

The Shliapnikoff elders and their six offspring who had chosen to flee with them, plus their respective families, lived in *Nahalovka,* the poor section by the rail tracks, where rents were lowest. Their accommodation was primitive. Each family managed to get a room with a kitchen of sorts. There was a coal burning stove but no plumbing, so water had to be carried from the hand pump in an adjoining yard. The toilet was an outhouse, shared by all the tenants in the compound. Winters were exceedingly cold in Harbin, similar to Siberia, just across the border. Olga, the daughter of Peter and Tanya Bakaldin, related her immediate family's experiences. *'It was hard for my father to find work. So he used his initiative like many other immigrants. He bought old clothes; my mother washed them manually on a washing board in a tub. Then she mended them. My father rented a table on a market place and sold them. There was a need for that sort of thing - Russian immigrants could not afford to buy new clothes. I remember carrying my father's lunch to that market place. I had to go across the railway tracks to reach it. I still remember passing through a lot of dead bodies by the tracks – these were the Chinese killed by the Japanese, so I knew how cruelly the Japanese were behaving during their occupation of China. Of course I was too young to understand the politics.'*

*'Many times my mother had to leave us early in the morning by ourselves.*

*She let us sleep and left our breakfast on a table. She had to go to the market place to bring some of the clean clothes and to stay there at the merchandise table while my father went to buy some more of the old clothes. Of course my mother could not afford a baby sitter for us. She just told us when we woke up to have our breakfast and play quietly. There were some things we did then; we were too young to understand how bad they were. Once, before my mother left, she put some dirty clothes in warm, sudsy water to soak in the kitchen tub. She had in mind to wash them when she would be back. When she returned, she saw a disaster – all the wet clothes were on the floor and my brother Nikolai was throwing, splashing the sudsy dirty water on me and laughing. At that time it was winter, we were both shivering, as we were wet and cold. My mother said she broke out crying. So she took care of us and proceeded with the task of clearing up the mess and washing clothes. She had no heart to scold us as we were too young and already punished being cold and wet. Another time, when my mother returned from the market, she found another mess. My brother, the mischievous one, somehow found the scissors, cut the pillows up and was throwing the down over me, having a lot of fun. What can you expect of unsupervised young kids?'*

Zina and Nikolai also ran a *baraholka* in Harbin, a street stall where they bought old clothes, washed, mended and ironed them for reselling. Zina also sewed and knitted clothes which her husband sold. She was always a very creative and resourceful woman. It could not have been an easy time for them but their eldest daughter Nina, my aunt, remembered her childhood in Harbin quite positively. They rented a house near the school where Nina attended until she was about 10 years of age. It was a small school of four classes, predominantly for Russian children, which Nina and her sister Julia (my mother) had to climb a fence to reach. The girls and their parents initially lived with their grandparents Artemy and Praskovia, or *'Babinka'* (an endearing form of *Babushka*) as was already known, and their teenage son Nikolai. Their house had two rooms and a kitchen. Zina and her family had one room and the senior family lived in the other. They had a large garden, which was perfect for the children. Polya (Pelageya), husband Volodya and their children lived nearby.

Nina related one of the ways they used to make a little extra money. Her father would buy cinema tickets in bulk and Nina would sell them on the street corner. She was less than 10 at the time and handed over all the money to her parents, who would buy a pair of shoes when there was enough. However, a teacher saw her one day and put an end to her little enterprise.

According to Nina, Babinka, despite raising eight children of her own, did not like having noisy youngsters around. No doubt remembering the din! However, she allowed Zina to live with them as she had *'two quiet daughters'*. When she was raising her own children she had been helped by a girl called Oxya who became like another member of the family and in time 'nannied' much of the next generation too. It is not clear what became of Oxya during those early years of struggle in Harbin but she too escaped Russia and later rejoined the family when they could once again afford to employ her.

The extended family lived in Harbin for three years but decided to leave in 1933 after a particularly bad year. There had been a flood and all their possessions, especially precious merchandise had become wet and spoiled. They kept their merchandise in padlocked crates at the markets to avoid carrying them back and forth. Each morning they would go to the market, unlock the crates and begin trading. The boxes and crates that held all their linen were drenched. Nikolai tried to retrieve as much as he could. Nina, relating this to me, remembered how she walked to the water's edge with her father. He undressed and left his outer garments with Nina, aged nine, and waded up to his waist to retrieve those of his crates that had not fully submerged or floated away. He succeeded in saving some items, which her mother dutifully washed and tried to make saleable again.

Polya and Volodya, who had not believed that the flood was coming, had stayed in their house and had to be rescued by small boats, salvaging only a few of their possessions in the process. Their three children escaped unscathed from this experience but by odd stroke of fate, their eldest son, Kostya, was to drown in a lake in his late teens.

After the flood they all left to live in another house on higher ground but it was only a temporary move. The flood was the last straw and the entire family decided to move to Shanghai, where they believed there would be better opportunities. They were a very close knit family and no one wanted to be left behind in Harbin on their own. So they all helped each other to move, family by family. The senior family members and their youngest son were the first to move. They opened a store selling used furniture, primarily intended for poor migrants like themselves. The next to leave were Peter and Tania Bakaldin, who also opened a furniture store on the same street. Soon most of the clan were reunited in the same vicinity of that vast and cosmopolitan city.

*Alexei Shliapnikoff.*

Alexei was one of the last of the Shliapnikoff siblings to leave Harbin for Shanghai. He had not been as successful as he had hoped and was therefore forced to borrow money from a local Chinese businessman to pay for the ship journey to Shanghai. It was too dangerous at the time to attempt the long trip overland. In due course he established a small goods factory in Shanghai and, having mastered the technique of smoking ham and making salamis, became affluent enough to repay his debt. He encountered a man who was returning to Harbin and gave him the money he owed plus a ham and meat to pass on to the Chinese businessman. Apparently, the lender was overwhelmed with gratitude and emotion at this stroke of fortune. He had never expected to see the money again, let alone with such attractive interest. But Alexei was a man of his word.

*Alexei, Ekaterina and their children, Yura, Vera, Volodya and Victor, c. 1934.*

# Mao's victory.

No sooner had our intrepid families arrived in the safe haven that they believed China to be, than they were caught up in yet another conflict. This time the aggressors were the Japanese, hungry for land and raw materials for their increasing population. In 1931 the officers of the Kwantung army, already in place in Manchuria, organised a military take-over of the whole of the province and 50,000 troops occupied the area. Despite vehement Chinese objections and a nation-wide boycott of Japanese goods, which now focussed anti-foreign feeling towards the Japanese in particular, they continued to press their advance further into China. By 1936 they controlled most of Northern China and were advancing towards Central China and Shanghai.

The Chinese people expected Chiang Kaishek to declare war on Japan and drive them out of the country but he was more concerned with wiping out the Communists. This would prove to be a catastrophic decision on his part. Zhang Xueliang, son of the former warlord of Manchuria, whose 'orderly' rule had impressed the French journalist, was no longer a useless wastrel. He had overcome his drug addiction and become an able soldier. Sent by Chiang Kaishek to destroy the Communists, he instead did a deal with them to fight their common enemy the Japanese. After all, Zhang was still smarting from their murder of his father, Zhang Zuolin, and wanted revenge. Also his men were Manchurians who would rather fight the foreign enemy than other Chinese. The Communists too, for their part, made much of Nationalist sentiment, using as their slogan 'Chinese do not fight Chinese'. It took the capture and imprisonment of Chiang Kaishek by Zhang's rebel forces to finally force him also to agree to form a United Front against the foreign aggressor. It was not a moment too soon. In 1937, the Japanese struck again, this time with the intention of invading and conquering the entire country.

The Chinese were to pay a huge price during the eight year Japan-China war. The city of Beijing was occupied in the first month and several months later, following a three month siege and heavy aerial bombing, from which the international community also suffered a great deal, Shanghai also fell to the Japanese. The capital Nanking followed shortly afterwards, forcing Chiang to retreat to Chongqing, a new base in the heart of the countryside, which subsequently became known as the most bombarded city in the world. By 1941 there were over 2 million Japanese soldiers in China but even at the peak of their power they never fully controlled the entire county. It was simply too vast; they did however control all the major cities and lines of communication. Nonetheless, the

Chinese suffered enormous casualties. It is estimated that 4 million were killed between 1937 and 1945 and a further 60 million made homeless, as whole cities were decimated when the Chinese fled from Japanese attacks. [9]

The Japanese behaved with barbaric ferocity towards the Chinese civilians, looting, torturing, massacring whole villages and working the people to death. Some were forced to work down coal mines for 13-16 hours a day. According to one survivor from the mines, when they became too ill to work they were thrown into a pit where dogs waited to maul them to death.[10] Despite such terrifying behaviour, the Japanese could not control the whole country and this failure played into the Communists' hands. When the invader moved out of an area, the communists could move in and take control. The barbarity of the Japanese further strengthened the communist cause because the more ruthless the Japanese were to the peasants the more likely they were to support the communists who were fighting them.

*Some of the effects of Japanese attacks on China.*

The GMD on the other hand, did nothing to ingratiate themselves with the peasants. They pursued a 'scorched earth' policy as they retreated, burning anything that could be of use to the pursuing Japanese, which served also to alienate the peasants whose property had been destroyed. According to Han Suyin, a noted author and supporter of Mao, Chiang had ordered the breaching of the Yellow River dykes to flood the land and stop the Japanese. It had not stopped them but a million Chinese peasants were drowned. [11]

By 1941 the uneasy alliance between the Communists and the GMD had ended and the country had become a battleground between the three military forces. The South and West were occupied by the GMD, the Northwest was Communist and the Japanese controlled the East. The Communists used their battle against the Japanese as an opportunity to organise the masses along strict party lines. They 'educated' the people in Marxism, formed unions, peasant associations and women's leagues, much welcomed in a nation which viewed women as second class citizens and still practised foot binding. That pernicious practice of tightly binding toddlers' feet, breaking their toes and leaving them crippled for life; just so women could have 'beautiful' tiny feet. The war undoubtedly helped the Communist cause just as in Russia where Stalin also profited from the enormous suffering inflicted upon the nation by the Nazis. Suddenly the home grown dictator was infinitely preferable to the foreign menace and at this point Mao did appear to offer 'liberation' from the hated Japanese.

The tide began to turn when America joined the war in December 1941 following the attack on Pearl Harbour. American supplies came into China along the Burma Road and, later, American airfields were built in Southeast China. By early 1945 the Japanese were already on the retreat and it is highly debatable as to whether or not the dropping of the atomic bombs was militarily necessary. Some historians suggest that it was a show of strength to their ally, the Soviet Union, whom they had never entirely trusted and with whom they were already in conflict over Berlin. On the 6th of August, the first bomb was dropped on Hiroshima, followed two days later, by prior agreement between Stalin, Churchill and Roosevelt, by the declaration of war on Japan by the USSR. The Soviet Red Army immediately invaded Manchuria. Those members of the ex-pat Russian community who had been forcibly conscripted into the Japanese army, many of whom were still wearing Japanese uniforms, suddenly found themselves in the very precarious position of being on the wrong side of a conflict with their former countrymen.

Both Chiang Kaishek and Mao Zedong were taken by surprise by the subsequent Japanese surrender and large parts of the country were still occupied by Japanese forces. The victorious Americans preferred Chiang to take control and US planes flew Nationalist soldiers to accept the surrender of Japanese garrisons. Where there were no Nationalist GMD forces, Chiang instructed the Japanese to continue fighting the

Communists until his men arrived![12] Such actions would clearly not endear him to the battered remnants of his people. No sooner had the world war ended then the GMD and the Communists resumed their Civil War, no less bitter than before only this time, although perhaps not immediately apparent, the Marxist forces had a strong chance of victory.

Despite numerical superiority, three million soldiers versus Mao's one million, and American support, victory would fall to the Communists. Why? The reason lay in the corruption and lack of direction of the GMD. Its soldiers practised theft and bribery, were cruel to the peasants and took every opportunity to steal resources from the war effort to sell on the black market. No one respected their officers, who in turn did not respect Chiang Kaishek. When this became blindingly obvious to the Americans in 1947, they withdrew their financial support, having already wasted 200 million dollars in aid.

The Red Army, now renamed the People's Liberation Army went on the offensive, abandoning guerrilla tactics in favour of open combat. A series of major battles secured their victory and as each province was won, more peasants were recruited to the cause. Areas under GMD control became increasingly impoverished and even the wealthier Chinese abandoned their support for them when inflation destroyed their life savings. Beijing fell in April 1949, Shanghai in May, and on the 1st of October, Mao Zedong proclaimed the establishment of the *Peoples' Republic of China* from the steps of Tiananman Square. For thousands of Russians who had already fled one Communist tyranny, this was an ominous development.

*Desperate Chinese queuing to retrieve their money and convert it into gold before inflation made it worthless.*

# Chapter 5

# Shanghai, city of wonder.

**Не место красит человека, а человек место.**

*It is not the place that graces a man but a man the place.*

# Background to Shanghai.

Shanghai in the 21st century is a thriving, vibrant, modern city of astounding dynamism and energy. The promising potential of its exotic and glamorous pre-war years has been more than fulfilled as China's tolerance of free enterprise unleashed the power of the market to transform this city. But it was not always so and this remarkable city has seen some immense changes of fortune in its long history. Its origins predate Christianity and records show of customs duties being collected from the port in the 13th century. Occupying a prime position on the Whangpoo River which flows into the great Yangtze, it had become an important and prosperous trading centre. Indeed, wealthy enough to attract many pirates, but its people proved to be not only good traders but worthy defenders as well and little harm was done to their city.

By the 19th century Shanghai had become sufficiently well populated and attractive to draw the attention of Western traders, eager to exploit this potentially huge market. The East India Trading Company sent trade delegations and by 1840 some 25 companies with 100 residents[1] had been established. Following the Opium wars of the mid 19th century, treaties established spheres of interest, or areas of the city where international trade could be conducted freely. Such *concessions,* as they were known, were protected by Western laws. By the 20th century the English, American and European concessions had been amalgamated to form the *International Settlement,* though the *French concession* remained distinct. An English map from the 1930's, included later in this chapter, shows three areas of jurisdiction: the International Settlement, the French concession and the Chinese city of *Nantao.* From this inauspicious start Shanghai was to grow into an exciting, dynamic and bustling city, reaching its heyday in the inter-war years of the 1920's and 30's; the decades some call its vintage years.

By the 20th century Shanghai's International Settlement of just nine square miles with a population of four million was firmly established as a unique enclave. It was known for its extreme wealth, a great hive of entrepreneurial activity where merchants of all races plied their business. This enclave was self-governing, by and large observing British law, as interpreted by its own administrative council and policed by Sikhs. Those proud, tall, turbaned Indians with warrior traditions, who found in this role an appropriate and lucrative outlet for their talents. The settlement had its own courts, currency and even its own language, the wonderfully varied and simple Pidgin English. Constantly adapted by its non Anglo-Saxon inhabitants, this archaic and arguably demeaning language was nonetheless an essential means of communication between the disparate groups. *'No wantchee'*: 'I don't want that'; *'savvy box'*: brain; *'maskee'*: 'never mind'. *'Chop chop'* and *'me no savvy'* are universally understood but a commonly used word to explain all manner of things was the delightful *'Mamafoofoo'*: 'any all how'. Today's equivalent might be *'Whatever'*. Irene Kuhn to whom I am indebted for the following information, worked for The China Press, owned by an astute Iraqi who had made his fortune in the opium trade before becoming 'respectable' in newspapers. Staff working for him received attractive salaries, which enabled journalists, like most other privileged salary earners, to employ a host of domestic servants. In addition to the reporters many other people were drawn to this magnetic, beguiling city. Merchants, bankers, lawyers, engineers, indeed any adventurer or seeker of fortune, frequented its many diverse clubs. Every nationality, profession and interest was catered for; drama, music, dancing and most popular of all racing, in a city that appeared to thrive on gambling. The French club was considered to be one of the most elegant and prestigious venues but the all male Shanghai club was the most exclusive.

Shanghai boasted hotels and restaurants catering for every taste and budget, from basic noodle stalls to the gracefully elegant St. Petersburg, managed by a former White Russian officer. The clubs and restaurants were famed as much for their dancing and decadent ambience as for the delectable food they offered. The two leading Chinese department stores, *Wing On's* and *Sincere's*, specialised in banquets on a grand scale, seating 500 usually and up to 2,000 for special occasions. The cooks had learned to produce international cuisine of every type in response to customer request. Ingredients were not just sourced locally but imported from all over the world. New Zealand and Australia supplied lamb, beef, *'Allowrie'* butter and citrus fruits. California and Hawaii provided fresh green vegetables, though these were expensive compared to local produce. Home grown vegetables however, had their own drawbacks since they always had to be washed first in potassium permanganate as farmers used raw sewage for fertilising. Irene Kuhn related the story of how she had paid a considerable sum of money for a difficult to obtain lettuce and celery. She had instructed the cook to carefully wash the precious greens in cool, boiled water. Imagine her horror when she found the cook scrubbing the celery with a decidedly old toothbrush. 'No, no!' Irene exclaimed, 'No brush!' 'Maskee, Missy' came the reply, 'No belong yours, belong my!'[2]

Shopping was a delight for those who had the means and Nanking Road its Mecca, where Chinese and foreign owned shops vied for the city's custom. The Chinese stores were particularly inviting, with their wooden signs painted in red and gold, distinct fragrances of herbs and the unique sound of the clicking abacus. Nanking Road was also home to the antique

*Nanking Road.*

dealers, purveyors of fine porcelain, curios and woodcarvings. One of the most famous shops was the great silk house of *Lao K'ai Fook*. He sold nothing but silk in every conceivable form, from delicate chiffon to the heaviest brocades. China had been the silk capital of the world for centuries and such shops capitalised on that illustrious tradition. The British department store *Whiteaway and Laidlaw* could also be found in Shanghai, side by side with an American ice-cream soda parlour. There was nothing that could not be obtained in this veritable shoppers' paradise - except perhaps for lettuce and celery.

Those who were fortunate enough to live in the city and enjoy a regular income found that not only could they maintain a large domestic retinue but indeed were expected to do so. Such privileged lifestyles would of course be familiar to anyone who had lived in the British Raj in India, colonial Singapore or Hong Kong. The mistress of the household typically employed *'A Number One Boy'* and a *'Number One Cook'*. If she entertained a lot then she would employ a *'Small Cook'* as well. There would also be a *'Wash Amah'*, a *'General Coolie'* (porter/servant), a gardener and finally the *'Rickshaw Coolie'* (the lowly servant whose job it was to transport goods, and people, by hand pulled cart). If there were children in the household then there would be a *'Baby Amah'* to look after them as well. In addition to this 'essential' help, many households would employ yet more servants, whether warranted or not. For it satisfied Chinese custom to employ as many people as possible, exemplified by the expression *'One does not break another man's rice bowl'*.

The Bund was, and still is, a magnificent boulevard of 19th century colonial buildings that swept around the teeming harbour of the Whangpoo River. Built by Western merchants, its name derives from the Urdu word *band,* meaning an embanked quay. At its northern end stood Garden Bridge, spanning Soochow Creek which flows into the Whangpoo and around which were clustered the British, American, Russian (USSR), German and Japanese consulates. From the British Consulate, with its immaculate green gardens, a verdant island in a sea of stone and brick the Bund stretched southward for almost a mile to the Edward VII avenue. In between lay the commercial houses that financed this great city and the luxury hotels where businessmen entertained their guests and the wealthy enjoyed the fruits of their success. Proceeding south from the British Consulate was the *Yokahama Bank*, then the *Bank of China* followed by the resplendent *Cathay* and *Palace* hotels. After them came the *Chartered Bank, American Bank* and *Central Bank of China,* the *Customs House* and *Hong Kong and Shanghai Bank*, known today throughout the world as *HSBC*. At the edge of the international settlement, at Number Two, The Bund, stood the distinguished *Shanghai Club*. Membership of this British Men's club was restricted to merchants, high ranking police and military officers and compradores (native born agents of the merchants). Overlooking the busy harbour, this imposing building contained beyond its gracious, lofty reception hall, the famous L-shaped Long Bar. At nearly a 150 feet in length it was reputed to be the longest bar in the world at that time. Members stood along its length in strict order of their rank in society and, over its polished mahogany surface, the barons of the great trading houses negotiated deals whilst enjoying their favourite cocktails.

The boundary of the International Settlement did not appear to be rigidly defined, passing as it did through densely packed streets and residential areas. In the north of the city it skirted Shanghai North railway station, crossed Soochow Creek, and then followed its course

*Garden Bridge over Soochow Creek.*

west for some time before again veering south. At its centre was the Shanghai Race Club and Recreation ground, bordered by the charmingly named Bubbling Well Road that became Nanking Road on the other side of the Race Club. This road ran perpendicular from the heart of the Bund. Here, amongst a myriad of other institutions, shops and homes were the Spanish and Portuguese consulates and the YMCA (the Young Men's Christian Association).

Avenue Foch, named after the WWI French General, ran parallel to Nanking Rd, separating the French Concession from the International Settlement. The French Concession was almost as large as the International Settlement and, despite its name, contained a microcosm of the world's nationalities, though Russians seemed to predominate. The principle road was Avenue Joffre, which ran east from the Bund, past the walled *'Chinese City' of Nantao*, to the west of the city. It should be explained that what distinguished Nantao from the rest of the city was not that it was the sole residence of the Chinese, on the contrary they lived and worked in all areas of Shanghai, but that international jurisdiction did not apply within its walls. It remained an essentially anarchic enclave, or so it appeared to foreign residents, where many Chinese criminals could and did flee to escape international justice. Avenue Joffre East consisted of mainly Russian businesses and was known as 'Little Russia'. The West of this huge thoroughfare was almost exclusively residential, with many beautiful homes and gardens owned by successful entrepreneurs of all nationalities.

The French Concession contained amongst many other things, the Polish and Chilean Legations and the Belgian, Dutch, Danish, Swedish, Swiss and Czechoslovak consulates. The famed French Park on the Route Vallon, which ran immediately behind Avenue Joffre, provided a rare and welcome splash of greenery amongst the urban sprawl. The area also housed a regiment of former Russian soldiers. There was no shortage of military men amongst the Russian community, since many of them

*Russian company of Shanghai Voluntary Corps, 1930.*

had fled the Bolsheviks and the Red Army. According to eyewitnesses there were several thousand former soldiers, many of whom had fought for the White armies.

There was also an association of former Cossacks, heirs to the tradition of free peasant warriors who formed proud military brotherhoods and eventually became soldiers for the Tsars. These men continued to revere the memory of Nicholas II as the following photograph shows. No doubt they distanced themselves from those Cossacks who failed to come to the help of the Tsar when he needed them most, in February, 1917.

*Shanghai, Union of Russian Cossacks, 1931.*

The Western institutions undoubtedly provided familiar islands in a remarkable and strange sea, but it was this very strangeness that captured the hearts of many of the foreigners who lived and worked in this unique city. For surrounding them everywhere were the signs of the dominant Chinese culture. The prolific Chinese engaged in every conceivable economic activity, from the successful and wealthy businessman to the long suffering coolie, bent under the weight of the load hanging from each end of his bamboo pole. They would be piled high with produce of every kind, supported by what must have been superhuman shoulders.

*Soochow Creek, Shanghai.*

Other, marginally more fortunate, coolies pushed even more enormous loads on barrows or piled high on bicycles or pedicabs (the ubiquitous tricycles that carried people as well as goods). All these people bustled between the warehouses of the harbour (the 'godowns') and their destinations, vying for space on the streets and alleyways crowded with thousands of cycles, motorbikes, cars, trams and even buses inching their way through the sea of humanity. On the water the picture was little different, the harbour thronged with boats of all kinds, from ocean liners to Chinese junks and every conceivable vessel in between. The Number One buoy was always reserved for the flagship of the British Navy, until it was handed over to the US Navy in 1946, in recognition of the shift in the balance of world power.

By the mid-1930's the number of foreign merchants, diplomats, soldiers and assorted expatriates, or *'Shanghailanders'* as they were collectively known, had grown to around 25,250. Of those, around 9,300 were British, 3,500 American, 1,800 French, 1,600 German[3]. The remainder were drawn from a wide range of nationalities, though mostly Western European. The vast majority of Shanghailanders enjoyed a privileged lifestyle, quite separate from the city's three million native Chinese, whom they considered to be an underclass. It was into this mix that the 25,000 Russian migrants settled, mostly in the French Concession, making them the second largest group of foreign nationals after the city's 30,000 Japanese.

It is hardly surprising then that this huge influx of largely impoverished Russian migrants was greeted with a degree of suspicion and resentment by the established and deeply class conscious Shanghailanders. Many Russians were forced to compete with the local Chinese for menial jobs and the most degraded and despised begged, stole, became drunkards or drug addicts; desperate women were forced to resort to prostitution. All of which undermined the illusion of white supremacy maintained by the old school Shanghailanders. Moreover, the sight of fellow educated, white Europeans reduced to this state made them feel deeply uneasy. But their perception of the migrant community was not entirely negative. The cultured and educated amongst the Russians, such as the respected opera singers, musicians and dancers, some of them ballerinas from the famous *Bolshoi* company, did indeed bring chic and glamour to the city. Former aristocrats and officers of the Imperial Army might, on occasion, even infiltrate the hallowed precincts of the Country Clubs, but, as a rule, it was frowned upon for a British member to be seen in the company of a Russian girl and marrying one would likely cost him his job.

The beautiful young Russian girls had little hope of marrying outside their own community and obtaining a coveted International passport, though many tried. One way they could meet desirable Western men, particularly Americans, and make a little money was to frequent the many dance halls of Shanghai and offer their services as 'taxi dancers'. In a city that generally attracted adventurous young men, there was a shortage of dancing partners and so the Russian girls would sell dance tickets (three dances for a dollar). Many a girl supported a large, extended family by such means. Yet even this activity would have been considered far too risqué by our puritanical, conservative family and the girls of the Shliapnikoff clan tended to work, socialise and marry within the narrow confines of their own community.

*White Russians guard a bank's armoured car*
*(many were forced to work in the 'security' business).*

Foreigners resident in Shanghai were acutely aware of the deep and pervasive poverty in China and some did their best to help alleviate it, though no doubt conscious that it would be but a drop in the ocean. Nevertheless, individuals and organisations initiated much worthy charity work and others helped by providing employment or giving to beggars. Begging was an industry in itself, efficiently organised by gangs who controlled the beggars in their area and demanded a cut of their takings. Some deliberately mutilated those in their charge to encourage greater sympathy. Irene Kuhn described one beggar that she constantly saw, dubbed 'Light in the head'. Aptly named, his bald head appeared to have a nail in it, upon which sat a candle, forever burning above his pitiful face. Pickpockets proliferated, particularly among the trams and buses and one could even find lepers on the streets.

Shanghai was not particularly healthy according to eyewitness and friend Irene Kounitsky, who said that cholera, typhoid and smallpox were prevalent. Everyone had to be vaccinated against these diseases and carry their vaccination certificates at all times. Police would periodically block off streets and vaccinate anyone found without a certificate there and then, not very hygienically either! Some resourceful Chinese would get vaccinated several times so they could sell their certificates. There must have been a flourishing black market for those precious documents.

Irene Kounitsky seems to have enjoyed a happy childhood In Shanghai. As the daughter of comfortably well off parents, she had an 'Amah' to look after her and she would take the children to the Chinese theatre instead of the park. There they would while away the time nibbling on pumpkin, watermelon and sunflower seeds while their Amah enjoyed the company of her friends. On Chinese New Year it was traditional to receive a new set of clothes. Each year the Grand Cinema opposite the Racecourse put on a special children's program, entry for which required one to bring a toy. These were most likely given away to poor children. Irene also recalled a visit to the *Hazelwood* Ice Cream factory in the Japanese colony of Hongkew, where they watched the manufacture of ice cream, ice fruit and *'maroon bean suckers'*. They enjoyed the samples too!

It seems the children were not without a sense of humour. The Kounitsky household's phone number was only one digit different from that of *Lungwha Airport* and they were forever getting wrong phone calls. However, knowing that many locals were very superstitious, the children would answer the phone with *'Kwisiling'*, meaning funeral parlour. The phone calls soon stopped.

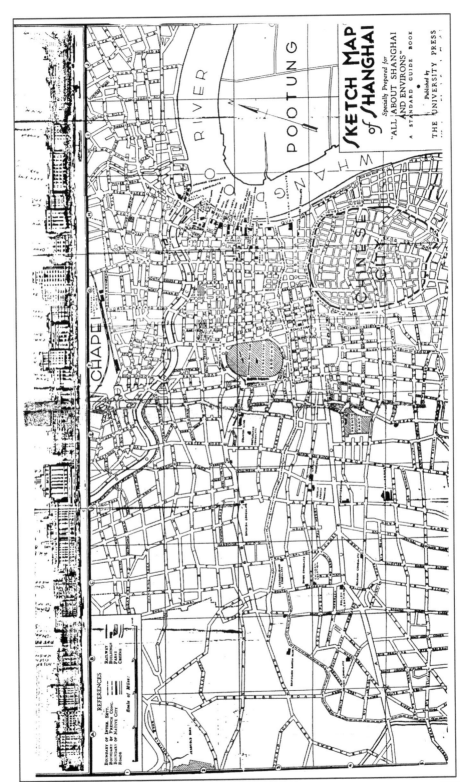

SKETCH MAP of SHANGHAI

Specially Prepared for
"ALL ABOUT SHANGHAI
AND ENVIRONS"
A STANDARD GUIDE BOOK

Published by
THE UNIVERSITY PRESS

WHANGPOO

RIVER

POOTUNG

CHINESE CITY

CHAPEI

REFERENCES
BOUNDARY OF INTER. SETT.
BOUNDARY OF FRENCH CONC.
BOUNDARY OF NATIVE CITY

RAILWAY
BUILDINGS
ROADS
CREEKS

Scale of Miles

# INDEX TO STREETS

# Japanese occupation and its impact.

For the people of Shanghai the Japanese occupation of China effectively began in 1937 when they began bombing the city. Children went to bed each night fully clothed in case they had to flee the bombs. One did fall near to Irene's home and their house shook but they were otherwise unharmed. However, their English tenant was not so fortunate. He had gone to check on the trams in the International Settlement and the rickshaw in which he was travelling received a direct hit. Irene's father had the gruesome and unenviable task of identifying his body. Slowly the occupation began to impact more and more on the Russian community. The Japanese forbade all Chinese from bringing their produce into the city and many goods became scarcer. When the Japanese fleet sailed into Whangpoo Harbour and took control then foreign imports were also restricted. The meat, fruit and butter from Australia disappeared as too, did vegetables from America. Irene described how the Japanese cruiser *Idzumo* sent an ultimatum to the foreign ships to surrender. The English gun ship *Petrel* fired on Idzumo and was promptly sunk, following which the American and French ships surrendered.

Curfews were imposed on the city, and people were forbidden access to their roof gardens, perhaps to prevent snipers attacking the Japanese. They also ordered holes to be dug, for people to jump into if bombed. These only served to trap unwary drunks who periodically fell in. Buckets of sand and water were also to be placed around, presumably against fire. Cars and many radios were confiscated, as were all buildings and businesses belonging to their wartime enemies, the British, Americans and Canadians, whose nationals also had to wear distinctive red armbands, stamped with the initial of their country. After 1943 Prisoner of War camps were established for 8,000 enemy nationals and Irene's convent school became a POW camp for nuns, both local and those brought from other parts of China. Interestingly, the French on the whole were not touched nor the Russians. The French because they had already capitulated to the Germans and by extension, to their allies the Japanese and so were no longer a threat. As for the Russians some claimed that it was because they were DP *(Displaced Persons)* and had no allegiances to any country. But a more likely reason was that the Soviet Union had not declared war on Japan, despite being allied to the Western powers, Great Britain, France and the USA. In fact, Stalin did not declare war on Japan until after the atomic bombs were dropped in 1945. Conflict with Japan had not been an option previously when the USSR had been engaged in a life and death struggle against the Nazis.

For their part the Japanese were preoccupied with conquering the Far East, which they were doing very successfully in the early years of the war, and would have seen no reason to antagonise the Russians. They even permitted them to keep their long wave radios according to another friend, Olga Kluge, who lived in Shanghai at that time. The Kluge family listened throughout the war to French daily news, broadcast from Shanghai. Following the fall of France the news was pro-Axis (Germany, Italy and Japan) and anti-Western allies. But, Olga recalls, *"we tried 'to read between the lines' and hoped for the best."* Short wave radios, however, were confiscated by the Japanese because, unlike long wave, they were capable of receiving Allied broadcasts from overseas. There would have been grave consequences for anyone found with one.

On the whole the lives of the Russians did not change as dramatically as it did for those members of the international community whose countries were at war with the Japanese. They were aware of the presence of armed Japanese soldiers in strategic locations such as on bridges and outside official buildings and they were expected to bow to them. Anyone who failed to bow or didn't bow sufficiently respectfully could expect to receive a nasty blow from a rifle butt. Nonetheless, few Russians at the time had particularly unpleasant memories of that period. Like most young people they tried to enjoy themselves regardless and continued to enjoy the cinema in particular, which was flourishing as more and more sought to escape the reality of war.

Bread, sugar and meat were rationed within the French concession where most Russians lived, by the French authorities, who incidentally also controlled water supply and electricity in their area. Food coupons were introduced in 1941 and often wages were paid in produce. Rice and beans featured heavily on menus and a daily bread ration for a family of four was only 325 grams. Cakes and buns could still be bought however, as could flour, so Russians continued to make their beloved pies as best they could. Beef was slaughtered exclusively for the Japanese and dairies were closed so there was no more milk and butter. The bombing had ruptured the gas mains and people were forced to resort to the variable 'Hibachi', a simple fuel burning container. In Irene Kounitsky's house they converted a ten gallon tin into a stove, fuelled by round balls of clay rolled in coal dust. Wooden fences were taken for fuel, in fact anything that would burn was considered. Cars had generally been requisitioned but the few that remained, as well as buses and trucks, were powered by a device attached to the rear of the vehicle, which converted them to run on gas. The Russians said it looked like a samovar, the traditional tea kettle. As might be expected, pedicabs became ever more popular through sheer necessity.

The Chinese were very kind to the Russian exiles on the whole. Shopkeepers trusted the Russians and allowed them to buy goods on a month's credit. Come the end of the month, the debt would be paid off and then they would start building up the next month's debt. This may not seem unusual today but before credit cards, most people settled purchases in cash. With the increasing shortage of goods prices rocketed and inflation became a serious problem. Naturally this affected the supply of credit as prices could rise significantly over the course of a month. While inflation rates were still tolerable goods could be paid for at the rate they were ordered, but only for very well known and trusted customers. As inflation increased those who were still fortunate to have jobs received their salaries in large bundles tied with string. These were quickly exchanged for silver bars, which could be converted to cash on the black market when necessary.

Russians continued to live their lives as normally as they could under the circumstances. Clubs and restaurants dwindled and in time disappeared altogether, so people started to visit each other more, taking their own tea and sugar. Ever resourceful, some people made their own peanut butter and sold it to neighbours. Jam was made from tomatoes and molasses. Rice became a staple food, with different kind of beans, red, brown or white. To this would be added vegetables, when available, stored tinned food and anything that could be bought on the black market. It was illegal to sell those scarce goods that were rationed but this inevitably led to a thriving black market in them.

*A traditional Russian performance, presented during wartime Shanghai.*

Showing considerable optimism in the face of ever increasing tension, Russians produced their own entertainments. Above is a photograph of a

'Spectacular' as they described it, that the community presented during wartime in Shanghai. The photograph was supplied by Olga and many of her family feature in this traditional play. This truly Kluge production featured her brother Kostya and his wife Tania, her own dear mother Natalie, brother Misha's wife Galia and the star of the show was her aunt Irene.

In 1944 American planes began bombing Shanghai and their Japanese overlords. This military breakthrough must have been viewed with mixed blessings by the international community. The planes flew low over their rooftops to avoid enemy anti aircraft as the locals cheered and waved. By August of the following year the war was over, and the arrival of the liberating Americans brought an end to food shortages. Before long the bars, restaurants and night-clubs were in full swing again, spurred on by the American GI's and their much needed dollars. Inflation however, steadily worsened as the rekindled civil war caused uncertainty about the future. Notes were issued in string bundles of thousands of Chinese dollars. Olga, still living fairly comfortably at the time, would go to the Park hotel with her boyfriend to dance on the penthouse floor under the stars. They would take a small suitcase of money to pay for a couple of expensive drinks. It was to prove a short lived but joyous euphoria. They were dancing on a volcano.

## Shalavins and Vanya's life.

From 1940 to 1943 Vanya and his brother Tolya lived and studied in a boarding school for Russian children, which may also have functioned as an orphanage, while their mother worked as a residential housekeeper in various Russian households to pay for their upkeep. One of her employers was the Shliapnikoff family, in particular, the eldest son Alexei who had become quite prosperous. For a while she also worked as a cook/servant in a hostel for Norwegian seamen. Before the war the school had been funded by nominal fees and charity from the local Russian community but by 1943 they were certainly beginning to feel financially squeezed. Conditions became steadily worse and food scarce. Students were fed only porridge and one slice of bread per day. There was no sugar, milk or other staples and the youngsters grew increasingly hungrier until they were forced to leave. Vanya was therefore obliged to leave the Russian College at 16 to seek employment, Tolya following soon after.

Tolya started an apprenticeship with a shoemaker and Vanya gained a position in a jeweller's shop. At first glance Vanya's job appeared to be very promising, offering not only the prospect of a respectable trade but also food and lodging, a very valuable commodity in wartime. The accommodation turned out to be just a bed in the kitchen. Nonetheless, as his mother had taught him to be grateful for small mercies in an insecure and harsh world, Vanya settled down to work hard and learn his craft. No doubt following her injunctions that without labour there is no reward - Без труда нет плода.

Vanya's apprenticeship in the jewellery trade was supposed to teach him how to repair watches, amongst other things. Though all he learned in the first instance was how to regulate fast or slow watches. The remaining time was spent looking after the shop, cleaning the silver, crystal and gold and even helping the jeweller's wife in the kitchen. But he was happy with the job and at least they gave him some clothing and fed him generously, which was very welcome after the long *'fasting'* at school as he put it. In due course, he did learn metal craft skills and found he loved learning about metals and precious stones and enjoyed the painstakingly detailed work of creating fine jewellery. He looked forward to a satisfying and potentially lucrative career but fate was once more to intervene. He would work only for a few short years as a jeweller but the skills that he acquired never left him and he continued to enjoy making beautiful rings and pendants. He also taught himself engraving and woodwork skills and took pride in being able to produce creative and interesting artefacts for his loved ones.

On quiet Sunday afternoons Vanya's employer's family enjoyed playing Mahjong, a very popular Chinese game loosely akin to Poker but played with ivory tablets (plastic today) beautifully decorated with Chinese characters and illustrations. The game is traditionally played for money but the family played simply for the pleasure of it. At one point a fourth player was needed and Vanya was invited to make up the numbers. Before long he was proficient enough to win on occasion, but win or lose he began a lifelong attachment to the game. Millions of Chinese enjoyed the game and across the city, indeed the country, those fortunate enough to have the leisure time played long into the night, evident by the distinctive sound of the clattering little tablets.

The owner of the jewellery shop, a Russian named Zaushin, had an affair with a Persian girl, resulting in a messy divorce and the break up of the household. Consequently, Vanya lost his job and 'home' but he managed to find a room in the same boarding house his mother and brother lived.

This was a large house in which Vanya rented a cramped, furnished room with no kitchen and a communal bathroom. Each occupant cooked on a Hibachi on the windowsill with charcoal and water obtained from the local Chinese. There was a bathroom on each floor with a flush toilet and

*Vanya in 1947.*

large bath, the hot water for which was bought from the street below and brought up in buckets. It must have taken a long time to fill the bath. The situation was not idyllic but Vanya was 18, independent and the war was over. There were better prospects for work and he had managed to pick up some rudimentary English from the American soldiers. Life seemed good indeed! Yankees were everywhere and so too were their American dollars. *'We lost all our girlfriends to them'*, he reminisced years later, adding significantly – *'almost'*. Those dashing looks must not have gone unnoticed by the young Russian ladies of Shanghai.

A hard adolescence had not quenched Vanya's optimistic and resilient spirit and now on the verge of manhood he was keen to accept life's latest challenge. He landed a job at the Central Motor Pool of the United States armed forces as a mechanic's assistant. For several months he enjoyed servicing ex-military vehicles, as well as cars, jeeps, weapons carriers and trucks of various sizes. He also relished the freedom a regular wage paid in the coveted American dollars brought. Conditions were improving daily in the immediate post war period, the restaurants and clubs flourishing once more and imported goods were appearing again. Although prices were high, Vanya could strike a hard bargain like a native, using local dialect to drive down costs to a fraction of their original asking price. His brother was also fortunate to find work with a foreign company - BAT, the British American Tobacco Company. He not only received a good wage but a regular supply of 200 cigarettes. Tolya quickly acquired the habit of smoking but those employees who did not had no difficulties selling their supply, which were far superior to the local cigarettes.

While he was at the Central Motor Pool, Vanya had taught himself to drive so when the night foreman asked him if he could move a weapons carrier from the third floor to the ground floor, he replied, with the cocksureness of youth, that of course he could. Well, driving a jeep in the car park was one thing, controlling a heavy vehicle several levels down a spiral ramp was quite another. When it inevitably crashed, so too did his employment with the U.S. military forces.

After this episode, Vanya went through a lean period, taking whatever itinerant work he could find, including amongst other things, making bread in a bakery. In early 1947 he met an old school friend by the name of Walter Sablinski who asked if he wanted to work with him on board a Danish ship. Vanya readily agreed and so they went to see the Captain. He took their details and told them to be ready to leave the port in two days. They went home, said their goodbyes to their families and friends, packed their belongings and prepared for a new adventure and life in the merchant navy aboard the *Laura Maersk*.

The ship, based in the Philippines, plied its trade in the South China seas and across the Pacific to the Americas. Their route took them to Hong Kong, then Saigon in Vietnam, Manila and several other islands in the Philippines. Then over to Japan followed by San Francisco and finally New York, via the Panama Canal. Vanya made two such return trips to America and recalled being suitably awed and impressed by the sheer size and ingenuity of the Panama Canal. His pleasure at seeing such

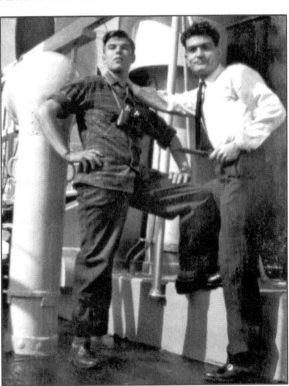

*Vanya with friend on the Laura Maersk.*

exotic places was tempered by his poverty, for the pay for an unskilled sailor working as a waiter/mess boy was a mere thirty American dollars a month. Although one could live 'nicely' on a USA dollar a day in Shanghai, their money did not stretch very far when they tried to explore New York. But far worse than the low pay was his horrific seasickness. For exactly three weeks Vanya suffered miserably before miraculously

*A pensive Vanya on board ship, 1947.*

acquiring the 'sea legs' necessary to endure the constant movement of the ship. It must have been excruciating serving food that he could not even bear to look at let alone eat. When Vanya returned home to Shanghai after a first short trip his mother was horrified at how gaunt he had become. Home cooking and *terra firma* undoubtedly restored both his appetite and appearance and he assured his mother that the next trip would be fine, and so it was.

Despite the excitement of visiting the various ports on his travels Vanya found life onboard very monotonous and decided a future in the merchant navy was not for him. Moreover, his position on the ship, as with the other three Russians, caused problems for the captain. For while he appreciated Vanya's hard work, he did not relish vouching for his 'white' credentials. In the tense new era of the Cold War between the USSR and USA, the Soviet passports that the Russians had been forced to accept in order to travel abroad were treated with suspicion in America. They feared spies everywhere and the captain was continually being called upon to explain that Vanya and his friends were not communists; in fact they were anything but. However, the Soviet Union passports seemed to be damning evidence against them. One Russian had jumped ship in New Zealand, asking for political asylum and received it, which did not help matters much. Vanya eventually returned to Shanghai in 1948, after precisely one year and 17 days at sea, and to his great pleasure, secured another position in a jeweller's shop.

In the year that Vanya had been away many Russians had left the country, terrified by the impending victory of the Chinese Communists and their fate under the new regime. They had found a temporary haven in the Philippines, but Vanya was glad to be back on dry land and the thought of sailing anywhere again was not attractive. Moreover, the prospect of paid work, especially in that uncertain period, was reason enough to stay put for the moment. Looking back he believes it was his destiny not to have returned to China earlier because then it is likely that he would have fled with the rest of the refugees and not met his future wife. As it was there were no more boats available and so Vanya had no means of leaving. The Americans had peacefully evacuated the country, having ceased supporting the Nationalist government, leaving the Chinese to their own devices. The Russians that remained had mixed feelings about the Americans' role, sorry to see them go on the one hand but grateful not to be caught in the crossfire of what would undoubtedly have been a bloodbath had they attempted to defend the city from the communists.

To the horror of the White Russian community, Vanya sometimes frequented the Russian Sporting club in Shanghai, an institution sponsored by the USSR. He was not politically motivated and attended purely for social reasons as he had friends there and to use the club's facilities. The official Soviet consulate used the club to drive home their message of 'returning' to the motherland, especially targeting the younger Russians. They were at least honest enough to admit that returning to the USSR would not be easy. "No rose strewn path awaits you, only hard work and a loaf of black bread". They were not joking. "Mother Russia needs you!" Vanya recalls that many cheered and agreed to go; however, *he* was not convinced.

*Working with friends at the Russian Soviet Sporting Club.*

Within the year, the Chinese Communist take-over of Shanghai was achieved without a single shot being fired as far as Vanya could see. He described how they woke up one morning to find Mao's soldiers standing on every street corner, armed with a machine gun or rifle. Trucks drove down the streets with loudspeakers announcing 'Congratulations! You have been liberated by the Glorious Peoples' Army. Do not be alarmed. Do everything as you have been doing yesterday.' Dutifully obeying the commands of the Peoples' Army, Vanya returned to his job at the jeweller's store. Oddly enough, this bastion of capitalist decadence, (for what could be more decadent than luxurious bourgeois jewellers?) was not only permitted to continue trading but actually flourished over the course of the following few years. Soviet advisors arrived in the new Communist China to provide technical and ideological assistance, bringing new funds with them. Not much to be sure, Mao said getting money out of Stalin was like getting food out of the mouth of a tiger! But there must have been enough high ranking Party officials with the means to buy watches or perhaps a trinket or two for the wife back home. Locals may still have been buying up gold and silver after inflation had wiped out their cash savings and trust in currency and banks with it.

Vanya's new position turned out to be quite fulfilling. His employer, Ivan Grigorievich Antipiat was a congenial man who treated him very well. He was married to Varvara and although they had no children of their own they had adopted three boys, to whom the jeweller had taught his trade. The eldest son was particularly skilled in the profession, having learned to set diamonds and other precious stones, something to which Vanya aspired. The second brother had been a successful businessman in China's relatively free market. Vanya had not actually met the sons because they had decided to return to Russia after the war, lured by the Soviet orators' persuasive pleas to their nationalistic feelings and desire for a motherland. In common with many others, the sons would come to regret catching the 'patriotic bug', as Vanya put it many years later; but once back in the USSR there was no escape for those that did return.

It was the departure of the sons, along with his experience at Zaushin's that provided Vanya with the opportunity to resume his promising career in jewellery. However, whilst the new regime did not immediately take control of the business their sentiments were clear, foreigners were no longer welcome and toleration would be short lived. So for many reasons, Vanya considered himself to be very fortunate to have lived through that traumatic period in China's history without serious repercussions. He survived comfortably under the protection of his kindly employer, right up to 1951, two years into the communist regime.

Relating his chequered work history to me, the varied jobs he had around the world, my father was most concerned that I should be ashamed of coming from such simple stock. Never. Nonetheless, he wanted to reassure me. *'Dear daughter, never worry that you come from such a plain family. Always remember that it is not the name that makes the man, but the man that makes his own name.'* Не место красит человека а человек место.

## Growing up in Shanghai, Nina and Julia's story.

Despite their tender years, Nina and my mother Julia had already travelled huge distances to arrive in Shanghai. Born in Kuznetsk, western Russia, their parents had soon moved to nearby Kuybishev. Julia had been just five and Nina seven when their parents trekked from there across the breadth of the vast country to flee to China. After a few years in Harbin the Shliapnikoff extended family moved to Shanghai in search of better opportunities. Upon arrival the entire family lived together for reasons of economy and security. Alexei and his family were the first to move out, followed by Zina and her family. Alexei initially sold second hand clothes, as too did his sister Zina, but he soon saved sufficient money to open his own store selling sausages and small goods – колбасную. Their grandfather Artemy opened a furniture store, as did Peter and Tanya Bakaldin. Zina continued with her 'commission' shop – комисионку, selling second hand clothes, blankets and general items. Nina remembered how the four of them lived in a quarter of the single room shop, the remainder given over to the goods they sold. Many years later she still recalled the smell of old, musty clothes though it was not long before they could afford to move to a separate room.

Although Nina and Julia were only ten and eight when they first moved to Shanghai they were soon earning and borrowing pennies to visit the cinema. Oxya, the nanny/servant that Babinka, the Shliapnikoff matriarch, had 'adopted' to take care of her own eight children had somehow managed to rejoin the family and was a favourite 'soft touch' when it came to cinema money. But if they were naughty she would complain about them to their grandmother and they would lose their cinema privileges.

Nina, Julia and their twelve cousins, Olga, Nikolai, Vera, Victor, Vladimir (Volodya), Georgi (Yura), Galina (Galia), Alexander, Kostya, Dima, Vera and later, little Tania when she appeared, all attended Ecole Remi, the French college for international children. There is 15 years between Zina, the eldest child of the Shliapnikoff clan and the youngest Nikolai, so Tania, his daughter is considerably younger than the rest of her cousins. But she fondly remembers Julia as a relative who was kind to her in her youth. Julia took her to a 'Laurel and Hardy' movie one day and bought her a sherbet ice cream with vanilla filling called 'Hollywood'. The children all became fluent in French as well as their native Russian. Some members of the family continued studying at the College Francais after leaving the Ecole at 16 but Nina and Julia chose not to pursue their education.

Photo by Z. Buchman.

10th class. 10-ый класс Школы Ремп в 1934-1935 учебном году.

| | | |
|---|---|---|
| 1) В. В. Кормилов, | 16) Вѣрочка Федина, | 31) Юра Солонин, |
| 2) м-me Баллеран, | 17) Катя Лысова, | 32) Володя Анкудинов, |
| 3) м-me Николе, | 18) Валя Носкова, | 33) Стася Новочинскій, |
| 4) Тамарочка Бурдина, | 19) Ганя Клеонкова, | 34) Леня Ежкин, |
| 5) Сусанна Кокая, | 20) Гина Овчинникова, | 35) Вова Шестопалов, |
| 6) Ганя Шестакова, | 21) Миша Петров, | 36) Боря Сарапулов, |
| 7) Ганя Потолокова, | 22) Тамарочка Халтузина, | 37) Коля Бочкарев, |
| 8) Ращила Илимсова, | 23) Маргорита Игошина, | 38) Саша Марич |
| 9) Лиза Лукьянченко, | 24) Валя Кунгина, | 39) Всеволод Неупокоев, |
| 10) Шура Рубчева, | 25) Олег Сенченко, | 40) Юра Попов, |
| 11) Галя Евсюкова, | 26) Женя Филиппова, | 41) Глэб Пискавитин, |
| 12) Ядвига Лысовская, | 27) Стася Якубовскій, | 42) Боря Кунавин, |
| 13) Шура Носков, | 28) Юля Каретникова, | 43) Миша Голубев, |
| 14) Шура Мезенцева, | 29) Тоня Ножина, | 44) Коля Демидов. |
| 15) Муся Канцевая, | 30) Таня Якобсон, | |

*Mother's class of 1934, Julia is number 28.*

The youngsters loved their school on the whole. They studied from 8 am to 5pm, with a two hour lunch break, in which to eat the free lunches provided by the school. According to Nina there were children from many different religions in addition to the Orthodox faith. Although Catholic, Protestant and Muslim children attended the school there is

134

little evidence of integration in their class photographs, which appear to be comprised predominantly of Russian children. Scripture lessons were held on Saturdays for each of the different faiths represented at the school. Of course, there was a huge variety of schools in Shanghai at that time including American schools and English Public schools.

*Ecole Remi – The French school the Shliapnikoff children attended in Shanghai.*

Galina provided the following information about Ecole Remi, which holds fond memories for most of its ex pupils. They studied three languages, four periods of English per week, four Russian and the remainder of the tuition in French. School life began with the nursery/kindergarten, or *Bebe* class, where they were fed and clothed, presumably as a service for working parents. Pupils then moved on to *Class Preparatoire*, followed by five more years of primary education. At the end they sat for their *Certificat d'Etudes Primaires*, a public examination. Secondary education continued until they were sixteen years of age. They had the same headmaster throughout their time at the school. Apparently he had been there since 1930 and served until the school's closure in 1946. A Frenchman, *naturellement,* he was always immaculately dressed and was fond of eau de cologne, the smell of which presaged his entrance into class.

Summer holiday camps were available to the children and Galia and her brother Alexander were fortunate enough to attend two. The summer holidays from late June to mid September were long and hot and too muggy to be spent on the streets of Shanghai. So the 40 children lucky enough to escape to the beach resort of Tsingtao, two days away by sea, undoubtedly appreciated the opportunity. Galia certainly thought her first trip in 1937 was a wonderful experience. Two years later she had the chance to go again, on what was to prove to be the last trip before war put an end to them. Again it was a joyous experience, this time in the mountains of Laushan, about 100 kilometres from Tsingtao. The children were aged between nine and fifteen and, at 13, Galia was in the older group and enjoyed special privileges. The children were required to write home weekly but when the weather was bad they wrote several letters at once and then handed them in one at a time. The parents in return, sent parcels of 'goodies', which of course the children eagerly looked forward to receiving.

There was a wealth of options for travelling around the city. As young children, Nina and Julia would usually walk to the nearby school because it cost nothing. When it rained their mother would give them ten cents for a pedicab, so the girls could travel together under the canopied seat of the tricycle, pulled by the cyclist in front. Occasionally, they would take a rickshaw, but the seat was very narrow so the smaller girl would have to sit in the other's lap. It was hard work for the poor rickshaw runner and so he would, quite reasonably, charge them extra. Nina commented how the rickshaw runners would have very sore legs. The discomfort was not worth the extra fare and so the girls preferred pedicabs. When she was older and working, Nina loved to travel on the top deck of an English *double decker* bus, from where she could admire the hustle and bustle of the teeming city. Trams and trolley-buses provided the other main alternatives although the Ford garage, virtually next door, ran a taxi service with Chinese chauffeurs. As kids they had played in its car park

but they had no idea that the name was that of a car manufacturer, they simply thought it was the name of the garage. They rarely used the taxis themselves, even when older, because they were too expensive.

*Julia, 13 and Nina, 15, with their parents Nikolai and Zina, 1938.*

When Nina left school in 1939, aged 16, she was advised to enter hairdressing, which she willingly agreed to and found fulfilling. After a year of unpaid training, she proudly spent her entire first week's wages on treats for the family, particularly cakes of which they were all very fond. This gesture was typical of her generous nature. Not long after she met the love of her life, Konstantin Miheev, and gave up hairdressing when she married him at 18. Thereafter she worked as a nursing aid for a while but throughout her working life in Shanghai Nina gave a large proportion of her salary to her mother.

*Nina in front of the beauty parlour in which she worked.*

*Nina and Zina in Shanghai.*

Julia undertook a secretarial course at an English business college, where she learned shorthand, typing and presumably English. Little did she know then that she would see out her days in an English speaking country. Many of that generation acquired a rudimentary knowledge of English from living in close proximity to the International concession and regularly attending cinemas, where they eagerly devoured Hollywood movies.

In the 1930's, as China was being invaded by Japan, the people of Shanghai were flocking to see Johnny Weismuller in *Tarzan and his mate*, advertised on billboards all over the city. The cinema was a favourite form of leisure activity for all the clan. They particularly loved the American films and the stars that featured in them – Deanna Durbin, Judy Garland, Jean Harlow, etc. Julia often skipped her business classes in order to go to the cinema and would be chastised by her mother when she found out, and who stopped her piano lessons as punishment.

As the sisters grew older, Nina and Julia, along with other young members of our family, started patronising the Russian Social Club, the *POK* (the abbreviated Russian name). It offered young people an affordable night out, somewhere where they could sit at tables and enjoy a cup of tea or coffee, perhaps a cake or a soft drink but strictly no alcohol! Their parents would not allow the girls to go to the city's nightclubs; they had heard about Shanghai's decadent reputation even in the far north of Harbin. But the *POK* was considered respectable; they could meet boys there and perhaps even have a dance, which the girls particularly liked. Their mother Zina had told them that they could go where they liked when they were married. Although both married at 18 they were no better off, in fact, they were poorer than ever, so there was still no clubbing for Nina and Julia.

When the girls were not being escorted to the *POK* by young men, who would be expected to pay for a taxi, they would take a pedicab, often travelling in threes to save money on the fare. When they spent all their money they would walk home, which they considered perfectly safe. They were still attending dances when Nina was 17, in 1940, during the war years and Japanese occupation. Only gradually did the clubs begin to close as the financial position of the city worsened and jobs became scarcer. Towards the end of the war life must have become more difficult for them all, though it seems hard to believe looking at their glamorous photographs.

*Party in Shanghai c. 1942. Julia in light dress on the right and Olga Bakaldin, bottom left.*

## Zina's life and achievements.

The French had been very helpful to the poverty stricken Russians when they first arrived in the city. French nuns invited the new arrivals into their monastery and gave them bagfuls of clothes, which Zina refashioned to fit her family. The bags continued to arrive – clearly the international settlement was very charitable. Once Zina was 'on her feet' she thanked the nuns for their help and, informing them that she no longer needed their charity, implored them to help others instead. Zina and the other members of the large family slowly grew more and more affluent and in due course Zina abandoned the clothes store and started her own business. She also acquired her own house, No. 89 Route Vallon. This street was immediately parallel to Avenue Joffre, a great thoroughfare that ran down to the Bund, the waterfront boulevard that formed the heart of the financial district. Zina's street is shown on the map earlier in this chapter. Nina remembered living around the corner from Avenue Joffre. Next door, in a different boarding house but in the same terrace block, lived the Chakalians. They owned the confectionery store, a popular business because Russians love their sweets. Their children also played with the Shliapnikoff children and eventually their son Rouben would marry into the Shliapnikoff family.

Housing in Shanghai was quite varied. There were large terraced houses and, what in the 1930's were considered to be, 'high rise' apartment blocks. The blocks had two sets of lifts, the front for residents and guests and the back lift and stairs for servants. Zina's house comprised three floors, her shop on the ground floor and eight residential rooms above. Initially she lived with her daughters and husband in the largest room which was twenty square metres. At some point, and it is not clear when, she separated from her husband. The girls continued to live with her until they in turn were married, whereupon they brought their new husbands to live in the house as tenants. Nina, being the first to marry, acquired a 20 square metre room but by the time Julie married there was only a 12 square metre room left. The remaining rooms were sub-let. They put up a "ROOM TO LET" sign in the window, English being the universal language of this polyglot community, but in practice they only took in Russian tenants. Zina would eye them up carefully with a landlady's practised eye – no drunks would be permitted! Zina's parents, Artemy and Praskovia, also lived like this, subletting rooms in their house, as did Peter and Tania Bakaldin. They recognised very early on that property was a good investment. One room of Zina's house was set aside for an Old Believers' Orthodox Church, with an altar built in to the corner, painted and decorated by Zina's brother-in-law and Aunt Galia's father, Ivan Cherviakoff. He was very artistic and was able to reproduce the beautiful artwork, woodwork and icons for which Russian churches are renowned.

There was one small kitchen of four square metres which only Zina was allowed to use. She had a gas hot water heater and a four ring gas range, from which she produced delectable treats. Gas was strictly limited and the other tenants were forced to boil water and cook meals on a kerosene fuelled primus stove or coal fired Hibachi, either in the corridor or on a bench near a window. Everyone kept a thermos as well to keep drinks hot and not waste precious fuel. At eight square metres the bathroom was comparatively large but there was only the one for all the tenants. It housed a bath with cold water, basin and a single toilet. Hot water still had to be bought from the street below and brought up by the bucket. Four buckets of steaming hot water, diluted with cold were sufficient to make a tolerable bath. A communal telephone was provided but its use was strictly controlled by Zina. Tenants were allowed 100 incoming calls per month, which Zina would presumably answer and then have to call the relevant tenant, plus a restricted number of outgoing calls. Each call was recorded on a piece of paper that hung by the phone. Zina furnished all the rooms, complete with curtains that she probably sewed herself, so that they were fully ready for tenants. Thoroughly methodical, organised and brooking no nonsense, she must have been a formidable landlady.

*Zina and Nikolai (on the right) with friends.*

In addition to running her house, Zina worked with her brother Alexei at one point, selling the goods he produced in his shop, which undoubtedly provided a steadier income than selling clothes. Zina was obliged to be financially astute since she had divorced and needed to support both herself and her two daughters. She may also have earned extra income sewing attractive clothes, for which there was a huge demand. Zina was a superb seamstress and was often called upon to amend or create wonderful dresses from apparently nondescript raw materials. In

141

addition she was an accomplished cook and baker, renowned for her delicious cakes and pastries, which I can still remember from my childhood with mouth watering relish. In short, she was a very flexible and talented woman who could turn her hand to most things, particularly if there was money to be made from it.

This trait rather embodies the attitude of many Russians at that time and goes someway towards explaining their remarkable success, first in China where they had arrived virtually penniless, then in the countries to which they subsequently fled. There was no question of them ever seeking any form of government assistance. Who was there to ask anyway? As stateless people they relied entirely upon themselves, their own strengths and their ability to produce goods that people wanted to buy. This was the only honest means they knew to make an income and survive. Their instinctive capitalist tendencies became their life-saving qualities in an alien environment. Whereas in the Russia they had been forced to abandon, under an ideology that despised individual and economic freedom, these same virtues had condemned them.

Zina eventually opened her own delicatessen, a 'Gastronome' where she sold what was known as small goods, e.g. sausages, teawurst, pates and other meat products, supplied by her brother's factory. In addition she sold home made wine, supplied in bulk by the producer who would be paid only for the amount sold; biscuits, sweets, cheese and other delicacies. Zina served at the till and was helped in the shop by a paid employee – a Mr. Kudrin, who cut up all the cold meats and sausages into slices. By this time Nina was also working from 7 a.m. to 7 p.m. for her mother. First thing in the morning she would go to the markets to buy fresh produce and then return to the shop to prepare the fresh salads, vinaigrette, herring and *zakuski* (vegetable snacks) that Russians love so much. This was

*Zina managing the delicatessen; this one is in Sydney a few years later, when she again worked with her brother.*

142

the 'fast food' of the day and everything was sold by the same evening, Nina recalled with some pride. Julie had married by then and had a daughter just a few months old. Neither she nor her husband worked but *'as they still had to eat'*, Nina noted without acrimony, their mother would pile a large plate high with food and take it to them.

## Happy times in Shanghai.

My mother's generation have fond memories of their youth in Shanghai; the parties, balls, trips to the seaside, activities centring on the very strong Orthodox Church and the many happy family reunions. No doubt because they were an expatriate community, living in an alien environment, the ties between the extended family remained very strong.

Shanghai was a large city but the lives of the Russian community were centred on a small part of it. Schools, sports grounds, swimming pools, parks and clubs were all within walking distance or people could hire bicycles cheaply when they wanted to go further a field. The YMCA, the Young Men's Christian Association, was a popular venue both for young Russians and other Europeans, as too were picnics in the countryside and train trips to the seaside, the Yellow sea being a favoured destination. Amazingly enough, some even managed to get to Japan for a holiday, evident in the following photograph.

*Zina (right) enjoying the sand 'baths' in Beppu, Japan.*

As the generation of young Russians grew up there were numerous opportunities for joyous family celebrations; engagements, weddings and christenings. The youngest Shliapnikoff sibling Nikolai, having fled Russia while still a teenager, grew to manhood in China and married in Shanghai. Nikolai and his wife Falia were blessed with a daughter, Tania. The youngest son of Alexei and Katya, Victor, was also born in China, as too was Elena and Ivan Cherviakoff's second child, Alexander. Born in Harbin just a year after their hasty departure from the USSR, like the others, he spent most of his childhood in Shanghai. Most of the children of the six Shliapnikoff siblings in China were to find love amongst the expatriate community and wed according to traditional rites in one of the city's many Russian Orthodox churches.

Only a few of the very wealthiest Russians could afford to patronise the international night-clubs and restaurants of the cosmopolitan city that was Shanghai in the 1930's. The vast majority lived quite frugal lives but they were masters of improvisation and avidly imitated the American film stars of the time. The women waved and 'permed' their hair in the fashionable styles, Nina becoming a proficient and popular hairdresser in the process. And they begged, borrowed or bought luxury fabrics which were often hand sewn into glamorous clothes. Photographs from the austere wartime 40's show immaculately dressed Russians enjoying their parties; the women in luxurious dresses and men in smart suits. Though not actually rich they tried very hard to convey that impression.

*Wedding celebrations, (Julia on the far left), c. 1941.*

144

Nina's wedding pictures, taken in 1941, show the radiant bride, resplendent in her sumptuous long white gown being crowned in the elaborate marriage ceremony, conducted in the ornate local Russian Orthodox church.

*Nina and Konstantin's wedding.*

The reception pictures show well dressed guests dining at a table laden with food and drink.

*Nina's wedding reception, 1941.*
*Her mother Zina is seated to her right.*

Nor is there any evidence of shortages two years later when Julia married Georgi (Yura) Nikulinski. Again, her mother Zina was able to arrange an elaborate wedding despite the rigours of wartime austerity. There were

*Julia's wedding in
1943 was a sumptuous affair.*

no limousines, however, and they arrived at church by pedicab, my mother no doubt being very careful to keep her long white train out of the gutters. *'How else could one travel then?'* She responded to my question many years later, as though a bride arriving in church by tricycle was the most natural thing in the world. How else indeed?

To Zina's delight her first grandchild (and my elder half-sister), Elena, was born the following year, to Julia and Yura. Another opportunity for a family celebration, though wartime shortages were finally beginning to impact.

*Julia's wedding party, with cousins and friends, 1943. Vera
Shliapnikoff behind her, poss. Vera Pravosudov to her left. The little
girl at the front may be Nikolai's daughter Tania.*

# The other Shliapnikoffs.

In 1935 Artemy, the patriarch of the Shliapnikoff clan died, to the great grief of the whole family. The father and grandfather who had risked death to escape Russia back in 1930, along with six of his eight offspring and their young families, would not live to see them permanently settled. They had only been in Shanghai a short time and were just beginning to become established. He was 62 years old and deeply mourned by all of his family, not least by his devoted wife Praskovia, who was to wear black for the rest of her life.

*Artemy's funeral, 1935.*

The youngest son Nikolai, who was 21 and still living with his parents at the time, now took his father's place working alongside his mother. As he was still relatively young the rest of the family provided help, emotional and practical assistance.

The extended family would often help each other out, particularly with loans to establish shops and businesses but also to rent or even buy apartments. There were clearly advantages to having such a large network of support. They were each others customers too and when established, their businesses primarily catered to the wider Russian community, despite living in close proximity to both the English and French concessions.

*Nikolai Shliapnikoff.*

Artemy had no doubt passed on his knowledge of the meat and small goods business to his eldest son Alexei, who established a successful industry producing them in Shanghai. As a factory owner, Alexei became the new patriarch of the clan following his father's early death. He opened a delicatessen shop as well as the factory. At one point he employed my paternal grandmother, Maria, to cook and prepare Russian dishes to sell in the shop. As his factory expanded he provided employment to both Russians and Chinese. His own sons, Georgi, Volodya and Victor, were teenagers at the time and did not immediately follow in their father's footsteps, but were presumably encouraged to pursue their education.

*Alexei's 'sausage factory', which also incorporated a delicatessen selling a wide variety of products. The caption under his photograph states that as owner and founder of the factory, he is a specialist in these goods, having worked in this profession since 1925, and in Shanghai since 1934. On the left he is pictured proudly "standing in front of his own automobile". Article reproduced from a Shanghai newspaper, c. 1936.[4]*

*Workers in Alexei's factory, c. 1940.*

Tanya Bakaldin, the third Shliapnikoff sibling, was also quite enterprising and, with husband Peter, established a successful furniture shop and became self-sufficient relatively quickly. The other brothers and sisters were not always so fortunate. Pelageya (Polya) for example, was often quite poor and sometimes worked for Zina. Other Russians were also not as successful as the majority of the Shliapnikoffs. Young

*Vera and husband Volodya Volski.*

men at the time, who were not enterprising and had no trade or profession often worked as volunteers in an organised armed force that helped the police patrol the city. Julia's husband Georgi (Yura) worked as one of these watchmen or security guards, as too did Polya's husband, Volodya. Nonetheless, they still managed to give their only daughter, Vera, an elaborate wedding, as this photograph (left) illustrates. Being a security guard was a common occupation for former soldiers, often veterans of both World War 1 and the Russian Civil War and the toughest men among them worked as body guards for rich Chinese, prey to kidnapping by gangsters

149

and secret societies. Such a bodyguard became a typical sight in Shanghai, standing on the running board of a car, with a gun slung over his shoulder.

In the absence of other employment, Elena Cherviakoff too was also obliged to work for her elder brother Alexei from time to time, though her husband Ivan's skills lay elsewhere. As an educated man and member of the Church, Ivan worked for a while in a Russian bank and later for the Russian newspaper. Pay was meagre, however, and Elena supplemented the income by working as a housekeeper for the Chief of French Police, another Russian as it happened. The Cherviakoffs also ventured into selling take-away home cooked food. Customers, often single men, would bring a *soudok*, a three tiered set of dishes, to buy a three course meal. This business folded after two years, whereupon Elena worked in her brother Alexei's delicatessen seven days a week, from 10 a.m. to 10 p.m., with a two hour lunch break. In 1937 Ivan began work as a security guard and painted icons and pictures in his spare time, which he sold through an art shop. Multi-talented, he also sang bass in the all male Kolchin's choir, renowned in Shanghai. During the war, the firm he guarded was taken over by the Japanese. Wages were poor and paid in rice, peanut oil, margarine, soap and eau de cologne. When he needed extra money to buy bridesmaid dresses for his daughter Galina's wedding, he sold caustic soda to make soap. Sometimes during his breaks at work he sketched his employers, who were happy with the result and probably gave him some extra rewards for his efforts.

In 1942 Elena and Ivan's sixteen year old daughter Galina began tutoring 12-14 year olds who were re-sitting the exams they had failed the previous year. Her parents also decided to produce soya bean milk for additional income, a very slow process Galina relates. She and her brother Alexander delivered bottles of milk on their way to school and then collected the empties on their way home. Galina left school to work in a real estate office, but she still kept up her delivery round for a while. With the end of the war things began to look up for the Cherviakoff family but their relief was short lived when Galina's mother was diagnosed with Tuberculosis. It fell to Galina to take her mother to the English clinic and act as interpreter between the English speaking medical staff and her Russian speaking mother. But Galina at 18 did not have the heart to tell her mother the truth about her condition. In 1947 Elena passed away, aged only 38, surrounded by her grief stricken and loving family. This brave woman had suffered the trauma of fleeing her native land as a 21 year old, with a young child in tow. She had survived revolution, civil war, exile and war again, but could not escape the cruel killer disease.

Galina was naturally heartbroken at her beloved mother's early death but found some comfort in her approaching marriage. Leo, an intelligent, proficient linguist who had been educated at the Kaiser Wilhelm School in Shanghai was totally devoted to his fiancée. The young couple were married at the Russian Orthodox Cathedral in June, 1948, followed by a reception for 35 people held at Leo's parents' home, the Ivanoffs. When Galina and Leo arrived at the reception, they were met at the door by Galina's father and her new in-laws with traditional bread and salt. That is, a small loaf with a tiny silver container of salt on top. The newlyweds took a bite of the bread, symbolising wholesome life and prosperity.

That same year, Ivan saw a post advertised for an Orthodox deacon in north-west Canada, offering assisted passage for himself and family. He applied and was accepted for the position. Since Galina was married by this time and therefore no longer considered

*Galina on her wedding day.*

'family', Ivan and his young son Alexander left Shanghai alone in 1949. Galina was distraught at losing her father and brother so soon after the tragic death of her mother but was consoled by her loving husband.

Life became increasing difficult for the extended family and they began seriously to consider leaving Shanghai, something which had been impossible to even contemplate during the war. Yet again they found themselves seeking the ways and means to escape. Alexei was the most successful of the clan and increasingly many were turning to him for help. *'But he could not feed them all'* commented Nina. One by one, Shanghai's shops began to close as their owners prepared to leave the country or had lost their assets to galloping inflation. Shanghai's once great infrastructure began to collapse. Zina closed the doors of her delicatessen for the last time in 1947, followed shortly afterwards by her brother's factory.

Whilst the family were jubilant that the war had ended, it was apparent that life could not simply return to how it had been before. Japan's defeat had marked the immediate resumption of the civil war between Mao's communists and the Nationalists, but this time a communist victory seemed imminent.

In 1949 the Communists did indeed secure victory and the residents of Shanghai awoke to find Red guards on every corner. Initially it appeared to be a peaceful take-over by the soldiers they referred to as *little cotton wool soldiers* (ватные солдатики) because of the padded jackets they wore. But when the public executions began, many conducted in the city's racecourse, it was clear that a new era had dawned.

## Post war period, hardship and happiness.

During 1944 Julia's husband Yura was working as a security guard. They received board and lodgings but very little pay and life was far from easy. This probably prompted Yura's decision to return to the outskirts of Harbin in the far north of China, where his family lived and where he could find work on the electric power station. My mother's idyllic childhood ended with that journey, for it was now that she began to experience true deprivation as well as an acute loneliness she had never experienced in the warm family cocoon. She detested her mother-in-law, who put the 19 year old young wife and mother to work on her hands and knees, scrubbing the bare wooden floors of the primitive timber hut that was now their home. There were no goods to be bought or sold on the black market, which had enabled her mother to overcome the restrictions of rationing. None of the distractions of Shanghai and what little money her husband managed to earn was spent on alcohol and gambling, leaving mother and baby daughter to exist on next to nothing.

Julia vindicated the commercial course she had studied by working as an administrative/payroll assistant for a while, but under the circumstances she could not enjoy her job. Life was exceedingly hard for them and Julia became increasingly disillusioned with her husband. There was no one to look after baby Elena, *Lyalya* as she was then known, while Julia worked. Sometimes she had to be left alone in a locked room, which was no doubt very traumatic for both mother and daughter. It was a dangerous, lonely interlude in the young bride's life as illustrated by a particular story related by Helen (Elena) many years later. Whilst living in the Northern township, Lyalya found a 'toy' that she thought looked like a bolt. When she threw it under the table it promptly exploded, causing a visitor's white shirt to be splattered with blood from superficial wounds and Julia's legs to be scarred for life. The 'toy' she had found was in fact a percussion detonator from a grenade!

The situation improved only marginally with the end of the war. In the wake of the dropping of the atomic bombs that signalled the defeat of Japan, Soviet Russians had swarmed over the border into Manchuria and behaved with wild abandon. These soldiers from the Far Eastern Army were often criminals who had been promised their freedom if they joined up. Regular soldiers had been totally absorbed in the life and death struggle against Hitler's Nazis on the Western front. But these so called 'soldiers', convinced of their victory over the Japanese, took out their vengeance on the Chinese caught in the middle of this horrific conflict. They raped and looted without mercy. White Russians trembled in their homes, their suspicions confirmed that Communism had indeed made monsters of their fellow countrymen.

Ironically, Soviet propaganda had warned that it would be the American soldiers behaving in this way and Julia had carefully hidden herself and her young daughter away from them too. But she was persuaded that they meant no harm when she did at last meet some. They treated her and her child with the utmost respect and gave them chocolate and other longed for luxuries. Until the war ended they had been living on near starvation levels. Helen recalled traipsing over fields to obtain desperately needed milk from a nearby village, until a Chinese woman was taken by a wolf and then they could no longer go. On another occasion the family found a drowned horse, which they cut up and ate.

Russians who had been forced into the Japanese army suddenly found themselves in the very strange and dangerous position of being on the enemy side. Totally unprepared for the Soviet invasion, they frantically destroyed their Japanese uniforms, for fear of being shot as traitors. One such White Russian caught in this unenviable position was Sasha Larionoff, who was to live out his years safely in Australia. He had been drilled and trained by the Imperial Japanese Army and forced to work for them, but had not actually seen action. Nonetheless, he was quick to remove his uniform. Years later, Sasha would tell his Australian friends, with his rather dry humour, how to remember his name – *"it's Larry 'on and off'."*

The soldiers of the Far Eastern Army were followed by official Soviet delegations. One of their tasks was to convince the Russian community to return and help rebuild the war torn *Motherland* that had *'suffered so much at the hands of the evil Nazi fascists.'* Rousing speeches and talks were aimed particularly at the younger members of the community, those who could offer hard work in return for living in their *own* country. It was intensely appealing to some of the more idealistic young Russians. They were not of the generation that fled the USSR in the 1920's and 30's. The generation that now warned them that it was all lies, that they could not trust the Communists and that they would end up dead or in labour camps for daring to leave in the first place. Wiser minds had noted the horror stories of the many Russian soldiers who, following Allied liberations, thought they would be free to remain in Europe. Instead, the Allies 'repatriated' them back to the USSR, where many were sentenced to a life of forced labour or death in the 'gulags'.

However, the generation that had fled the Soviet Union as babes in arms or young children knew nothing of the terrors of which their parents spoke. They perhaps thought that they were exaggerating simply to justify their own exodus and refusal to return. What they *did* know was that China was a volcano poised to erupt and that sooner or later they would all be exiles once more. What could they do? Where could they go? Barely in their 20's, they were keen to be independent and not just follow in their parents footsteps. They had grown up in an alien environment, firm upholders of Russian traditions as their elders had strictly enforced and, to a lesser extent, members of the broader international community. But they had most definitely not integrated into Chinese society. Not surprisingly, it was this same Chinese community that was now rejecting them. The only language and culture they were familiar with was that of a country they had never seen or barely remembered and here was *Mother Russia* welcoming them back with open arms whilst the rest of the world seemed to be turning its back on them. Bear in mind that all *White Russians* were in China illegally. They had no official nationality or citizenship. The vast majority had destroyed any 'communist' identity papers they may have had, secure in the knowledge they would never return, unless or until the evil despotism that was Bolshevism was destroyed.

So here they were, a stateless, nation less people, like millions of others caught up in the post war turmoil of Europe and Asia. The rest of the world was preoccupied with its own reconstruction and the 12,000 or so 'lost' Russians still remaining in China at that time were the least of its problems. The older generation may have dreamt of settling in the *land of the free* but the USA was not opening its doors to them. Only Mother Russia beckoned. Some 2,000 families, Nina and her new husband Konstantin amongst them, heeded the call and returned to their Motherland - and ten years of internal exile! The once strong and unified ex-pat Russian community in Shanghai was split asunder. The White Russians viewed returnees as communist sympathisers and Konstantin immediately lost his factory job as a result.

*Nina and Konstantin (Kostya).*

Julia's husband Yura had abandoned her and their young daughter, Lyalya, on a number of occasions during their time in Manchuria and by the late 1940's it was clear to Julia that their marriage would not survive. Julia related the heartbreaking story of when she and Lyalya were sitting in a station café and saw Yura for the first time in several months. Lyalya called out *'Papa, papa'* in delight but he completely ignored her. The child was devastated by her father's indifference and Julia resolved to divorce him and return to her family in Shanghai. But travelling across country in that confused and violent period was very dangerous for an unaccompanied woman; moreover it would take time to find the means.

When Julia finally arrived back in Shanghai in 1950 she was to discover a very different city from the one she had left six years earlier. During that time World War II had ended, and with it the Japanese occupation. The Chinese Nationalist armies had been defeated by Mao's triumphant communists and the American soldiers had returned home. The greatest shock, however, was the discovery that her sister had returned to the

USSR and her mother had divorced her father and fled the country, along with most Europeans, her relatives included. What a bitter blow it must have been to the single mother and her little girl. The Shanghai she had missed so much was now a mere shadow of its former glory and the family she so desperately needed were scattered around the world.

That there had been no contact between Julia and her close family during her six years in Manchuria may seem utterly astonishing today but it must be remembered that communications were all but impossible throughout the war torn continent at that time.

*Elena and Julia in 1950.*

Julia managed to locate her father, who had remained in Shanghai and coincidentally married another Zina. Nikolai took them in and gave them a tiny room under the stairs. It was then that Maria Zinovyevna, a former housekeeper to her mother's family who had helped prepare Julia's wedding, rediscovered this frail, pretty divorcee. It occurred to Maria that it would be a good idea if her eligible young son were to meet her. And so, Vanya and Julia were introduced...

What followed was something of a whirlwind romance; they both quickly became smitten with each other. Vanya's inherent generosity, loving nature and deeply held masculine trait to nurture and protect the weaker sex, as he saw it, were awoken by this helpless and vulnerable young woman. For despite being a divorced mother, Julia had lived a sheltered life and was still naïve in many respects. Notwithstanding the unhappy experience of her first marriage, Julia was still keen to seek happiness in marriage and in Vanya she could see a solid, dependable man who would never betray her in the way her first husband had. Although he had little material wealth to offer, she recognised his potential and sensed that he would work hard to provide for her and her daughter. Moreover, he was physically appealing. How could she resist? The differences in social position no longer seemed relevant, nor did the fact that, at 23, he was two years her junior. As a 16 year old school boy

156

he vaguely remembered his mother helping to cook for the lavish wedding of this 18 year old girl, the sort of girl that would have seemed unattainable to him then. He could never have imagined in his wildest dreams that within seven short years she would be his.

Vanya had been forced to rely upon his wits from an early age. Poverty, perseverance and his travels in the merchant navy had forged a strong and independent character. Even so, he was ready to commit to a lifelong companion, someone who would be his soul mate and partner in the uncertain days ahead. The casual acquaintances of a sailor long behind him, Vanya had been imbued with the strong, conservative values of his deeply religious mother and longed for the security and blessings of a proper Russian Orthodox marriage. *'A person is not whole until they are married'* he believed. Thus, their common cultural and religious ties and desire for one another overcame the mere accidents of age and social status, as they embarked on a joyful and fulfilling relationship.

On learning that his protégé was in love and intending to marry, Vanya's employer, Antipiat, in his chosen role as surrogate father, helped arrange the wedding. Despite the recent exodus of Russians and an atheistic Communist regime in power, he managed to find a functioning Russian Orthodox church and a priest. So, following a short courtship, the happy couple married on the 28th January 1951. Even in that tumultuous time, Julia managed to find a bridal dress, not a long one this time but as attractive as she could muster in the circumstances and without the invaluable help of her mother. The wedding was conducted in the traditional Orthodox manner, with all the attendant ritual, Vanya standing proud and solemn in his dark suit.

The new regime must have allowed some vestige of free enterprise to flourish because Antipiat arranged for their wedding photographs to be taken in a Chinese studio.

*Russian Orthodox church, Shanghai.*

A small reception, undoubtedly a sit down supper, was organised by Vanya's mother, the indefatigable Maria Zinovyevna. It was not as large as they might have liked because, by then, the vast majority of Russians had already fled the country.

After their wedding Julia went to live with Vanya in his modest room until they could complete the laborious negotiations necessary to leave China. Zina was to play a major role in this event, despite having left China two years earlier.

It was still not apparent in 1950, a full year after the Chinese communists' victory, whether or not all foreigners would be evicted. But other relatives, having seen the writing on the wall, had already left in 1948. They had been

*Vanya and Julia's wedding, 1951.*

aided in this diplomatic and logistical nightmare by the International Refugee Organisation (IRO), which initially sent them to Tubabao in the Philippines for onward embarkation to those countries that were prepared to offer them residency, such as Australia, Canada, America and Brazil. This was quite an adventure in itself and will be related in the next chapter.

Zina had already left for Australia in 1949, via Tubabao, and had been negotiating to obtain a visa for her daughter and granddaughter to join her. She had naturally been very perturbed to leave China without either of her daughters but the Russian community had negotiated long and hard to be admitted to safe havens and so she did not feel she could afford to miss the opportunity when it was presented. Particularly as they were stateless refugees and it was far from clear when, or if, another chance would come along. Nina had already returned to the USSR, despite Zina's pleadings to the contrary. Julia seemed almost as far away in

Harbin, though Zina believed she was at least safe with her husband and his family. Years before, it had been foretold that Zina would see out her days with one of her daughters so she was very alarmed that they were in different countries. Who would she die with in Australia? Thus, upon arrival in Australia, she immediately set about arranging a visa for Julia.

She was surprised to discover that it was not only Julia and Elena who needed a visa but her new husband as well. However, the documents had already been sent off in Julia's first husband's name – Nikulinski. There was no time to change the names on their visa applications and Julia was obliged to travel using her previous name. Zina, always the conservative, status conscious mother wrote back in alarm. *'You must not live with your new husband on the boat, without his name. People will think you're not married!'* Needless to say they ignored this particular piece of advice.

In the absence of an Australian consulate in Shanghai, the newlyweds were interviewed at the English consulate and granted permission to enter Australia. The next problem was how to get there. The IRO had paid the fares of the émigrés that had travelled via Tubabao but the Shalavins had literally 'missed the boat' and would therefore have to pay full fare on a passenger liner. Vanya and Julia had to borrow from several people, some leaving with them and others already in Australia. Zina most likely gave them some assistance.

*Vanya and Julia (back, right) enjoying a party with friends from the jewellers, possibly a farewell to Shanghai.*

*SS Changsha.*

The first leg of their journey to Australia was by train to Hong Kong and then on to the ship 'Changsha'. The first 4-5 days at sea were not so bad but the remaining ten days were horrible and much of the time they were seasick. When they crossed the equator Lyalya wrapped her parents in streamers as they lay on their bunks, as part of the festivities. Of course they were delighted when they eventually arrived in Sydney, though Julia, who was lying ill in her bunk, was disappointed to have missed their entry into the spectacular harbour. She remembers the engine cutting out and then silence. Now we are all going to drown, she thought (mother never did like water). But on being told that they had arrived in their new country she joined in the delirious celebrations. Tugs pulled the large ship effortlessly under Sydney's iconic Harbour Bridge, much to the relief of the passengers who did not believe it would actually fit. Upon seeing the enormous clown's face that is the entrance to Sydney's harbour side amusement park, Luna Park, Julia promised her excited daughter that they would visit it as soon as possible.

It was September 1951 and they had arrived in their new home, Australia. The young family, now adopting the English names of John, Julie and Helen, spent a short time in Sydney before travelling north by steam train to join Zina in Queensland. John wondered what had become of his former employer, the jeweller Antipiat. Had he managed to escape? What happened to his money and the shop? John had nothing to lose he claims. What remained of their life's possessions, and all they had to begin their new life in Australia with, had managed to fit into three suitcases.

# Chapter 6

## Tubabao, Philippines - a tropical interlude.

## Коли хочешь себе добра, никому не делай зла.

*Treat others as you would have them treat you.*

# Arrival in the tropics.

The expatriate Russian community became increasingly alarmed in 1948 when it became apparent that Mao's Communist forces would be victorious in China. The North had already been taken over with the aid of the USSR, whereupon the Russian Secret Police, the KGB, had arrested and deported many Russians back to the Soviet Union, to face internal exile or the labour camps. In Europe thousands of former soldiers had already been forcibly returned to the USSR at Stalin's insistence. They had begged the British and American authorities to be allowed to remain but were refused. It is true that some White Russians had collaborated with the Nazis in order to bring down the Soviet regime. A few had even formed a Fascist party in China and took to wearing black shirts and giving the *Heil Hitler* salute. They hoped to return to Mother Russia in triumph, *'riding on white horses'*, following the defeat of the hated Communists by Germany. In view of such collaboration, *all* Russian soldiers and exiles were suspect and likely to be punished, or so they reasonably believed. 40,000 Cossacks returned to the USSR from Austria faced certain death, according to members of the Russian Historical Association.[1] Some soldiers even committed suicide rather than return. When news of these events reached the Russians in China they quite naturally became desperate to leave their adopted home and seek refuge in the free world.

The Russians in Shanghai formed the *Russian Emigrants' Association* to co-ordinate their émigré community's efforts to seek asylum elsewhere. Their dynamic and charismatic leader was a Cossack and former Colonel in the Russian Imperial Army called Grigory Bologoff. He appealed directly to the United Nations and every country of the free world to grant them refuge. The preferred destination of many refugees was the USA but it was to take a further two years for America to pass the enabling bill required to permit entry to refugees. Australia offered to take anyone prepared to work for two years in a job, possibly as a labourer, and location of the government's choosing; an offer which only about 1,500 chose to take up at the time. The South American countries of Brazil, Argentina, Chile and Paraguay, however, were prepared to accept them without condition. The only prompt response, however, came from the Philippine government, which offered the virtually uninhabited island of Tubabao as a temporary residence and, most importantly, a safe haven from Communism. The *International Refugee Organisation* (IRO), a department of the United Nations, was charged with arranging their transit to the island.

The last meeting of the Russian Emigrants' Association was held in May, 1948. 2,500 people were present as well as representatives of the American and other consulates, the secretary of the Mayor of Shanghai and an IRO representative from Geneva. The President of the Association stressed that his members would not live under any form of Communism and decisively announced that *'We can be broken, but not bent'*, which was met with long and thunderous applause.

The immediate priority was to save those Russians who were still living in the North of the country around Peking and Tientsin. Accordingly, an appeal for help and support was sent to General Douglas MacArthur and in particular to Admiral Badger of the US Armed forces. Badger agreed to the request and MacArthur allowed a few hundred of the refugees to fly to Japan but the remaining refugees scattered about China was still a concern.

As far as organising transport to Tubabao was concerned, the IRO was only offering to evacuate 500 responsible leaders and those prominent in the White community. The Association emphatically rejected this. There were some 6,000 Russians waiting to be expatriated and the President declared *'Evacuate all the White Russians or none'*.

By November, little had been resolved, though the first group of refugees from Tientsin had arrived in Shanghai aboard an American war vessel, to the jubilation of the community. Perhaps they would transport them all to Tubabao now. By then most folk had already sold off as many of their possessions as they could and were witnessing a rapid decline in their funds as the Chinese dollar sank lower in value by the day. More urgent letters were sent off to governments around the world. The IRO was still insisting that they could only transport 500 people. Eventually there was a showdown between the IRO representative, a certain Mr. Clark, and the Association's President. In this meeting Bologoff declared *'Gentlemen, if you will not reject this idea in spite of my report....I, as a sign of protest against this, shall kill myself in this office (and pulled a revolver from his pocket). I trust that this question will not be raised here again, and that I shall not be forced to take more effective steps in regard to the people working in this office.'* Mr. Clark rose and asked nervously *'What do you mean?'* A short reply followed: *'What I said'* and sealing his answer with a light hit with his fist on the table, he left the meeting.[2]

Whether he was bluffing or not, his outburst seems to have had the desired effect because the IRO eventually agreed in principle to help all the refugees.

One of the nine Committee members of the Emigrants' Association was Konstantin Kluge, a former officer of the Russian Imperial Army who had fought in the Russian Civil War. Born into a distinguished Russian family, of noble heritage, his election to the committee undoubtedly reflected the community's faith in his energy and ability to co-ordinate the massive tasks ahead. The following information was translated by his daughter, Olga, whom I am pleased to consider a close family friend.

Mr Kluge had to liaise with the IRO and he lamented that the organisation was influenced both by the United Nations and indirectly by their old enemy the Soviet Union. To add insult to injury the Soviet Consulate was located right next door to the IRO offices and Soviet officials were known to infiltrate the organisation. Moreover, the Association found that thousands of Soviet citizens living in China suddenly realised that they too could escape China *and* the USSR by becoming 'stateless' and joining the ranks of the desperate refugees. Thus, this new group were casting away their Soviet passports, some publicly confessing their new allegiances in the newspapers. Their applications flooded into the IRO offices with yet more requests for assistance to leave. The IRO, who could not cope with the previous numbers, asked the Shanghai Emigrants' Association to help process these people as they had been impressed by the Association's organisational ability. What a dilemma faced the committed White Russians. In Mr. Kluge's own words:

*'Such a position was not to our liking, as those individuals who so recently were Soviet citizens had changed their beliefs like a pair of gloves. Our hearts were not in it and frankly we could not trust them. On top of that, we understood that the Soviet Consulate freed them easily and willingly from their obligations, by all accounts not considering these people of any value. On the other hand, it would be to the Soviets' advantage to scatter their own, well checked out citizens throughout the world.'* [3] Nonetheless, despite their misgivings they were forced to accept these dubious citizens and include them in the plans for evacuation.

The city was divided into sections, each headed by a representative, who liaised with the Association to register and organise intending evacuees. Many members of the Shliapnikoff family were in these lists, including my grandmother Zina, her niece Galina and her husband Leo, who also worked with the IRO. Mr. Kluge continued processing the documents of the thousands now in the care of the Emigrants' Association though there was still no news about when, where and how they were to be evacuated.

At last, the news arrived that they had been granted temporary accommodation on the island of Tubabao in the Philippines. This was a tiny island, which had until recently been a US Navy base, connected by a wooden bridge to the larger island of Samar. There would be an established camp the IRO informed them and everything would be in readiness for their arrival. The intending evacuees were naturally pleased with this news as conditions in China were deteriorating by the day. Throngs from the countryside invaded the streets and Chinese troops roamed aimlessly. Meanwhile, the Russians' life savings were whittling away in value and they feared being caught in the middle of a revolution. Finally, after many months of anxious waiting, they heard that the *SS Hwa Lien* was on its way to take the first group of passengers to safety on the island. Colonel Kluge was asked to lead this first group of settlers and to ensure their safety.

There was still much to be done before departure; medical examinations, form filling for the Philippines consulate and document processing for the Chinese police and customs. Finally they were ready to depart, only to find that there was more confusion and disorder, particularly with the allocation of cabins. To their dismay they discovered that the passenger lists they had prepared had simply been ignored. They were convinced that Soviet citizens had been deliberately smuggled into that first party by the Soviet Consulate and allocated cabins alongside the White Russians. Colonel Kluge and his wife were left without a cabin at all and spent the first night sitting with their hand luggage in the lounge room. Nonetheless, they were delighted to be under way. A Russian Orthodox Archbishop, who was also a good friend of the Kluges, blessed the evacuees at the dockside and prayed for their safe journey. The remaining Russians, stood as a crowd on the shore, waving and shouting their farewells; pleased for them and sure that their turn would soon follow. The traditional *'Oora'* echoed in the passenger's ears as the ship sailed away and they in turn waved the Imperial Russian flag back to those left on shore.

As the first contingent of 500+ men, women and children sailed away from Shanghai, a working party of single young men flew ahead to prepare the island for their arrival. One of those men was Oleg Miram, to whom I am indebted for the following account of the first days on the island.[4]

Mr. Miram recounts how he happened to be walking along the Avenue

Joffre one day when he bumped into a Mr. Digeau, a committee member of the Shanghai Emigrants' Association. He asked Oleg if he would be interested in leading a 'working party' of about 50 young men to Tubabao. The only stipulation was that they all had to be single, young and ready to go in two days! Two days later the keen and willing party, presumably there was no shortage of volunteers, flew to Manila airport on an American army transport plane. They had no time to obtain any documentation, carried a maximum of 50 pounds of luggage per person, and had absolutely no idea of what they were letting themselves in for. They were supposed to be met by a Captain Price of the IRO but when they arrived there was no sign of anyone from the IRO, just American reporters. They were led away to a large empty room and told to sit on the floor, whilst armed guards with machine guns were posted at the entrance.

With no sign of assistance and his men becoming hungry Oleg decided to take matters into his own hands. He called the officer in charge of the guards and asked him to take him to the airport restaurant. There he asked to speak to the owner. A middle-aged American woman emerged and Oleg politely requested that he would like to order dinner for 50 people. He would sign the bill but the IRO, care of Captain Price, Manila hotel would pay. To his great surprise and relief, she agreed and the 50 unshaven, dishevelled men, overdressed in warm clothes for a tropical climate, some even wearing army boots, sat down to dine in this comparatively prestigious restaurant. Air travel was still in its infancy at the time and only the rich could afford to fly. After dinner, they returned to their bare room to sleep on the floor. For a further two days they ate lunch and dinner in the restaurant and slept on the floor. On the third day they were evicted from their room by the airport authorities who informed them that they were to be moved, under armed guard, to an unfinished building located across from the airport. Naturally, they objected vehemently to being treated as prisoners. At this point, Oleg relates, pandemonium broke loose and the officer instructed his guards to aim their guns at the hapless refugees. But they stood their ground and refused to move until it was agreed that they would be allowed to walk as free men to their new accommodation, having agreed not to 'escape' en-route. At last, a Filipino gentleman appeared and informed them that the camp, equipped with electricity and all other conveniences, was ready and that they were to be flown to Tubabao that same day. How wrong he was.

Upon arriving at Guiuan airport the working party was met by more armed guards and a dozen old jeeps. After loading their luggage, the long motorcade wound its way to the island of Tubabao, where they were simply dumped in the middle of the jungle and left to fend for themselves. An inauspicious start for the working party that was to prepare for the arrival of the first of what was to eventually become a population of 6,000 people! Oleg writes lightly of his reactions to the desperate situation but one can imagine that a lesser man might have felt quite daunted by it. However, Oleg and the group would not give in to despair; they had been chosen for their abilities and energy and so set about investigating the island.

They spent their first night on the floor of an old Quonset hut (a lightweight semi-circular prefabricated structure made of corrugated steel) that the US military used during the war years. They found water from a little creek and so were able to drink and wash themselves, but there was no food. However, guards with about a dozen jeeps had been left behind to keep an eye on them. Remembering his success at Manila airport, Oleg instructed the entire group, plus the guards to whom they were now accustomed, to drive to the city of Guiuan, about 5 kilometres away. There they found the first restaurant, a Chinese one, and explained their situation and that they could sign the bill, but IRO would pick up the tab. It is an extraordinary testimony to human generosity, given the uncertainties of the post war period, that the restaurateurs agreed so readily. They were able to do this for a few days, but it soon became clear that they could not afford to waste valuable time driving back and forth between Samar and Tubabao for food. The SS *Hwa Lien* was due in two week's time and the refugees onboard would expect to find a working camp.

The situation was clearly critical; here were 50 young men, resourceful to be sure, but with no equipment, tools or building materials with which to build a camp for hundreds of people. Shelter was of paramount importance, for even though it was warm, the tropical climate meant that it rained a few times every day. Once again Oleg's initiative came to the fore. On their dinner expeditions to Guiuan he had met a Filipino entrepreneur whom he approached with a proposition. Namely, that if he could provide them with a supply of provisions, he would eventually be paid by the IRO. Perhaps it was stressed that this organisation was under the auspices of the United Nations, which made the request seem reasonable. Whatever the reason, the provisions were duly supplied and delivered to their island. Thus the working party could survive the two weeks themselves and begin to think about how to prepare for the newcomers. They found an old army pot in which they could boil meat and vegetables, using leftover army tin cans as plates and wooden chopsticks for cutlery. They also discovered some Filipino natives on the island who were persuaded to lend them their spades and picks. The party could then press on with the construction of toilets and a rudimentary kitchen, with water piped from the creek. But that was all they could do in the time they had available. They could not do anything by way of providing shelter because the tents on which they would have to rely were being transported in the same ship as the passengers.

In due course the *SS Hwa Lien* arrived with her cargo of anxious, tired and apprehensive families. The ship anchored off shore and passengers and supplies, including the precious tents, had to be ferried to shore on barges. The tents were offloaded first so that the working party could start erecting them, otherwise the passengers would have nowhere to go. The working party were dismayed to find that the tents were just a collection of old discarded wartime surplus, in dreadful condition. Many had holes, some didn't have ropes or pegs and they were all different sizes. Erecting this motley collection was to test the working party's energy and resourcefulness to the limit. They worked 16 hours a day, with the help of able-bodied people from the ship, erecting them as quickly as they could on the nearest available level ground. The result was a haphazard 'shanty town' of tents of all shapes and sizes, ranging from two-man right up to 20-man. When the IRO camp director finally arrived a week later he reprimanded the settlers for their shoddy camp.

They were expected to have erected them in lines, with walkways between, as in a military style camp. However, when the circumstances were explained, the director was sympathetic. Similarly, when Oleg explained why he had chalked up such huge bills to the camp's finance officer, he had the grace to be understanding.

After all the problems they had encountered creating a working camp out of the jungle, it came as something of a shock when some time later they discovered a deserted US Navy base on the neighbouring island of *Manikani*. It was built like a small town and possessed all the necessary facilities. There were rows of Quonset huts formed into streets, huge warehouses, furnished officers' quarters, even churches and a swimming pool! It would have been ideal for the refugees. Perhaps it was this base that someone had in mind when they had been falsely promised all conveniences on their island. It appears however that the refugees were victims of Filipino corruption. They later discovered that Tubabao belonged to a friend of the President and the IRO had paid him per head for the use of the land. However, the *Manila Times* (it is believed) reporting on the arrival of the refugees, said that the *'600 hectare reservation (of Manikani) may be turned over to the refugees if they find Guiuan too crowded.'* Well, neither Guiuan nor Manikani were ever offered to the evacuees and their lives would have been considerably different had they have been. But the same report did end with the inspiring observation about the lesson to be learned from the refugees' flight: *'It had to do with man in such a need of freedom that he would go into exile to keep it.'* [5]

## Life on a Filipino island.

Meanwhile, the group of refugees who had been allowed to go to Japan, as guests of General MacArthur had a different set of experiences before they too, eventually ended up in the Filipino island. Irene Kounitsky was among the first group of 50 to leave Shanghai.

The select group arrived at Lunghua airport in Shanghai for the flight to Tokyo on the 28th of December 1948. However, the Chinese authorities refused to validate their departure visas - put their *chop* on them, and so they were forced to remain in the city. Their suitcases were loaded onto the plane but they were taken to the French barracks at Route Frelupt where they were to remain indefinitely. Irene, an attractive young lady, had only a handbag with her, containing her comb and make-up. There were entire families with mothers and young children, bitterly disappointed, tired, cold and hungry. After another false start they were finally permitted to leave, at their third attempt, on the 5th of January. In Tokyo, they were taken by US Army buses to a depot two hour's drive away, where intelligence officers questioned them all. The women were segregated from the men and their barracks guarded 24 hours a day by military police. Why were the Americans treating the Russians with such suspicion? These were the days of the fledgling Cold War and the Americans obviously felt they could not run the risk of Soviet spies infiltrating the group. The females could only meet their men folk in the mess hall where they had their meals, or in the square, surrounded by a twelve foot fence, where they were taken for daily exercise. At least they were well fed, Irene noted. Not until the 27th of February were they finally allowed to go to Manila, stopping at Okinawa for refuelling. At Manila airport, they had to endure a hot and humid night, sleeping in army cots in a public hall. The final leg of their journey was made in an old army troop transport plane that flew them, rattling and shaking its frightened passengers, to Samar, the nearest airport to Tubabao. Finally, the weary but grateful throng arrived at their temporary abode. Conditions in the camp in those early days were still harsh and it would be some time before the ingenuity and energy of the refugees transformed the barren island into a tropical haven.

Another refugee, Kyra Tatarinoff related her memories of the journey to Tubabao on board the second ship, *SS Cristobal*.[6] She made the poignant observation that the Russians were so frightened of betrayal and forced repatriation to the USSR that even when on the ship they diligently watched which way the ship was sailing, by sun in the day and stars at night. The ship was old and enormously overcrowded. Not only were the 518 passengers far more than it was intended to carry but they also carried the excess luggage of the first boat *Hwa Lien* and the luggage of those transported by air. People slept in hammocks in the hold or sat upright in the lounge. It listed to port and people would get wet from waves washing on to the lower deck. One alarming night a ship loomed straight at them out of the darkness heading directly for the *Cristobal*, then changed course quickly at the last minute. A pirate ship that thought better of attacking them? They could only speculate. At Manila harbour in the beautiful coloured sea they gazed in awe at the grim reminders of the war, row upon row of masts sticking out of the water, all that was visible of the sunken ships below the surface. By now the tropical sea was calm and glorious but they could not become complacent yet and, sure enough, their worst fears were confirmed when a teenager observed that the moon was on the wrong side of the ship, confirming that they had turned back. However, there was no cause for alarm, the decrepit ship's boiler had blown and they had been forced to return to Manila for repairs. Finally, after 20 tense and uncomfortable days, they reached Tubabao.

Disembarking was the first major hurdle faced by the new inhabitants, who were shocked to find nothing in readiness. As with the *Hwa Lien*, their luggage was unceremoniously dumped in the middle of the square and, after being issued with their tents, camp beds and mosquito nets, they were left to their own devices. Those fortunate enough to know one of the earlier arrivals would at least be welcome with a cup of tea. One resourceful mother, prepared for any eventuality, arrived clutching her own kettle full of hot water, which she clung to throughout the entire disembarkation process. This involved climbing down the ship's unsteady stairs to the Army DUK's (amphibious landing craft) ladder, clambering onto the beach and then the bumpy bus journey along the rough jungle roads to the camp site.

The early days were hard and awful Irene Kounitsky related. She was allocated a place in a tent for 12 people, adjacent to the ravine that had to be guarded at night because natives crept out from the jungle, carrying dreaded bolo knives, to rob the refugees. After dark, Filipino military police would shoot at any noise in the jungle. The food was terrible, mouldy bread and tins of hash – leftover army supplies. Water had to be obtained from a stream at the bottom of the ravine via a steep descent that became slippery and muddy when it rained. There were queues for everything; hot water, meals, medical treatment, inoculations and all the administrative paraphernalia required to migrate to a new country. Some, like Oleg and his new wife, were fortunate enough to receive their visas to the US after only a few months at Tubabao, though it had still taken four years since he had first applied. Others were to stay there for nearly three years. Accidents, illness and serious disease were commonplace as was typhoid fever, dengue, tuberculosis and skin ailments of all kinds. People frequently fell over the tent ropes and pegs, particularly at night when there was no light. Cuts and scrapes turned septic in the humidity and they had no disinfectant. Toilets were just canvas enclosed large pits covered with wooden boards into which several holes had been cut. There was one for men and one for women per district.

In time, conditions improved as the 6,000 or so inhabitants applied themselves to the task in hand. The camp was divided into 14 districts, each with its own leader who was responsible for the facilities. They built communal kitchens, installed hot water boilers, toilets and even showers. Electricity was eventually provided as well but the supply was limited and very erratic. A hospital, sanatorium, supply office, cemetery and several churches of different denominations were also built. For the camp contained not only Russians of predominantly Orthodox faith, but also Poles, Ukrainians, Armenians, Turks, Latvians, Lithuanians, Estonians, Romanian, Czechs, Yugoslavs, Hungarians, Germans and Austrians.

The camp authorities, IRO and Filipino officials became more responsive to the needs of the camp's population. Fresh meat was obtained after the camps' scouts performed a well-received skit, ceremoniously burying a few tins of the detested hash around the campfire. In due course, there was even an open-air theatre where dances were held as well as performances displaying the myriad talents of the assembled population. Brass bands staged concerts; there were dramatic performances, operettas, poetry readings, acrobatic displays, singers and dancers. *Entertainment Square*, as they named the large open area, even showed movies at night under the stars. Everyone brought his or her own seating, a wooden box or stool if one was fortunate enough to have such a luxury. Some of them elaborate affairs with roofs and canopies and drop down sides to keep out the inevitable rain, others just makeshift affairs with improvised umbrellas. When movies were not shown they danced at night under the stars in their wooden clogs, their own shoes having long since worn out or else having been carefully put away for the big day of their departure to a 'civilised' country.

*Entertainment square,*
*the recreation area for the refugees.*

Young and old alike managed to find moments of joy in their primitive surroundings and adapted to their Robinson Crusoe like existence. They danced at night to the music of Mickey Kay's band, even during the tropical downpours.

On the 31st of October, 1949, The Russian Emigrants' Association took great pride in staging a special concert, with Maestro P. Tebneff conducting the brass band, to bid farewell to the first people leaving for Sydney, Australia aboard the *General Greely*.

In May, 1949 Oleg married his fiancée in the most lavish ceremony they could manage to organise on the tropical island. Photographs show the bride in a long white dress, complete with train that she must have brought with her for the occasion. The seven bridesmaids' dresses on the other hand show evidence of creative and colourful improvisation. Frilly skirts, off the shoulder flounced blouses, sandals and tropical flowers in their hair, combined to produce a suitable effect for an island wedding.

Oleg and his wife, now living in America, recently celebrated their 50th anniversary but he still has fond memories of his time at Tubabao. For his generation he recalls, it was an adventure but he appreciates that it must have been very difficult for many older people and for those with young children, as sickness and disease was rife.

*Oleg and his bride.*

*Bridesmaids at Oleg Miram's wedding.*

He remembered another particularly poignant story about the day he was called to the Filipino security office. Two men were handed over to him and he was asked to find them accommodation amongst the camp's Russians. Thinking nothing of it, he said, *'Let's go'* to the men and led them out to the camp, taking a short cut through the jungle. Halfway there, the men, with fear in their eyes, asked where they were going. It dawned on Oleg that they had believed he was taking them out to be shot and when he later learned their history he could well understand why.[7] They were defectors from the Soviet Union. The tall, blonde younger man of the two had been a military pilot who had simply flown his plane east, without any navigational charts, until it ran out of fuel and crash-landed on a Japanese island. The other, a short, dark, stocky man had escaped from the USSR on a raft, which he sailed for days before being picked up, close to death, by Japanese fishermen. Both men had been handed over to the American authorities and interrogated. Having decided they had no valuable information they were sent to Tubabao. These brave young men had risked death to escape Soviet tyranny and they could not believe their luck when they at last found themselves in a safe haven.

Oleg Miram's wedding was not the first to take place on the island. On the 13th February 1949, just a few weeks after the arrival of the first shipload of refugees, Olga Kluge, the youngest daughter of Colonel Konstantin Kluge married her fiancé, Alex Pronin. The Orthodox ceremony was conducted in *'a canvas covered chapel'*, according to the report in the Manila Times the following day. Sadly for the young bride, Colonel Kluge and his wife were not present at the ceremony. There had been a dispute with the Filipino authorities who alleged that they had failed to comply with government regulations and as a result, they were refused permission to enter the camp. The senior Kluges were returned to Manila where they stayed until they received their visas to enter America. The situation left the Kluges in something of a quandary

regarding their youngest daughter, Olga. A son, Konstantin, was studying Art in Paris, another possibly already in USA and another daughter was also married and independent. But Olga was just 17 and her parents were naturally concerned for her safety, alone in the inhospitable and possibly dangerous circumstances of the refugee camp. She was given the choice of either going with her parents or getting married promptly, so that they could be reassured that she would be safe with her husband and his parents. Olga and Alex did not hesitate and so it was that the Russian Orthodox priest was called upon to officiate and bless the first of many weddings on the island.

*Olga Kluge.*

The resourcefulness and ingenuity of the refugees was to be demonstrated time and time again in this difficult and challenging environment. They had no fresh food for the first four months and the staple diet was military issue hash, tipped into huge cauldrons and boiled with lots of water. Dried vegetables were also issued and special rations of evaporated milk and canned fruit salad for the children. Living conditions of course were very basic but they continually improvised and found new uses for a variety of objects. Apart from the camp beds there was no furniture, so crates functioned as stools, a trunk as a table, or if placed on its side, as a chest without the drawers. Many handy men fashioned benches and tables from young trees, using only a sharp kitchen knife and lashed the poles together with vines. They scavenged for string, a nail, canvas to repair tents, cans to carry water and bits of wire for handles. Tents were very close together and the sides often rolled up altogether so there was absolutely no privacy. Many people built themselves reed fences around their tents, complete with padlocked 'gates'.

To settle the inevitable disputes that arise when people live in such close proximity to each other they set up their own Arbitration Board, from those residents with a legal background. They also set up their own police force, to maintain order, keep the peace, resolve petty squabbles and deal with drunks. Filipino military police and security guards guarded the camp from natives with criminal intent and the threat of pirates. The Russians recorded at least one occasion when pirates landed on the island, stole a 44-gallon drum of petrol and were chased by the police through the jungle. The drum was abandoned as they disappeared into the darkness.

By and large relations with the native Filipinos were amicable. There were some fishing villages near the camp where the local people lived in simple huts built on stilts. They fished in outriggers and sailboats, planted taros, the indigenous vegetable, harvested coconuts and bananas and lived basic but seemingly pleasant lives. Women, young and old, wore bright dresses of printed cotton, even under the open showers they fashioned from old oil drums which collected the daily fresh rainwater. Elevated on a few poles, a plug in the bottom allowed the water to flow when required and cleaning the dress and oneself was combined in one simple operation. On Sundays the girls wore full, colourful skirts and pretty blouses, with a white lace scarf over their heads for the walk to church. High heeled wooden clogs with bright straps and fancy carving completed the picture. Filipinos were converts to Catholicism from their former status as a Spanish colony and church services and religious processions had become part of their regular rituals. The men wore shorts on a daily basis but on Sundays they too would wear their best sharkskin pants and embroidered shirts. Many of them also carried the *bolo*, hanging from their hips. A formidable weapon and tool, it consisted of a sharp blade, about 20 inches long, with a wooden handle. It was used to cut down trees, open coconuts, dig the ground, slaughter pigs and occasionally attack their opponents. This was the weapon that struck fear into the refugees when they were threatened by robbers and made the presence of the Filipino guards necessary. In nearby Guiuan where some of the refugees had to go from time to time to attend the hospital if they were seriously ill, as some were with Tuberculosis, even the doctors carried guns for their own protection. According to my aunt Galina, almost every night a Filipino was stabbed or shot and had to be admitted to the hospital.[8]

## A new birth.

Galina had very mixed experiences during her time in Tubabao. Her husband Leo was employed by the IRO so there were some privileges to be had. They had a first class cabin on the *SS Hwa Lien* and he continued to earn wages throughout their time on the island. This enabled them to buy goods from the locals as well as in Guiuan. Galina and Leo were able to attain passes on occasion to visit the town, which had two restaurants, a market place, a telegraph office and a hospital, one of the few solid buildings in the town. Most of the other buildings were on stilts, so they could be quickly replaced after they had been demolished by the frequent typhoons. They thoroughly enjoyed their rare visits to 'town' but passes were difficult to obtain and they still had to be back in the camp by 6 p.m. However, when Galina contracted TB she had to spend four months in the Guiuan hospital – Dr. Montero's, whilst awaiting the birth of their first child. It could not have been an easy time. At least the conditions there were better than in the camp hospital and Galina could amuse herself listening to the nurses' gossip. She remembers an incident when they ran out of toilet paper, the nurse said, *'Don't worry, I'll run to the market and get some'.*

Leo worked full time, taking mail to the post office, receiving and sending telegrams on the mainland as well as many other jobs. Whilst at Guiuan he befriended the Filipino employees at the Telegraph office. Thus, Galina and Leo had Filipino meals cooked for them whenever they visited town, a treat indeed and no doubt a welcome relief from the standard fare of the refugee camp. In time, the locals realised there was money to be made from the camp dwellers and set up stalls along the main road from the jetty. Simple huts built in a few hours; they sold everything from fresh fish to fancy dresses as well as much needed kitchen equipment. Some even established little restaurants where one could eat and drink – beer, wine and even spirits. San Miguel beer becoming very popular! Cold soft drinks and ice cream were also undoubtedly coveted items amongst young and old alike. For those so inclined, there were also local ladies on offer. At night the stalls with their portable kerosene lamps offered a welcoming scene of illumination. The

178

stall holders were very enterprising Galina notes, and always offered alternatives if they did not have something you wanted. Inevitably, it would be available *'Manyana'*. Galina was and is adept at improvisation herself and learned to make both *pelemeni* and *piroshki* with tinned Spam (Supply Pressed American Meat); the former, being the ever popular dumpling and the latter a traditional meat pie, rather akin to a fried pasty.

After a few months' treatment and convalescence in Guiuan, being looked after by the good doctor himself, who always carried his gun during his rounds, Galina returned to the camp to await the birth of her baby. By this time the first ship bound for Australia was ready to go and Leo was kept very busy with arrangements for the departing refugees; checking luggage and clearing passengers for embarkation. It must have been a very exciting time for the fortunate leavers and an exhausting time for Leo. What a coincidence to have the baby decide to come on that very night! Leo was ready to drop when Galina announced that she would need to go to the hospital that evening. Nonetheless, he arranged for a nurse and driver to take her to Guiuan by jeep. It was 1.30 am and she had to endure a 32 km ride through the pitch-black jungle, with only the headlights of the jeep showing the way. Not an experience to be forgotten in a hurry related Galina. Her first son, Alexander, my second cousin, was born that afternoon and ten days later, mother and son were back in camp. Just a few days after that happy event the island was lashed by a terrible typhoon, with winds of up to 140 miles per hour. Leo was working at the Headquarters and the anxious mother clung to her newborn baby's cradle, as the wind raged around them, grateful that he seemed to sleep through it all. The following morning a scene of terrible devastation greeted them – collapsed tents, uprooted palms and general havoc. They cleaned up as best they could and life resumed its now familiar pattern.

A typical day on the island began with an early breakfast, when the morning breezes kept the temperature relatively cool. Those who could afford to buy it had their own coffee, similarly with canned milk. Leftover bread was issued along with some sugar and jam, when available. Eggs were inedible as both they and the native chickens that produced them smelt of fish. While the staple meals were cooked and served by the communal kitchens, many people had acquired their own little primus stoves on which they could cook additional food. Galina related how she shared such a stove between three tents. An accomplished cook, she was likely to have been one of the many camp dwellers to produce traditional Russian fare from the most challenging ingredients. After all, if she could make *piroshki* out of Spam, she could make anything. Like everyone else she collected water in buckets, made from converted kerosene tins with makeshift handles. Each section had several taps installed, but electricity was only connected to the huts used as offices, hospitals and the police station. Even then its supply was rather erratic. Galina also related how a resourceful Chinese man from Guiuan had built a canteen on the island, selling everything from ice cream to beer. He also had a radio that was on every day from 10 am to midnight. The hit song of the day was *Manyana*, epitomising the attitude of the locals as indeed, it did of the whole plight of the refugees. Tomorrow they would get their products, fulfil their dreams and attain their freedom...

By 8 am people started work. Everyone had a job allocated to them in the schools, hospital, kitchens, motor pool, various offices or general camp maintenance such as garbage disposal, shower maintenance or the least popular task of all, digging the toilet pits. Using them was universally disliked as well, as they were public toilets and one simply squatted side by side with total strangers. Those with extra funds sometimes 'bought off' their allotted duties by paying someone else to do it for them, which nobody seemed to object to. The vast majority were willing workers as it undoubtedly helped to pass the time as well as providing an opportunity to exchange gossip. *'It is strictly between us – I saw last night Nikolai N. walking near the tent of Anna X'... 'They say in the third district that the D.P.* (Displaced Persons) *bill was approved in America'. 'Tomorrow the material for dresses will be issued – two yards each – no selections.'* [9]

Children enjoyed themselves most in the relative freedom of the island's daily activity. They attended school in the mornings, where learning the English language played an important part but they also had additional lessons in Russian. When not in school, they enjoyed swimming, 'scouting' along nearby jungle trails, foraging for shells, crabs and lizards and even the threat of snakes did not dampen their adventurous spirits. Elderly now, they reminisce fondly about their island experiences.

By noon it was already very hot and long lines would form at the kitchens under the shadows of the palm trees. *'What is it today? – Macaroni again! No!'* Some were fortunate enough to be able to spice up the macaroni with their own canned sardines or something else but many had to eat it on its own. Nonetheless, it was still preferable to food and conditions in many of the Displaced Persons camps in Europe. After lunch it was far too hot for work and the camp sank into a welcome siesta for a few hours. Hardly anything moved and even the camp dogs stretched out in the shadows. The camp began to stir again after four o'clock. Filipino vendors arrived, selling clogs, coconuts, fish, blouses and playing musical instruments to promote their wares. A favourite of the camp was Pedro, a boy of about 12, who sold fresh coconuts and played an instrument of his own construction. It consisted of a bamboo frame on which different bottles were hung, filled with water to various depths. When struck, each bottle produced a clear musical note and so he was able to play different tunes.

Before supper some people went for a swim, others to the *bazaar*, the market stalls, if only to window shop, to see the variety of goods on offer. Dinner at about 6 p.m. was usually quite bland and unappetising – meat hash, rice or a macaroni casserole. After their meal, watching the beautiful sunset was a popular activity. The girls liked to refresh themselves and dress again for the evening's entertainment in the square. By 10 p.m. the camp was asleep, to be ready for another busy day.

## Halcyon days.

In many respects it was quite an idyllic life, particularly amongst the
young singles who viewed it all as an adventure. Amid the lush surroundings, romances blossomed in the glorious sunsets and moonlit nights. Weddings were taking place almost every week and so the refugees built themselves a church for this purpose and for regular services. They were particularly thrilled when Archbishop John Maksimovich of Shanghai visited,
on his way to Washington DC to help promote the passing of the *Displaced Persons Bill*. This encouraged them all greatly for he was renowned as being an achiever as well as *'a priest of great virtue'*.

Most of the Russians in the camp appeared to sincerely follow the practices of the Orthodox faith. A makeshift chapel of canvas and native foliage had been constructed almost immediately. In time this became a

*Makeshift Orthodox cathedral.*

comparatively elaborate cathedral, with solid timber walls, what appeared to be a tin roof and the obligatory onion dome, with traditional Russian tri-bar[10] crucifix atop. Inside the cathedral the refugees built the iconostasis, the elaborate screen that separates the altar from the main body of the church and in which their beloved icons are kept. They even constructed 'bells' from empty gas cylinders partly filled with water to adjust the tone. Hung on an 'H' frame they rang loud and true, in celebration of holy days and the many marriages that took place. On some of these occasions a military jeep would be pressed into service as the wedding 'limousine' and a truck for the guests. At the peak of the camp's existence there were in fact three Russian Orthodox churches. Other nationalities also constructed Catholic and Protestant Churches and there were assembly tents for the Pentecostals and Baptists. There were even a few Muslims who also had their place of worship.

The devout Orthodox lovingly recreated those ceremonies established many centuries earlier in Mother Russia. On Palm Sunday they were able to use real palm fronds to commemorate the entry of Christ into Jerusalem. In the colder climate of Russia the 'верба', pussy willow, had long been used to symbolise the unobtainable palm and, ironically, some lamented its absence. Interestingly enough, years later, when given the choice, they would return to using the pussy willow for this important service of remembrance.

The Easter service figured most prominently in the religious calendar. At midnight the congregation stood in the night air, clutching their candles of hope and deliverance and listen to the glorious sounds of the choir raising their voices to celebrate the message that Christ has risen. The choir was particularly good in Tubabao, as there were plenty of people with time to practice. After the service some of the camp inmates somehow found or improvised the ingredients to produce the traditional *kulich* cake and *paskha*, a creamy cheese dessert. Even the fish smelling eggs were painted in bright colours and displayed around the *kulich* in the customary manner.

The refugees who were most in need of their faith were those diagnosed with the dreaded disease Tuberculosis. Known in the camp as *Teebeeshniks*, they had a particularly difficult time. It was especially devastating news because only medically fit people were allowed into the countries of choice and diagnosis of a single family member could condemn the entire family. One woman seriously contemplated suicide in order not to jeopardise her family's future but was luckily talked out of it. Many questioned how it was possible that, having been cleared in China, around 500 of them managed to contract the disease in Tubabao. A meeting with the IRO Geneva representative reassured them that about 90% could be cured with the necessary treatment, for which a special budget was required. France offered to take TB patients for treatment but most of those in the non-infectious category refused to take up this offer as they correctly inferred that they would not then be able to go to the USA or Australia.

The treatment of TB consisted of Streptomycin injections and Amino Acid pills. The TB ward in their newly built sanatorium was full of rumours about who was getting better, or worse, based on the doctor's conduct. Those to whom he said *'You are getting better'* were genuinely improving; those to whom he said *'Well, it looks like you are getting better'* were not and those to whom he simply gave an encouraging pat on the shoulder were tragic-

ally, hopeless cases. A number of refugees ended their days on Tubabao and so the camp gained a Russian Orthodox cemetery as well.

One such unfortunate, dying in the 'infectious' ward, was a very noted artist. He began but did not live long enough to finish the *White Mother of Christ*, a Madonna figure attired purely in white with the pale face of a TB sufferer. Painting this icon enabled him to accept his own approaching end and he was much admired for his spirit and faith. A former *Habarovsk Cadet* dealt with his impending death in a very different way. A strong man with attitude, he broke all the hospital rules, frequently got boisterously drunk and fought both nurses and doctors, who had to wrestle him to administer a tranquilliser. The hospital also had a small *'coo-coo'* house for mental patients, three cells with barred windows, where this chap spent time sleeping off his hangovers.

# Dreaming of the future.

The uncertainty of their futures must have weighed heavily on the camp inmates. Much of the conversation revolved around when the US Congress would pass *The Bill* that would allow the Tubabao refugees to enter the USA, the preferred destination for most of them. But it would be almost three years before the last of them were permitted to enter.

To speed up the checking of immigrants and the issuance of visas a branch of the American consulate, complete with FBI agents, was established on the island. Along with medical checks, refugees had to submit to mental tests, resulting in some poignant and amusing moments. One very staid, plain woman who spoke no English was asked by the doctor, via an interpreter, *'from what end would she start washing the stairs – upper or lower?'* Her response: *'I will wash all the stairs in America and will not ask for his advice.'*. An agent, interviewing a beautiful woman of dubious reputation, asked where she had spent the previous night. Without hesitation she pointed to another FBI agent. Her visa was granted at once.[11]

*Queue for US visas.*

Galina and Leo with their newborn son had initially tried to get visas for Canada, where Galina's father and brother had relocated, but they were unsuccessful. Australia was more forthcoming.

By 1951 most of the refugees had finally relocated to new homes in Australia, the USA or South American countries. Those suffering from TB were the last to leave but they too were given clearance eventually. As the camp shrank to the last 250 or so people, a horrific typhoon passed over the island. Everything was destroyed – the tents, barracks and even the road to Guiuan. As sheets of corrugated iron flew dangerously around, the inhabitants placed the children in the walk-in refrigerator which, with the power off, was just nicely cool. When the typhoon passed the remaining camp inhabitants were moved to the mainland. Areas that had been cleared for tents now reverted back to jungle or were used to grow taro. The camp ceased to exist and a critical rite of passage for some 6,000 Russians was over.

# Chapter 7

# Australia, the promised land.

## Без труда нет плода.

*Without labour there is no reward.*

# The Shalavins in 'Oz' – early days.

John, Julie and Helen arrived in Australia in 1951, thrilled to have arrived safely in a country which welcomed them, where they could at last live in freedom, safety and perhaps even prosper. Most of mother's relatives had preceded them so there would be welcoming arms and help if necessary. Rented accommodation was soon found, boarding with other Russian families, but even that proved too expensive for the impoverished immigrants and so they were obliged to head north to where my Grandmother Zina lived in Brisbane, Queensland. Zina, always the shrewd businesswoman, had landed on her feet and quickly acquired her own small property and was therefore in a position to offer the young family lodgings in her own home.

Julie was soon pregnant and I was born three months prematurely in the local hospital in Brisbane. I was promptly placed in a humidicrib and my poor mother, after due time for recuperation, was sent home without me. To give credit to both the medical staff and Julie, they must have taken good care of me, since the survival rates of three pound babies were not good in those days. Nonetheless, I thrived and was eventually allowed home.

Early photographs of those days show we lived in a wooden bungalow built on stilts. Later, it would seem rather rickety to me, but it was typical of the houses in that area. We never found out whether the stilts were to protect against flooding or snakes, or just to keep the house cool. However, it had lovely gardens, where I learned to toddle, and a magnificent mango tree next door that dropped its succulent fruits into our garden every summer. The first time this happened, Dad carefully gathered them up and returned them to their rightful owner, as he tried to explain in his broken English, heavily accented with Russian and a touch of American, to the astonished neighbour. After all, his mother Maria had taught him never to take anything that did not belong to him. The neighbour's response was something along the lines of *'Strewth mate, if they fall in your yard, you can keep "em"'*. So, much to their delight, the family gorged themselves on the most magnificent fruit they had ever tasted in their lives.

After a few years, Zina, John and Julie decided to return to Sydney, where the rest of the extended family had settled. Once again, it was rented rooms in someone else's home. To their pleasure they found that their neighbours were friends they had known in Shanghai. Nadia and Boris Koslovsky were fond of playing Mahjong, a game my parents had also learnt to play in China. They soon established a regular routine, an annual habit they continued for decades, of playing through the night after a traditional Russian meal, accompanied by much jovial laughter and social chit-chat. I recall falling asleep at night after a very special dinner to the gentle click clack sounds of the ivory bricks falling on the table. Life was not all hard work and grind though it must have seemed that way to my father at times. He was forced to take any menial labour he could find to make ends meet, repay their passages and support his family – his wife, the new baby girl he doted on and his eight year old step daughter. At barely 25 he had considerable responsibilities. Accordingly, he worked ceaselessly and without complaint, even when obliged to work nightshifts. When his little girl jumped on him in the early mornings, not understanding why Papa still wanted to sleep, he just smiled tolerantly.

John would have loved a jeweller's job and he did have such an opportunity in Australia. But although the pay was comparable to manual labour there was no overtime and therefore no chance to earn those vital extra few pounds. Heavily in debt, he had to forgo this chance of a worthwhile career. He had not had the benefit of free passage from Tubabao and the cheap bed and board other Russian immigrants received in exchange for a two year work contract. Instead, he was constantly forced to work in one physically demanding job after another. Long hours, often extended by overtime, left him too tired to attend evening classes and acquire new skills. Besides, he undoubtedly wanted to spend what little free time he had with his family. At one point he did take English lessons by correspondence, which he was very serious about, doing homework and practising on the family, though it must have been very difficult. John persevered with the daily grind. Yet he had an exemplary work record, never took days off and took pride in his punctuality and the quality of his work. For many years he worked as a sheet metal worker, learning the art of cutting and shaping metal. He commuted to work by bicycle when it was relatively close, or more commonly by rail, until he was eventually able to buy his first car, a second hand green Holden. Julie too, went to work, travelling by train to *Buckle and son*, where she worked for many years making belts and, yes, buckles.

Finally, their industry enabled them to settle their debts and buy their own land. Land! This was the dream and the promise of the new country and now they had achieved that too. John and Julie were ecstatic to have a property of their own and couldn't wait to move into their new home.

Their new plot was located in the south western suburb of *Cabramatta*, some 20 miles from the city centre. Land there was still comparatively cheap compared to the genteel northern suburbs, where the earlier English migrants had settled, or the more convenient but congested eastern suburbs. It also offered good rail access to the city and industrial centres; all of which made it attractive to new migrants. The south west of Sydney had been settled for quite some time by that stage, in fact the nearby township of Liverpool dates back to the early 19th century when Australia was still an English penal colony. That former convict settlement was just two stops down the rail line, after the racecourse at Warwick Farm. Heading the other way, towards the city centre, Canley Vale was followed by Fairfield. But unlike those quintessentially English names, John and Julie's new home suburb had a decidedly Australian ring to it. In fact the name derives from two aboriginal words, *'Cabra'* meaning a fresh tasty water grub and *'Matta'* a jutting out piece of land.

They bought, what for them must have seemed like a huge plot, roughly two thirds of an acre (about 300 x 100 feet or 92 x 31 metres). It was a superb plot with several mature pine trees in the front, the ubiquitous gums, beautiful bougainvillea bushes in the middle, a massive willow tree at the back and a magnificent mulberry tree, to name but a few. A veritable gardener's paradise and John was eager to get his hands in the soil again, as he had done in the wilderness of Manchuria.

However, buying a plot of land did not necessarily mean it came with a house. *That* would have to wait until much later. What it did have however was a prefabricated garage, for the car that so few could afford. The garage was made out of *fibro* (Fibrous Asbestos Cement) with a metal *Tiltadoor* at one end. Fibro was a common building material at the time, a substance that came in thin, brittle sheets, rather like plasterboard. It was used extensively to build both garages and houses because it could easily be sawn and nailed directly onto a wooden frame. One layer on the inside and another layer outside and *voila* - instant garage or house! It was hot in summer, freezing in winter and no doubt a determined person with a heavy boot could kick a hole through it, but it was cheap and thousands of Australian homes were built this way. In the 1980's building restrictions imposed covenants, obliging people to build in brick. After that it became illegal to build fibro homes and new house prices shot up as a result.

At any rate, John and Julie did not even have a fibro house. They had a garage and that would have to do for the moment. If memory serves me correctly, I was only about four at the time, the *'cottage'* was already habitable before we moved in. That is to say, the Tiltadoor had already been sealed off from the inside (another layer of fibro) and there was a kitchen/bathroom extension at the back. This consisted of a medium sized room with a concrete floor, a stone tub in one corner with a cold water tap and a shower in the opposite corner – a concrete trough, with a metal pipe leading to a tin can with holes in it. This was heated by kerosene, which exploded alarmingly into action when lit by a match. On summer days we much preferred to use the outdoor shower, a rubber hose hoisted over a rough frame or tree, another tin can and a curtained screen for privacy. The kitchen was also equipped with a kerosene primus cooker, a huge table for preparation and a pantry for storing food. A second hand refrigerator must have been acquired fairly soon, a necessity in the Australian heat. A large wardrobe delineated the remaining space into living and sleeping areas. A double bed and my cot filled the sleeping area and in the living area there was a couch, presumably Helen's bed, a dining table and chairs. Very soon we acquired a *'buffet'*, that indispensable piece of furniture that contained the glasses, cutlery, crockery and the treasured knick knacks we were already beginning to accumulate. This was our first home and we were delighted with it. The local Russian Orthodox priest was invited to bless it and an icon was ceremoniously mounted in a top corner of the room. Beneath it, a candle floated in oil, a perpetual flame illuminating the faces of the saints. The priest sang his hymns and prayers while we all stood reverently and thus our home was acknowledged as a Christian abode.

*A party, shortly after moving into the 'garage' in Cabramatta. John, Julie, Uncle Tony, Tania, Grandmother Maria and new Dutch friends.*

John quickly laid out the garden, leaving a large area in the middle for the house they would eventually build *when* they could afford it. A concrete path was laid at the front with flower borders and shrubs around. The huge pine trees of course were left, for the vital shade they provided and the privacy they afforded, also their branches would be useful for Christmas trees. The dwelling was already adorned by bougainvillea shrubs and their beautiful purple flowers were encouraged to grow over the side of our home. A little porch was added to the front and in no time it began to look more like a cottage nestling in the woods than a garage. The willow tree defined an outdoor socialising area where we spent many idyllic hours. A swing was hung from the tree's branches and a home-made table tennis table placed underneath, which could be quickly converted to a dining table for outdoor eating and parties. Most of the rest of the land was turned over to productive use. Growing fruit and vegetables was not just a pastime for John but an economic necessity. He grew (with a little bit of help from his daughters) sweet corn, tomatoes, carrots, cucumbers, potatoes, pumpkin, horseradish, eggplants, beans and even watermelon. Helen remembers watering strawberries with a bucket during droughts. At the very back of the garden he built a chicken pen, so we could have fresh eggs and the occasional chicken. Now that was an aspect of self-sufficiency I could not come to terms with. I vividly recall Dad chasing a hapless chicken around the yard, axe in hand. Even when decapitated the chicken would not stop running.

Last but not least, the toilet or *'dunny'* as Australians call it, deserves a mention. Connection to a main sewer pipe was still a long way off and, while wealthier landowners installed septic tanks, most people relied on the *'dunny man'*. This shadowy figure had the unenviable job of collecting waste in the early hours of the morning, usually once a week. The toilet had to be located some distance from the home, not so far that you would take forever to get there, when needs must, but far enough away to avoid the odour. This was another little fibro building that we tried to disguise with trellis and flowers but there was no disguising its function. The wooden seat lifted up to reveal a cavernous black receptacle, like an oil drum, which the dunny man would bravely hoist on to his shoulders and empty out into a specially built truck. It was customary to leave him a well deserved special treat at Christmas – money and/or beer being most common. Incidentally, one always lifted the toilet seat to check for spiders lurking underneath. The story about *Redbacks* on the toilet seat is no joke; they can give a nasty bite and even be fatal in certain cases. Personally, I found *Funnel Webs* and *Huntsmen* more frightening. When illuminated by candlelight (there was no electric lighting) spiders appeared very ominous indeed. Visiting the loo at night could be a traumatic childhood experience. Still, if that was the only cloud on my horizon, I really had nothing to complain about and life as a child in Cabramatta was very sweet indeed.

Russian parties featured prominently in my childhood. While our immediate extended family was small – Dad had his brother and mother only, my mother had a substantial array of cousins, descendants of the Shliapnikoffs, who had all fled Russia together back in 1930. To these must be added the friends they had made in Shanghai, a large number of whom had relocated to Sydney. They all kept in touch on a regular basis, at first with any excuse, but then at Weddings, Christenings, Easter, Christmas and eventually funerals, as the older members began to pass away. While we lived in the garage, parties could only be held in the summer, under the great willow tree where the table tennis table could be covered with a huge tablecloth and all the food laid out, covered until the last possible moment – fly swatters to hand. Home made benches and blocks of wood on bricks, covered with blankets served as chairs, for it was imperative that everyone should be seated around the table in order to eat and drink properly. No matter how many people were invited, *'buffet'* style eating was unheard of in Russian tradition. The guests sat or squeezed around the table, depending on numbers, and socialised – ate, drank, talked, continuing for many hours. Any hot food would soon get cold – no

*Four generations – Praskovia, (Babinka), Zina, Julie and Helen.*

matter, another vodka and no one would notice anyway. A really successful party would have them singing as well. Who said Russians were morose?

We were beginning to adapt to life in Australia and to Cabramatta in particular. At the age of four and a half I was sent to English school. I had no hesitation about going though it must have been daunting because I could not speak a word of English. However, I am informed that I was quite an independent child. My parents often told me that one of my earliest phrases was 'Masik masya'. Masik being the affectionate, shortened version of my name the family used and *masya* being my own corrupted form of *sama*, meaning *myself*, or *don't help me – I'll do it myself*. So, off to school I went, escorted by an old biddy whose presence I no doubt resented. But it was a good long walk of about a mile, on the other side of the railway station and there was no question of going alone. In fact, I had led quite a self contained life until then since we had such a rich, domestic life centring on the Russian community and very little contact with Australian children. I recall feeling very shy and intimidated at first, but picked up English very quickly. I soon integrated and do not recall feeling out of place for very long. We were a multi-ethnic community and there would have been lots of children in a similar position. We probably helped each other and by the time I befriended Erina and Tania in the second year of infant school and could walk to school with them (no more old nannies), we were quite comfortable with the language and ourselves. The infant teachers seemed a bit harsh and cruel – rapping one on the knuckles with a ruler for making mistakes, but junior school was a pleasure with Mr. Kynaston.

Following in my grandmother Zina's footsteps, I learned to sew in school on a Singer treadle sewing machine, the same American company that had sold so well in Russia in the 19th century and in Shanghai in the 20th. It was on such a machine that *Baba* Zina had produced such wonderful clothes. My mother acquired a hand-operated version, but our school still had the archaic model.

We learned our times tables by rote and spelling tests abounded, which were no problem as I had quickly become a prolific reader of English books. In assemblies we sang 'God save the Queen' with gusto, followed by 'Santa victorious, happy and glorious'. What Santa Claus had to do with the Queen we did not know but decided it was just another strange aspect of Anglo/Australian culture that we had to get to grips with and accepted quite readily. (It took some time to realise that it was actually 'Send her victorious...'). We also learned to march in pseudo-military formation around the dry, dusty earth that served as our playground. Little wooden benches were dotted around the ground where we ate our lunch under the baking sun and even torrential rain when the heavens opened, but the most coveted benches were those placed under the few gum trees. Though even these would be avoided like the plague when a nest of grubs was found beneath them and the caretaker had to be called to remove them. These fat, slimy creatures seemed to breed in colonies of thousands and a small mountain of them would suddenly erupt under a tree. We watched them in ghastly horror as they writhed in a revolting mass. The caretaker could only burn them off by pouring petrol on them and setting the mass alight. They would burn and pop like firecrackers, emitting the putrid smell of scorched flesh. Yes, junior school was fun.

Eventually John and Julie saved enough to begin building the house. It would be a cheap and cheerful common fibro bungalow, built by contractors specialising in basic layouts. A little covered porch led into the large open plan living area, from which radiated three bedrooms and a bathroom on one side and the entrance to a kitchen dining area on the other, the latter located behind the front room. The lounge had impressive floor to ceiling windows overlooking the long front garden and the cherished pine trees. Shrubs and a flower-bordered path had already been established and the view from the living area did justice to much of Dad's gardening efforts. It may have been a simple house but we were overjoyed, most of all my mother who was expecting her third child, so the timing was just perfect. Helen and I had our own bedrooms and when our little brother Michael (Misha) arrived he slept in a cot in our parents' room for a time. Of course we all loved him dearly and he was 'mothered' mercilessly by his sisters. In fact, as soon as he learned to

*Baby Michael and his sisters, in front of the new house, 1960.*

195

toddle he was running about the garden furiously trying to escape the hugs and kisses of his overly affectionate siblings.

Once again, the local priest was called in to bless our new house and the icons were placed in a corner of each room, the largest in the lounge and smaller ones in the bedrooms. The kitchen was as modern as one could get in 1960, or so we believed. The bathroom contained a separate bath and shower, but alas, no toilet. Sewer pipes had still not extended to Cabramatta. But there was a laundry area with enormous concrete troughs, useful for anything from washing vegetables, boots, the baby or plucking chickens. It also held the indispensable wringer washing machine and a huge boiler, so that we always had instant hot water on tap. The Shalavins had come a long way from those buckets in Shanghai. From humble beginnings this little house would grow and grow. First, another large porch/veranda was added to the back, with the new flush toilet, when it finally arrived, taking pride of place in its own little cubicle at the side. No old fashioned chains for us, we went straight from the dunny man to a push-button job. However, it could not be located in the bathroom as there was no room and in any event it was considered far too close to the living area. Still, it was undercover and part of the house, a vast improvement on the loo halfway down the garden. Then, a larger laundry area was added, the original having been used to extend the kitchen. Finally, my grandmother Zina arrived to live with us, having become too frail to live on her own and maintain her detached bungalow and garden. The funds raised from its sale enabled her to build her own 'granny flat', which further increased the house size significantly. She built on her own kitchen, large lounge and separate bedroom, bringing with her much of the furniture and treasures she had accumulated over the years.

Having moved out of the old 'garage' it was let out to Uncle Tony, John's younger brother. He lived there for a few years with his second wife, Tania, and sons Nick and George. Nick was actually Tania's stepson but to give this generous woman her due she brought him up as her own. This dwelling also continued to grow, Tony and John building on an extra bedroom and modernising the kitchen/bathroom. So, once again we were living in an extended family household. Our two families often went on outings together, to beaches, picnics and a favourite venue, Lake Wallacia, which could only be reached by dirt track in those days. This bottomless lake, or so it was rumoured, nestled in a wooded valley with huge stone escarpments creating a waterfall at one end and sandy beaches at the other. For us youngsters, it was a rite of passage to swim across the full length of the lake with the adults, once we had abandoned our safety rings. Those adults who could not swim usually wore old tyres for, try as we might, no one had ever reached the bottom of that lake. Happy days. With the arrival of a third son, Tony and the family moved to a house in a different neighbourhood. But the garage never stood empty. After all, my other grandmother was living on her own and that would not do. So Maria Zinovyevna took over the garage from her youngest son and enjoyed the comfort of her own 'granny flat' in our garden, not to mention the security and love of her family nearby.

## The matriarch – Babushka Maria, a woman of the land.

My exuberant paternal *Babushka*, Maria, thrived in Sydney and adapted well to her new situation, though this did not extend to learning the language. Maria's inability or lack of desire to learn English was not without its humorous moments. I recall shopping with her one day in the local grocer's shop – one of those cornucopias of delight alas, no longer seen today. Sacks of grain lay along the floor in front of counters of small goods and delicacies, pies, sausages, salamis, lamington cakes and huge jars of sweets. Babushka would point to the buckwheat on the floor and tell the owner in perfect Russian that she required a pound of this and two pounds of that, and he would smile knowingly and fetch exactly what she asked for. *'Why learn English when he seemed to understand Russian so well!'* She would exclaim triumphantly in her booming voice, while I, a self consciously bilingual child cringed beside her. The owner, a stalwart Australian, undoubtedly served his Italian, Greek, Polish and Ukrainian customers with equal aplomb and tact. Thank you Mr. Watford – you were a treasure – your store was and is much missed. The language may have defeated my grandmother but she had no such problems with the currency and always ensured that she received the correct change. How odd the English system of twenty shillings in a pound (or twenty-one in a Guinea) and twelve

*Maria and her grandchildren under the willow tree in Cabramatta.*

197

pennies in a shilling must have seemed to her. Never one to waste a penny, she knew full well the value of small change. As the Russians say, Копейка рубль бережёт - meaning *take care of the pennies and the pounds will take care of themselves.*

*Maria, 1956.*

It is often commented that it is the women who are the stronger members of typical Russian families and that was certainly the case with my grandmother, who survived not one but three husbands. The first one had left Siberia with her to start a new life across the border in Manchuria. Though widowed early, the chasm that divided her from her parents' family was now impossible to surmount in the early 1920's and she was forced to rely entirely upon herself. With no husband, no family, no country, no education, no qualifications, in fact, no status as a person who belonged anywhere at all, life could have become impossible for her. Certainly, women in similar circumstances would have been abandoned to die in many cultures around the world at that time. But, Babushka was nothing if not resourceful and quickly adapted to her surroundings. She found work, supported herself and remarried in due course. Her marriage to Ivan Shalavin was successful for many years and, for the sake of the boys, she had tried very hard to make it work. Ultimately, she was forced to give up on him, having correctly decided that she could be a more successful parent alone than she could ever be living with his drinking problem.

After the failure of her second marriage, Maria lived independently for many years in three countries. She lived in Canada for a while, where an appreciative family had taken her following the fall of Shanghai, but she missed her sons too much and made her way to Australia. Eventually, thinking that she might ward off a lonely old age she remarried in her 60's. The groom was a widower named Andrei Ignatich. They wed in an Orthodox ceremony at her local Old Believers' church, a converted shop in Sydney's western suburbs. As children we all joined in the celebrations, not thinking it odd at all to be attending grandmother's wedding! Alas, it did not last – *'He just wanted me to cook and clean for him for nothing!'* she declared indignantly. *'I didn't work hard all my life just to be someone else's slave in my old age!'* Babushka may have been oblivious to the protests of the Women's Liberation movement that was making itself heard in the 1960's but she instinctively shared many of their sentiments.

John doted on his mother but there were issues upon which Maria and her son disagreed and diet was one such bone of contention. My father was and still is, very health conscious whereas Maria clearly was not. As a devout Christian, she had no shortage of willpower when it came to giving up meat for the Great

*Maria (right) at a friend's funeral. (Russians think it is perfectly acceptable to take photographs at a funeral, indeed they expect it).*

Lent, numerous shorter lent periods, Wednesdays, Fridays and any other day decreed by the Church to be holy and for which fasting was to be observed. However, if it wasn't forbidden by the Church then she ate with gusto and in quantity. Like many other Russians who had endured poverty and deprivation in their youth, the abundant produce available in Australia meant that eating could be enjoyed and so they did. Grandmother's normal meat pies – prime mince, fried in oil with onions and then baked into a rich buttery pastry, would be replaced first by equally rich and delicious fish pies and, when that was not allowed by the Church, potato or cabbage pies. Large oven baked pies were often replaced by traditional *piroshki*, deep fried until golden and succulent. These could be supplemented by mountains of pancakes (*blini*), stacked layer upon layer with lashings of butter between them. These could then be individually wrapped around a stuffing of one's choice – mince (on Lent free days) being most popular, and then fried again. Small wonder that many 'New Australians', grateful to be living in an affluent society, keeled over with heart attacks instead of living to a ripe old age. But this is not to denigrate Russian food, which can be healthy and nutritious in moderation. (Yes, Dad I hear you.) The vegetable *zakuski*, predominantly starters but also served as accompaniments, made in various combinations from carrots, peppers, onions, garlic, cabbage and of course beetroot. The wonderful soups, *pelemeni* (at least they are boiled) and last but not least, tasty fruit pies and compotes are all part of this rich and varied cuisine. Russians abroad faithfully reproduced their traditional dishes, recipes surviving transport through China and beyond. But nobody made pies better than my Babushka.

Looking back, it seems to me now that she was recognised as something of a 'wise woman' as they were perceived in earlier centuries. Coming from a very remote country area where scientific medicine was virtually non-existent, people like her developed skills that were much in demand. I recall her administering herbal drinks for all kinds of stomach ailments as well as removing ear wax in a time honoured way. This involved applying a large cone of paraffin soaked, stiffened cloth to the ear, which burned furiously at one end, whilst sucking out wax at the other. This is not unusual apparently and commonly practised in China. She also practised traditional Chinese *cupping* which too, seemed shocking in the 20th century. Glass jars, into which a paraffin light was introduced to burn off the oxygen, became vacuums. They were then immediately clapped onto the patient's skin which sucked up to fill the void, discolouring as it filled with blood. Before long, the patient would have an angry back covered with these glass jars stuck firmly to their skin. People who have it done swear it alleviates back pains and rheumatoid and arthritic conditions. Who could argue with that?

I still vividly recall a vision of her trudging along the street in her sensible men's shoes, carrying a saucepan of home made *borsch* to some poor friend or invalid neighbour, her hair covered in the customary scarf. She was large and plain, but not unattractive in her youth, though a hard life meant that she never had time or inclination to care about her appearance. Simple, practical clothes made her look prematurely old at 40, but then again she looked much the same at 70. A truly remarkable, self-sufficient woman, she continued to live independently into a reasonable old age, considering she had no notion whatsoever of healthy eating. She died mercifully quickly, following a sudden heart attack, aged 74, in her son's arms.

A kind soul, who always thought of others before herself and generously dispensed food, advice, homespun wisdom and peasant remedies; she had become enormously popular amongst the Russian community in Sydney. Her funeral was incredibly well attended in that same little converted shop, which overflowed with stricken mourners. Not for her the fancy Orthodox cathedral, just a few miles away, with its huge onion domes and the ornate Byzantine artwork. Her church, like her faith, was simpler and the people who stood for hours, packed together in the stifling heat of that tiny space, seemed to recognise that with her passing a little bit of old Russia had gone forever. The moving and beautiful Orthodox service, with its incense and chanting priests clad in medieval garb, seemed to last interminably, clearly

*The interior of Maria's Old Believers' church.*

not intended for the Australian heat. When it finally ended we proceeded to the cemetery. I recall sitting in the back seat of my father's car watching the funeral cavalcade as it slowly wound its way to the enormous Russian Orthodox section of Sydney's Necropolis, where Maria had thoughtfully and responsibly bought her plot in advance. I think I gave up counting after 30 cars. We were all so sorry to see her go.

*Uncle Tony saying goodbye to his mother.*

Many people had loved her but she had a particularly close bond with my father, who absorbed much of her inherent generosity, consideration towards others and resilience to outward misfortune. Both had been uprooted several times and never acquired the skills necessary to succeed in a materialistic world. Yet neither of them coveted the advantages of their wealthier friends or relatives and were always grateful for the blessings they had. John is fond of saying that if he looks up there are always people better off than him, but if he looks down, there are many, many more that are less fortunate and who deserve his help. Babushka had taught him that *'a kind deed never burns in fire or drowns in water.'* Доброе дело в огне не горит и в воде не тонет. For Dad, that was an injunction to charity, for compassion really does begin at home and means nothing if forced. Such was the nature of her legacy.

## Growing up as a Russian Australian.

As residents of Cabramatta, we were part of a very broad international community of migrant settlers. There were Italians, Greeks, Poles, Ukrainians, Yugoslavs, Dutch, Czechs, Hungarians, Estonians, Latvians, Lithuanians, Germans and undoubtedly many others of whom I was unaware. The English Australians were by no means outnumbered yet and vast numbers from 'the mother country' were encouraged to migrate to Australia in the 1950's, lured by the promise of an affluent, growing country and a subsidised £10 fare. It is undoubtedly true that one values less those things obtained for little or nothing compared to those for which one has paid. So the English migrants were often disappointed that the streets were not paved with gold and that life was not automatically easier than it had been in the Glasgow tenements or London terraces. They were provided free accommodation in a hostel, former army barracks made of tin huts, located behind Cabramatta high school. Poor food (provided) and rumours of hepatitis outbreaks must have contributed to this dismal start and undoubtedly lent weight to complaints about the *'whinging Pom'*[1].

However, the European settlers were under no such illusion. They were well aware that they would have to work and work hard to fulfil the promise of the new country and grasped the opportunity with eager hands. The Russians in particular, who had completely burned their bridges as it were, and had nowhere to return to, were most committed and enthusiastic about their new home. Some had even literally burnt the Soviet passports they had been obliged to accept by the Australian authorities, who would not take in 'stateless' people as a general rule. (Though those with formal international refugee status were exempt.) So when the migrants were permitted to become 'naturalised' Australian citizens after five years of residency, they were both overjoyed and relieved. No one could force them back to the Soviet Union now!

They enthusiastically participated in the Naturalisation ceremonies, joyously swearing allegiance to their new beautiful, young Queen Elizabeth. Many have remained committed monarchists ever since, just as previously most had been committed Tsarists. Mother related how during the ceremony when the speaker asked the new citizens to repeat after him *'I, your name…'*, the large group dutifully repeated *'I, your name'*. It is probably true that the people who carried the vote against Australia becoming a Republic in the recent referendum were migrants such as these.

*Julie and John receiving their Australian citizenship.*

So John and Julie became proud Australian citizens, living the Great Australian dream. They continued to socialise with their original Russian friends and relatives but also formed new relationships within the local community. Mainly Russians initially because language was still a barrier and whilst they had learned English after a fashion, they continued to be more comfortable with their mother tongue for quite some time. They discovered the local Russian Orthodox priest, Father

Gan, lived several houses away and I attended the local school later with his son, who also became a priest for a while. Father Gan had the unenviable task of educating the new generation of Russian/Australian children in the traditions and customs of the Orthodox faith. My family attended church regularly at first, less so as the years passed. But the children also had Scripture lessons at the local state school. While my peers learnt about the Catholic, Church of England, Presbyterian or Lutheran faiths, Father Gan was given a room in the school where we Russian children were taught about the Orthodox Christian religion, in our own language.

Father Gan would address me imperiously, Ты что? *'What are you Maria Vanna?'* using both the wrong Christian name and a demeaning form of my patronymic. The polite form being Marina Ivanovna (daughter of Ivan) but it seemed to me that he deliberately shortened my name inaccurately in order to remind me of my place. And what was that place? A humble child, not Russian born and not an Australian either; nor in his eyes would I ever be allowed to become one. I would dutifully answer, *'I am a Russian Orthodox Christian.'* *'Good, never forget that'* he would reply sternly. Worse would follow if one met him on the street – which, living only a few doors away, I would frequently do. When anyone in the Russian community met him in public one was supposed to approach him for a blessing. The priest would make the sign of the cross over one's forehead and shoulders then give you his hand to kiss. Perhaps people born and brought up in the old country thought nothing of such customs but a tradition that was commonplace in a Siberian village was oddly out of place in suburban Australia. Nonetheless, the peer pressure was such that it would be many years before I became confident enough to rebel. This in turn was linked to my growing disenchantment, not only with the Orthodox faith, but religion in general. Though I would continue to be impressed by the aesthetic beauty of the services.

*Cabramatta church, built c. 1960's.*

The Church was a familiar beacon for the exiled Russians. They lovingly rebuilt them with the exotic Byzantine onion domes in brilliant colours, all the more striking against the bright Australian sky, and filled them with the precious icons that so many had risked their lives to bring to the new land. Customs were faithfully recreated; the services in Slavonic led by the rich bass and baritone voices of the priests, enhanced by glorious choirs, voices resplendent in their musical harmony.

By the time my parents arrived in Sydney the Orthodox cathedral of Saints Peter and Paul had already been built in the leafy, inner city residential suburb of Strathfield, which our family chose to attend. Wealthier Russians had settled in that area and the surrounding suburbs of Homebush, Croydon and Burwood, so the church was well endowed and frequented. Weekly attendance was not on the agenda for my family though because the church was at least 10-12 miles from Cabramatta and we had no transport. Besides, my parents undoubtedly felt that, having worked hard all week, they deserved a day of rest on Sunday. And, as my father never ceased to remind me, you don't have to go to church every week to be a good Christian. He undoubtedly felt guilty about this because his own mother had never failed to attend church every week and on the additional occasions of a particular saint's day.

The Cathedral of Saints Peter and Paul was set in its own large grounds. There was a meeting hall behind it used for social occasions, the beloved dances, balls and especially festivities for the youth of the congregation. A number of smaller buildings were used as classrooms for the education of Russian youngsters at Saturday school. I attended this school for four years from the age of 11, when my parents deemed I was old enough to travel alone by public transport. It was a good 30 minute walk to the train station, then the same again on the *'red rattlers'* (affectionate name for the red rail carriages) and a further walk to the church. We had three lessons; a language lesson, where I learned to read and write using the Cyrillic alphabet and was briefly introduced to the great works of Russian literature, a history lesson which never went beyond the 18th century and, last but not least, the obligatory scripture lesson. The latter was only memorable for being conducted in the cathedral itself, where I imagine it was presumed we would somehow soak up the holy atmosphere. Certainly, I appreciated the beauty of the impressive architecture, the artistry of the medieval icons depicting morbid saints and often gruesome scenes and the magnificent gilt altar. But, somehow the lessons left me cold and seemed incomprehensible and irrelevant even then.

Sadly, the elderly men and women who believed it to be their duty to educate the Russian youth seemed to have no notion of making it interesting and enjoyable, which one might expect from voluntary attendance. They probably viewed attendance as a necessary moral duty for us, a way to save our Russian heritage, if not our immortal souls. To be fair, there were undoubtedly exceptions and Mrs Irene Rezaeff, who later taught at the school in Cabramatta, was an exceptionally gifted and popular teacher but there were none of her calibre in my experience. I persevered for four years but my attendance became sporadic as I became increasingly rebellious in my teens and I finally stopped going altogether at 15. I would not have endured it for that long had it not been for the friendship of Maria, Irene and John. Thank you.

The school's intentions were to continue the traditions of Mother Russia wherever the young generation were located and in that respect, they were probably similar to Russian Saturday schools in San Francisco, New York or Buenos Aires. Portraits of the last Tsar Nicholas adorned the walls, as did the flag of Imperial Russia. To the stalwart denizens of this thriving community it was as if the Russian revolution had never taken place. If it ever was referred to at all it would be in hushed tones of disgust and contempt. Some individuals even tried to recreate the old class structures of Tsarist Russia and former aristocrats tried briefly to enforce the deferential attitudes to which they were accustomed. I remember particularly, one old lady, reputedly a member of the Russian nobility who insisted that Russian girls curtsy to her in the street. This could not have lasted long in the democratic environment that Australia was renowned for, any more than their English counterparts would have continued tugging their forelocks or doffing their cloth caps.

But there were some positive and enjoyable aspects of growing up as a Russian Australian, particularly the concerts, plays and festivities. The annual 'День Русского Ребёнка' – day of the Russian child, celebrated their accomplishments in song, music, dance and theatrical

performances of all kinds, in the native tongue of course. Christmas concerts, the 'Ёлка' performed a similar function but with the added bonus of presents and a visit from Santa Claus – Father Frost in this case. Every child would receive a gift

*A typical children's performance.*

bag, often of coloured cellophane paper containing fruit, nuts, sweets, little toys and perhaps trinkets for the girls. Everyone had to perform at these Christmas concerts and I was a rabbit one year, complete with grey furry costume with pink, floppy ears – *Baba* Zina's sewing skills having been pressed into action again. Another year saw me as a much more sophisticated flower, a vibrant peony with a pretty dress of red petals and garlanded long tresses, my hair freed from its traditional two plaits. This was a speaking part too and I can still recall the opening lines of the poem I recited; it was customary for Russian children to learn poetry by heart. My friend Maria was an equally vibrant blue flower.

Older youths, teenagers over 16, could join a dance troupe, which performed its way around the country, singing old Russian ballads and dancing traditional folk dances. Their costumes were resplendent, the boys in flowing shirts pulled in at the waist by a broad sash and the customary boots. The girls had colourful long dresses, traditional *sarafans* with frilly blouses and bright scarves. My sister Helen performed in one of these troupes and as a child I was terribly envious of her, particularly her freedom to travel around Australia. Melbourne and Brisbane seemed very exotic at the time.

*Helens's dance troupe, Helen is last on the right.*

The schools continue to thrive and new generations of Russian Australians have passed through them so perhaps the teaching has improved and they have become more flexible to the needs of children. Furthermore, cultural diversity is more valued now and a new generation may relish their differences rather than feel the pressure to conform and integrate, as many of us did in the 1950's and 1960's. After all, we were growing up in the height of the Cold War between the Superpowers –

USSR and the USA. I well remember having to reassure my Australian friends (allies of the USA) that I was a White Russian, not to be confused with the dangerous and aggressive Red Russians that now had nuclear capability and appeared to be threatening to blow up the free world! We had ample reason to be wary of our heritage at that potentially explosive time. Many of my cousins refused to speak Russian at all; one had been accused of being a 'spy' in the wake of the Petrov affair[2], youthful banter of course. Nonetheless, Alex would no longer want to be known as *Sasha*, and from then on focussed on becoming Australian like so many of my generation.

## Goodbye to faith.

Notwithstanding the whole family's gradual alienation from regular worship, we continued to attend the cathedral at Strathfield for the fabulous special services at Christmas and Easter. The midnight mass on Easter Sunday was particularly inspiring. We youngsters would be sent to bed early and awoken around 11pm. Easter falls in the Australian Autumn when evenings can be quite chilly and so we would dress in our best warm clothes – pom pom hats, mittens and muffs and embark upon the exciting event. Within a block of the cathedral it would be evident that this was no ordinary service. The entire church was filled to capacity and the overflowing congregation spilled out, first into the yard of the cathedral, then onto the pavements outside and finally into the street itself. One could not move for the many thousands that attended. However, one could hear the glorious choir from inside the church and the deep voices of the Deacon, priests and their assistants singing the sacred hymns. Then they would emerge from the church bringing the service to the throng outside, each person holding a lit candle in the darkness, with its paper collar to prevent wax dripping onto fingers. The bells would chime as the Deacon announced triumphantly *'Christ has risen'* and the multitude replied as one *'Indeed he has risen.'* The high priests and their attendants holding enormous crucifixes and icons would parade solemnly around the perimeter of the church, so that all could see them. As they did so they swung the incense in its brass container held by a long chain and proclaimed that Christ has risen, all rejoice. When the service was over, and as the bells continued to chime, people would search out those acquaintances whom they only saw once a year. Each happy reunion followed the same custom: the first person would state 'Христос Воскресе' (*Christ has risen*) and the other would reply 'Во истину Воскресе' (*Indeed he has risen*) then they would kiss three times. The previously solemn crowd now erupted in joyful embraces and conversation. What did the neighbours think of this annual event I wonder? For the cathedral was located in the centre of a quite affluent, middle class residential area. The Australians presumably watched bemusedly or disappeared for the night if they wanted some peace and quiet.

Finally, when it was all over the congregation would return home to begin yet more festivities. For only now could one partake of a genuine 'breakfast', though it was still the early hours of the morning. The devout would have

'zakuski' – appetizers.

fasted through the Great Lent of 40 days during which time they would have given up meat and fish. The more devout, like Babushka, would also have given up all dairy products, effectively becoming vegan for the period. But even those who had not fasted would have prepared the traditional Easter foods in happy anticipation of this early morning feast. All across Sydney and indeed most capital cities of Australia, tables groaned under the weight of ham, salamis, pork, chicken, liverwurst and beef, the traditional vegetable salads of beans, cabbage, potato, beetroot and the much loved herring, caviar and sour cream to accompany it all. Eggs symbolising new life were boiled and painted in different colours.

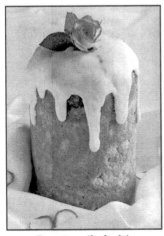
*Russian 'kulich',*
*traditional Easter cake.*

But the piece de resistance would be the desserts – the obligatory *kulich* and *paskha,* the special Easter cake and traditional cheese delight. The kulich cake would have been made well in advance - a light, well risen cake loaf, fragrant with vanilla, cinnamon and sultanas, baked in special tins that gave it a distinctly cylindrical shape. Its golden hue topped with white icing and icing also used to form the crucial letters on the side – X B. The Cyrillic letters standing for Christ has risen. But it was the paskha that was my favourite. Rich curd or cottage cheese strained through a muslin cloth then pressed into a special wooden mould (also with the letters XB carved into the side). To the cheese would be added butter, eggs, sugar, vanilla, aromatic mace or nutmeg and the whole blended together to produce a delectable melt in your mouth concoction. Bliss.

Easter may have been the most important holy day in the Orthodox calendar but Christmas was next and naturally very appealing to children. We celebrated Christmas according to the pre-Revolutionary Julian calendar, so what for us was the 25th of December was actually the 7th of January for pretty much everyone else. After all, White Russians were not going to follow the example of the non-believing Bolsheviks and change their calendar to the Gregorian one. The annual festivities began on Christmas morning with the exchange of gifts around the decorated tree. Dad having climbed up one of the huge pines in our front garden and cut off a branch for this purpose. When my cousins lived in the 'garage' our morning ritual was for the children to exchange presents. My cousin Nick and I would go to and fro between our respective homes laden with gifts. The gift exchange was followed by the church service, always well attended on this special day when we would dress up in our best clothes; the children often receiving new garments for the occasion. The temperatures may have often reached 40$^C$ but the men still wore their starched collars and suits while the women wore their smartest frocks, stockings and accessories. I can still recall sweltering in the crowded hot church along with hundreds of others, trying to keep our best clothes wrinkle and sweat free. At least Christmas lunch could be served cold; unlike the the Anglo Australians, 'cooked dinners' were not part of our tradition. Our meats and chicken were cooked beforehand and served in cold slices.

While I was progressing through the 'English' school system I continued to lead the life of dual identity common to so many migrant children; Russian at home and increasingly Australian at school and outside. Cultural links with my roots centred on religious practices. For much of the older generation, the first 'new Australians', the church offered a vital link with their past and cultural identity. As for me, it played an important and rewarding, albeit temporary, role in my childhood.

While regular services could be incomprehensible to our generation and tediously long, nonetheless, I experienced something of a religious revival in my pre-pubescent and early teen years. I was beginning to search for answers to the deeper issues of life and felt a need to be 'good', in a fundamental, philosophical sense. Not having any other frame of reference at that time, the church appeared to provide the answer, as indeed it had for centuries. I was also influenced by my best friend Erina and her family (who also lived up the road in a converted garage) and who were much more conventionally religious than our family. Cabramatta had by now acquired its own Orthodox church – a little hut to be sure but somehow this seemed to make it even more spiritual than the great Cathedral at Strathfield. Services followed the same rituals of prayer and song but in the small church there were no open spaces to impress and awe you. Instead, a hot, packed environment, where the heady smell of the incense, the candles and the chanting of the priest combined to produce an almost hypnotic effect. Certainly it was captivating and for a while I was totally seduced. I attended Confession and admitted to 'sins' where I felt I had deviated from perfect moral behaviour and then, purified by this admission, I could receive Communion with a clean heart and conscience. No paltry wafer and sip for us, we were given a good swig of port like wine and a chunk of home made white bread to represent the blood and body of Christ. Was it symbolic or an actual miracle taking place, as the Catholics believe? No such Reformation conundrums polluted our thinking. The niceties did not matter, only the result - a pure person.

I attended this church regularly with Erina and her sister Tania (now a teacher and doctor respectively), their mother (another strong Russian woman bringing up children on her own) and their grandmother. For a short, critical period I really did try to live up to the ideal of being a virtuous example of a Russian Orthodox Christian. But however hard I tried, the services provided no genuine answers; the priest's sermons were still meaningless and despite the undoubted beauty of the singing and the ambience, the novelty eventually wore off. I stopped attending, even as the congregation grew. I had failed to be transformed into a saintly person and the secular pastimes of a normal Australian teenager beckoned. The regular churchgoing was dropped for Sundays at the beach or at least the local swimming pool – much cooler in scorching temperatures of up to $40^C$. Clearly other people did not feel the same way and the small church was in due course replaced by a larger cathedral, as funds from the Russian community poured in. Everyone from that community was encouraged to participate in its construction and I remember my father helping to lay the foundation stone. When it was built, a Russian artist was commissioned to paint the Byzantine murals of the interior. The impressive result featured in the local newspaper.

I had long since discovered the pleasures of reading and enjoyed going home after school and collapsing on my bed after a long, tiring day and immersing myself in books. British children's books were my favourite at first and I was quite convinced that I was gaining an insight into English culture through them and longed to see the real country for myself. After all, if one had to adopt a new culture as one's own then surely the original would be preferable to a second hand version? My newfound Australian friends tended not to see things this way and so I kept my long-term ambition to myself. One day I would see England… The novels painted a picture of lush green fields, quaint villages, picturesque meadows, pretty tea shops that always served scrumptious scones and of course endless adventures with polite boys and girls – perfectly enchanting. (Years later, my English husband, who was born in urban Manchester, would guffaw at this rosy coloured image of an England so far removed from his own experiences.) Children's books gave way to mysteries, historical fiction, adventure books, science fiction and eventually to philosophy. At 16 I discovered the works of Ayn Rand and my world changed forever. At last my search for meaning was over. Her philosophy of reason, individualism and freedom brought together all the different strands of my background and experiences into one harmonious, integrated whole. Her depiction of life in Lenin's Russia in *We the living* brilliantly dramatised this crucial period in Russia's history, when individual life was subordinated to the state. Whereas, *Atlas Shrugged* taught me, as it has taught millions of others, the dangers of state control and what really moves the world is the energy and drive of individuals working for themselves, benefiting society as an unintended consequence.[3] Rand showed that virtue was not a monopoly of religion, that integrity to one's self was paramount and that nothing could be placed above the sanctity of individual human life. These were the principles I would come to accept should be at the heart of all human endeavour and the church became an increasing irrelevance. I did not dispute the vital function faith played in many people's lives but it would no longer play a part in mine.

Before I had reached my formative teen years of course, I had progressed to secondary school where Cabramatta High beckoned at age 11. There was no question of going anywhere but the local state school; my parents did not have the knowledge, time or finances to consider any alternatives. As it turned out, I believe I had a relatively fine education, primarily because of the influence of one superb teacher who taught me English in the early years then Modern History in 5th and 6th form. Those of us who were fortunate to be taught by him gained immeasurably from his dedication and scholarship. My life long love for both subjects is due directly to his inspirational teaching. Thank you Mr. Lambert.

So we settled down to life in 'big school'. As might be expected from a large *comprehensive* of nearly 2000, the teaching was very variable, even in the coveted top classes. I enjoyed English, with Mr. Lambert naturally, but also with Ms. Watford, daughter of that wily grocer who charmed my grandmother by appearing to know Russian. Mathematics was quite tolerable and I liked French too. Sad to say, I was a late developer with History. My early experiences of it with something called *Social Studies* were less than inspiring, but I did enjoy a field trip to a 'very old' Victorian church, though we called buildings of the 19th century *colonial*. I still remember the cold, dark stone and the tight, winding staircase through its misty interior. So solid, so *old* – it was magical and I was hooked. The intellectual fascination with history came in the fifth form, by which time our initial entry numbers had dwindled to about 60 from the original 400 (10 classes of 40, strictly set by ability). Most had struggled through to the end of four years of school, when they sat for the School Certificate, but only the top sets stayed on the further two years to sit the Higher School Certificate, our passport to University. Many pupils in the lower classes did not even make it through four years and left the day they turned 15, some to work in factories or the building sites springing up everywhere. Many others undoubtedly, succeeded in the myriad avenues of life that do not require an academic education.

It was in the 6th form, that school and intellectual issues really became important to me. Advanced English literature opened new perspectives and History became an abiding passion. I even liked the rigour and problem solving of Mathematics, which stood me in good stead when I later studied Formal Logic. I also resumed my study of Russian which I had neglected since leaving the Saturday Russian School. We were not offered Russian as a matriculation subject at the school, which was strange as there would have been no shortage of people to teach it. If the school could find a teacher for our Scripture lessons, a language teacher would have been simpler. At any rate, the three of us who opted to take it as a Higher School Certificate subject had to do it by correspondence and the Deputy Head supervised our lesson time. The lessons arrived by post and our homework had to be returned in the same way. I found it an enormous challenge since four years of weekly lessons had left me with only a superficial knowledge of the language and here I was expected to read and critically analyse Lermontov in the original. Dear Mrs Irene Rezaeff, a graduate from Harbin University and a wonderful teacher, who also happened to be the wife of my father's best friend, Victor, came to my rescue. With her extra tuition I managed to gain a creditable pass in my final exam and thus matriculate.

School had become more enjoyable in the 6th form because we were given more privileges and independence. Some of us became prefects and enjoyed the benefit of our own prefects' common room. The uniform became smarter. Previously we had green pinafores over grey shirts, worn with blazers, ties, grey stockings, green gloves and berets. The full uniform mandatory when we went away on school hockey matches, sticks thrust through our briefcases. The junior uniforms were now replaced by white blouses and green mini skirts, which in the *Swinging 60's* became very mini indeed. Fashionable tights at last replaced stockings and high-heeled shoes or platforms completed the picture. Not dissimilar in fact to the uniforms of 6th form girls in the UK today! Though Cabramatta High in the 21st century is a different story altogether.

## Cabramatta – a typical Sydney suburb?

Cabramatta's multi-ethnic society continued to grow and prosper in the 1950's, 60's and 70's. But the waves of migrants from old Europe were gradually replaced by immigrants from Asian nations closer to the great continent, in particular those fleeing Vietnam. During the 1960's, Australia in alliance with the USA, had sent soldiers to support South Vietnam in their bitter Civil War against the Communist North, led by Ho Chi Minh. Some Australians, in common with their American counterparts, believed in the *Domino* theory of successive countries falling under Communist influence, one by one, like a collapsing stack of dominoes. They believed that China, North Korea, and North Vietnam were just the start and that the rest of South East Asia was weak and vulnerable and in need of Western protection. Australia was considered particularly susceptible because it was perceived to be a Western island in an Asian sea. For many Australians the war against the Communist threat merged with a greater fear of the *yellow peril*. 'White' Australia would be flooded with millions of Asians who would undermine the traditional Anglo-Saxon culture according to this view. Such a notion lay behind the previous *White Australia* policy which had officially discriminated against non whites through restrictive immigration. I disagreed with that view then and still do. The free migration of people of any hue, providing they are prepared to support themselves and abide by the law, is an enriching influence on a country not a burden. It is both sad and ironic that many white European migrants, who themselves had benefited from the opportunity for a new life in Australia, supported that policy, thereby depriving others the chance to better themselves too.

Following the defeat of the South Vietnamese state and the subsequent withdrawal of American and Australian forces, Australia, to its credit, abandoned the White Australia policy and allowed refugees from the conflict to settle in the country. Vietnamese, as well as Chinese that had been living in Vietnam, fleeing the newly established Communist state were granted asylum. From the late 1970's and throughout the 1980's many hundreds of thousands sought a new and peaceful life in Australia, particularly in its economic capital, Sydney, which offered the greatest opportunities for work and advancement. In time migrants from Laos, Cambodia and Thailand swelled their ranks. Interestingly, the new migrants were drawn to that same area of Sydney that had for so long been so desirable to impoverished migrants – Cabramatta. Very quickly the Italian, Greek, Yugoslav delicatessens, milk bars and shops gave way to Chinese emporiums, Asian food markets and oriental stores and the suburb became known, rather notoriously, throughout Sydney as 'Vietnamatta'.

*Cabramatta Plaza, traditional Chinese architecture features in the local shopping centre.*

Cabramatta became the new *Chinatown*, complete with Buddhist temples and a pedestrian plaza decorated with a traditional carved dragon arch inscribed with the words *'The world is for all to share and to respect'*. Indeed – my sentiments exactly. But Russians of my parents' generation and those with longer memories, found the inscription somewhat ironic. *'Not what they said when they threw the foreigners out in 1950'* muttered a few bemused Russians, *'then it was, China for the Chinese.'* Most Russians, however, appear to be quite accepting of this strange twist of fortune and live happily alongside their neighbours.

Some older immigrants even relish the opportunity to again savour the sights and smells of their childhoods in Shanghai or Harbin.

However, the problems of crime and violence have made integration of the Asian and European community in Cabramatta difficult, at least during the 1980's and 1990's. Some Australians blame the Vietnam War for brutalising and uprooting an entire generation that had never known peace in its own country. For whatever reason, it is a sad fact that this once very safe and friendly community had by then become the drugs capital of Australia, and since this is an illegal commodity, the area was rife with gangland warfare and all the horrors that entails. Shootings were common and prostitution, heroin addiction, burglary and violent crime rampant. The police were accused of corruption and not a day went by it seemed without some new scandal being uncovered, as the following collage of Sydney newspapers later in this chapter demonstrates. People I know had even witnessed a drive-by shooting.

It was particularly poignant when a second-generation East European Australian politician attempted to 'clean up' Cabramatta with tragic consequences. In September, 1994, the State Member of Parliament for Cabramatta, John Newman, was gunned down and killed outside his own home by two assassins. They were later identified as two Vietnamese hit men and charged with his murder. Mr Newman, whose original name was Naumenko, was actively working to eradicate corruption in the area.

When I left Australia in the late 1970's to travel on my own to England and Europe via the *Overland* route, taking several months to explore Asia and the Far East, my father was most concerned that it would be very dangerous. Stay at home, where it's safe he pleaded. Cabramatta – safe? Who was he kidding? '*Marochka, vot for you travel so much? It doesn't vorth it.*' It is Dad, it is. It is not relevant here to describe my experiences in Asia. Suffice to say the fascinating places that I saw and the wonderful people that I met confirmed my fundamental belief in the goodness of human nature, the value of individual liberty and the power of the free market to improve peoples' lives. I thoroughly enjoyed my time in Indonesia, Singapore, Malaysia, Thailand, Burma, Nepal, India, Afghanistan (when it was still beautiful and peaceful) and Iran (before it became fundamentalist), Israel and Turkey.

The civil war in Vietnam ended in ignominious defeat for South Vietnam and its American and Australian allies, who abandoned their South

Vietnamese 'collaborators' to a harsh fate. The nation was subsequently reunified by the Communists, led by Ho Chi Minh. However, history shows that tyranny cannot hold sway indefinitely, no matter how brutal the dictator. Sooner or later even the most statist socialist bureaucrats realise that in order to earn money, if only to keep themselves in comfort and power, some degree of free enterprise must be permitted. Lenin discovered that in 1921, Gorbachev and Yeltsin in the 1980's, Chinese communists also in that decade, even Castro in Cuba is finally permitting some economic freedoms. For Vietnam to have suffered the horrors of indiscriminate bombing and such obscene tortures as *napalm* and a*gent orange* is doubly tragic, in the light of the transformation that is now taking place peacefully.

Having won the war against 'capitalist' South Vietnam and the world's greatest superpower, Vietnam has increasingly permitted more and more economic freedom. In the 21st century it is openly embracing tourism and the dollars it brings, which in turn stimulates the growth of an infrastructure, providing hotels, leisure facilities, improved transport and so on, all of which provide employment and higher incomes for its people. It is hugely ironic that US veterans are returning to that once scarred country, now reverting to its natural beauty, drawn by curiosity or a desire to exorcise their guilt at the horror their government perpetuated in the name of freedom. Such veterans are taken down into the myriad tunnel systems where peasant guerrilla fighters hid from US military might and shown precisely how they were defeated - for a fee of course. The power of the market works in strange ways.

CRIME ON OUR STREETS THE REPORT

# Resignation call 'ridiculous': Ryan

**RICHARD BASHAM**

By NAOMI TOY

POLICE Commissioner Peter Ryan yesterday accepted ultimate responsibility for the policing crisis at Cabramatta but refused to take any of the blame.

It is only in his capacity as the boss that he will answer to the breakdown in policing, he said.

"The buck does stop with me," he said.

"You can't be everywhere at once but at the end of the day I am the Commissioner of Police.

"I can only do as much as I can do. We've said we could have done better. That does not mean we failed."

Mr Ryan angrily rejected calls for his resignation labelling the suggestion "ridiculous".

He said he was unable to comment on the contents of the report as he had not been provided with a copy and angry that reporters had access to it before him.

Mr Ryan denied that he had ever mismanaged Cabramatta & pushed the theme that eve should instead concentrate the future.

We've dealt with the man arrested people at Cabramatta, we've put 14 new commanders in, three new duty officers and now resources are going to move on to the road.

"Let's look to the future instead of constantly carping on about history."

Mr Ryan conceded communication between police and resources and frontline officers had been a problem but that he was improving.

"I do agree there is a problem

and I do try to talk to the front line as often as I can by visiting peace stations.

"But the important thing is we are trying to look at the best ways of developing our leaders and managers now and in the future so that communication problems are eliminated as much as possible.

Mr Ryan promised that officers like Sergeant Tim Priest who spoke out about the crisis would not be victimised nor would their careers suffer.

"I am hopeful that Sgt Priest will decide to stay on in the service and contribute to its ongoing reform," he said.

Sgt Priest said he felt vindicated by the report and praised Ms Shaw Ho for doing "an impossible job brilliantly".

"It doesn't only but many

## KEY RECOMMENDATIONS

❑ Police service to ensure it has sufficient resources to investigate gang activity
❑ Interpreters to be made available to assist officers 24 hours a day
❑ Police Assistance Line, assisting callers from a non-English speaking background, to be randomly surveyed
❑ Recruitment and retention targets ... lished of officers from non-... backgrounds ... to exceed

## Putting blame where it belongs

IN contrast to the Premier and some senior police officers who have suggested that frontline police "took their eye off the ball" the Parliamentary Committee makes it clear the primary responsibility for police failure in Cabramatta lies at the top of the service, not with Tim Priest and the other officers who risked their careers to ... forward.

### Tales from the war zone

### Two arrested in drug house

TWO people were arrested and syringes and knives seized after a raid on a fortified drug house in Cabramatta yesterday.

The pair will face a number of charges under the recent old Police Powers (Drug Premises) Act.

Police alleged that when they entered the unit one person was found fleeing drugs onto a sink and that officers confiscated hundreds of syringes and balloons.

Eight knives, including two described as commando type weapons, three machetes and a blade tapered to a length of metal were also seized.

The latest raid takes to four the number of warrants executed this month under the new laws.

## Credibility of police diminished

THE credibility of senior police has been badly tarnished by the level of drug related crime in Cabramatta and the use of worth ... statistical evidence by police to try to show crime in the area is diminishing.

That police accepted these statistics instead of the evidence of their own eyes beggars belief.

"It is strange as it seems, up until several months ago police ranked Cabramatta as 31st out of 80 suburbs in the level of criminal activity. According to the list, areas such as Roseville had higher levels of crime than Cabramatta despite the ... suburb's thriving illegal drug trade ... and gang related violence.

## Betrayal on the beat
### Officer tells his story

### So fed up he quit

### HORROR STORIES

- A Year 8 student fails at school because he's home guarding his parents' property.
- A primary school class tells of addicts with "purple lips and stuff coming out of their mouths" lying outside unit blocks.
- A teacher taking a sick five-year-old home is circled by pushers trying to sell heroin.

### The secret evidence of life in Cabramatta

### Horro... Fro...

made him stay home to guard against break-ins.

A primary school student at ... school was circled by drug ... teacher walked him home.

A local doctor said he had ordered ... not to visit him at his clinic because of assault.

And commuters said that every morning at Tain they were harassed by addicts desperate at the railway station as they tried to work.

Their testimony is the human backdrop to a key finding of the report — that a community neglected because senior police management failed to communicate with or simply ignored frontline officers.

And, in a damning finding, the report condemned attempts by senior police management to besmirch frontline police, including Detective

## failure lies at the top: Richard Bash...

us, the buck stops with all of ...

... Leader Kerry Chikarovski and ... and Andrew Tink said the Police ... ould be sacked.

... ounts Mr Whelan is a big F — failure — ... time for him to pack up and leave." Mr ... said.

# Other Russian 'Aussies'.

It is my considered view that, whilst Communism is an evil and impoverishing doctrine, it is futile and counterproductive to fight it with military force, except in self-defence. Nothing encourages people to back a regime, however despicable, more than outside invasion, even when it is for the best of motives. Instead, free nations need only uphold their institutions of liberty as a shining beacon to the world, an example and inspiration for oppressed people everywhere. Tyrannies cannot be perpetuated indefinitely; left to fester they will inevitably collapse sooner or later. The disintegration of the former USSR, as we shall see in the next chapter, is a clear illustration of this.

Many Russian Australians would disagree with my interpretation. They supported their new country's involvement in the tragic war in Vietnam, believing it to be a necessary step in the world wide struggle against Communism. After all, they had not fled Marxist states in two countries only to see it spread, via the Domino effect, to their new found bastion of freedom. One such enthusiastic patriot was Eugene Konashenko who could not wait to gain his Australian naturalisation so he could *'fight the commies'*. His life story provides another interesting insight into the experiences of Russian Australians.

Born in Harbin, China, in 1920, he is the son of a former officer of the Russian Imperial Army, who had fought on the Eastern front in WWI. Like many Russians, his father fled the Bolshevik revolution by travelling across Siberia in a cattle train and then making his way to China. His future wife fled the same way and they met and married in Manchuria. In due course the couple with their young son, Eugene, made their way to Shanghai, where the family prospered. Eugene attended a French university, the Aurora, gaining a degree in law and economics. He married Julie Vertoprahoff in 1948, the same year that Russians were desperately trying to leave China as a Communist victory in the civil war was imminent. Eugene was given the opportunity to lead one of the first groups, permitted by General MacArthur, to be flown to a military camp in Japan. From there they flew to Manila and thence to Tubabao where the remaining displaced Russians had settled. In Tubabao, his legal background ensured Eugene's appointment as legal assistant to the camp's Arbitration Board. Having lived in the Filipino island for about a year, they departed for Sydney on the US transport ship *Marine Jumper*. Immediately upon arrival, they were sent by train to the Department of Immigration Reception and Training centre in the NSW country town of Bathurst and from there to Wallgrove Migrant Camp near Blacktown.

Many *new Australians,* particularly the English, were horrified at the conditions in these camps, where they slept in barrack like accommodation, often segregated, ate in communal halls and hiked to basic latrines. For the Konashenkos of course, it was no hardship after their experiences in the Philippines and they were simply happy to have at last found a 'home.' As with all migrants who were given fares to Australia, they had to fulfil certain conditions, one being that they were obliged to work for two years wherever they were sent. Julie was assigned an office job in the *Silknit* factory and Eugene became a process worker in a chemical factory manufacturing rabbit poison; Australia was at that time plagued by rabbits. Though conditions were hard and the hours long Eugene appears to have no regrets at this change of status and welcomed the attractive salary. Other professionals were not nearly so magnanimous. To their horror and dismay Doctors, whose qualifications were not recognised, were given menial jobs and a few even committed suicide as a result.

*Gene Konashenko in the RAAF, 1968.*

The processing job was followed by a stint as a store man but in 1955 Eugene found a niche worthy of his talents and aspirations. Against very challenging odds, he was accepted into the Royal Australian Air Force as an Equipment Officer. Now he could show his gratitude to his adopted country and he threw himself wholeheartedly into his new position. By all accounts his efforts were appreciated by his new employers, who gave a glowing recommendation when he retired after 21 years in the service. He had even had the opportunity to fight against communism in Vietnam; Korea having been out of the question because he was not yet an Australian citizen but by the 1960's his credentials were in no doubt. Eugene served 12 months with Number 9 RAAF helicopter squadron as a Supply officer in Vung Tao airbase, where he was promoted to the rank of Squadron Leader in 1969. He had found fulfilment in his work for the

Air Force and in his adopted country, fathered an Australian born daughter and now delights in the accomplishments of three grandchildren.

Olga Pronin, whom we first came across in the chapter on Tubabao, is another Russian Australian with a fascinating story. Olga is the daughter of Konstantin Kluge, a former officer in the Tsar's White Army and a Russian noblewoman. Her elder half-brother is Konstantin Kluge, the distinguished Parisian artist awarded the *Legion d'Honneur* for his services to France.

*John, Marina, Olga and Gene, celebrating the 79th anniversary of the founding of the Sydney Russian Club.*

He was sent to Paris to be educated whilst the rest of the family were in Shanghai, only returning to China just before the outbreak of war in Europe. His autobiography is extremely illuminating. He had three wives, the second, Mary, was the daughter of Canadian missionaries to China and still lives in Paris, according to Olga who keeps in touch with her. Olga's other half brother, Michael, worked in transportation in China and eventually made a significant contribution to the development of containerisation throughout the world. He became a wealthy man in New York, where he settled. Olga's sister also resided in America.

As children in Shanghai, Olga and her sister attended the same school as my mother and her cousins, the Ecole Remi. Olga was a bright pupil and was promoted to the same class as Galia Cherviakoff and Vera Shliapnikoff, though they were a few years her senior. The family had servants and lived in relative luxury. Olga's education and indeed, her life, were disrupted by the urgent need to leave China when Mao Zedong's victory seemed imminent. But by that time she had fallen in love at the age of 17. She travelled to Tubabao with her fiancé Alex Pronin and his parents, where they married in the lush tropical surroundings of the Filipino island. In due course the young couple were allowed to immigrate to Australia.

On arrival in Australia, as part of their obligatory two year contract, Olga and Alex were sent to work in a hotel in Bathurst. They were fortunate enough to have their food and accommodation provided and so were able to pocket their wages. As a result they were probably amongst the first to be able to buy their own property. The Pronins lived for many years in the quiet town of Bathurst before moving to Sydney with their three sons. They bought a house and a news agency and worked long and hard to succeed. Their diligence and efforts paid off and, prompted by frequent requests for school texts, they diversified into selling educational books as well. Alex and Olga had correctly recognised that here was a market to be supplied and the educational books venture became such a lucrative business in its own right that they were able to relinquish daily operation of the news agency.

After the death of Olga's husband, their eldest son took over the business and, with the help of his wife, expanded it. Today they import books from around the world and the international company is thriving. Olga is justifiably proud of the flourishing business that she and her husband established and of the success that her family enjoys.

As part of the Darling Harbour redevelopment project in Sydney, there is a section of wall from the original passenger terminal called the *Welcome Wall* where the names of foreign born Australians are honoured. Immigrants are invited to submit details of their country of origin and how they came to arrive in Australia. This information is stored in a computer database and their names engraved on the wall for posterity. Following Alex's death, his sons recorded the story of their parents' arrival and Olga is proud to point out their names.

The arrival of the Shalavins in 1951 is also commemorated by their appreciative children. Those of us who were fortunate to be born in the new country pay tribute, through this small gesture, to the strength, determination and magnificent efforts made by the Russian refugees to successfully establish new lives and homes in an alien country. In honour of their achievements, we thank John and Julie, Alex and Olga, Leo and Galina, Vadim and Vera, Alexei and Katya, Dima and Polya, Victor and Irene, Tony and Tanya, Boris and Nadia, Gene and Julie, Axi and Louise, Zina, Maria and many, many more.

# Chapter 8

# World War II and its aftermath, the people left behind.

## Что посеешь, то и пожнёшь.

*You reap what you sow.*

# China 1949-1976, life under Mao.

*The collective earth is an orphan, the private plot is a child.*
(Chinese proverb)

So what *did* happen to China in the years after our families, and thousands of other Russian exiles, fled the country?

Once in control, the new Marxist state proceeded to bring the country in line with the dictates of the Party. Agrarian land reform took 47 million hectares of land, about 40% of all cultivated land, from landlords and richer peasants and gave it to the poorest peasants.[1] Communist Party members went out to the countryside to teach the people how to distinguish between the four 'classes'. The *landlords, rich peasants* (like the Russian Kulaks who may have owned a few animals of their own and occasionally hired others to work for them), *middle* and *poor* peasants. The landlords were stripped of their land, but so too were many rich peasants. Just as in Russia, redistributing land from the most productive farmers to the least would have unfortunate consequences. The poorest peasants were encouraged to hold *'speak bitterness'* meetings where they could criticise and condemn landlords and others who had treated them badly in the past. Unsurprisingly, this often became an opportunity for personal vendettas and the settling of old scores. After all, Mao had proclaimed that China was now a *'Peoples' Democratic Dictatorship'*. That is, in his own words, *'democracy for the people and dictatorship for the reactionaries'*. In practice, *'reactionaries'* meant not just landlords and Guomindang members but anyone who stood against the new regime. Such people were dragged before *People's courts* where they were humiliated and forced to confess to their 'crimes'. Many were condemned to death, estimates vary between two to four million people killed by the People's courts.[2] Of course this was all with Mao's approval, as he had written: *'Local bullies and evil landowners have killed peasants without batting an eyelid. In view of these crimes, how can anyone say that the peasants should not now rise and shoot one or two of them, and bring about a small-scale reign of terror in crushing these people.'*[3] The luckier ones were sent to prisons or special camps to be 're-educated'. 'Thought reform' was another of the more sinister aspects of this social revolution; camp inmates were forced to study the writings of Mao, Lenin and Marx. They also had to attend large meetings where public self-criticism was expected.

Peasant ownership of land lasted an even shorter time than it had in Russia. By the early 1950's it had become apparent that peasant ownership would not automatically lead to increased agricultural production. Many peasants simply lacked the skills or agricultural equipment necessary to increase productivity. This led to increased pressure on them to amalgamate into co-operative farms. At first co-operatives were small in scale, typically pooling the land and resources of 30 to 50 families (who still legally owned their land). However, the demands of the 5 year plans in industry required greater food output. In any case, a free peasantry selling food for profit was not compatible with Marxist ideology. Some peasants might become successful bourgeois capitalists all over again! Like the Russian Kulaks – they had to be stopped. The Party put pressure on the remaining peasants to join yet bigger co-operatives. Not only were these much larger, involving 200-300 families, but the peasants were forced to sign over the title to their land, animals and equipment to the co-operative. They would no longer be paid rent for the use of their land but would be forced to work for wages. By 1956, 95% of peasants belonged to such co-operatives. The peasants, betrayed by the false promises of their government, were landless again.

This betrayal was neither necessary nor beneficial to the demands of industry. Following the Soviet Union's example and advice, the Chinese drew up 5-Year Plans to develop their heavy industry, particularly coal, iron, steel, oil and cement. China was now a command economy, whereby all decisions about what goods would be produced were made by the government and it decreed that heavy industry would take priority over consumer goods. As with Russia, industrial production did increase but living standards did not improve. Mao was still convinced that simply by releasing the *'tremendous energy of the masses'* all manner of miracles could be accomplished. Perhaps the success of the *'Swat the fly'* campaign (every one of the 600 million citizens was asked to kill ten flies a day, resulting in their virtual eradication) had led him to believe that the economy too, could be bent to his will. How wrong he was.

In 1958, Mao declared the *'Great Leap Forward'*, a second 5-Year Plan, which was meant to overtake the British economy in 15 years and the American in 20 to 30 years. Co-operative farms would not be sufficient for such grandiose ambitions. The Chinese people were now organised into huge Communes, consisting not only of farms, but also centres of industry, commerce, education – in fact all aspects of life. Four million communal eating halls were set up to free people from cooking. Infants were placed in nurseries and children in schools so that both parents, freed from the responsibilities of raising their own children, could

СЛАВА ВЕЛИКОМУ КИТАЙСКОМУ НАРОДУ
ЗАВОЕВАВШЕМУ СВОБОДУ, НЕЗАВИСИМОСТЬ И СЧАСТЬЕ!

*The Russian state welcomes the Chinese people into the brotherhood of Communism.*

concentrate on work. Communes were run by Party members and soldiers, who controlled schools, clinics and, above all, work brigades and ensured that Party policy was followed at all times. By the end of 1958, 90% of the population, approximately 700 million people, were living in one of 26,000 communes, varying in size from a few square kilometres to the size of a British county.[4] All this collectivisation was encouraged and indeed abetted by the USSR who initially welcomed China's regime, as this poster shows.

Did the communal experiment work? Many Chinese were undoubtedly enthusiastic and laboured long and hard, with little or no equipment, to build their country. Huge dams were built, canals dug, often with bare hands scratching at the earth and carrying away the soil in baskets passed from hand to hand. The results appeared impressive, particularly the *'backyard steel'* campaign that sought to increase steel production by setting up thousands of small scale furnaces in villages right across China. By the end of the first year 11 million tonnes of steel had been produced, a huge increase over the previous year. But they could not congratulate themselves for very long.

By the late 1950's it became apparent that the Party's propaganda urging everyone to work harder and faster may have resulted in targets being met but at a huge cost in quality. Old, overworked machines fell apart, factory workers fell asleep at their benches and accidents were rife. Nearly a quarter of the backyard steel that had been produced was useless for industry and had to be scrapped. Worse still, the effort required in producing it had taken people away from the fields, so less food was produced.

By 1959 even Mao had to admit that the *'Great Leap Forward'* had failed and he was honest enough to say so to the Party leaders. *'I am a complete outsider when it comes to economic construction, I understand nothing about industrial planning.'* [5] Was this meant to console those who had to face the consequences? Diverting labour from food production to useless steel manufacture was to have disastrous results. Working to unrealistic targets also encouraged Party officials to lie and distort figures to avoid recrimination. In 1959 they falsely claimed that there had been a record harvest. Commune officials congratulated themselves and gave out generous meals, using up valuable food stocks. In 1960 the combination of the chaos caused by the *'Great Leap Forward'* and bad weather, which caused floods in some areas and droughts in others, resulted in a famine that claimed nine million lives. Strict rationing did not help and the famine continued – by 1962 some 20 million people had died.[6] We must never become inured to the human horror and tragedy that such bald statistics fail to convey. 20 million people, more than the total population of Australia in 2006, *died* of starvation within living memory and, most horribly of all, for largely avoidable reasons.

After the *'3 bitter years'* of 1959 – 1961, as the Chinese called them, Mao's influence declined and power shifted to the 'moderates' – Head of State Lui Shaoqi, Party Secretary Deng Xiaoping and Prime Minister Zhou Enlai. They abandoned the disastrous state-led *'Great Leap forward'* and permitted peasants their own private plots again, thus reversing the tragic collectivisation. Communes were reduced in size and the *'backyard steel'* peasant farmers returned to the fields to do the work they knew best. Peasants were permitted to sell their surplus for profit, recognising that only such incentives would actually increase food production. As with Lenin and his *New Economic Policy*, they had finally recognised that profit *is* the key to production.

Mao quite accurately condemned such policies as going down the *'capitalist road'* and fought to put people back on to the 'right' road to Communism. In the early 1960's people simply refused to listen to him, until, that is, he gained the support of Lin Biao, the Minister of Defence who commanded the four million strong People's Liberation Army. He issued each soldier a copy of the *'Quotations from Chairman Mao'*, known as *'The Little Red Book'*, and encouraged them to study it. With their help Mao made his comeback in 1966, in what became known as *The Great Proletarian Cultural Revolution*. This time Mao would launch his revolution with the very young, to ensure that the spirit of communism would not die out with his generation. One might have thought that the recent horrors would not so easily have been forgotten. But by targeting the youth of the city, people who had escaped the famine of the countryside, Mao and his wife, Jiang Qing, revealed not only their ruthlessness but also their political acumen.

The movement began among schoolchildren and students in Beijing in 1966. They were formed into military units, called *'Red Guards'*, and encouraged to commit themselves wholeheartedly to political activities designed to destroy all traces of 'capitalist' influence. Schools and colleges were shut down for this purpose. As might be expected the kids simply went wild. From innocent beginnings with monster parades and poster campaigns attacking the *'4 Olds'*, old ideas, old culture, old customs and old habits, they quickly progressed to using violence to further their ends. Shops selling anything resembling Western style consumer goods, such as records, chess sets, cosmetics, fur coats, any 'luxury' items, as well as examples of their own culture, were destroyed. Bookshops and libraries were burnt and museums, galleries, churches and temples closed down. Even girls with Western haircuts had their heads shaved and Western 'capitalist' clothes were ripped off their wearers. Mao relished and encouraged these children running amok in his name, as once again the cult of Mao was re-established. Pictures, busts and statues of him were erected all over the cities and 740 million copies of his book were printed and distributed between 1966 and 1969. Mao took his revenge on the moderates who had ousted him from power and imprisoned both Deng and Lui, who was to die in captivity.

Mao, the power hungry tyrant who had admired and was inspired by the brutal and bloodthirsty First Emperor, Shi Huangdi, looked on with pleasure as the youngsters turned on their elders. Everything of worth was destroyed by the fanatical children vying with one another to demonstrate their love of Mao. For three years, millions of Chinese people lived in fear of Mao's teenagers as scenes like the following were reported across the country. *'It was a time of terror.... We knew the Red Guards would one day come to our house. At 11 o'clock one night the knocks finally came, loud and sharp... There were 7 or 8 of them... all wearing white cloths over their mouths and noses and dark clothes. Their leader carried a whip. He struck it against the table with a loud bang. "Liang Shan", he said, "Is there anything feudal, capitalist or anti communist in your house?" Father stammered: "No, no." "Pig!" The man sliced the table again. "What you must understand is that this is a revolutionary action. Right?" said the man. "Yes, yes, a revolutionary action." I had never seen my father plead with anyone before......'* [7] Before leaving they burned all their books, including Chinese poetry, history and Chinese legends and stole their money.

Anyone suspected of being a *'capitalist-roader'* was humiliated, tortured, occasionally tried but more often summarily executed. A famous writer, Lao She, was simply held head down in a muddy pool until he drowned. Thousands of people committed suicide in this period. Eventually the Red Guards turned on each other and, having acquired guns, machine-guns and even anti-aircraft missiles, battles broke out across China as the country sank further into the abyss. It is estimated that over a million people died during the *'Cultural revolution'*. [8]

Finally, even Mao was forced to curb their excesses by sending in the People's Liberation Army to restore order. Mao called on young people to go to the countryside, to be 're-educated' by the poorer peasants. Many went willingly at first, believing they would *'plough, plant, eat what we grew and be able to respect ourselves again.'* They were told the peasants would welcome them, but that was another lie. The peasants, barely able to feed themselves, resented these useless city youngsters.

The Cultural Revolution was to have even more devastating effects in addition to the huge loss of life and property. So many young people had missed out on their education that by 1981, the New China News Agency claimed that there were 140 million illiterate Chinese. But there were also some consolations from the bitter experience. Many millions, who had previously been devoted Communists, lost all respect for the Party. A noted author, imprisoned for 13 years by the Red Guards, summed up the effects: *'The great Cultural Revolution was the revolution that sent culture to its death!'* [9]

Fortunately for China, it also discredited Mao once and for all. Even his former friend and supporter, Lin Biao, the Defence Minister, wrote in a secret document that Mao *'..is a paranoid and a sadist….the greatest dictator and tyrant in China's history.'* [10] No truer words were written. However, he still wielded immense power, and a plot to depose Mao by Lin was thwarted, followed by the mysterious crashing of Lin's plane.

In the ensuing years a power struggle took place between the Left, supporting Mao (chiefly his wife Jiang Qing and her three supporters known as the *'Gang of 4'*) and the Right, led by Zhou Enlai and the freed Deng Xiaoping. Following Mao's death in 1976, the moderate Rightists wrested control of the country and China entered a new historical period.

## The 'Great Patriotic War' – Russia's agony.

The Second World War would have a huge impact on both China and the USSR, bringing a Communist dictatorship to power in the first country and strengthening its iron hold even further in the second. While the fortunate Russians abroad settled into new lives and new challenges, those remaining behind faced yet more horrors. This time the threat came from the West, as the Communists had always believed it would, but it was not the 'capitalist' West seeking to destroy them. The threat came from Germany, in the grip of the *Nazis* - the National Socialist German Workers' Party, led by the fanatical megalomaniac, Adolf Hitler.

During the 1930's Stalin continued to consolidate his control over the country, eliminating the last of the Bolshevik old guard and indeed anyone he considered might have even the remotest chance of supplanting him, as well as hundreds of thousands who did not. The former were removed in a series of well publicised 'show trials' in which the victims, after torture and dire threats to their families, confessed to absurd and fanciful crimes against the state. By 1937 the 'trials' had extended to the military, claiming war heroes like Marshal Tukhachevsky and many other generals of the Red army. All three branches of the armed forces were affected, every Admiral was shot and over half of the total officer force of around 25,000 was either shot or imprisoned.[11] Among the population at large, dissidents were summarily dispatched to the ever-growing *gulags*. Yet at the same time, Stalin's regime was attempting to detract from this terror by publishing evermore pro-Stalin propaganda, which many Russians appeared to be taken in by.

In June 1941 the Nazis launched their attack on Russia, code named Operation Barbarossa. Stalin was reportedly horrified and disbelieving of the initial reports of wholesale destruction. After all he had signed a Non-aggression Pact with Hitler two years earlier and they had secretly agreed to carve up eastern Europe between them, starting with Poland. Although Stalin did not trust Hitler, the pact had bought him vital time in which to prepare his forces, yet still he was unprepared for the Nazi onslaught. Within a week the Germans had virtually destroyed the entire Soviet Air force on the ground, like sitting ducks, and taken over half a million civilians prisoner. The preparations for the attack by three million German soldiers could hardly have gone unnoticed by the Soviets, yet Stalin had done nothing to prepare his people for the *blitzkrieg*. Moreover, by so drastically purging his own military a few years earlier, he had effectively undermined their chances of mounting a defence.

By October the three German armies had virtually achieved their objectives, encircling Leningrad in the North, threatening Moscow in the centre and Stalingrad in the south. It seemed that Russia was theirs for the taking and that Hitler had been correct to state that he had only to '*kick in the door and the whole rotten structure will come crashing down.*'[12] In the light of Stalin's repressive regime some actually welcomed the Nazis as 'liberators' from his tyranny. In the Ukraine in particular, grateful villagers offered the traditional bread and salt to the German soldiers as they advanced. But the Nazis failed to take advantage of these tentative gestures of friendship and pressed on with their brutal invasion. In keeping with the fanatical hatred of Russians that Hitler had inculcated in them, they showed no mercy to civilians and soldiers alike. Very quickly the welcome turned sour and Russians and Ukrainians alike rallied around their own home-grown tyrant. The Fuhrer had failed to take into account the Russians' deep determination to repel foreign invaders and their capacity for endurance and suffering.

Infuriated by the Nazis' brutality towards the 'subhuman, inferior Slavs' as Hitler perceived them, the Russians now revealed their true grit, much to the surprise of the Germans. As they retreated before the advancing invader, the Red Army implemented the same *'scorched earth'* policy that had so weakened Napoleon's advance over a century earlier. By destroying everything of value to their foe they forced the Germans to rely on their own ever lengthening and increasingly vulnerable supply lines. And, like the French army before them, the Nazis found that failure to conquer Russia before the onset of winter would also prove to be their undoing. As temperatures plummeted to $-30^C$ German soldiers froze at their posts, their tanks became useless as fuel solidified; even attending to bodily functions was dicing with death as frostbite took its toll.

A vital aspect of the scorched earth policy was not only the destruction of food but the removal of all industrial resources, especially ammunition plants and the like. Entire factories were dismantled and transported by rail to safety beyond the Ural Mountains, where they were reassembled and the vital production of munitions resumed. Another crucial factor was the assistance of the Americans. Under the *Lend Lease Act*, they provided the Russians with the necessary funds and equipment to withstand the Nazi onslaught. From November 1941 the USA supplied over a billion dollars worth of food, weapons, fuel and medical supplies via the Soviet port of Archangel. By 1945 the Americans had sent 16.5 million tonnes of material to the USSR and according to at least one historian: *'without this aid it is unlikely that the USSR could have continued fighting.'* [13]

Nonetheless we should not underestimate the monumental contribution of the Russian people themselves. For three years they bore the brunt of the Nazi war machine, until the D-Day landings in June 1944 finally opened the new western front and the tide began to turn in favour of the allies. In Leningrad especially, Russians showed outstanding heroic fortitude. Surrounded on all sides by the unrelenting Germans, men, women and children defended their city against all odds for the three bitter years. They were reduced to eating wallpaper, soup made from glue, cats, dogs, rats, sawdust, jelly made from soap, machine oil, anything the desperate people could scavenge from the dying city. Still the Leningrad Symphony Orchestra played on, at least those spared by famine and bullet. The weakened musicians dragged their instruments to the concert hall to lift the morale of the city's besieged populace, and momentarily distract them from their gnawing hunger. The city was mercilessly bombed, despite attempts at camouflage, the domes painted green in summer, grey in winter. When the plumbing was destroyed, water was carried in buckets by human chain from the canals to the bread factory. The only lifeline to the outside world was the famed *'ice road'* across Lake Ladoga, which evacuated some of the children and brought in desperately needed supplies. The brave truck drivers drove with their doors open so they could leap out when bombed. Shostakovich managed to escape but dedicated his 7th Symphony to the city's defenders, a work which has enormous symbolic value for the survivors of Leningrad.

There is no denying the immense sacrifices the people of that city endured and it is a tribute to their gallantry that the city never succumbed. A third of Leningrad's three million people died of starvation alone, significantly more than the total number of British, Australian, Canadian and American soldiers and civilians killed throughout the entire war. One girl's diary entry, tells us of her family, *'All died. Only Tanya remains.'*

During the four years of Russia's valiant stand against the might of the German *Wehrmacht* it is estimated that over 23 million soldiers and civilians died, roughly the same as the military deaths of all other countries combined. How many of that number were attributable solely to the Nazi invasion and how many to Soviet tyranny and incompetence is a minefield of an issue. There is little doubt that Stalin's failure to act upon warnings of impending invasion, coupled with his previous destruction of the upper echelons of the armed forces, contributed to the early heavy losses. There is also no denying that it was the enormous sacrifices on the Eastern front that tore the heart out of the previously invincible German war machine. Evidence appears to suggest that the Russian people withstood the Germans *in spite* of their supposedly revered leader, rather than because of him. Yet the Soviet media would continue to promote Stalin as the great patriot who had saved his people in their hour of need, just like Churchill in Britain. Tragically for the Russian people, the war would consolidate and extend his power further so it became nigh on impossible to be rid of him.

So Stalin emerged from the *Great Patriotic war*, as the Russians called it, stronger than ever. The fragile alliance with his Western allies began to crumble as the deep suspicions between the two opposing systems of government resurfaced. Even in the latter stages of the war the distrust was evident as both forces raced to be first to capture the German capital Berlin. The allies could not take the surrounding countryside in their bid for the city. And while they succeeded in taking much of the capital, it was left to the Soviets to capture the eastern part of Germany as well as key parts of Berlin, including the *Reichstag* (the German Parliament) and Hitler's bunker. Thus it was that Berlin and the country found itself occupied by different allied forces, a division that would become permanent for much of the second half of the century.

## From hot war to cold war.

With the defeat of Nazi Germany in 1945, the wartime alliance between the Soviet Union and the Western countries broke down irretrievably. Berlin and the rest of Germany was split into separate zones by the victorious nations; the USSR controlling the eastern sectors and Great Britain, America and France the western ones. Efforts to reunify the country, as intended by GB, USA and USSR at the Yalta conference, by Churchill, Roosevelt and Stalin, broke down in the face of opposing aims. There were to be no free elections in the countries of the soviet controlled Eastern Europe after all, the USSR claiming continued control was necessary to act as a buffer zone against a hostile Western Europe.

The Baltic states were simply annexed, Eastern European nations had a semblance of freedom but in practice Communist governments were installed in Poland, Hungary, Czechoslovakia, Romania and Bulgaria. The borders of these countries effectively drawing an *'Iron Curtain'* between them and the free states of Europe, as Churchill described it. The Soviet Union, having suffered so many more casualties than the West, intended to weaken Germany permanently and mercilessly plundered the remaining resources of the vanquished nation as compensation for their losses.

1949 was a critical year in what had now become known as the *'Cold War'* between the Soviet Union and the USA. That is to say, a conflict marked by tension, propaganda, economic sanctions and a dangerous arms race; building up to warfare without the actual *'heat'* of battle. For it was in that year that the USSR developed its own nuclear bomb, destroying the monopoly of mass destruction that America had enjoyed for four years. The division of Germany also became permanent with the creation of the soviet puppet state the *German Democratic Republic*, with its capital in East Berlin. Taking their lead from America, the Western allies established the democratic nation of the *Federal Republic of Germany* in 1955, with its capital in Bonn. Although West Berlin was part of the FRG it was completely surrounded by the Soviet controlled GDR.

With US financial aid and the encouragement of a free economy, West Germany quickly prospered. The Western powers had decided that a weakened Germany would only be a burden on them. Moreover, they had learned the lessons of World War One, when the desire for revenge and harsh reparations had simply led to resentment and further conflict; ultimately enabling Hitler to rise to power by capitalising on the Germans' deep hatred of the vengeful peace treaty. So, in the Western part of Germany there was to be no retribution, despite the disclosure of the full horrors of the Holocaust revealed at Nuremberg. It was to prove to be a sensible, humane and successful approach. The German people quickly put their Nazi past behind them and within a few years took their place in the European family of nations. A salutary lesson learned from the past - revenge achieves nothing.

1949 also saw the establishment of the new Communist state of China under Mao Zedong, which announced its friendship with the Soviet Union, another alarming portent for the world at large. The news of USSR's successful atomic bomb explosion encouraged the USA to develop ever more powerful nuclear capabilities, and thus a deadly arms race between the two superpowers began. Each side spent billions in an attempt to gain the upper hand over the other. The first 'hot' war between the two groups was fought in Korea the following year, with Communist North Korea[14], supported by the USSR and China, fighting South Korea, supported by the USA and UN forces from the UK, France, Canada and Australia. Although ostensibly a civil war, it can reasonably be viewed as a proxy war between the USSR and USA. Despite lasting four years and costing many lives there was no conclusive outcome and the ensuing armistice more or less restored the original boundaries between North and South Korea.

# Back to the USSR, the 'motherland'
# – Nina's exile in the northern Urals.

When the long, bitter Great Patriotic war mercifully ended the battered remains of the Russian people set about reconstructing their war torn country. With so many of her young dead and industry destroyed, the plea rang out to expatriates to *'return to the motherland'* and help rebuild *'your country'*. A small number of White Russians from the expatriate community in China, my aunt Nina and her husband Kostya amongst them, answered the call. They were stateless, suspected that they were in imminent danger of being expelled from China and eager to carry out their patriotic duty for a country that most had never even seen.

When Nina, Kostya and his family left Shanghai to return to the Soviet Union in 1947, the whole Shliapnikoff family came out to bid them farewell. Her mother Zina was undoubtedly distraught at the thought of losing her daughter to that hateful regime she had risked her life to escape, but Nina and Kostya were adamant. It was whispered that he must have been a *'secret Communist'* to want to return, but he was also a charming, independent and strong willed young man whom Nina adored. If it was his desire to live in *'Mother Russia'* then she was prepared to sacrifice her strong family bonds to be with him.

Six ship loads of expatriates made the voyage to Russia. 2,000 families, many with young children, first sailed to Vladivostok and thence on to destinations unknown. I later learned that all the children were separated and transported on the first ship, essentially they were used as hostages to ensure their parents did not change their minds whilst they waited for their ship to arrive. Nina and Kostya travelled on the second ship, along with his mother, his sister Tamara and her family, his other sister Lolya, now in Sverdlosk, plus a number of other friends, such as the Belkin family, who we will return to later.

Such was the prejudice in the White community against *returnees* that some considered them to be 'the enemy' and refused to have anything to do with them. Most, however, wished to keep in touch and letters were exchanged between the anxious families. The Soviets clearly censored all letters so the correspondents took to writing in code. Returnees would describe, with wry humour, how they were missing the wonderful Chinese moon cakes, which had been universally detested by the Russian community, implying that they now had much worse. Others wrote how they should join them in the 'Motherland' as soon as so-and-so has had her baby, when the person in question was far too old to conceive! One famed actor wrote back in rhyme to a friend who had warned him, admitting that she was right and that now he was chopping wood. Катя, Катя, ты права, я теперь рублю дрова.

Stories circulated about returnees' belongings being confiscated. As indeed had been the case in 1925, when exiles had been offered Soviet passports and encouraged to return, and again in 1935, when control of the Manchurian branch of the Trans Siberian railway passed to China and those Russians who had been working on it were repatriated. On those occasions returnees had been encouraged to pack all their possessions: clothes, furniture, even animals – pigs and chickens, onto separate rail trucks. These were then disconnected from their train and promptly disappeared. Some said that returnees were stripped of their good clothes and given rags to wear, others that they were left with only the clothes on their backs, which quickly became dirty and worn. They were then paraded through the streets, ragged and filthy to show Soviet citizens how poorly Russians lived abroad! The Soviet Union had been rocked by the effects of Stalin's collectivisation policies and subsequent famine in the 1930's, so the authorities had no qualms about milking naïve expatriates for all they were worth. Many of these experiences only emerged many decades later when families were eventually reunited. Nina at least, suffered no such ignominy in 1947.

In Tsarist times, those dissidents that didn't merit imprisonment or hanging were punished by being sent to live in the wilderness areas of Russia, usually remote outposts of Siberia. However, the Communist regime had intensified this punishment by establishing harsh labour camps, the infamous *gulags*, right across Russia. Returning Russians who had obviously been tainted by Western values, or were known to have extensive contact with Westerners, were immediately despatched to these camps. Others, like Nina and Kostya, were simply ordered to live in a remote village for an unspecified period, for their 'crime' of having lived abroad. The sentence must have come as a terrible shock to those who believed they would be welcomed home as long lost sons and daughters of the motherland.

Nina and Kostya were sent to Severuralsk, near Ivdel and Serov, in the northern Urals. By all accounts it was quite a primitive village, typical of the Russian countryside, with none of the material comforts that they had become accustomed to in Shanghai. After a year or so they managed to buy their own little house of 24 square metres, similar in size to Julie's garage in Sydney, having *'sold a few things'* as Nina recalled. By some miracle, Nina had managed to cling to her possessions and was able to sell some of her Shanghai crystal and silk lingerie. Clearly attractive goods if sufficient to buy a house with. It is interesting to note that the concept of private property continued in some remote areas.

Home photographs show a simple wooden hut with a decked outdoor area, presumably to keep the mud out of the house. Water had to be brought from a distant well in huge barrels, which they wheeled along the street. One can only imagine how treacherous that must have been in the bitterly cold winters when the town lay under snow and ice. Their toilet consisted of an outhouse built around a hole in the ground. The streets were unpaved and when the spring thaw melted winter's snow and ice, the roads would turn into a quagmire. Still, it appeared that most traffic at the time was horse drawn carts and pedestrians.

*Nina and Kostya beside their house.*

*Village street in Severuralsk.*

*Pleasure trip to the mountains.*

Life must have been very difficult for them at the beginning of their exile. Nonetheless, Nina and Konstantin were young, strong and very much in love and so took all the hardships in their stride. They made friends amongst the local community and lived in the village for about twelve years. Photographs eventually reaching Australia showed them entertaining friends at jolly parties, with home-grown food and the ever-present vodka. Undoubtedly there were moments of pleasure too, occasions when seemingly the whole community went on trips to the countryside. Here they are seen enjoying a trip to a popular beauty spot in the mountains on an open top charabanc.

*Beside the lake, Nina and Kostya on the right.*

Nina was one of life's optimists, a warm hearted and genuine person who always looked at life positively and took great pleasure in small delights. She had a wide, generous smile and indeed a matching girth, but that did not appear to bother her. If she could obtain enough food to satiate her and a bit more besides then she simply considered herself to be very fortunate. She continued to be devoted to her handsome, athletic husband whom she had married 'for love' at the tender age of 18, and who

*Party in Severuralsk.*

reciprocated those feelings. Despite living behind the 'Iron Curtain', the impenetrable barrier that closed off the USSR, she wrote regularly and prolifically to her mother and other relatives scattered around the world. Possibly through pride or stubbornness, not once in all those years, did she admit to experiencing difficulties or utter a word of regret about their decision to return to Russia.

We never did find out just how committed they were to the Communist cause and whether it was political idealism that had led Kostya and his parents to return to Russia. There is one revealing photo of Kostya with some male companions at a demonstration, one is holding the red banner and the other is wearing the distinctive red ribbon. Whether attendance was voluntary or obligatory we could not ascertain. Nina said that he simply went along with his colleagues and even refused to attend on occasion, apparently without consequence. She claimed that he never joined the Party. He was invited to but diplomatically declined, saying *'he was not worthy'*. However, being a fully-fledged, card carrying member of the Communist party conveyed prestige and would undoubtedly have brought material benefits. She

*Kostya (centre) attending a pro-Communist demonstration in the USSR.*

did admit though, that he was a patriot and although he saw injustice around him, he hoped it would improve. He had marched in demonstrations from time to time, both in Severuralsk and later when they moved to Dnepropetrovsk, but at the end of the day she did not think he truly believed in Communism as an ideal. Was Nina being diplomatic to me as a 'Westerner' or was this her genuine view after all these years? I like to believe it was the latter, after all it was 1998 when she made this comment and by that time it was surely safe to reveal her true feelings.

*Nina attending a Mayday demonstration in Severuralsk. 1959.*

Both of them were clearly pressured to at least go through the motions of supporting the socialist state. On the *'Mayday'* celebrations each year, the international day of labour and the working classes, good Soviet citizens were expected to show their 'solidarity' with the communist state. The previous two photographs show the village of Severuralsk demonstrating their loyalty to the cause, under the banner of Lenin. Nina in her distinctive hat is clearly seen amongst the demonstrators.

As a vivacious, sociable woman, Nina shared the pleasures and sorrows of her new found friends in the Urals village. Particularly in the absence of her warm extended family who were facing their own challenges around the world. The following photographs, from one of her many albums, provides a rare glimpse of rural life in the 1960's.

*A friend's funeral (typical of a rural Russian Orthodox burial).*

241

# Life in Dnepropetrovsk.

Around 1960, after some twelve years of internal exile, Nina and her husband were given permission to relocate to a place of their choosing. This period was presumably the length of time considered necessary to rid them of their false foreign ideas and show that they were indeed loyal Soviet citizens. Or perhaps it was simply due to the death of Stalin and the comparative freedom that his successors permitted. Nina and Kostya chose to move to the warmer climes of Dnepropetrovsk in the Ukraine.

In the cities there was no question of buying your own house. Everyone lived in identical high rise apartments, built by the State to the same specification, whether it be Leningrad, Moscow, Vladivostok or Dnepropetrovsk. So they applied for, and in due course received, what she describes as a modern flat, with which they were extremely pleased. After all, it had central heating, running hot and cold water, an indoor toilet, a bath with shower and a kitchen with a cooker and oven. What more could they want? No more collecting water from the well or braving the Siberian winds to attend to one's basic functions. This seemed sheer luxury to the young couple after their isolated village life. Moreover, Dnepropetrovsk was a congenial, bustling city on the banks of the river Dnieper, with all the leisure facilities that a large river affords. They

loved to swim, and Kostya to fish, and often took holidays in the nearby Black Sea resorts on the southern coast of the Ukraine or in the Crimea. The Ukraine had a much milder climate too and fruit and vegetables were readily available. Nina's letters were full of joy and happiness about her new home.

Indeed, it was a considerably better situation than many in the USSR were experiencing at that time. Property in the classless socialist paradise was allocated by the State and despite a massive building program of nondescript high-rise flats, there was still a shortage of accommodation. Many families in the 1960's, 70's

*Nina in 1965.*

242

and even 80's were still living in one room and sharing basic kitchen and bathroom facilities with other families. Such communal flats, *Kommunalki,* were still commonplace when Nina and Konstantin received their flat. Although they had their own private kitchen and bathroom the bedroom and living room were still combined. The sofa by day became a double bed at night, though to be fair this is no different to the ubiquitous bed-sits of London or studio flats of Sydney, perhaps even better if the kitchen is entirely separate. Though in Soviet Russia, couples with children, and sometimes also a grandparent, lived in such accommodation. Small wonder then that generations of Russians only had one child.

Nina and Kostya settled down to live happily in their new home. Kostya's sister, Tamara, also lived in the city and it was probably she who had recommended it. Nina quickly made new friends, as her friendly and exuberant nature was wont to do. A former teacher named Zoya became a life long friend as did Genia, a lovely lady with the most amazing operatic voice. In due course they discovered Ida, another expatriate from Shanghai, who had also somehow made her way to this city and was married to a Frenchman, Joseph, who had been reluctantly trapped in the USSR. Their story follows later. Nona was another acquaintance who would have preferred not be living in the Ukrainian Soviet Socialist Republic. Like Ida and Nina herself, she too was an ex-*Shanghai-ka.*

Quite possibly, the only serious regret of Nina's life, which she only momentarily alluded to, was that she never had any children. She loved them and would clearly have made a wonderful mother. She would not speak of it herself but her mother and sister knew that in the turbulent years after her wartime marriage, when no one knew for certain where they would end their days, Nina and Kostya had made the harsh and painful decision not to have any children then. Contraception was not readily available in those pre-Pill days and Nina undertook a particularly dangerous course of action which left her permanently infertile. My mother related the following sad family dilemma. When Nina and her husband were about to return to the Soviet Union, possibly never to see the rest of the family again, Nina asked Julia if she could take her daughter Elena, then three years old, and raise her as her own. It was a desperate and forlorn hope but she argued that Julia was young and fit and could have many more children, as indeed she did, whereas this was Nina's only hope of motherhood. My mother was shocked by Nina's request and would not entertain the idea of parting with her only child.

Even though, having been abandoned by her husband, life must have seemed very precarious to her at the time. Nina and Kostya returned to the USSR childless.

Nonetheless, they appeared to have a full and satisfying life, making the most of the hard conditions, seeking pleasure and escape whenever they could. They led an active social life, centring on very warm friendships, congenial company and their careers. Nina worked as a hairdresser, the trade she had learned as a young girl back in Shanghai, and progressed to being the senior 'manager' of her state run shop. She loved her work, creating attractive hairstyles for people and enjoying the convivial atmosphere of a beauty salon, where she had many loyal customers. She was awarded several medals of distinction for her services to the state, which was the former Soviet Union's method of rewarding hard work, in the absence of 'elitist' and 'divisive' pay increases. After all, in this egalitarian society no one was to be richer or poorer than anyone else. When I visited her, she proudly, though a little shyly, showed me her medals, no doubt aware that this would seem very odd to a Westerner.

At some point Nina was able to establish contact with her Aunts Alexandra and Klavdia, the two Shliapnikoff siblings who had chosen to remain behind when the others fled to China.

Alexandra (Shura) had remained in Samara with her newlywed husband Grigori (Grisha). Like most of his generation, Grisha had served in the war, as this photograph they sent to Nina shows.

Nina learned that the other sister Klavdia and her husband Vassili had moved to Leningrad and by the 1960's Nina was also in communication with their daughters, her cousins Lara and Taissia, as well her cousin Irina

*Alexandra, Grigori and their daughter Irina, c.1948.*

in Samara. At some point they also rediscovered Vera, Pelageya's (Polya's) daughter, who had found her way to Chelyabinsk, after also returning from China in similar circumstances to Nina. Nina could at least rejoice in their offspring and followed the birth and growth of each child with great interest. This photograph given to Nina, of a young girl at Russian New Year, may well be a relative. She is standing in front of the traditionally decorated tree beside Father Frost, the Russian equivalent of Santa Claus. The former Soviet Union, which was officially atheist, did not celebrate Christmas. However, they did welcome in the New Year with festivities, the exchange of gifts and even a tree, much like their Western counterparts.

*Father Frost with a young friend of Nina's at New Year, 1963.*

## The family from Kuznetsk.

Following the flight of her six siblings, Klavdia remained in Kuznetsk, the place of her birth and also that of my mother and so many of the Shliapnikoffs. She and her husband Vassili remained for many years in the town they loved and called home. Their two daughters,

*Klavdia and Shura (Alexandra), Samara 1931.*

Larissa (Lara) and Taissia (Taya), were born there and Lara has fond memories of her early years in the town. Kuznetsk was not so far from the city of Samara where Shura, the other sister that remained behind in the USSR, lived and so the sisters were able to visit each other. Of course they had also visited Samara two years earlier, on the occasion of Shura's wedding, when the last portrait of the entire family was taken (refer to Chapter 3).

Perhaps surprisingly, given the circumstances, Lara stated that she and Taya enjoyed happy childhoods in their home town of Kuznetsk. There was a garden, they had fresh air and they could ride bicycles to get around. The town was small, unlike the big city of Samara nearby, where Grisha and Shura lived. The children were most likely shielded from the political turmoil of the times though Lara acutely remembered some of the consequences. Food was scarce during the 1930's and bread was rationed. Lara recalled *'little Taissia'* taking her *lepyeshka* -bread patty (лепёшка), furtively taking a bite from it then hiding it, believing that it would be all she would get that day. They laughed at her, saying there would be another at lunchtime and more food in the evening. How much more I wondered, when millions across the country were literally starving to death. Lara also recalled the apparently groundless arrests and sudden disappearances of people; the mass arrests and deportations to the *gulags* in Stalin's Russia must have affected a huge number of families.

During the war years everyone was forced to dig trenches in preparation for the German onslaught and they were warned about bombers. Children were taught to recognise the distinctive high pitched sounds of the Fascist planes and run for cover. However, Lara did not say if they were actually bombed in Kuznetsk though Samara, as an industrial centre, may well have been. Certainly they heard German planes overhead and wounded German soldiers were treated in a local hospital. Lara distinctly remembered seeing them with their heads covered in bloody bandages. The family experienced real hunger then - again. As the food situation worsened, many families had to resort to making their *lepyeshki* out of grass and some added potato peelings.

By the time the war began for Russia in 1941, Lara was 18 and had already finished school. Throughout the war years, she worked in a munitions factory, just as women were encouraged to do in England and Germany. At the same time she trained as a bookkeeper / accountant, though her sister tried to convince her to enter medical school. It seems many young people were advised to do so in those years as the USSR was probably desperate for doctors. However, Lara was not inclined that way.

Whilst still in Kuznetsk, they received parcels of clothes and food from their relatives in China, for which they were grateful. Though these simple acts of charity from their well meaning kin did cause them problems. Gifts from abroad were treated with suspicion and Lara's husband Sasha was hauled *'over the carpet'* by the Soviet authorities as a result. Life was made very uncomfortable for them because of their ties with 'foreigners' and perhaps for this reason, amongst others (Lara couldn't say for sure after all these years), Sasha decided to move far away. He decided to move to South Sakhalin, a territory that had been won from Japan after their defeat in World War II. Sakhalin is a large island in the Far East, off the coast of Russia, just north of Japan. The Soviet government encouraged migration to that area to establish it as a Russian settlement and young couples who could breed and therefore *'Russify'* the territory were particularly welcome. Lara was already pregnant at this stage and so they had no problems obtaining permission to move there.

They travelled across Siberia to Vladivostok on the East coast in cattle trucks; about 15 people to a wagon, with cold and hard wooden bunk beds the only concession to human use. Interestingly, it must have been around the same time, in 1946-7, that Nina and Kostya were making their fateful return to Russia, also through Vladivostok. The rest of the family who had fled were now once again uprooting from China to the Philippines and beyond; the respective branches of the family oblivious to the whereabouts of the others.

Lara and Sasha had to endure difficult conditions on that journey. There was no food, water or facilities on the train. They had to carry everything they needed, including their own chamber pots which they used as best as they could in the confined areas. The women put up curtain screens around themselves to use the pots while the men urinated out of the slightly open door. When the train stopped they all rushed out to defecate in nearby fields. Once, Lara very nearly missed the train when it started without her. Luckily the train pulled away very slowly and she was helped up by willing hands. Sasha who had got off to look for her was shouted at to get back on board. Under the circumstances it was perhaps not so surprising that Lara sadly miscarried her baby during the journey. It must have been a terrifying ordeal in the cattle truck. Fortunately, there was an older woman on board with experience in these matters who took the young wife in hand, pushing the others away and curtaining her off for privacy whilst she tended to her. All was fine in the end.

The final part of the journey was made by ship. Lara recalls trying to board the ship from a small motorboat, climbing up the ship's rope ladder – a very daunting experience as both boats moved precariously with the wind and waves. The height of the ship was frightening and she was ordered not to look down as she climbed.

They finally arrived at their destination and were offered rooms in Japanese homes. There was no privacy, the walls were thin and the houses were open plan, which the Russians found unfamiliar. But the local people were remarkably polite, calling Lara *'Madame'*, and so they settled down in this new environment. After six months or so Lara was homesick for her parents and Kuznetsk. She was an independent, spirited and even stubborn young woman as she proclaimed herself. She had agreed to travel with her husband but when things did not work out as she

*Vechislav and Irene, 1954.*

had hoped she was quite prepared to return all that way without him, which she did. However, he soon followed her and once again they lived in her childhood home of Kuznetsk for a while. Over the course of these years Lara and Sasha had two children, Irina born in 1947 and Vechislav two years later.

They could not live long in one place for long it seemed, and this time they decided to migrate to central Asia as Lara described it, to live in Tajikistan. Tajik people were quite welcoming and Sasha quickly succeeded in finding work there, as too did Lara. By 1963 they were on the move again, this time to Latvia, where Sasha's mother and sister lived. They had hoped to move to

*Lara working as a bookkeeper, 1955.*

the capital, Riga, but could only find work in the much smaller city of Liepa. However, they settled down there and Lara grew to like living in this congenial coastal town. The Soviets had established a naval base there after the war and it became a city closed to foreigners. Even other Latvians could not move there – another iron curtain behind *the* Iron Curtain. Here, as in Sakhalin, Russians were again encouraged to settle and Russify the area.

The other sister Taissia had quite different experiences. After the war Taissia, in her 20's, had her heart set on studying medicine in Leningrad. She moved there in 1945, arriving by goods train. She began working and studying in a medical institute and in due course qualified as a doctor. Taissia met Yan in 1954 and they married the following year. Their daughter Anna was born in 1956. She appears to have had a contented childhood and, as an only child, was very close to her parents.

*Taissia working as a doctor, c. 1960.*

Anna provided the following brief history of her father's life, prior to meeting her mother. Yan Yakovlievich Klyuevskiy was born in the Caucasus region in 1914, in the town of Slavyansk, near Krasnodar. He left his homeland, aged 14. One of six children, they were literally starving in 1928 so he went to Rostov where he found work in a tractor factory. (It was believed that tractors were to be the key to modernising agriculture in the new USSR.) He managed to earn enough money to feed himself and send money home to his mother. By 1932 he had moved to Leningrad.

*Taissia and Yan, after their marriage registration, Leningrad, 1955.*

By now committed to Leningrad, Taissia urged her parents to move there as well, quite possibly to help bring up Anna while she worked; a common Russian tradition. Much as they had loved Kuznetsk, Vassili and Klavdia were now the last members of the family living there. Since their other daughter, Lara, was also moving even further west to Latvia at about the same time they agreed to the move.

Somehow they managed to acquire a summer house on the outskirts of Leningrad, which they called *Melnichny Ruchey* (Mill Stream),

249

as there had once been a mill nearby. It was unfinished but Vassili was skilled at carpentry and able to make the necessary additions that would enable them to live in it all year round. They appeared to have been extremely fortunate to have been able to acquire this appealing wooden house and its large plot of land. Perhaps it was considered undesirable because it was in the 'country' and had no facilities; no water, except for a well in the garden, and no sewer. Vassili and Klavdia were in their sixties by then and may already have been pensioners when they moved to the house, so they would have had time to devote both to the house and their granddaughter.

Lara and Sasha's two children, Irina and Vechislav, grew to adulthood in Latvia. Irina, a bright and studious girl, had decided to follow in her aunt's footsteps and study medicine in Leningrad. She moved into the house on the city's outskirts with her grandparents, Vassili and Klavdia, and commuted to and from the city every day, a trip of about two hours. The alternative was student accommodation in the city's universities but it was very poor, students typically sharing four to a room, and a very cold room at that. At least there was some heating in the downstairs rooms of Klavdia's house and perhaps a little more space than Irina would have had in a dormitory.

Lara and Sasha eventually returned from Latvia to nurse her parents in Leningrad, as they grew older. They continued to live in the house at Mill Stream after her parents passed away. It has lots of fond memories for them all. Their son Vechislav remained in Latvia for a while but also returned when his marriage broke up; his ex wife Galina and their son Sergei remained behind in Latvia. As he grew up, Sergei would often travel to Leningrad to keep in contact with his grandparents and Lara doted on the boy. Many family photographs bear witness to the happy times he spent seeing the sights of that great city with his grandmother.

Like people everywhere, my relatives in the USSR tried to live normal lives, maintaining their close family ties as best they could. The clan in Russia were far fewer in number than their counterparts abroad and lived under a shadow of pervasive disquiet. Soviet media encouraged fear of the West which, they were constantly told, was out to destroy their way of life, if not the nation itself. The events of the 1950's and 60's certainly seemed to support this claim.

# The Cold War intensifies.

The division of Germany soon showed the world the clear difference between nations giving their people freedom to trade as they see fit and a command economy where all economic decisions are made by the state. West Germany experienced a phenomenally fast recovery, and the devastation that had been wrought upon the country by continuous allied bombing was nowhere to be seen within a few short years. The people rebuilt their country, transport flourished and West Germans quickly reached a standard of living that was as high, if not higher, then the victorious western powers. East Germany, on the other hand, languished under the dead hand of the Soviet state. Nowhere was the difference as obvious as in West Berlin, that island of capitalism in the sea of Communist East Germany. Throughout the 1950's Berliners could move freely between the two parts of the city and so could see only too clearly the results of the competing ideologies for themselves. 20,000 defected from the East to the West each month and by 1960 two million refugees had fled to the Western part of the city[15], many of them professional and skilled people, causing a *'brain drain'* in the East. It was a particularly embarrassing situation for the Soviets whose propaganda claimed that only their socialist societies catered for the common good, while the heartless capitalist societies resulted in misery and oppression for the workers. Something had to be done.

Stalin died in 1953. He had engendered so much fear among his peers that not one of his associates or doctors dared, or perhaps desired, attend him when he endured his last fateful heart attack, and so he perished alone. It was a fitting end to the tyrant whose actions had led to the deaths of millions of his own countrymen. Yet as a tribute to the success of his propaganda, the country mourned the loss of *'their father'*, no doubt many quite sincerely, clearly oblivious to his inherent evil. At first glance his eventual successor, Khrushchev, appeared to be more approachable, at least to Western eyes. But he too had no intention of allowing Soviet domination to slip, either over his own people or that of its satellite nations. In 1956 a spontaneous, nationwide revolt in Hungary against its Stalinist government and Soviet-imposed policies was brutally suppressed on Khrushchev's orders. Russian tanks rumbled onto the streets of Budapest and in the ensuing fighting 2,500 Hungarians were killed and 13,000 injured[16]. Around 700 Soviet troops also lost their lives, some having been executed for refusing to fight civilians. In the reprisals that inevitably followed, tens of thousands of Hungarians were arrested, imprisoned and deported to the USSR, often on the basis of mere heresay. An estimated 350 were executed and a further 200,000 fled the country. The Cold war continued in earnest. The Soviets were convinced that the West in general and the USA in particular, was determined to undermine and eventually destroy their system of government. The Americans for their part were convinced that the Soviets intended to make the whole world Communist, as indeed Marxist doctrine said would inexorably happen. The tragic irony is that both sides claimed to be acting defensively and in the process came very close to nuclear Armageddon.

The 'problem' of West Berlin's 'brain drain' was resolved when the Soviets decided to erect the Berlin Wall in 1961, a massive concrete wall that completely encircled West Berlin, to prevent East Germans escaping. In fact it was two walls with a deadly corridor between them. Anyone breaching the wall would be shot on sight. It was to remain in place for the next 28 years and become the most potent symbol of the Cold War. A new, young, American president came to Berlin to show his support for the people of Berlin, but Kennedy was not prepared to do anything else. The risk of war was too great. Khrushchev drew the false conclusion that Kennedy could be intimidated and the following year a nuclear holocaust was only narrowly averted in what became known as the *'Cuban Missile Crisis'*.

The Cold War led to the birth of the Central Intelligence Agency (CIA) in America and encouraged the proliferation of thousands of spies on both sides. The CIA's equivalent in the USSR, and its main adversary, was the KGB (being a Western transliteration of the initials of Комитет государственной безопасности, meaning Committee for State Security). The KGB had, at its height, employed over 25,000 people with agents in over 90 countries.[17] In 1962 American spy planes detected the presence of nuclear missiles in Cuba, aimed at America. With additional nuclear material arriving by ship from the Soviet Union, they had the power to destroy cities across the American continent including New York, Washington, Chicago and as far west as California. The prospect was quite simply mind boggling and terrifying. During that fateful last week in October 1962 the world held its breath while the two leaders confronted one another. Khrushchev refused to turn back his armed ships, just days from his bases in Cuba. Kennedy was poised to strike at Cuba but reluctant to give the orders that could begin a third world war and the most frightening one ever known. For the arms race had led to a situation known as MAD, or Mutual Assured Destruction. In the end both sides backed down, each claiming to his people that the other side had. Khrushchev agreed to remove the missile sites from Cuba and Kennedy agreed not to invade the Communist island nation that was uncomfortably close to Florida and the mainland of America. Kennedy also quietly agreed to remove missile sites in Turkey that had threatened Moscow and other Russian cities, the situation which Khrushchev claimed, perhaps justifiably, had provoked the crisis. The world breathed a huge sigh of relief, for there were many on both sides of the Atlantic, who had believed that they would not see November arrive.

Yet there was a positive outcome to the potential holocaust. Both sides recognised that they had responsibilities and should learn to peacefully co-exist. Neither party wanted to use the weapons arsenal at their disposal, and the first treaty banning nuclear testing came into existence. During the 1970's a period of *détente* came into being, a relaxation of tension, which appeared to bode well for future relationships between the superpowers; but it was not to last.

# Chapter 9

# Coming full circle - happy reunions.

# Доброе дело в огне не горит и в воде не тонет.

# *A good deed endures.*

# A Soviet citizen visits Australia.

Contrary to public perception, some Soviet Citizens were permitted to travel outside the USSR and, following a long and drawn-out bureaucratic process, Nina was granted permission to visit Australia in 1970. One can only deduce that to be allowed to visit a 'decadent capitalist country' she must have been considered trustworthy. Consequently, when she arrived in Australia she would not be drawn into political discussions, much to the frustration of her firmly anti-Bolshevik relatives. She would not criticise the system nor show any inclination towards defection, even though it may have been possible should she have expressed the slightest desire. Nina was of course well aware that her beloved husband was still in the USSR and undoubtedly vulnerable. In fact, these were the only circumstances under which Soviet citizens could travel, that is, if a family member remained as a hostage. Nevertheless, there were still many defections. But Nina returned to Kostya after a two month visit, never once betraying either him or the 'motherland' through word or gesture.

Naturally, she had a wonderful time visiting her mother, sister and all those members of the extended Shliapnikoff family living in Sydney. She was wined, dined and feted by each of the respective families, who of course had never expected to see anyone from the Soviet Union again. After 23 years it was a particularly joyful reunion for Zina, delighted to have both her daughters together in the same country. By that time Zina was too frail to live on her own in her large bungalow and had moved in with Julie's family. She had sold the bungalow and used the proceeds to build herself a comfortable self-contained flat on the back of John and Julie's house. Here she believed she could live out her twilight years, in relative independence, with the companionship and security of her children and grandchildren, as was the Russian custom. So John, Julie and Zina welcomed Nina with open arms and tried to make her stay in Sydney as enjoyable and enlightening as possible. Little Michael too, at 10, participated in the round of parties, reunions and visits to places of local interest, the beaches: Manly, Cronulla and Bondi; Sydney Harbour Bridge and Circular Quay. She also saw the El Alamein fountain at King's Cross but one wonders if she realised that the World War II memorial is located in Sydney's red light district.

They also took her further afield to the beautiful Blue Mountains; Katoomba, the peaks of the *'Three Sisters'*, the scenic railway and the cable car over the attractive blue gummed valley. All were obligatory tourist sites for those venturing to the stunning capital city of NSW.

Helen and I were not so involved at the time as we no longer lived at home. Helen was married with three young children and I was at University and living in the Eastern suburbs. However, I do remember being impressed by Nina's hearty and jovial manner, giving the lie to the notion that Soviet citizens were morose and depressed. Her winning smile and eagerness to please charmed everyone, and of course Australia dazzled her, particularly the huge choice of consumer goods. Nina did not cry when visiting a supermarket for the first time but other people from the Eastern bloc had been known to do so. Seeing the wondrous display of food, totally unlike the blandness and lack of variety typical of the USSR at that time, was an overwhelming experience for some.

*Nina (second left) visiting family in Sydney.*

Nina visited the rest of the clan on my mother's side, many of whom had become quite rich by then and lived in comparative luxury. Zina's brother Alexei, who had long since become the patriarch of the family, was retired from his small goods factory and shop, which had seen considerable success as an independent small business in Sydney. Alexei had refined the art of making meat products and his factory produced hams, salamis of all kinds, teawurst, their own mouth-watering pates, frankfurts and many other delectable products. The goods were sold on the site but it was predominantly the wholesale business that became so successful. The *'Burgomaster'* factory in Burwood was clearly visible from the train on the city to western suburbs railway line and became a familiar landmark amongst the Russian community. Alexei and Katya established a fine home in the genteel, leafy suburb of Strathfield, an elegant brick bungalow, not far from the main Orthodox cathedral and enjoyed the fruits of their labour and hard won success. They threw a large party for Nina and she was undoubtedly impressed by the lavish event. Not to be outdone, the eldest son George (Yura), also entertained her in his opulent house in the fashionable suburb of Hunters Hill, on Sydney's waterfront. Whereas his father's house was luxurious in the traditional 'English style'; carpeted, chandeliers and antique furniture (I loved that house), the son's home was modern; polished wood and large glass windows framing a simply breathtaking view, according to my mother. Nina also caught up with an old school friend from her days at *Ecole Remi*, having found that he too lived in Hunters Hill. Another successful businessman, he was engaged in friendly rivalry with Yura over who had the best house, or so it seemed to Nina, who found the whole thing rather amusing, as she related to me many years later.

*The Shliapnikoff clan, Sydney, c. 1968.*

*Back row, from left: Victor and wife Valya; Vadim and wife Vera, Victor (Vera & Vadim's eldest son), Katya and husband George, Volodya with baby Misha and wife Olga.*
*Centre row, from left: Nina (Victor's daughter), Victor (Valya's son), Tony (Victor's son), Vad (Vera & Vadim's second son), Alexei and wife Ekaterina (seated), Nicholas (Katya & George's son).*
*Front row, from left: Kathy (Valya & Victor's daughter), Vovie (Vera & Vadim's youngest son), Tania (Olga & Volodya's daughter).*

Nina returned to the USSR effusively grateful for the hospitality shown her but remained committed to her country of origin. Zina had pleaded with her to apply to emigrate to Australia but she would have none of it. It was clear that she would undoubtedly have enjoyed a more affluent lifestyle in Australia but whether she would have been any happier is another question. Nina clearly belonged to that fortunate group of people who find happiness in whatever situation they find themselves in, within reason.

Nina took great pleasure in receiving members of her extended family in the USSR as, one by one, a few cautious and curious relatives returned to their country of birth. Inspired by her sister's visit only a few years earlier, my mother Julie was the first of our clan to visit the USSR. John and Julie had just made a handsome profit from selling their first home, that wonderful large plot of land in Cabramatta. Though they had not intended to move, particularly since my grandmother had invested her money into their property, the offer was too good to refuse. The suburb was expanding at breakneck speed and many other houses around them had already been sold off for apartment blocks, which were seen as the answer to Sydney's burgeoning population. The street was changing character as yet more waves of new immigrants were pouring in and demanding cheap housing. We watched uneasily as 'low rise' blocks of 10 to 15 flats, for rental or purchase, replaced neighbours' houses. The property next door, inhabited by a single old woman, which comprised a wooden house with a veritable jungle at the back, into which we used to creep surreptitiously to play, was demolished and replaced by such a block. All neighbours' talk was of who could get the best price and from which developer. Families who had 'granny flats' or their married children living in the 'garage'; were offered two apartments in the block that would replace their house.

Zina and my parents went to look at the apartments next door, where an enthusiastic young estate agent tried to convince them to buy two flats, one for them, one for Zina. They could afford two and still have ample money left over from the sale of their house. *This is what the Communists did after the Revolution'*, Zina muttered darkly, if rather over dramatically. *'They took your house away and let you live in one room of it'*. Anyone who has seen *'Dr. Zhivago'* will remember the poignant scene when Yuri returns from the war to his elegant house to find a multitude of tenants occupying it and his family confined to the obligatory number of square metres. *'Much fairer arrangement'* agreed Yuri diplomatically in response to the grim, accusing faces. However, in Australia the redistribution was accomplished through the forces of supply and demand, the only truly equitable method. Unlike Yuri and the thousands of 'bourgeois' individuals his fictitious character represented, my parents were duly compensated for their property. John and Julie bought another house in Cabramatta, further out from the station and with less land; they had no need to be self sufficient in vegetables any more. No sooner had the sale been completed than Julie was planning a world trip. She had many relatives to visit but Nina was naturally her first priority. It was still very difficult to travel to the USSR as an individual but tours were arranged by *Intourist*, the Soviet travel agency, eager to exploit a valuable source of much needed hard foreign currency. Mother found a suitable package tour advertised in the Australian Woman's Weekly.

*Nikolai, the youngest of the Shliapnikoff siblings, visiting his eldest sister Zina at John and Julie's home in Cabramatta, Sydney.*

## Reunions in Russia – the sisters meet again.

After a 43 year absence, Julie finally returned to the country of her birth, which she had last seen as a five year old. She had been in exile in China, then settled into life in Australia; if one can describe their struggle from rented rooms to garage to own house as 'settled'. Her travelling companions were largely middle aged people, many of them of European origin, who were also visiting their countries of birth after many years absence. In addition to visiting the USA and England, the European leg of the tour would take in the Baltic states and so there was a fair contingent of Estonians, Latvians and Lithuanians, who had fled to Australia in the wake of the Soviet take-over of their countries at the end of the Second World War.

The Baltic people were often suspicious, if not hostile, to Russians - with good reason. Their ancient cultures, which had more in common with the Nordic Scandinavians than with the Slav Russians, had enjoyed only a brief period of independence in the inter-war years. Throughout the Second World War they were caught in the middle of vicious fighting between the Nazis and Russians, before finally being 'liberated' by the Soviets. A mixed blessing as one tyrant had simply been substituted for another. Not even granted the pretence of self rule, as the other Eastern bloc countries were, these nations became the Estonian Soviet Socialist Republic, the Latvian SSR and Lithuanian SSR respectively, their governments destroyed and their unique cultures systematically undermined. So there was not much love lost between the Baltic migrants of Australia and Russians. But they had the good sense to realise that their fellow Russian travellers were equally victims of the same regime and bore them no ill will. Julie happily shared her time with a congenial Latvian lady.

Julie, of course, had a wonderful time seeing the sights of Europe and the USA, where she caught up with her cousins Olga and Nicholas Bakaldin and their families in California, as well as her Uncle and Godfather, Nick Hatton, as he now called himself (from Shliapnikoff, as *'shliapa'* means 'hat'). But the fondest reunion was to be with her sister, Nina. Mother's tour would only visit the Russian cities of Moscow and Leningrad (St. Petersburg as it had formerly been known), so Nina arranged to meet her in Leningrad. This she was happily to do, particularly as there were other members of the family to visit there.

Nina travelled overnight, via Kiev, to Leningrad and met Julie at the prestigious four star hotel, the Astoria, where the tour party was staying. Julie and her Latvian friend conspired to smuggle Nina into the hotel initially but when the two sisters tried to leave to visit their other relatives the horrified and officious Intourist guide exclaimed *'You can't go off on your own – it's not permitted!'* But Mother, having breathed free Australian air and secure in her Australian citizenship, scoffed at her and with words to the effect of *'Just watch me'* left to spend a few days with her cousins. She knew when the party was leaving and ensured that she was back in time for the next leg of the journey. Meanwhile, she had a marvellous time exploring the city with her long lost family. She related the story of how she and Nina went into a *Berioska* shop to buy those coveted consumer goods that are only available to tourists paying with 'hard currency' (the dollars or pounds the Soviet economy so desperately needed for international trade). The two women went in, chattering in their native tongue, only to be accosted by another officious lackey. *'Where do you think you're going?'* he rudely demanded. *'This shop is for tourists only.'* Mother drew herself up to her full 5'2" and retorted in her impeccable Russian, *'I **am** a tourist'* and waved her Australian passport triumphantly in his face. He was suddenly all ingratiating smiles and apologies.

Yet this is how Soviet shopkeepers/bureaucrats commonly treat their customers, as anyone who has travelled to the former Soviet Union can testify. The notion of customer service and politeness is a feature of free, competitive economies. It is not that Russians are inherently rude, they are not, but living in a society controlled by fear, where your basic needs are met, whether you put yourself out or not, has resulted in such anomalies. It is interesting to note that when McDonald's opened their first restaurants in Moscow they had to 'teach' their staff to smile at customers. Communism has indeed corrupted generations of Russians and it could be some time before its pernicious influence is eradicated. After the reunification of Germany, West Berliners observed the same phenomena in East Berliners.

When the party travelled on to Tallinn, Riga and Vilnius, the Baltic passengers also temporarily abandoned the trip to indulge in joyful family reunions with their long lost relatives. The Intourist guide ranted and raved in exasperation but could do nothing to stop them.

So Nina had a wonderful time seeing her younger sister again, even enjoying the luxury of a four star hotel, something most Russians could only dream about at that time. She also introduced Julie to the cousins she had last seen when they were all young children. Her only memory of them had been when they were all together for that last family portrait taken in Samara in 1929. The younger generations were not included in that picture but they were playing in an adjoining room. Over forty years had passed but the reunions were heartfelt and genuine. Taissia and Lara, warm and exuberant personalities, much like Nina, were ecstatic to see both Julie and Nina again and they were invited to the suburbs of Leningrad. Here, their Aunt Klavdia and Uncle Vassili still lived in the modest wooden house at Mill Stream, with its lovely large garden where they grew vegetables, kept chickens and lived in rare, private seclusion.

Klavdia was a sensitive and sentimental member of the family. She had cherished her copy of the family portrait until her death. After all, she saw very few members of her family after they left Russia. In 1974, a few years after Julie's visit, Klavdia decided to write down for posterity who they all were and their ages at the time of the photograph. The first part was written when Klavdia herself was 67 and already conscious of life's fragility, though she was to live on for a further twelve years.

The notes read as follows:

*Aunt Klavdia writes,*
        *Friends!*
*Remember the time we passed in Samara and the events we witnessed on the 22nd September, 1929. (The wedding of Shura and Grisha.)*

*Further Aunt Klavdia writes On the 16th of February.*

*45 years have passed since we were photographed. In that year when we were recorded, my parents were – Father – 54, Mother – 49, my eldest sister Zina – 30, Lyosha – 28, Tania – 26, Polya – 24, Klavdia – 22, Lena – 20, Shura – 17, Kolya – 15, sister-in law Katya – 26. The brothers-in-law – Kolya, Peter, Volodya, Vanya, Grisha, I do not know or remember their ages. Vasya was 26. For remembrance, I have written this at the current time, that is 1974 when I reached 67, Vasya 74. In 1972 we celebrated our Golden Wedding anniversary. Our parents have long since died. After them followed from life, Lena, Vanya, Kolya (brother-in-law), Volodya and Lyosha.*

The notes are a poignant testimony to the family's former closeness. Many years later Nina copied Klavdia's notes onto the back of another copy of the photograph and took it upon herself to document the passage of time and lives lost. She added the list of relatives and their dates of death. Klavdia's passing in 1986 is recorded on the fifth line of the list.

*Vassili and Klavdia in Leningrad, c. 1980.*

Nina was to travel to Leningrad several more times after that initial happy reunion with her sister. Olga, from San Francisco, was the next to visit. She had been in close correspondence with Nina for years and often sent her food parcels, for which Nina was very grateful. Olga's brother Nick Bakaldin and his wife Natasha were the next to visit from the USA. Then Olga returned again in the 1990's, this time with her cousin Vera from Sydney, as part of a tour of Churches and monasteries. Each time, Nina would happily embark on the huge overland journey to rendezvous in St. Petersburg. She was more than pleased to do this and it also gave her an excuse to visit her cousins. Besides, nobody could visit her in Dnepropetrovsk. At that time it was a *'closed city'*, one of many the Soviets considered too strategically sensitive to permit entry to foreigners.

*Olga from USA, second from right, with Irina, Vera and Boris in front of Smolny Cathedral, Leningrad.*

*Standing (from left): Yan, Nina, Anna (Yan & Taissia's daughter), Nick, Irina (Alexandra's daughter). Seated: Sergei (Anna's husband), Taissia, Natasha and Lara. Sisters Lara and Taissia are cousins to Nick, Nina and Irina.*

By the late 1990's Nicholas in the USA was the last remaining family member of his generation, the only survivor of the portrait. Four had lived to 1991 but only Alexandra in Samara had witnessed the collapse of the state that had split our family asunder. She was to live but a few months into the new era that saw the implosion of the Communist superpower and the disintegration of the USSR.

*The Russian clan about 1990 - standing (from left): Sergei (Lara's grandson), Irina (Lara's daughter), Boris (Irina's husband), Lara and husband Sasha, Nina and Irina (from Samara); seated (from left): Anna & Sergei, Natasha, Taissia & Yan.*

## The end of the Soviet Union.

In 1979 the Soviet Union invaded Afghanistan, to prop up a Communist regime on its borders, whose leadership had been threatened by extreme Islamic rebels. These rebels, known as *Mujahedin*, were fighting to set up a Muslim state along similar lines to the recently established regime in neighbouring Iran. To do so they would have to destroy the pro-Soviet government. The USSR decided that this would set a dangerous precedent so close to the Soviet Union and sent in thousands of troops, in the false belief that the movement could be quashed comparatively easily, as had been done in Hungary in 1956 and again in Czechoslovakia in 1968. How wrong they were. Despite the deployment of 80,000 Soviet troops by February of 1980[1], it quickly became apparent that this would be far from a simple operation. The Soviet government, now under Brezhnev, had seriously underestimated the skill and determination of the Afghan guerrilla fighters, defending their faith and homeland. They were also aided by soldiers from many other Arabic states, among them a charismatic and determined young Muslim extremist, known as Osama Bin Laden. Moreover, the *Mujahedin* were given financial assistance and support by America, still keen to prevent the extension of Soviet influence anywhere in the world. So with professed good intentions the US government itself indirectly contributed to the rise of Al Qaeda.

The war soon became bogged down in a vicious bloodbath, with atrocities committed on both sides and the young teenage Russian conscripts becoming increasingly disillusioned with their role. As thousands upon thousands of boys perished in the mountains of Afghanistan it began to look more and more like Russia's Vietnam. That is, a war that could not be won, fought by reluctant young men who had no belief in their cause, fighting an unseen enemy using guerrilla tactics rather than open warfare. Throughout the 1980's the war took its toll on the reputation of the USSR and its meagre resources and would ultimately play a large part in its downfall, as indeed did the arms race in general. Détente with the USA broke down irretrievably as the Soviet bear writhed in its final death throes.

In 1985, following the death of three leaders in as many years, Mikhail Gorbachev, a fresh and young leader by Soviet standards, took control of the USSR. Gorbachev realised what dire straits the country was in and attempted what he believed to be the fundamental reforms necessary to improve the situation. The country was absolutely broke. Industrial production was falling, agriculture was inefficient, there were few consumer goods, food was scarce, leadership corrupt and, to cap it all, inflation was destroying the value of the rouble. With little money, they could not maintain the high cost of controlling the eastern European satellites and would have been hard pressed to prevent them gaining their independence, which, unsurprisingly, they kept demanding. There seemed to be no end to the Afghan war in sight and military spending was consuming 25% of the country's budget. The country was clearly bankrupt, the reasons being only too apparent to responsible economic thinkers outside the USSR and perhaps to some thoughtful ones within.

The USSR had been founded on socialist principles that decreed that all people should have the same level of income, so that there should be none of the pernicious class differences that had permitted the existence of rich and poor. Since remuneration was based on need, and people's basic needs are fundamentally the same, there would be no inherent wage differences between a doctor or a cleaner, a maths professor or a waiter. *'From each according to his ability, to each according to his need'*, Marxist doctrine had proclaimed. In practice of course, there was never really equality, for Communist party officials received 'perks' and creamed off what few consumer goods were available for themselves. An elitist system developed with government bureaucrats and high ranking party officers obtaining the best flats, food and luxury *dachas* – holiday homes in the countryside. Corruption flourished, as did the black economy, with scarce goods selling for many times their official price. For no amount of legislation can ever really destroy the market, only drive it underground.

It stands to reason therefore, that with no financial incentive to work harder, many people did only the barest minimum in order to gain their meagre wages. Of course, this is not true of all people and to give Russians their due; they continued to produce fine doctors, mathematicians, indeed scholars and scientists of all kinds. Such people were and are often motivated by personal pleasure, intellectual curiosity or respect for peers; indeed anything but financial inducement. The trouble is that many are not. In a free society we can choose what motivates us and every individual is driven by their own motives. But this is what a command economy fails to recognise and respect. Without financial inducement, business, trade and the accumulation of capital from profit languished. It was only a matter of time before the lack of such capital would impact the economy. The Soviet Union had to rely increasingly on food and technology imports from the west. This had to be paid for in 'hard' currency, dollars or pounds, not the worthless rouble, for a currency is only as strong as the goods or wealth which it represents. Without goods for which there is a demand, or gold, behind it then paper money is just that, paper.

So how did the Soviet Union obtain some of the essential foreign currency it needed to pay for imports? Borrowing was necessary and to reduce the country's debt foreign tourists were encouraged to visit and pay for services in their valuable currencies. *Berioska* shops were established (named after the birch tree - a symbol of Russia), to allow foreigners to buy scarce consumer goods not available to most Russians. Soviet exports, on the other hand, were laughable. Who wanted a Lada car? The Russian people had few consumer goods, but what they did have was strictly price controlled. It was true that rent for the tiny high rise flats that most city people dwelt in was cheap. Transport was subsidised and even the opera and ballet were cheap by western standards. But as that popular saying amongst freedom-loving people goes, TANSTAAFL or *'There ain't no such thing as a free lunch'*. The 'free' goods and services that Russians enjoyed, such as they were, still had to be paid for and the country could no longer afford them.

Such was the state of the nation that Gorbachev inherited. He believed that he could turn the situation around by reforming the country along two parallel principles, *Perestroika* and *Glasnost*. *Perestroika* or *'rebuilding'* the economy aimed to reduce corruption, provide consumer goods, remove central planning and encourage people to do their jobs 'properly', just as Lenin and Mao had been forced to do before him, albeit temporarily. *Glasnost* referred to *'openness'* and would permit more democracy in government, freedom of speech and a leadership that would be open to criticism. Noble intentions which, if carried through to their logical conclusion, must bring down a Communist government because they are essentially incompatible with a command economy. He had unwittingly opened Pandora's box and the outcome was inevitable.

One other factor made a significant contribution to the demise of the Soviet Union. In 1988 Russia celebrated a thousand years of Orthodox Christianity. The millennium celebrations attracted millions of supporters, which was a direct affront to the state and visible evidence of a much deeper legacy than the transient Soviet rule. The celebrations seemed to remind Russia that it was still a Christian country and the cry for religious freedom, as well as political freedom was strengthened.

The first challenges to Gorbachev's authority came from the satellite states who, by the late 1980's, needed little encouragement to throw off the hated Soviet yoke. First in Poland, where waves of strikes by the Polish union *'Solidarity'* eventually led to their union leader becoming leader of a free Poland. When it became clear that the Soviet Union would no longer send in the tanks to suppress popular revolt the remaining states quickly began to throw off their Communist masters; East Germany, Hungary, Czechoslovakia, Bulgaria and finally Romania. In Romania, the hated Stalinist dictator Coucesceau and his corrupt wife were tried and executed on live television. As each nation chose to go 'their own way', the process became known as the Sinatra doctrine, after the famous crooner's song, *'My Way.'* One of the first exit points that had been opened up was the border of Hungary, where guards had literally cut through the wire fence that had formed their section of the 'Iron Curtain.' Almost immediately, thousands of desperate families, many in their own Ladas or Trabants, packed all their belongings in these little cars and fled through the gap to the West. Many others grabbed whatever vehicles that could still move, tractors or trucks, and did likewise. World media showed their jubilation and excitement at finally being able to leave. But the excitement of that exodus paled into insignificance compared to the destruction of that most hated symbol of oppression, the Berlin Wall.

By late 1989, the East Germans had reached boiling point. Having been forced to live apart from their families and friends for so long they were desperate for freedom. The city had been violently split into two by the construction of the wall. Since then, many hundreds had died trying to escape over it to the west. Others had succeeded by tunnelling under it, flying over it in home made kites, balloons, hang gliders, or had been smuggled through checkpoints in furniture, suitcases, under cars - all manner of ingenious contraptions. With Gorbachev proclaiming freedom openly, the East Germans wanted to see this translated into action. When it was announced on live TV that borders would be opened, thousands massed at the checkpoints to see for themselves. It was still barred and the bewildered guards, who had been told nothing, were at a loss. Finally, on the stroke of midnight, the gates opened to scenes of wild delirium. Thousands poured through the gates ecstatic and triumphant. They climbed over the wall, helping each other over amidst tears of joy and happiness. It was a truly momentous occasion and all those who were watching the scenes on television could not fail to be moved. Determined individuals took pickaxes and hammers to destroy this symbol of their enforced imprisonment once and for all. For that is how it must have felt to the people of East Germany, that they had finally been let out of prison.

The end of the wall meant not only that Germany would be reunited, but that all the countries behind the Iron Curtain could now experience the freedom they so desperately craved. The following month, the leaders of the two superpowers, Gorbachev and President Bush, met and declared the Cold War officially over. Events may not have unfolded as the Russian leader had expected, but nonetheless, it was a great triumph for this charismatic and dynamic reformer.

The Soviet Union's domination over Eastern Europe had evaporated and it now had to concentrate on achieving the reforms that Perestroika and Glasnost had promised. But Gorbachev found that he had unleashed forces beyond his control. Following the example of the satellite countries, the 15 Soviet Socialist Republics that made up the USSR declared their independence. But Gorbachev's harshest critics would come from his own state, amongst them Boris Yeltsin, the first President of the Russian Soviet Federated Socialist Republic and the first popularly elected President in Russian history. He condemned Gorbachev for being too slow with the pace of reform. Yet diehard Communists feared the changes and attempted a coup in August 1991, which was only put down with the help of Yeltsin, who emerged from the fiasco as the popular figure of the moment. Eventually, with the disintegration of the USSR effectively stripping him of his authority and power, Gorbachev was forced to resign as leader of the defunct state. Yeltsin, as leader of the new Russian Federation, promised an end to Communism, the introduction of democracy and a free market economy. The Communist era in Russia had finally come to an end after 74 years. As a political system, Communism had been incontrovertibly proven to be morally and economically bankrupt.

## 1992 - A year of change for Russia and my first visit.

In the first year of Yeltsin's rule, between 1991 and 1992, 82,000 state-controlled companies were privatised and 42% of Russian workers became employed by private companies.[2] Initially, the privatisation process was carried out by distributing shares to a company's employees. Price controls were removed for most goods, enabling profits to be made, and shops began to stock goods. As was to be expected, with prices no longer restricted or subsidised, they rose by 250%.[3] To buy basic necessities, many people sold their shares to those with money, hence the rise of the oligarchs. Some of these financial magnates also gained huge windfalls from their political connections.

*Mikhail Sergeyevich Gorbachev.*

The changes were moving at breathtaking speed and there was, naturally, resentment and conflict. Yeltsin also faced opposition from old Communists in the Russian parliament, though the party's power had been broken. When they tried to thwart his reforms the following year, he dealt with them in a fashion that was thoroughly undemocratic, though recognisably Russian. He simply shelled the Parliament building until they capitulated. In subsequent years Yeltsin's enormous popularity was to decline as he battled to transform the nation and his own alcoholism – ultimately the attempt was to break him as well. He resigned his office on the 31st December 1999 and died seven years later, aged 76.

Years of stagnation could not be reversed overnight, as Russians found to their dismay and disappointment. 'Freedom', far from bringing instant prosperity, created a sense of anxiety, insecurity and in many cases, despair and hardship. Whilst many welcomed the opportunities a freer economy brought, others found the whole process alien and impossible. After all, for years they had been provided with basic necessities, not much to be sure, but enough to survive on. Now, it seemed this was under threat. For those who lost their life's savings or their uneconomic jobs, it must indeed have been a difficult time. Moreover, in the absence of an effective legal and judicial system, endemic corruption did not disappear. On the contrary, it was exacerbated as Party officials and bureaucrats simply took over former state run concerns, in many cases merely substituting a state monopoly for a private one. Although many new managers became fantastically wealthy very quickly they were more thief than entrepreneur. Little wonder then that 'Mafia' gangs quickly emerged, using violence and intimidation to protect 'their' turf and demand a cut of even legitimate business.

There was no precedent for dismantling such a monolithic state and so Russia's transition was always likely to be difficult and fraught with problems. Most would agree, however, that an effective system of law is vital to the process. Businesses, as well as individuals, require stability and recourse to an impartial third party to settle disputes regarding fraud, theft, breaking of contracts and such like. That degree of law and order seemed a long way off in the early 1990's.

Notwithstanding Russia's inherent problems, some advances have clearly been made and I can offer some personal observations. I had been keen to visit Russia for a long time, to see for myself the country of my roots, visit relatives and observe the impact of Communism first hand.

My mother had been warmly welcomed in Leningrad and I knew that same welcome awaited me too, especially from my aunt Nina and her cousins.

So in 1992 I finally ventured to Russia for the first time. That year had been particularly difficult, with sudden dislocation of the economy and it was far too early to see any signs of improvement. Sure enough, the decrepit state department store *GUM* limped along with near empty shelves and products of dubious quality. Food was scarce, especially meat, and lard was commonly used as a substitute. Indeed I saw butchers' shops stocked high with boxes of lard and a friend staying with a family was served it as a main meal – with sour cream yet. St. Petersburg (recently reverted to its former name by a narrow vote of its citizens) was more dismal than Moscow and even tourists could not find takeaway food at any price. I searched in vain and found one grotty little shop selling fried sausage on black bread, enormously popular judging by the queues. None of this came as a surprise but even then there were positive signs. Littlewoods had just opened a branch and locals were queuing to buy British clothes. The first McDonald's had opened in Moscow, though mostly aimed at tourists as few Russians could afford their prices. Nonetheless, the queues of curious locals had stretched around the block, though they were probably disappointed when they received their order. We heard of one poor man who had stood in line for some time to buy the one basic hamburger that no doubt took a fair chunk of his salary. He took it home carefully to share with his family, where the wife meticulously cut it into quarters so all could have a try. They probably wondered what all the fuss was about.

By fortunate coincidence the tour I was travelling with would first take me to St. Petersburg, where my mother's cousins lived. My aunt Nina lived far away in the south in the Ukraine but she arranged to make the lengthy train journeys to meet me and introduce me to the rest of the clan.

Taissia lived with her husband Yan in a flat in the city. It was there that I ventured for my first reunion with the family, something I had been eagerly anticipating for some time. I remember tentatively knocking on the door, unsure if I had the right place. The door opened and I was greeted by a beaming, larger than life Aunt Nina, whom I had known from her visit to Australia many years before. There was no mistaking her, and she proudly introduced me to the rest of the clan. The members of both families had turned out for this rare visit of someone from the west. The little lounge/dining room was filled to capacity but they warmly welcomed my companion, the host of the *'home stay'* I was staying at, who had insisted on accompanying me to this hard to find corner of St. Petersburg. The table was attractively set with as much finery and good food as could be mustered: Russian pies – my favourite, alongside vegetable salads, *zakuski*. We passed a convivial if noisy few hours, with much animated conversation, laughter and questioning on all sides. Taissia and Yan's daughter, Anna, was there with her husband Sergei and newborn son, Slavik. As was Aunt Lara, her daughter Irina and her husband Boris. Only Lara's husband, Uncle Sasha, was missing, possibly being too frail or unwilling to travel into the city. Uncle Yan was certainly there and (gently) reprimanded me for wearing jeans. Not that he was concerned that I wore them to his home but because I admitted to having been that morning to the Hermitage, the famous art gallery, and previously the Tsar's winter palace. Apparently that did not show due respect for St. Petersburg's finest treasure, and I duly accepted the reproach from my host who had obviously gone to great pains to entertain. Russians tend to dress well in public and I was clearly not pulling my weight as a 'rich' westerner. As for me, I was more concerned to be warm and comfortable in this bitterly cold spring April, when the snows were just melting and icy mud and slush lay everywhere.

Nonetheless, when I went to visit Uncle Sasha in the outer suburbs of St. Petersburg a few days later, I took care to wear a smart skirt, tights and shoes. What a mistake. The freezing wind whistled round my legs as I stood waiting for the train at *Finlandski* station. The very train that carried Lenin back to Russia after the first revolution was still there, complete with commemorative plaque. I am no lover of Lenin, but it was still exciting to see such an important historical artefact before my very eyes. The train was late, so I had plenty of time to satisfy my curiosity and chat to Aunt Nina. The journey itself was comfortable and I caught glimpses of the *'Road of Life'*, or signs to it. That famous lifeline across Lake Ladoga that brought food to the besieged Leningraders during the three bitter years of encirclement during World War II.

We eventually arrived at the little station in the woods near to my Aunt Lara's house. I was very excited to see this house, partly because my mother had told me so much about it from her visit, but also because it was so refreshing to see some real Russian countryside after the hustle and bustle of the cities. I was to taste rural life very quickly however. There was no raised platform at the station so we descended from the high steps of the train to ground level, causing some inconvenience to a not-so-lithe Aunt Nina. Then we had to walk across the tracks and along a muddy unpaved road for some distance through the woods. On a sunny day it would have been a delightful walk amongst the pines and silver birches, but negotiating those icy paths in my flimsy shoes was both treacherous and very cold. Nina, in true Russian stoic tradition, thought nothing of it and even managed to work up a sweat.

We were greeted with characteristic Russian warmth and hospitality by Aunt Lara, Uncle Sasha and their daughter Irina, the dining table having already been laid out with a simple but wholesome meal. But first there was the outhouse to negotiate. I had not seen an outside loo since my childhood in Australia, with the possible exception of backpacking in Asia where one could expect anything. But this was very much like the Australian version, and my hosts were very gratified to hear me say so. We washed our hands from a simple bucket and plunger tap, with water from the garden well. We then sat down to enjoy a convivial supper, Uncle Sasha commenting that I did not seem to be sufficiently warmly or sensibly dressed for their climate! The house did not disappoint. A traditional two-story wooden structure with a wood-burning stove in the corner of the living room and a closed chimney that extended the full height of the house. I believe, in theory at least, the stove could heat the top floor as well but it would have been expensive and so that floor was only used in summer. Lara and Sasha lived in three comfortable ground floor rooms all year round, but in summer the house also served as a *dacha* (holiday cottage) for the other members of the family. It must have been far from comfortable in the depths of winter but they must have considered it preferable to the lack of privacy typical of small town flats.

On a first visit it hardly seemed appropriate to discuss politics, and in the few short hours available to us we were happy to talk about our families and general social chit chat. They gave little away about their own conditions, though Lara and Sasha appeared to live more spartan lives than their counterparts in the city. Even the dinner table had more frugal fare, though they had clearly tried their best. I had a wonderful time in their company and all too soon it was time to return to my 'home stay' in the city. I was staying in an attractive flat belonging to Vladimir and Lyuda, who were paid to accommodate foreigners. They were a charming couple and more forthcoming about the situation in their country. They did not seem unduly alarmed by the galloping inflation, though they did comment wryly, almost jokingly, about the bag of money needed to buy a bag of sugar. They were obviously quite privileged themselves, having a large three room flat, from one of which they could generate income. Most other Russians, however, were not nearly so fortunate and expressed their discontent quite publicly.

Out on the streets the next day, I stumbled quite by accident upon a pro-Communist demonstration. There had been a pro-Yeltsin demonstration only that morning, with supporters showing their loyalty to the president in the face of ever increasing criticism. A peaceful, happy show of solidarity I was told, with music and singing. I had heard people say later that, yes, the transition had been hard, but a necessary economic pill they had to swallow. Yeltsin at least had made it more 'bearable'. The demonstration I saw, by contrast, was bitter and hostile. Many of these people were understandably angry at the sudden devaluation of the rouble, which had destroyed their savings and pensions. But there were many others who could not relate to the new economy and who saw competition as a threat to their lives. They looked back to a Communist past which they believed, as they had been taught, would always take care of them. It did not surprise me to see Lenin pictures amongst the banners but an alarming number carried Stalin's portrait as well. Surely enough of his infamous exploits would be common knowledge by now, I thought. But no, people believe what they want to believe, against all evidence to the contrary. I mingled with the crowd trying to pick up as much of their mood as possible. The red flag flew uncomfortably close, even blowing into my face and against my mouth at one point! Never in my wildest dreams did I imagine myself to be present at such a gathering. I resisted the temptation to spit it out. Regrettably now, I also refrained from taking photographs. But since the atmosphere was hostile, I did not want to draw attention to myself – this was no time for holiday snaps.

Despite my reluctance to be in such company, I recognised the unique historical moment and longed to stay. Nonetheless, I tore myself away to meet people with whom I had made prior arrangements. As a member of a *'Good Will'* tour, an association created during the Cold War to foster British/Soviet relations, I was in the company of a diverse mix of British students, journalists and academics. A packed and very interesting itinerary had been arranged for us, and we met Russians from different levels of society. A particularly memorable experience was a meeting with senior Russian economists, who quite frankly seemed baffled by the current economic situation. Nothing taught to them in their Marxist view of history had prepared them for the new Russia.

On another occasion we were given the opportunity to visit a warehouse of space rockets and memorabilia of the space race, abandoned during the political turmoil and closed to the general public. There I was actually able to climb inside the very space capsule that had returned the last cosmonaut of the Union of Soviet Socialist Republics, Krikalev, back to Earth.

*Inside Krikalev's space capsule, 1992.*

All in all, it had been a fascinating trip and a veritable eye opener into my parents' homeland. I was eager to return!

# Chapter 10

# Russia and China moving into the 21st century.

## Что прошло, того не воротишь.
## *What has passed cannot be returned.*

# China – post 1980's, from doom to boom.

China had seen momentous changes since the departure of our relatives. The nation had embraced Communism and found, after the dismal 'Great Leap Forward' had resulted in mass famine and the so called 'Cultural Revolution' had wrought havoc, that violence and death were the only victors. A drastic U-turn was required to change China's fortunes.

With Mao's legacy increasingly abandoned during the 1980's and 90's, reforms were introduced to establish *'Zones of Free Enterprise'*. Initially in a few restricted areas, they steadily extended across China. The reforms quickly led to an improvement in the standard of living of many Chinese people and today, in the 21st century, a booming middle class is emerging; demanding, producing and purchasing consumer goods of all types. In fact, the speed with which the Chinese economy, at least in the cities, has been transformed has been phenomenal.

In 1983 when I visited the country for a month (en route from Australia to England where we had decided to settle) there was still little evidence of progress. There were markets in the larger cities where farmers from the country brought their surplus produce to sell, as much as they could physically carry on the back of a bicycle, which could be an enormous load nonetheless. Ubiquitous restaurants fared well, particularly for the fledgling tourist market, though visitors were not yet encouraged, except as members of organised and comparatively expensive package tours. All the more opportunity to make them part with valuable foreign currency. But we chose to travel independently, to see as much of the country as we could in the time available, recognising that travelling by public trains was inevitably going to be time consuming. We, being my husband, our one year old son Daniel and myself, embarked on this mini adventure after first having spent time in Hong Kong.

Hong Kong was a vibrant and exciting city and we thoroughly enjoyed ourselves, observing the frenetic hustle and bustle of its unique blend of East and West. For Hong Kong, until 1997, was a British *Crown Colony*, administered by a British appointed governor under English law. Like Shanghai in the 1930's, Hong Kong was dynamic, innovative, enterprising, colourful, exotic and supremely successful. If some chafed at 'foreign' rule, the vast majority simply ignored the British presence; Chinese industrial magnates no doubt benefited from their association with their British, and indeed international, counterparts. The myriad skyscrapers bear witness to the success of this tiny capitalist island, which had no natural resources beyond a deep harbour, no foreign aid, no reason to be wealthy at all, except by the industry of its inhabitants, living under a relatively benign government. Hong Kong flourished as a gateway between East and West trade, certainly aided by the light tax burden imposed on its companies. Of course, not everyone was wealthy. As in any free society, there will always be winners and losers. For every *tai-pan* enjoying the fruits of his success in the night-clubs, luxurious hotels and golf clubs, there were hordes of poor Chinese eking out an existence in a sweat shop or noodle stall. Yet even they appeared to be grateful to live in this bustling metropolis where they were at least free to pursue their dreams. One only has to look at the constant battle fought by the authorities to repel illegal immigrants from mainland China to appreciate its appeal.

In this inspiring city, we marvelled at the colour, the noise, the traffic (so many cars and yet nowhere to drive) and the seemingly endless shopping opportunities - from the enormous department stores to glamorous boutiques and tiny craft stalls in dingy allies. There was no shortage of ways to

*The 'Jumbo' restaurant, Hong Kong Harbour.*

part people from their money, locals and travellers alike. When one tired of the hectic activity, one could escape to the surrounding islands by ferry, admiring the Chinese sailing junks on the way, where a peaceful wood or beach awaited. In the city, we were struck by how sophisticated, urbane, chic and simply beautiful the Chinese women were. No different, of course, than people in any big city and I make the point not to be patronising in any sense but simply because all this was to disappear the moment we crossed the border into the Republic of China.

Suddenly, the glamour, sophistication, enterprise and energy evaporated into thin air. We had expected the skyscrapers, the visible symbols of capitalist enterprise, to disappear but we had not expected such an obvious and marked difference in the *physical* appearance of the people. For the oriental beauty of Hong Kong had vanished in this land of drab, colourless beings. Men and women alike dressed in the same sexless blue uniforms, their faces devoid of make-up, colour and oftentimes, even

281

expression. Here were a people still living under a totalitarian regime, forbidden to work, except where the state decreed, forbidden to live, except where the state assigned you a home, forbidden to speak or even dress freely. And it showed. It showed in their faces - submissive, beaten, wary and most apparent, with the women, lacking in femininity. Indeed, quite often we simply could not tell women from men. In the past, Chinese women paid bitterly for being the 'weaker' sex, abandoned to die, sold as slaves, crippled for life by the cruel practice of foot binding, and to give the Communists their due, the lie of 'equality' had at least raised the status of women. But at what price we asked ourselves, gazing at these asexual creatures, so different from their sisters in Hong Kong.

But the human spirit cannot be beaten and even in this oppressive society we found instances of warmth, generosity and courage. We had been warned not to travel independently, the authorities telling us that China was not welcoming to, or geared up for, individual travellers. Certainly it was not easy and we had to argue long and hard to buy tickets and arrange accommodation. But throughout our journey we found that obstinate officials would suddenly relent when we perched a blonde baby on their desks, their faces breaking into welcoming smiles. Indeed, our child enabled us make contact with local people far more readily than we would otherwise have been able to do. It may seem difficult to believe now but millions of Chinese people had never seen a blonde, blue eyed baby before and it was hard not to laugh when they quite literally fell off their bicycles at this strange sight. Simply walking along a public street became an adventure as people craned their necks to look at us, and the moment we stopped we would be instantly surrounded by a curious, but polite, throng of people pointing and gaping at this unusual phenomenon. Some would push their own children forward and take a photograph of East meets West, usually accompanied by much laughter and general appreciation. In fact photography, or more accurately, taking photographs of each other with ancient cameras, was a popular pastime.

Few spoke English and Cantonese or Mandarin was just too daunting for us to attempt, but we did meet one intrepid man who spoke beautiful English, having learned it by listening to the BBC world service. He was a delightful host and a mine of information; he gave us a grim insight into the reality of living in China at that time. He told us how he was a graduate whose outspoken comments had consigned him to work six days a week in an iron foundry, which he hated. He had taken us to some gardens that weren't open to the public, negotiated our entry and was then mysteriously man-handled away. We sincerely hope that he did not have to pay a heavy price for his 'indiscretion'. Another amazing individual we met who spoke good English was a traditional Confucian scholar. His long, flowing moustache marked him out almost as much as our own appearance. He proclaimed to the large crowd that we were *'from the land of Shakespeare'* and had *'honoured China by bringing a child'*. Following which everyone smiled at us and applauded enthusiastically, much to our bemusement as he had not yet translated what he had said.

*Promenading on the Bund in Shanghai, 1983.*

A waiter at one restaurant was so enchanted by Daniel that he begged to be able to show him off to the cooks in the kitchen, at least that's what we think his sign language was trying to convey. Reluctantly I agreed and handed over my son. The minutes seemed to stretch forever and I was beginning to panic. After what seemed like an eternity he returned, in the arms of the cook, smiles from ear to ear all round as our little boy turned up sporting a traditional pigtail!

In Beijing we pushed the buggy up the Great Wall of China, or at least the segment open to the public. Once again, we were besieged by curious onlookers, many just as intrigued by our ultra lightweight, state of the art

*McLaren* buggy that folded neatly into an umbrella as the child. For the majority of young children we saw were transported en-masse in a curious affair made from bamboo and resembling a small cage on wheels. Anything up to half a dozen toddlers stood, clinging to the sides, being pushed by what we presumed to be a state nanny. In an effort to reduce the burgeoning population the all-pervasive state had decreed that families in the cities could only have one child each, though country folk were permitted a licence for more, providing they paid extra for the privilege. Special 'spies' were employed to seek out women who dared to have more than one and state sponsored abortions were not only encouraged but sometimes inflicted right up to full term of pregnancy. Generations of children have grown up without siblings, uncles or aunts, and the old prejudice against women

has once again reared its ugly head, as countless little girls were mysteriously 'stillborn' so that their parents could try again for a boy.

On a practical note, it was impossible to buy disposable nappies in China. Their children wore split pants that simply separated when the child squatted. I must admit the idea seemed quite tempting initially, until that was I saw an infant relieve itself on its doting parent.

Whenever possible we travelled by public transport as it affords an ideal opportunity to meet local people, especially on longer journeys. By and large the Chinese rail service was not

*Pushing the McLaren
up the Great Wall of China.*

bad, used as it was by vast numbers of people; private car ownership being virtually non existent at that time. Sadly, the dour and unresponsive high ranking soldiers we shared a compartment with on the overnight journey from Shanghai to Beijing not only glared at us the entire time but hardly even spoke to one another. On another occasion, we were forced to take an internal flight when no alternative was available. However, it quickly became apparent that this was a mistake, for we really did feel we were taking our lives in our hands. We took off into a severe storm that lasted for hours and I have never seen such abject fear as I saw on the faces of the passengers and crew packed into that little plane as it was buffeted from side to side. China, like all Communist states, is officially atheistic, but it seemed to us that many of these passengers were praying. State control of the media means they do not have to report crashes and we wondered nervously how many such planes simply disappeared without trace. After an interminably long journey we touched down in Shanghai to great relief and joy. We were very fortunate that the plane was a British built Trident and wondered if the Russian planes the Chinese also bought would have withstood such a battering. In later years, when I travelled to the Soviet Union on their national airline, *Aeroflot*, shoddy workmanship and poor engineering would be evident as the plane roared and rumbled into the sky. Not for nothing was it known as *'Aeroflop'*.

Travelling in China in the 1980's was certainly an eye-opener in many respects, and a far cry from the country that my parents knew in the 1930's and 1940's.

In the years following our visit, China moved with considerable speed towards a freer and less economically regulated state, ironically under the auspices of the still dominating Communist party. It has become far more prosperous as a result, but human rights, political freedom and freedom of speech remain firmly stifled. Even the economic progress has not been without trauma, as competing ideologies came face to face with each other. For example, there had been reports that the freeing of restrictions on farming, specifically the right to earn profits from surplus produce, had allowed some more enterprising farmers to become hugely successful. Suddenly the old spectre of 'inequality' re-emerged. A development that a generation of Chinese, raised on communist propaganda, considered inherently evil and something that should be stamped out. We heard, sadly, how such people were beaten up, sometimes even killed by their less successful 'comrades'. Envy can be very vicious indeed.

Following the break up of the Soviet Union in 1989, Chinese students optimistically believed that the time was ripe for political reform in their country too, and staged huge peaceful demonstrations in Tiananmen Square in Beijing. In the world's largest public square, where displays of military might and mass displays of collective 'harmony' had been showcased under the watchful eyes of Chairman Mao, thousands of students gathered to peacefully ask for democracy and greater freedom. In response, many hundreds, possibly 2,500 according to the Chinese Red Cross, were gunned down in full view of the world and their appalled countrymen. Economic freedom notwithstanding, China was still a totalitarian state.

In light of these events, the return of Hong Kong to Chinese rule in 1997 had been greeted with dismay by many of its residents, who clearly preferred to live under liberal British law than restrictive Chinese communist rule. As with Shanghai in 1949, there had been a frantic departure of wealthy Chinese, with much gold undoubtedly spirited away by people who desperately sought ways and means to escape the country before it was swallowed up by the mainland. Much of the small nation's five million plus population had fled China as refugees during the 1950's, 60's and 70's and clearly did not wish to return. A privileged few received British citizenship, others succeeded in emigrating to Australia or the USA. But the vast majority had to take their chances with the new regime and hope that it would keep its promise to Britain, as part of the take-over deal, that its way of life would be preserved.

To give the Chinese authorities their due, they appear to have adopted a gradualist approach to the incorporation of the island, no doubt reluctant to destroy the 'golden goose'. It continued and expanded its role as the commercial powerhouse of the region, stimulating and developing trade between the expanding number of free economic zones in China and the rest of the world. Some claim that the island has indeed become impoverished, and there are still elements who lament the loss of their democratic freedoms. But on the whole it appears that the transition was not as devastating as it could have been. The once obvious distinctions between the two 'nations' now appear to be blurring and this is due to the enormous changes taking place in China itself.

It is undoubtedly true that an economic revolution has taken place in China towards the end of the second millennium. The right to trade for profit, which the Chinese communist party has paradoxically embraced, resulted in an unprecedented upsurge in economic activity. Small businesses have flourished, some undoubtedly becoming large concerns as international investment increased, with foreign companies

*Nantao, the 'old city' regenerated.*

keen to take advantage of the huge labour market of the most populous nation on earth. The results, at least in the major cities of Shanghai and Beijing, have been phenomenal. The shabby and decrepit cities we saw 20 years ago have metamorphosed into gleaming metropolises of high rise skyscrapers, shopping malls, glamorous night-clubs, restaurants and boutiques. Shanghai is once again regaining its pre-war image as a vibrant, exciting, pleasure loving city, but on a much grander scale.

China's transformation was irresistible to me and in 2007 I stopped over on my way to visit Australia for John's 80th birthday. Shanghai did not disappoint. The colonial buildings of the historic Bund are well preserved and on the opposite bank of the Whangpoo river, in the former derelict district of Pudong, stand the gleaming new skyscrapers, including the iconic Oriental Pearl Tower. Shanghai Municipal Council is conscious of its heritage and, to its credit, there were lots of fascinating museums, one of the best being in the basement of the Oriental Pearl Tower.

*Pudong, Shanghai, 2007.*

I hired a young Chinese student as a guide/translator and armed with my old Shanghai map (seen Chapter 5) and a modern one, courtesy of *Lonely Planet*, we tracked down my family's Chinese past. We succeeded in not only finding Route Vallon, now Nanchang Road, in the former French Concession, but the very house that my grandmother Zina had owned - Number 89. I was delighted to discover that the whole area, far from being demolished as I had feared, is actually being regenerated as a cosmopolitan enclave. Trendy boutiques and cafes are reviving the once neglected area and the leafy ambience of the 1930's is still evident.

*No. 89 Route Vallon, the house that Zina owned in the 1930's.*

*Nanchang Road today.*

For my last night I splashed out on a relatively expensive hotel, the Rui Jin Guest House, a gardened complex in the former French Concession, with buildings of historic significance. It turned out to be the former Morris estate, home to the editor of the North China Daily News in the 1930's (17 The Bund). Some of our family's wedding parties had even been photographed by journalists from his newspaper. Later the estate became the Mayor's residence and many notable dignitaries stayed there when visiting China, including Richard Nixon. On checking in I found that I had been upgraded to the suite that Chiang Kai Shek had stayed in. (Tricky Dicky's was next door.) In fact, Chiang had married Madame Kai Shek in the beautiful lobby downstairs so this may well have been their honeymoon suite. Their wedding photograph adorned the reception area of the suite and a plaque outside the rooms commemorated their stay.

My all too brief stopover had been truly memorable. I had walked the streets where my relations had lived, and where many, like my parents, had grown up, fallen in love and married. And I was able to take to Australia pictures of buildings and areas which members of their generation could identify and remember.

*Oriental Pearl Tower, Shanghai.*

Capitalists are now officially permitted to join the Communist party. Whatever next? China's embrace of free markets, even partially, must have die-hard Communists writhing in agony. But they still have a considerable grip on the country. A successful businesswoman declared in a western television interview that she loved China and the Chinese Communist party! This fashion designer who owned her own business was clearly prospering as Chinese women in their millions clamour to replace Mao's peasant garb with the latest fashion styles. Yet the spectre of Tiananmen Square still haunts the people of China and encourages them to at least pay lip service to the Party. So they prudently call this increasingly competitive society 'Communism' and remain tight lipped about the lack of political freedom. Increasingly, young people have become disenchanted with politics anyway. Like youth everywhere, given half the chance, they want to have a good time, look smart, enjoy themselves and, above all, crave money, as they freely admit themselves. A free(er) market economy has given them that opportunity.

Of course, not all people seek material wealth, whether Chinese or otherwise. Man is a complex being with spiritual needs as well and it is undoubtedly true that for many people such needs are far more important than possessions. The Communist Party of China now appears to reserve its greatest wrath for those who wish to pursue religious freedom. So the grip of the state is still heavy on dissent, judging by the brutal suppression of the *Falun Gong*, a benign, peaceful religion. Harsh persecution, including torture, is now reserved for its practitioners rather than economic dissidents; for sound reasons by the logic of those in power, as it is here the state will face the greatest defiance. After all, people will not die for the right to eat at McDonald's, but they will to practice their faith.

The only solution to seemingly irreconcilable aims is to recognise and uphold the freedom of the individual to engage in any activity that does not impact anyone else without their consent. Thus, the freedom to practice any religion or none at all, the freedom to pursue material wealth – honestly, without fraud, or the freedom to practice charity – sincerely, without force. After all, compassion is only meaningful if given voluntarily. Are these Western liberal values? Yes, but not exclusively. Liberty is founded on basic humanitarian principles that apply to individuals of all nations, races and faiths. The right to life, liberty and yes, property, the fruits of one's labour. Those peoples and nations that recognised this in the past have advanced. The same will hold true in the future. Chinese people, at long last, have taken the first steps towards liberty in their own country. Let us hope for their sake and ours that they can continue.

## Nina's friends in the former USSR.

As China was opening up, so too was the former Soviet Union and I was very keen to return when the opportunity arose. I particularly wanted to visit my congenial aunt Nina again. She had always enjoyed seeing her cousins in Leningrad, especially if it coincided with the visit of foreign relatives, but by 1998 she was too ill to make the long and tedious journey from the Ukraine. By that time Dnepropetrovsk, in the newly independent republic of the Ukraine, was no longer closed to Westerners and so I was able to visit her in her hometown. Whilst there, I was honoured to meet some of Nina's friends, many of whom had also left Shanghai back in 1947, and all of whom had an interesting tales to share.

One such friend was Ida Nizewicz neé Belkin, born around 1930 in Shanghai she was a little younger than Nina. She had attended the same school, *Ecole Remi*, as my mother's generation and fondly remembered my mother and aunts and uncles. Very few Western tourists travelled to Dnepropetrovsk and so these ex-Shanghai residents felt very isolated from the rest of the world and Ida was keen to relate her story and delighted to be reminded of her happy childhood.

Her father was a photographer and photojournalist, who worked with Shanghai's foreign community, particularly the Americans and English. He was quite well known and certainly well patronised by Russian friends wanting family portraits or to record special occasions. Business had declined during the war years and after the war he saw no prospect of improvement now that most of the international settlement were preparing to leave. So when the Soviets called on the stateless Russians to return and help rebuild 'their' country Ida's father was seduced by their plea. Perhaps he should have suspected something was amiss when all the children, his daughters Ida and Irina among them, were separated from their parents and sent back on the first ship. Ida believes they did this to ensure that their parents would not change their minds. The ship made six journeys in all, shuttling returnees from Shanghai to the Russian port of Vladivostok.

Upon arrival in the USSR their father was promptly arrested for the 'crime' of fraternising with foreigners. It had been barely two years since the collapse of the wartime alliance between the USA and the Soviet Union and the two countries were by then locked in the potentially deadlier Cold War era. The Soviet regime did not believe it could take the risk of allowing 'tainted' citizens to spread American ideas, and so he had to be sacrificed. He was to die in the hostile conditions of the camps in some frozen wasteland. The rest of the family, like Nina, were initially exiled to an isolated village until they had 'earned' the right to live where they wanted, whereupon they also chose Dnepropetrovsk. Ida's sister Irina married a doctor called Boris, who was also arrested upon their return to the USSR, but luckily he managed to survive the camps. Interestingly, their son Sasha grew up to become a successful businessman, one of the breed of *'New Ukrainians'*, who, like the *'New Russians'*, knew how to survive in the freer post-communist economic climate. Ida believes he is quite wealthy and helped his mother financially until her death, though he is now estranged from the rest of the family. Ida is bitter about her parents' decision to return to the USSR and laments the fact that she never had the opportunity or means to leave the country in which she has always felt trapped.

Her husband's Joseph's story is even more poignant. He is the son of a Ukrainian woman and a Polish man, who had left the USSR to live and work in France. Joseph was born and spent his first 16 years there, considering himself French, of Slavic extraction. His parents' decision to return to the USSR may have been prompted by the Nazi conquest of France. Whatever the reason it had serious repercussions on Joseph's life. Not only does he have to endure living in a country where he feels alien, but also had to spend much of his life convincing others he was not a foreign spy! He had few decent job opportunities and was forced to work in manual labour, such as mining. However, like all Soviet citizens, he still had to do the compulsory military training and spent three years in the army. He related the story of how he returned home triumphantly after two years, having won a driving competition. He had a wonderful incentive to win – his wife had just given birth to their daughter.

His daughter, Katya, is now married to a General in the Army and they live in Armenia. It shows how times have changed, Joseph commented wryly; previously a high ranking officer could never have married the daughter of someone 'tainted' like himself. Ida and Joseph also have a son, George (Zhorik). When George married, his parents gave the newlyweds their two room flat and moved to a one room flat, which seemed like a sensible thing to do since he would have a growing family. However, in due course George separated from his wife and left her with the children in their flat. So where could George live now? Back home with his parents of course. Property is difficult to obtain, or used to be, and many newlyweds simply move in with their parents. Divorce is commonplace and cramped living conditions must play a part in this. However, Ida and Joseph now live in one room with the obligatory sofa bed and a kitchen that is just large enough to take a table and chairs. Where could they accommodate an adult son entitled to some privacy? Why, on the balcony of course. Fortunately they had a slightly larger than average balcony, which was duly glassed in, the walls covered with thick veneer and the floor carpeted. A small chest of drawers and bed was squeezed in and it was quite habitable – in summer at least. But when the Siberian winds comes howling in from the East in winter, the unheated

balcony cannot be used and a makeshift bed is arranged for him over a storage chest. Their flat was immaculately maintained and beautifully decorated with mementoes of their Chinese and European childhoods.

*Ida, Ira and her son, Natasha, Victor and Nina.*

Nona was another of Nina's friends that had grown up with our relatives in China. I was surprised to hear that she spoke perfect English, albeit with a slight American accent. She had also attended the *Ecole Remi*, following which she had studied at the American Institute in Shanghai.

Like Ida, she was very bitter that they had returned to the USSR – after all it had been their parent's choice, not theirs, and, as teenagers at the time, they felt that their youth had been destroyed by the move. Nona's father had died in Shanghai and her Ukrainian mother

*Nona, Marina, Zoya, Genia and Joseph.*

decided their future would be more secure in her land of origin. But the daughter, who had grown up in Shanghai, felt an alien in this strange land. She and Ida would reminisce about the happy years of their youth and play records from 1946 – their favourite year, when the war was just over and before they left Shanghai. They fondly remembered jazz music, the Glen Miller band and Hollywood films; and would spend their days listening to the music and dreaming about the past. When they had arrived in Vladivostok, the enormity of their act struck home. What *had* they done?

Nonetheless, Nona was a survivor and in due course was in demand as an interpreter and later as a teacher of English. Compared to her contemporaries she earned relatively good money and continues to teach at 67 to supplement the family income. It is typical that parents can and do help their children all their lives, particularly since many families continue to live together, even after marriage. Russians traditionally have elaborate weddings. But with divorce rates being so high, living together as 'partners' is now becoming more commonplace and acceptable to the older generation, the expense of weddings overcoming traditional moral scruples.

Nona's sister, Alla, who managed to emigrate to Australia is a reminder of missed opportunities. Alla now lives in Switzerland and has a daughter, Larissa, who was born in Australia. Nona's two brothers, Julian and Vitaly, had also returned with Nona and both spent several years in labour camps, for being 'foreign'. They were some of the fortunate ones who survived the camps and lived on for several years. However, both had long since died before my arrival, the camps having surely taken a toll on their health.

Nona brought treats for the party in my honour, as is customary; she gave me the tin of caviar she kept for special occasions and Nina a tin of ham. She moaned about having 'nothing' though on closer questioning she seemed to live well enough. As far as I could ascertain her husband was still in paid employment so they still had two incomes, and their children were comparatively independent. Incomes are however, very low, and Nona was obviously working not just for her own satisfaction but also because she knew living on a pension was well nigh on impossible. Nona was particularly proud of her daughter, Ira, who arrived with her young son; a delightful boy who was keen to try out his school English on me. Ira is an accomplished pianist, a graduate of the Conservatoire. She is an attractive, ambitious and rather assertive woman. Wild horses would not have kept her from a gathering with a foreign visitor, though some people in the city looked at me as though I had two heads – they had *never* seen a foreigner before. Hard to imagine in this age of international travel.

Ira was desperate to get out of the Ukraine. Although travel was certainly permitted by this time, obtaining visas was a lengthy and expensive procedure. She was frustrated and argumentative about the lack of prospects in the Ukraine and almost came to blows with Zoya, who is a loyal citizen and very proud of her country. According to her it was always possible to travel abroad, even before 1989. After all, *she* had, and was promptly accused of being a member of the KGB by Ira!

Not all of Nina's friends were refugees from Shanghai. In fact her best friends, Zoya and Genia were very much diehard Soviet citizens. Zoya had impeccable Communist credentials. Both her parents, a Ukrainian father and Russian mother, had been engineers and had worked, amongst other places, at the Kremlin in Moscow. She had attended school with Stalin's daughter and was a committed member of the party herself. *'Her family did not suffer much'* observed Nina. A very young, energetic 70 (she took me on a walking tour of her city – *'we'll walk until you're tired!'*), she had grown up a firm believer in the Soviet state and was a devoted follower of Stalin himself. Even following the revelations of his tyranny, many Russians refused to believe that Stalin could have been personally responsible for the gross miscarriages of justice and the deaths of millions. After all, they had been taught since childhood that he was their *'shining sun of humanity'*, a *'universal genius'*. In the eyes of many he was almost a god.

Zoya is a capable, intelligent and dogmatic History teacher; passionate about her country and, like many others of her generation, still obsessed with World War II. She had lived through the horrors of that conflict and the suffering imposed on the USSR by the Fascists. (Soviet Russians always refer to the Nazis as Fascists, associating them with evil, imperialist, capitalists; never Nazis which stood for Nationalist, *Socialist* Workers Party). She was genuinely concerned that the current generation would not be capable of defending their country. *'From whom?'* I asked, but did not get a satisfactory reply. She showed me around the war museums, complete with elaborate diorama displays of the heroic struggle of the Russian and Ukrainian peoples against the Fascist menace. Zoya had written her thesis on *'The role of Stalin in World War II'*. But his death in 1953 and the subsequent revelations of his misdeeds a few years later by Khrushchev meant that she would have to write Stalin out before she could submit it. This she refused to do and so she

was unable to obtain the higher degree that would have allowed her to teach at a University. Instead, she had to teach in what she called a *Technica* - presumably a technical college for boys. However, she enjoyed it, was popular with her students and did not regret her decision - truly a woman of principle. She provided me with a good example of why the Communist state had endured for so long. The successful fusion of the Soviet State with the survival of the Russian nation, which had so clearly been under threat during the war, meant that to question the former became treason. Years of being constantly bombarded with propaganda had also borne fruit.

*Zoya standing proudly in front of a war memorial.*

Nina suffered from a permanent inoperable hernia and heart condition. When she became too weak to walk far herself, Genia, who had befriended her upon her arrival in 1960, cleaned her flat and did her shopping. Genia also had a magnificent singing voice and treated me to a private operatic concert that nearly blew Nina's windows out. Yet she only sang in a choir and rarely as a soloist. I was very impressed. Genia was also a former member of the party though, unlike Zoya, she did not seem particularly committed and implied that she had only joined because it was expected of her, indeed she seemed completely apolitical.

Genia was a very warm and friendly person and she also took me around the city; this time to the many busy markets filled with shoppers and to the stores, which had goods for sale but considerably less people buying. She particularly enjoyed our foray into the bank on Karl Marx Street, a prestigious area of luxury shops, how wonderfully ironic. Two burly, scowling, armed muscle men barred our way. *'Where do you think you're going, silly old woman?'* one snarled at Genia. Banks are not for ordinary members of the public it seems. *'We are going to the American Express office'*, I replied, *'It is this way isn't it?'* The key words *'American Express'* worked their magic and we sailed in, to ingratiating smiles and disbelief (my two heads again). Genia positively skipped past them in triumph then perched up on a tall stool, swinging her legs and admiring the plush office surroundings where the new businessmen conducted their financial transactions.

Tamara was Nina's sister-in-law by her first husband Kostya, who had also returned to the USSR with them in 1947. Although 85 she was still very active. She had baked a beautiful cake for me and brought it on the bus, which she travelled on frequently. She was very busy cooking, playing the hostess and sadly did not have a great deal to say, though I am certain her life could have been a book in itself. Her son Victor also came with his wife, Natasha. They both seemed very congenial people and very fond of each other. Despite the fact that there was Russian champagne, a considerable amount of wine and a little vodka on offer Victor did not touch any alcohol. I asked why, whilst refusing once again the offer of 'best' Napoleon brandy. It seems that, in common with many Russian men, he had had a problem with drink. Natasha had put her foot down and said, choose the drink or me. He chose her and has never had a drink since. Victor was an engineer but there was little work in Dnepropetrovsk at the time. A once comparatively prosperous industrial city, the huge plants had become inefficient and without the Russian economy propping them up they were mostly lying idle. Victor was lucky to receive sporadic factory work. Natasha worked at a Children's Educational Centre and invited me to visit her there. She was delighted when I did so and showed me around and introduced me to her colleagues. They were very curious about my school and were most surprised that there were many similarities. My hosts were also most impressed by the knowledge that my teenage sons in England earned a little extra money whilst students, one of them working in McDonald's. They were all familiar with this store though few could afford to patronise it. Three outlets had already opened in the city, one of them a drive-in.

*A sign of the times, "Macauto" – 'Fast, tasty, convenient". Nina and her friends found the idea of a drive-in hamburger shop quite remarkable.*

## An interlude in Kiev.

On my way to Dnepropetrovsk I stopped off in the Ukrainian capital Kiev, where a moving experience awaited me at the wonderful and mysterious Monastery of the Caves, *Pecherskaya Lavra*. Monks that had reputedly become saints are interred in the caves, which has been a centre of religious pilgrimage for hundreds of years and which mercifully escaped destruction in the communist era and war. The site of this intriguing monument to Orthodox belief was easy enough to find, but once within its venerated walls, discovering the entrance to the caves themselves was quite a challenge. The entire place seemed deserted, despite the existence of a few souvenir shops, catering for pilgrims more than tourists. I eventually located one of the elusive entrances to the actual caves. A monk at the gaping hole in the wall that served as a door sold the obligatory candle and motioned me to enter. I gazed into the impenetrable darkness and hesitated. There was no one else around and I would have only my little candle for light. What if it went out? Did I really want to be alone in the dark, in an underground cemetery, with only the bones of former monks for company? I am not the slightest bit superstitious but practical concerns suddenly presented themselves to me. How could I trust the tunnels not to collapse? Who would notice or care if they did? The indifferent man at the door made no record of my entrance, gave no indication that I should be out by a certain time or that they would come after me. Indeed, I had the distinct feeling that as this was a holy place; all considerations of health and safety were to be left entirely in the hands of God!

I considered who would immediately miss me. Aunt Nina was not expecting me for two more days at least and would probably not find it unusual if I were delayed. My husband and sons were not expecting me home for another week, plenty of time to be buried with the monks. Fortunately, three other women appeared at that point. They too peered in and hesitated. Finally the boldest of the three marched in, declaring that as we would be *'walking in the footsteps of the saints'*; no harm would come to us. So, they trooped in and I followed at a discreet distance. We descended deep into the bowels of the earth in total darkness, with only the flickering candles clutched in our hands for illumination. As we reached a level area my eyes became accustomed to the dark and I perceived that there were many tunnels leading away with stronger illuminations emanating from them. Drawn by curiosity, all sense of danger having now disappeared, I had allowed myself to part company with the other ladies when I heard the distant murmur of voices and what sounded like singing. The first illuminated spot revealed a little niche in the walls of the tunnel totally surrounded by flowers and more candles. I could see that they were encasing a long glass window set in the earthen wall, behind which lay the robed and covered remains of presumably one of the monks. It is said that as each monk died, his body would be left unburied for a period of time. If the remains putrefied as would be normal, then he would be considered just a man and interred. However, if the flesh remained whole it showed he was holy and deserved sainthood. Then he would be given an honoured place in these catacombs where surviving friends, monks and later visitors could come to pay their respects and pray to the saint. I read that some monks even buried themselves voluntarily, starving and dying in religious ecstasy, as they sank into the earth.

I peered inside the glass, a whole figure appeared to be lying there, but it was impossible to tell what lay behind the robes, after all this time it should only be a skeleton. Fortunately even the face was covered and I gave the pilgrims the benefit of doubt. There is not a mystical bone in my body, being a devotee of reason and logic, but I could appreciate the wondrous nature of this place and allowed myself to give over to spiritual musings. Tunnel after tunnel revealed hundreds of such niches harbouring more and more monks. I roamed for what seemed like hours amongst these shrines, some more elaborately decorated than others. I was rarely alone as there were others wandering too, singly or in small groups, whispering in awe to each other. Every now and again we would come upon an especially large shrine, which would have an entire cave devoted to some particularly well loved saint. Then, to my delight, an impromptu service would take place as the faithful pilgrims burst into a song of prayer, in the Orthodox style. There they stood in the semi dark with their candles lighting up ecstatic faces, before the tomb of a favourite saint, singing the familiar hymns in his honour and revelling in their spiritual devotion. I stood to one side, huddling in the dark, an unbeliever to be sure, but grateful and honoured to be sharing in this magical spectacle.

I wondered if my parents would have been happy to come here. With my grandmothers there was no doubt. They would have relished this atmosphere and surely known about all the saints. I could imagine Babushka singing here with gusto and prostrating herself in religious devotion before the holy tombs. She would have loved this place. There were fresh candles available around every corner and I lit one and placed it before the shrine in her memory and for my dead mother. It was their religion not mine. But I owed it to their memory to maintain this vital cultural link. Continuing to wander the endless tunnels I passed the time in contemplation of my rich heritage and even richer legacy of loving family. I was temporarily alone but never existentially alone. I was fortunate to have a loving husband and sons, a dear father, brother, sister, aunts, cousins and friends. I am strong, healthy, happy and lucky enough to still live in a free society. I counted my blessings, the closest I can come to prayer, and emerged from the darkness of the earth feeling elated and emotionally rejuvenated.

*Ukrainian dancing by the Monastery.*

# The end of a vital link with the past – Nina's passing.

Nina had long grieved the loss of her beloved Kostya but eventually embarked upon another relationship. She told me about her second husband, Volodya, whom she had married for companionship in their old age, though she was to outlive him as well. He had also been previously married and had two adult children and grandchildren. She enjoyed her role as stepmother and step-grandmother, even after his death. They had much in common as he had also been in both Harbin and Shanghai, though she had not known him at the time. He had been a good scholar in China, a student of English and French, and managed to continue his studies after his return to the USSR, gaining the coveted *'Red Diploma'* for being an outstanding scholar. He went on to become an academic in Russia but despite his achievements he was arrested in 1953 and sent to the camps, where he endured six years of hardship. Why was he arrested? I asked. Goodness knows, replied Nina, probably because he had come from abroad and taught foreign languages. He did not tell her very much about what he had endured because, she said, he was of *'nervous disposition'* and did not like to remember it. But snippets revealed that he had worked in cold forests, cutting down trees, and that it was from that time he had developed rheumatism and poor health in general. He was just 35 when he was incarcerated and after his release he was often ailing even though he was only 41. It is sad that he had managed to evade arrest throughout the Stalin years, only to be taken away a few months after the tyrant's death. Things did not improve immediately observed Nina. Perhaps he had been informed upon by a jealous colleague, or his past had simply come to the attention of the secret police. A valid reason was never necessary to the overzealous upholders of the Soviet dictatorship, merely being accused of being an *'enemy of the state'* was reason enough. A knock on the door, usually in the dead of night, and the accused was taken away by the dreaded secret police often never to be seen again. The death rate in the camps was very high so Volodya was one of the fortunate ones to return. He even managed to eventually return to work as an academic and in due course became a Professor of Languages. He died in the 1990's, leaving Nina a widow for the second time.

Nina's delight in small pleasures was evident in her prolific letters, in which she always related everyone's news to each other from around the world. She was genuinely pleased, for example, when my father visited me and my family for the first time in the UK, and wanted to know all the details of his journey. She was astounded when Dad and I sent her a small financial gift of 265 Ukrainian Griven, about £100 at the time. She explained what that was worth to her. She received a pension of 50 Griven a month, so this represented over five month's pension. (The equivalent for a pensioner in the UK at the time would be about £1000, a considerable sum of money.) Nina was not conversant with English pounds but was fully aware that the sum of money represented 150 American dollars, a fortune in her eyes. She was immensely grateful and did admit that to live on a pension in the Ukraine was very difficult. She supplemented what she could buy with her pension with other financial gifts from relatives and the food parcels they also sent her. Her cousin Olga in San Francisco was particularly generous with food parcels and Nina showed me her stash of tinned meats, hams and such like that she had sent from America. Some enormous chicken legs that had somehow been sent over particularly impressed us. During the presidency of George Bush Senior, in the early 1990's, there had been a surfeit of chicken in the USA and so it had become extraordinarily cheap. Some of this surplus chicken duly found its way to the Ukraine, where it was known as 'Bush's legs' - Ножки Буша. Nina prepared a meal for me of this luxury item. I am convinced it was turkey not chicken, never have I seen such enormous drumsticks.

She relished receiving her parcels, but pointed out that money was preferable now that goods had become available. The trouble was she just did not have the money with which to buy them, unlike in the past when she had the money but there was nothing to buy. I ventured to a local 'department store' to see what was on offer. In a rather shabby 'warehouse' style shop I found that one could indeed buy a wide variety of goods, many of which were imported. Prices were cheaper than in the UK, though not significantly so. When one considers that her weekly pension was about the equivalent of £5 or $8, it is little wonder that pensioners could not use such stores. It would have bought her the equivalent of about a kilo of beef or perhaps five loaves of bread.

Nina was admirably almost self-sufficient in fruit and vegetables, which, in time honoured tradition, she pickled or preserved in summer in readiness for the coming winter. Friends with *dachas* – summerhouses that could be as humble as a shed on a vegetable allotment, supplied her the produce and she made her own preserves and compotes – fruit puddings, with berries, plums, and blackberries; whatever was available. She also salted and bottled tomatoes, cucumber, eggplants and other vegetables that were in season or received from farming friends. Her nephew Victor, Tamara's son, kept her supplied with potatoes and onions, to store on her balcony along with her huge bottles of home-made berry cordials. Nina proudly showed me an enormous store of bottled produce, which enabled her to live in winter when goods were scarce and she could not venture through the ice and snow to the markets. She kept them in all the bottom cupboards of a display cabinet that ran the full length of her lounge room. Vegetables from her bottled store, a tin of spam from her American parcels and some bread and she had a ready meal.

In her 70's Nina found it increasingly difficult to get around. She says she used to go to Church but as she could no longer walk far, she prayed at home, like her mother did in Sydney. I was reminded of my grandmother Zina's devout formal prayers – morning and night. She would stand in front of the icons in the corner of her room, the oil lamp lit underneath, and chant the hymns and prayers of the Orthodox faith in the Old Believers' style, bowing and crossing herself frequently. She emphasised that our family had always been very religious and seemed keen to show that she had not lost that faith, despite living in an officially atheist country. I was intrigued to see that since the demise of the Communist state, the church had experienced something of a revival and new generations of Russians were returning to the Orthodox faith. The churches themselves were being lovingly and lavishly restored and services were attended by large congregations. I observed a particularly moving and beautiful ceremony in a Kiev cathedral that brought back fond memories of my devout youth.

Though confined to her flat Nina remained in touch, by phone or letter, with all her friends and relatives. She watched television a lot and kept abreast of world affairs. She informed me that *'the whole country'* grieved when Princess Diana died tragically in the Paris car crash. *'So young, so beautiful, such a shame'*, Nina lamented. She wrote to me about the financial crisis that in 1998 sent their prices skyrocketing, undermined their currency and wiped out life's savings. Ever the optimist, she hoped *'things would improve soon'*. She mentioned how happy she was to hear from Galia in Sydney who was celebrating her Golden Wedding (50th) anniversary and enjoying a visit from her brother in Canada. Nina knew of, and sent wishes to, everyone on their birthdays and anniversaries, rejoiced at new births and kept the scattered family informed. She may well have been the first to realise that four of her generation were now Great grandmothers - Lara in St. Petersburg, Olga in San Francisco, Galia in Sydney and Irina in Samara.

She still considered herself to be very fortunate with her home, *'the best home she has ever had in her life'*. She had moved into this two-roomed flat with her second husband and at some point they had actually managed to buy it. Whether purchase meant actual freehold or simply life long tenancy was not clear but certainly she could bequeath it, and did so to her nephew Victor and his wife Natasha. When Nina had written her letter of invitation to the Ukrainian Embassy – a necessary bureaucratic process to obtain a visa for me, she had emphasised, almost proudly, that she had a *'spare room'* for me and so we would not have to share rooms. In fact, it was the sofa bed in the lounge. Her bedroom, an entrance lobby, and a tiny kitchen and bathroom completed her abode. To be sure it was warm and comfortable and the lounge was attractive and homely, containing the treasured knick-knacks she had accumulated over the years, and a formidable collection of books from her late husband.

It was the communal areas of the building that I found appalling. The entrance to the large, multi-storied apartment block had huge holes in the ground and concrete slabs randomly lying about, all of which had to be negotiated to reach the stairs or lift. The area was not lit and was absolutely lethal for the elderly, frail or very young. The lift was ancient, dirty and often broke down, stranding people inside. I refused to use it, preferring to walk up three flights rather than risk being stuck in this tiny, pungent box that stank of urine. Stray cats and dogs roamed around the surrounding barren 'garden' where some enterprising tenant had tried to grow vegetables; however they were constantly stolen, so he gave up. No doubt this was no worse than many public housing estates in the West, but Nina assured me that this was a desirable area in which to live. We walked to Ida and Joseph's flat, in a nearby block, for a dinner of traditional *pelemeni*, and the communal areas there were much the same. Joseph though, being fit and 'handy', had painted and papered the entrance area immediately outside his and his neighbour's flat, in marked contrast to other communal areas.

Nina, however, could not do anything to her block's entrance, though she did go down there on warm days and sat passing the time with other elderly residents. For a while she used the walking stick/convertible chair that I brought her, with which she was very thrilled, having never seen one like it before. Every day a friend would call her or she would call them, to check on each other and be reassured they were all okay. She said she had heart murmurs on occasion but was otherwise *'fine'*, though I knew that this was not true, as she had already had a few blackouts, which may even have been mini strokes, in my presence. 'First-aiders', or paramedics, had to be called and they treated her with injections obtained from a filthy medical box. Fortunately, on each occasion she seemed to make a full recovery.

After my departure in April, Nina continued to write prolifically, thanking me profusely for my visit and keeping up a running commentary of family news, both from the past and present. She wrote furiously and uncharacteristically haphazardly, perhaps realising her end was near. She readily admitted that, at 75, her strength and health were diminishing, though even then she *'did not mind'*. Truly one of life's treasures, she passed away in October, 1998 after a sudden stroke. Zoya informed me by telegram that she believed Nina's passing was free from lengthy suffering and requested me to pass on the sad news to our relatives around the world. Nina bequeathed her very desirable two room flat to her beloved first husband's nephew whom with his wife and son, were naturally delighted with their windfall. *'Out of misfortune - fortune'* they later said; now they and their adult son could move out of their one room flat. Nina is sorely missed.

*Nina in her kitchen, 1998.*

# Post communist Russia – some observations.

I would not have believed the astounding changes to the economies of Russia's two major cities that had taken place in the short space of six years had I not seen it for myself. It was not so apparent in the Ukraine, as Dnepropetrovsk still seemed to be in economic decline, but a few months after that trip I revisited St. Petersburg and Moscow.

Phenomenal changes had taken place since my last visit in 1992 and I could scarcely believe these were the same two cities. Considering there had been yet another 'economic crisis' and I very nearly did not go, for reasons that I explained in an article I wrote at the time[1], the progress I witnessed was impressive. Moscow especially had been transformed beyond recognition. Advertisements abounded for all types of goods and the fact that they were clearly targeted at local consumers demonstrated a degree of choice unheard of under the old system. Massive department stores had sprung up, under European or international control to be sure, but catering to the Russian populace rather than just tourists, as had previously been the case. Littlewoods was no longer alone, *Next*, *Benetton* and a host of other big Western names had also appeared. Electrical goods stores had opened up all over as more and more people discovered the delights of labour saving domestic appliances. As for food, the choices were as abundant and diverse as in any European city, perhaps even more so. And, whilst expensive *a la carte* restaurants may still have been the prerogative of the privileged few, at the bottom end of the market there was a bewildering array of budget fast food. Ironically, much of it modelled on the McDonald's chain. Yes, here were the look-a-likes, selling very similar products, even to the milkshakes and apple turnovers, not to mention the ubiquitous *gemburger*. Considering Russia had just experienced a severe economic crisis, during which the value of the rouble had plummeted, there was already sufficient infrastructure to soften the blow, at least for considerable numbers of the capital's citizens. Shops and expensive cafes still buzzed with Russian voices, they could not *all* have belonged to Mafiosi.

On the occasion of my third visit in 2005, it came as no surprise to find that the two cities had continued to thrive, but the speed and extent of change was nonetheless still astonishing. Most of my impressions were gained through first hand observation but I also talked with locals and official guides, who offered pertinent nuggets of insight. A particularly valuable source of information came from Andrei and Olga, cousins of

Russian friends back in England. We had arranged to meet at the Hotel Ukraine, where I was staying. A flamboyantly luxurious Soviet era construction, it is the tallest hotel in Europe and second tallest of Stalin's *'seven sisters'* group of skyscrapers. Built in an elaborate combination of Russian Baroque and Gothic styles they are also known as *'wedding cakes'* because of their multi layered appearance. The interior was very smart, with beautiful high ceilings, polished floors, lots of marble and a lovely dining room, all rather art deco in appearance. Whilst many of the *sisters* were built to house state ministries, some were allegedly built to house the new *'socialist hero'*; the mythical superman that the communist paradise was supposed to produce. So the doors are ten foot high and far too heavy for mere mortals to shift. The revolving doors are hazardous but still easier to negotiate with suitcases than these huge conventional doors. The bedrooms had seen better days, though there was an impressive ceiling plaster with a bronze trimmed ceiling rose. On the 29th floor there was an observation deck (100 roubles entrance fee) with stunning views over the city and Moskva River.

A lovely couple, Andrei and Olga took me to the Russian Historical Museum on Red Square. It is an interesting traditional museum, housing artefacts from the Stone Age to the 19th century, including a beautiful throne, traditional sled, an unusual globe and lots of ancient icons. Whilst we admired the displays they talked a lot about their lifestyle. They have a son called Daniel, as do I but their's was only six years old. They limit

*Traditionally clad 'boyars'- nobles, entice people into the museum on Red Square.*

his time on the computer as well as television - it seems lots of Russian children, like their counterparts in the west, are becoming obsessed with computers. Andrei works for a large catalogue company, *'like your Littlewoods or Burlington'* he said. He holds some sort of middle management position that involves a lot of travelling, in fact he was off to Germany shortly after our meeting. He picked me up in a very smart BMW and his wife also has her own car, a Toyota if I remember correctly. He explained that many Russians in the provinces want to buy goods but the only decent shops are in Moscow and St. Petersburg. So they order from the catalogue and have their goods delivered a few weeks later. Mail order is apparently a booming business and his lifestyle certainly seemed to support that claim. Olga is a freelance lawyer (*yurist*) doing conveyancing, if I understood her correctly. They travel every year, mostly in Russia, but also Europe. They had bought a plot of land and were in the process of building a house on it. Not just a *dacha*, but a house for year round living. They had considered buying a larger flat in the city, but decided they would rather have land for their son to play in and commute into the city by car instead.

*Andrei and Olga in the Russian Historical Museum.*

It was so encouraging to speak to a thoroughly 'normal' and happy couple. No Russian angst or bitterness here, they were independent, responsible, ambitious people, just like thoughtful couples anywhere. He at 33 and she 27, still remembered the communist times, though she was only 13 when the regime ended, Andrei 19. His mother had forced him to join the *Komsomol*, the young communist league. He was not the least interested in communist activities, but she insisted it was a necessary step in order to go to a good university. Eventually he gave in only to please his mother, just before he began his student life. The couple's general view is very positive but they freely admitted that Russia is two countries – Moscow and the rest. Their personal prospects seemed exceedingly bright and they were looking forward to completing their house, which was their next priority. It had been a very enlightening encounter with this couple and I am very grateful to have met them.

Much of what Andrei had told me was confirmed by a Moscow guide, who additionally gave me some interesting statistics. Before 1991, she claimed, there were half a million cars in Moscow. By 2001 that had increased to over a million and by 2005 to three million, one for every three people in the city. Surely that is an indicator of prosperity if nothing else. As a result, the city is noisy, brash and filthy as all those cars take their toll. The *Ladas* and *Moskviches* are largely gone; replaced with Japanese and European models. As befits a booming economy, the amount and quality of housing was also growing, though as might be expected in a capital city, prices were exorbitant. Still clinging to old traditions, domestic space is measured in terms of square metres. The going price, that year, for property in Moscow ranged from £2,000 to £3,500 per square metre. Under the old regime people had been allocated five square metres each and flats had been 'free', though Muscovites often had to wait up to ten years for one. Now, new apartment blocks were springing up all over the city, with enormous dimensions by comparison, and even on the outskirts people were beginning to buy land

and build houses, just as Andrei and Olga intended to do. On the way to the new airport, we saw evidence of many new developments, the start of a suburban society - though the guide claimed they were only for the rich. St. Petersburg, too, is now experiencing a similar property boom.

*The flagship of the Bolshevik revolution, the Aurora, now a museum, has her guns trained on a construction site of exclusive harbour side penthouse apartments.*

The Moscow guide was under no illusions about the dark side of Moscow's prosperity and pointed out that corruption was rife in her beloved city. Her comments on Russian lifestyle were quite revealing. For example, she believed that in the UK we respected the law and would only consider a person to be innocent if they had committed no crime. Whereas in Russia, where people were so used to being controlled by oppressive laws that they always sought to evade if possible, they had the saying: Не пойман - не вор, meaning *'You are not a thief until they catch you'*. So, if you can get away with theft, dishonesty and corruption then you are still innocent until you are unlucky enough to be caught. This illustrates an interesting contempt for the law, which my virtuous grandmother Maria would have found horrifying. Moscow police are notoriously corrupt, and there are conventions about how to agree an acceptable bribe when they catch you for something like speeding. The going price is often expressed as so many tickets for the Bolshoi!

My personal impressions of Moscow were very encouraging, though I am well aware that I was seeing only the affluent face of the city. Nonetheless, any prosperity is better than none. Whilst walking back to the hotel from the Revolution Museum I inadvertently wandered into yet more shopping malls, built underground around the metros and full of shoppers. There were also plenty of fruit machines (one armed bandits); indeed, amusement parlours and casinos seemed to be very popular. Shopping complexes are the same everywhere it seems, one could just as easily be in London, Sydney, Paris or Berlin - same goods, same expensive prices and same crowds of course. It was late Friday afternoon, after work and Moscow was full of people strolling on a warm spring day, drinking and eating in cafes. There seemed to be a pleasant holiday mood of perfectly normal, comfortable people, coming out of office buildings, ready to enjoy the weekend. Some people were at booths looking to buy tickets for the theatre, just as in London. The old state department store, *GUM*, is now very trendy, with lots of designer shops, wonderful cafes and patisseries for weary shoppers and Italian pizzerias doing a roaring trade. New visitors could be forgiven for thinking that Moscow had been like this for years. I was particularly intrigued by the proliferation of interesting *Matryoshka* dolls on sale. Russian entrepreneurs had quickly discovered the market appeal of these traditional dolls and produced examples to satisfy every taste and trend. Creative artists appeared to relish painting animals, politicians, sporting heroes and celebrity figures from every culture.

*'Matryoshka' dolls for every taste…*

On another occasion, an English acquaintance and I were determined to sample traditional Russian fare but we had to search long and hard to find it amid this plethora of international cuisine. We eventually found an enormous food court in yet another massive shopping mall, built under Red Square. We had difficulty finding the entrance because it was hidden away next to McDonald's, which we had been avoiding. Here, amongst more plush, expensive shops, was a veritable cornucopia of delightful takeaway food counters. One could choose from appetising Russian salads, pies of every description, huge pieces of fish, meats, kebabs and soups. The food was dished out at the counters and eaten on communal tables in the centre of the mall. In short, the kind of fast food outlet that is reasonably priced in England and cheap in Europe or Australia. Not so here. It had seemed cheap at first, then it dawned on us that the prices were quoted for 100 grams. They made sure to give you huge plates, weighed them down and then presented you with the shocking bill. My friend thought they saw us coming, but Russians were charged the same prices I noticed, though they were doubtless a lot more careful about stipulating the portion sizes. We sampled a few dishes, sharing a beetroot/mixed salad, a bowl of *pelemeni*, a wonderful pie and mushroom dumplings.

McDonald's was very popular and comparatively cheap though it seemed to be more popular with young business people rather than families, and loud music was commonplace. A *'Big Mac'* was less than half of the English price; good value on the World Economist test, according to my guide. There were advertisements everywhere for a *Big Teysti*! Later, the guide introduced us to a popular Russian food chain, called *Moo Moo* - yes, complete with a big plastic cow outside. But food inside was genuine home made traditional fare, served from counters that people filed past with trays. There were huge queues as it was very popular and prices were reasonable. Rustic style décor, excellent value and filled with young professional Russians eating in their lunch breaks. *Yolki Palki* (Pine sticks), once a curse I used to hear from my Uncle Tolya, is a similar chain with Russian forest themed décor.

Of course there were, and still are, enormous numbers of people who do not share in this general prosperity. It is unheard of in the countryside outside of the capital cities, and too many industries are controlled by former Party *apparatchiks*, often in cahoots with local gangsters. The State pretends to oppose this but often supports the gangsters. Indeed, many would argue that the biggest gangster of all is the Russian government. Today, in the early years of the 21st century, the war in Chechnya shows no signs of abating and the ugly sceptre of conscription still hangs over the youth of Russia. The Chechens themselves are treated as sub humans, to be bombed into submission and Russia is in very real danger of becoming a Fascist state. That is, a state where individual freedoms are suppressed except those economic interests which benefit the government. This dire situation should never be confused with Capitalism[2]. Sadly, the current administration in the USA in 2007, also appears to be heading the same way.

The political climate in Russia today is still very ominous, with suppression of rival political parties and of free speech, evident in the murder of critical journalists (RIP Anna Politkovskaya) and businessmen. Russia is returning to an authoritarian system of government that in many respects is as sinister as its predecessors. Let us hope that economic success will see those who wield financial power join forces with human rights groups and the voices of democracy to exert pressure on the state to perform its proper role of defending human rights rather than trampling them.

Nonetheless, in the new century, many people appear to have real hope - though how much of this is due to the current administration in Russia, let alone the influence of the President himself, is difficult to determine. I have met Russians in England who claim things are improving considerably in their home country and one asserted that, for the first time, she actually felt proud to be Russian. Generously low tax rates have encouraged real investment and the major cities, Moscow and St. Petersburg, are positively booming. It is probably safe to say that such success as Russia has shown has been in spite of its government rather than because of it. Economic progress is also readily apparent in countries from the former Soviet bloc. I can vouch for the Czech Republic and Poland, which I have had the privilege of visiting recently and was excited to see a massive Tesco, not just in the capital, but in a relatively provincial city. Department stores were unheard of in Communist times, so this represents real progress, giving the people of those beleaguered countries genuine choice in food and consumer goods.

So where does that leave Russia today? With some way to go before the country as a whole will reap the benefits of material progress. Perhaps due to its vastness, some parts will always remain backward. But in the cities there is real promise. Moscow and St. Petersburg are exploiting their heritage effectively, from Tsarist palaces magnificently restored to themed restaurants offering a 'spy' experience! There are even enterprising Lenin look-alikes, indeed any historical figure is fair game when it comes to parting tourists from their money.

*'Lenin', 'Putin' and 'Marx', from three different centuries conjoin to make a rouble. No one seems to mind the anachronism.*

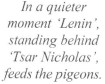

*In a quieter moment 'Lenin', standing behind 'Tsar Nicholas', feeds the pigeons.*

Moscow is forging ahead at breakneck speed. The city is buzzing and many urban Russians appear not only materially wealthier but also brimming with confidence. There is no end to the myriad opportunities available to unfettered imaginations if only the violence of the gangster culture can be curbed. In the provinces there is still despair, yet Russia is a country of vast natural resources. If those resources can be utilised by market forces for the benefit of its people, that is, if Russia's industries can be revitalised, then the countryside should also see economic advancement.

Already Siberia's gold and mineral resources are transforming the lives of Russians in that remote far Eastern region of the country. The city of Blagoveshensk, Babushka Maria's birthplace, whose people prided themselves on their independence, due in no small part to its sheer distance from Moscow, is beginning to flourish. It is the nearest Russian city to China, separated only by the river Amur; in winter it is possible to walk across the frozen border. Today Russians from the city take day trips across the river to go shopping for bargains in China. Huge shopping malls, catering exclusively to the *nouveau riche* Russians, have sprung up on the river's banks, full of designer clothes shops, electrical goods, toys, trainers and many other goods once considered luxuries; and no visa required!

As the culture of dependence on the State fades from living memory, new generations of Russians will live freely and openly, travelling abroad and bringing back valuable ideas, experiences and skills to further enrich their nation. I am cautiously optimistic for its future.

# Chapter 11

# Next generation, bringing the families up to date.

## Живёшь сам, дай жить другому.

### *Live and let live.*

# Our family in Russia.

The clan in Russia, descendents of Klavdia and Vassili and Alexandra and Grigori are surviving in varied circumstances. I remain in closer contact with Klavdia's offspring living in St. Petersburg, though both she and her husband Vassili passed away in the 1980's. They had lived to ripe old ages, still devoted to one another. Vassili died at 81, followed five years later by his beloved wife. In less than ten years the next generation would begin to follow them. Over the course of the 1990's, Uncles Yan and Sasha then Aunt Taissia passed away. Dedicated to the end, she was still working as a doctor when she succumbed to cancer. Uncle Sasha was barely 69 and it was regrettable to see the passing of that generation of my mother's cousins. Then we heard the tragic news that even Irina's husband Boris had died, at just 55. Lara had been forced to move out of Mill Stream, the lovely old house in the forests, when it became too much for her to look after on her own. It must have been with some regret that she moved into her recently widowed daughter Irina's flat. Though both continued to spend the hot summers at Mill Stream, a welcome breath of fresh air from the confines of the flat and the bustle of city life. Lara continues valiantly to present a cheerful attitude, as her naturally warm personality decrees, but, following two heart attacks, she is now completely housebound. Under the circumstances she is remarkably buoyant and is still generally optimistic in her letters and phone calls. When I last visited her in St. Petersburg she was as warm and welcoming as ever, a bright and perky 85 year old.

Another distant relative that we know of in Russia is another Nina, now living in Pskov, who was still active and vibrant in 1998, despite advanced years. When I travelled to Russia that year, she was visiting Lara at her home. She is the daughter of my great grandmother's brother, that is, Praskovia's niece and a distant great aunt to me. She informed me, quite out of the blue, that her father had been killed by the Communists in Stalin's Russia in 1930. So Artemy, the head of the

*Nina from Pskov with her grandchild, Vera Volski, Vera from Sydney, Irina from Samara, Sergei.*

Shliapnikoff clan at the time, appeared to have lost both his brother and his brother-in-law that fateful year, little wonder then that he decided to leave the country. Interestingly, she volunteered this information about her father to me within ten minutes of our first meeting! Family reunions evoke memories of family tragedies, even after seventy odd years. Perhaps she wanted to make sure that we family members in the West knew of this vital event. Though news to me, her particular tragedy came as no great surprise, alas.

By the time of my third visit to St. Petersburg in 2005 my only surviving relatives were my Aunt Lara and two second-cousins Irina (Lara's daughter) and Anna. In previous visits it had not been possible to talk to the family in any depth but this time, probably due to their reduced number, they were far more forthcoming.

I arranged to meet Irina in the city centre, where she worked. We then travelled to the flat she shares with her mother and where my other second-cousin Anna would be waiting. Irina's amiable young driver, Sasha, drove us north of the city, over the River Neva and into the suburbs, where Irina lived in a typical soviet style, 17 story, block of 85 flats.

*Irina's block, on the far right.*

Thankfully the lift awaited us and we were soon entering her apartment on the 14th floor. The front door opened onto a small entrance hall, where one took off one's outer shoes and put on the obligatory slippers, *tapochki*. The flat had a large kitchen, big enough for table and chairs as well as all the essentials. But Irina had set a dining table in Lara's bedroom, producing a cosy and very attractive ambience. The traditional oriental carpet on the wall above Lara's bed/settee framed the table upon which Irina and Lara laid on a superb three course meal, with wonderful Russian champagne, light and sweet. They offered smoked salmon, ham, salmon salad, fried chicken and vegetables, followed by a beautiful torte – a veritable work of art, and I was honoured by their generosity.

*Marina, Aunt Lara and Anna,*
*in Lara's home, St. Petersburg.*

As we ate, they told me a little about themselves. Both Irina and Anna were doctors but neither still practiced. Anna now works in medical insurance from what I could gather. It is administrative work so, as she put it *'no-one is going to die if I take an afternoon off'*. She also suggested that the work was less stressful and slightly better paid. Doctors it seems were not well paid, though she did concede that there were some in the new Russia who did make money but *'they charged their patients',* she said in horror. That was against her principles and so she chose not to work in medicine at all. Whilst there was clearly a considerable gulf between her views and mine, I, nonetheless, had to admire her conviction.

We talked about the consumer boom that has transformed the city centre, where I had seen lots of new western style shops appearing, fashionable boutiques, cocktail bars, expensive restaurants and many others. Nevsky Prospect was a far cry from the city I remembered from 1992, when all one could buy was a sausage sandwich. It appeared to me that lots of affluent new Russians were shopping in the new malls but according to Irina and Anna, most people would only be window-shopping because they would not be able to afford to buy anything. How then could all these shops remain in business I wondered?

Anna, the daughter of Taissia and Yan, also lives in St. Petersburg. She is strikingly beautiful, with the distinct facial features of her father's people, who hail from the mountainous Caucasus region of Southern Russia. She is married to Sergei and they have a son, Slavik, born in 1992. Sergei graduated in Philosophy, a useless subject in the new Russia she intimated.

*Anna and Sergei on their*
*wedding day, Leningrad,*
*c. 1980's.*

He now works as some kind of Safety or Protection officer and continues to pursue his interest in Philosophy as well as poetry. Anna was bitter about the economic reforms that had taken place. Her father had saved all his life for their futures but the devaluation of the rouble in 1992 had wiped everything out. Fortunately, she suggested, he had not lived to see that, having died just a few months earlier.

They had wanted to emigrate to either America or Canada. But it was very expensive and they could not afford English lessons. French speaking Canada was considered because French lessons were cheaper. Though Anna did admit to being reluctant to start a new life in a foreign country where she could not speak the language, so maybe that had been the deciding factor in them remaining in Russia. She views her life in two separate eras – until 1991 when they had lived comfortable lives, not luxurious to be sure and always in the same two room flats. Then it all changed with the demise of the Soviet Union, which happened to coincide with the death of her parents. Suddenly in place of security there was uncertainty about the future. Prices rose dramatically but their wages failed to keep up and their quality of life plummeted accordingly. They

used to enjoy the theatre but that is now out of their price range, except on very rare occasions. They do have a computer, but she doesn't use it much and said that it had been bought mainly for her husband and son.

Sergei and Anna were extremely concerned about the fate of their 13 year old son and his impending conscription into the army at 18. Officially 1,270 conscripts died in 1997 from suicide and brutality inflicted by their own officers, though some observers put the figure at five times that.[1] The guide in Moscow had assured my tour party that it would be abolished in 2008. It was also claimed that only volunteers would be sent to Chechnya in future. A concession won by the campaigning of the Mothers' Committee (of Chechnya soldiers), many of whose sons had been killed. But, according to my relatives this was not so and the only way out of this dreadful dilemma for Anna, would be to keep Slava studying with higher degrees until he was married and

*Anna working as a doctor, Leningrad, c. 1970's.*

had a child. Apparently they did not send fathers. However, she hoped he could escape it by going abroad. Slava (affectionately known as Slavik) is a bright boy, who did well in school, preparing for exams in Russian, mathematics and two optional subjects in Year 9. He continued on to class 10 and 11 and is finishing school aged about 16, a little younger than his peers. He can then choose to go either to university or an academy. If he passes the necessary exams, his parents hope he will gain entry to the Military medical academy, where he will continue the family tradition and become a doctor. It remains to be seen whether or not this ambition will be realised. Slava seems to be quite a mature, independent teenager with strong views; he could be successful in many fields.

In August 2005 Anna and her son travelled to the Krasnodar region from

where her father's family had originated. They visited the graves of her grandparents and the house she used to live in, now occupied by others. They had a wonderful ten days on the Black Sea in the village of Lermontov, named after the famous Russian poet, where they bathed, swam and Slava dived. The family grew healthy and tanned and it seems to have been a very pleasant interlude.

*Slava, Anna and her husband Sergei in the garden of the family's summer dacha.*

Irina has a managerial position in the area of health, the environment and safety. She had her own chauffeur to take her to work each day. Having a 'chauffeur' does not mean luxury travelling by any means. It was a very basic car, probably shared by many employees. Sasha, the driver, was very congenial and glad of the opportunity to speak with a foreigner; he talked of going to America one day and seemed very positive and hopeful that he would be able to do so. In the meantime he was happy to work as a driver. Whilst holding down her important position, Irina also nurses her mother and finds solace in the church, having become more religious since her husband, Boris, passed away. Though apparently better off than Anna, she too, seemed rather pessimistic about their general situation.

As a highly valued medical consultant, Irina appears to enjoy the respect of her peers and is frequently sent on business trips across the breadth of Russia and, previously, within the former satellite countries. She has been to the Baltic States, the Ukraine, Czechoslovakia, East Germany, Poland and even abroad to Sweden, Finland and Holland.

*Irina and her mother Lara.*

Someone in a comparable position in the West would enjoy tangible economic benefits but salaries still seem to be lagging behind, even in the new Russia.

*Irina in St. Petersburg, 2008.*

Nonetheless, by the time of my last visit in 2008 it appeared that the gap in our respective lifestyles had narrowed significantly. My relatives are now able to partake of all manner of western goods never before available to them; from English tea and cosmetics to laptop computers. Even the Avon lady comes to call! Aspiring Russians now dream of owning a '*kotej*' in the new suburbs, a house with a garden *and* proper plumbing. Our relatives are no exception and this ultimate symbol of prosperity may even be within their grasp one day. I certainly hope so.

During an earlier visit I had the opportunity to speak with Irina in Samara and Vera in Chelyabinsk. My cousin Irina rang each of them up to tell them I was visiting and then thrust the phone into my hands. It was an unexpected, albeit slightly awkward, pleasure to speak to people I had never met in person, though I knew something of their backgrounds.

Irina is the daughter of Alexandra, the youngest of Artemy and Praskovia's daughters. Alexandra had married Grigori at 17 and chosen to stay behind in Russia with him when the rest of the family fled. The couple remained devoted to one another and passed away within two years of each other, both at around 80 years of age. Irina still lives in Samara, the city from which the Shliapnikoffs fled. She has two daughters, Elena and Galina, who are both married with children of their own, Elena has two girls and Galina two boys. Galina's son Artemy, has a son of his own, so Irina is now a great grandmother. Her voice sounded strong and confident and Anna assured me that she was still an attractive, commanding woman. This branch of the family appears to be thriving and growing in numbers as one might normally expect; more great grandchildren for Irina to enjoy.

Vera Volski is the daughter of Polya and Volodya Pravosudov, who also escaped to China but returned to Russia after the war and now lives in Chelyabinsk, a little to the east of the Ural mountains. Vera had been one of the family beauties growing up in Shanghai, as is evident from her wedding photograph in Chapter 5. Returning to post war USSR could not have been easy and I would dearly have liked to know her reaction to that fateful decision made in 1947. But a brief phone conversation hardly seemed the opportune moment to ask about the events of 60 years earlier, perhaps we shall yet meet. She had two sons, one of whom died tragically young and the other is married with children of his own.

As for remaining Shliapnikoffs in Russia, I have no firm knowledge of Russians with that name that are related, but Internet searches reveal a young man who is the spitting image of Great Uncle Alexei. Could this be another descendent of this illustrious family?

## Expatriates around the world.

Sadly, none of Artemy and Praskovia's children are still with us but their descendants who had fled Russia are thriving around the world; in Australia, Canada, England and the USA.

Their eldest daughter, Zina, passed away in 1978, succumbing to stomach cancer, which she had denied until the very end. But she had lived out her life with one of her daughters as had been foretold and when death came she accepted it with pious dignity. Her funeral was a traditional Orthodox affair in an Old Believers' church in Sydney and I still recall my mother bitterly weeping for her *'Mama, mama'* as she clung helplessly to my father. The bond between them had been particularly strong. John too was grief stricken at the loss of the determined, capable woman Zina had been; the person who had helped them so often through the tumultuous early years of their marriage. She was the last of their parents to die and at that moment they seemed conscious of life's fragility, recognising that the mantle of the older generation had now passed to them.

John and Julie continued to live in the house at Cabramatta for some years, Zina's 'granny flat' becoming Michael's den, eminently suitable for a teenage boy as Helen and I had long since moved out. After Michael also grew up and left, the family home became indeed, an 'empty nest'. By the 1990's as they became older, John was finding it increasingly difficult and expensive to maintain their large house and so it was agreed that he and Julie would sell up and jointly buy a property with Michael and Karen. A suitable house was found in the quiet Hills district of Sydney's north-western suburbs, far from that hotbed of crime and violence that Cabramatta had become. It had a large two bedroom self-contained flat, with its own entrance and veranda for John and Julie. With characteristic energy and enthusiasm John set about recreating their cherished home in this new environment. Many of their superfluous accumulations would have to be discarded but there was room enough to keep those treasures that held such sentimental value for them. Zina's glass buffet with its precious crystal and their own sideboard with the various souvenirs Julie had collected on her trips to Europe, America and above all Russia. Again, the precious icons received place of honour in corners of each room and before long the familiar furniture and possessions personalised their new home.

John was delighted to be living with his son and family and especially enjoyed the unfettered access to his beloved grandson. Now that he was retired he had plenty of time to enjoy with the toddler, in a way he could never do with his own children. The little blond boy was the image of his father at that age and John considered himself to be blessed to have this second opportunity at fatherhood as it were. He quickly took the title of *'Deda'*, a shortened form of *Dedushka,* the Russian word for grandfather. Not only to David but seemingly to everyone, including the mothers of the local toddlers group which met at their house and with whose youngsters he soon became a firm favourite. Later when Michael and Karen's second son Jack was born, he too would grow up with the great privilege of knowing that the door to his devoted grandfather would always be open. Never one to sit still, John helps both Michael and Karen with a score of activities, from babysitting to house painting, gardening to shopping. In fact, Karen's friends declare they also want a 'Deda' and the joke in their household is that, should they ever divorce, heaven forbid, Karen would keep Deda! A great compliment for any in-law surely but one that comes as no surprise to those who know him.

A supreme optimist, despite enduring a harsh life and numerous setbacks that might have left a lesser person bitter, Dad rose to life's challenges and turned them to his advantage. Very much like his mother, he considers it necessary and desirable to always work hard and he has not stopped working just because he is retired. On the contrary, he considers it even more important to be productive and useful, though he can now choose his work rather than being at the mercy of an employer. He rises early each morning and does 50 or so press-ups, eats sensibly, drinks only in moderation, does not have an ounce of fat on his body and consequently looks remarkably fit and healthy. For years he has suffered from tinnitus, that persistent ringing in the ears that can drive some people to distraction. John has decided that it sounds like the ear splitting cacophony of noise made by cicadas, so redolent of the Australian bush. When he goes to bed, rather than letting his malady keep him awake, John welcomes his familiar friends and drops off happily with the sound of the countryside in his ears. Just one such example of his ability to turn misfortune to his advantage.

Zina's eldest daughter Nina passed away in Dnepropetrovsk, far from her family, as previously related. Her younger daughter, Julie, lived for 44 years in Australia and bore two of her three children there. Julie had never attained her aspirations of working in an office environment, using the stenographic skills she had studied in the Shanghai Commercial College. Her lack of confidence in English probably contributed to this yet she had a much better command of the language than she gave herself credit for, read prolifically, excelled at crosswords and could defeat anyone at 'Scrabble'. Nonetheless, she worked for many years in various menial jobs then succeeded in obtaining a good position at *'Cablemakers'* where she worked in quality control, being responsible for product standards. She was valued as an efficient, methodical and dedicated employee. Eventually she found some fulfilment working in a Russian convalescent home as a nursing aide. At the St. Sergius home in Cabramatta she was greatly appreciated for her concern for her patients and the very valuable asset of being able to speak to them in their mother tongue, something which many of the younger, qualified nurses could not do. Julie could joke and cajole the elderly patients, chatting to them about their common childhoods in China and Russia which the increasingly senile people often remembered more clearly than recent events. Julie had a great sense of humour and often regaled us with amusing stories about her patients.

Julie passed away in 1995 aged just 70, of a heart attack. She had suffered minor strokes before and had been ailing for some time, with various conditions causing her considerable discomfort. High blood pressure and diabetes contributed to a desire on her part to avoid a lengthy, distressing old age and her wish was granted with a painless, quick death on the morning of August 20, 1995. I was visiting Australia that winter, as I try to do every 2-3 years, and was awoken by my agitated sister-in-law Karen, a nurse, who had been trying to resuscitate her with the help of my brother Michael. Ambulance men had arrived and also tried to revive Julie but to no avail. She was pronounced dead in our presence. A forlorn John, numb with shock, covered his wife of 44 years with their duvet. Helen, who had been summoned urgently in the early hours, Michael and I tried to comfort him and each other as best we could. It had all been so tragically sudden and we were bereft of words in our grief and horror. We kissed her farewell and she was taken away.

*Julie's grave, over her mother's, as requested. To the left is Zina's mother Praskovia and next to her is Pelageya (Aunt Polya).*

325

I stayed in the country long enough to see my mother's coffin laid to rest on top of her own mother's, in the overflowing cemetery at Sydney Necropolis. She was given an Orthodox funeral. John had chosen to waive the formal ceremony in a church and so the last rites were conducted by a priest at the graveside. In time honoured fashion, each of the bereaved took a handful of dirt to cover the coffin before it was swallowed by the earth.

Dad and I returned a few days later with my young sons to tend the grave and tidy the mass of flowers. He gasped at the sight of the flower strewn grave, crossed his arms on his chest and stood in silent reverence; I think it was only then that he realised his lifelong companion had really gone. After arranging the flowers and paying our respects, we went for a stroll amongst the tombstones.

*Daniel and Stefan with their grandfather, in Sydney Necropolis, 1995.*

The Russian Orthodox section of the cemetery is huge and unlike many other denominations, it is not a grey and morbid place. On the contrary, it is colourful, vibrant and almost cheerful. There were many people about on this warm and sunny winter's day. Widows, widowers and family, fondly tending the graves of their relatives; putting out fresh flowers and dusting away any debris that had accumulated since their last visit. People normally bring a small brush and broom, bucket and sponge for this purpose. The result is a clean and sparkling scene. Each tomb has its own distinctive Orthodox cross, with its two extra cross bars, usually painted white. Hundreds upon hundreds of these bright crosses thrust themselves into the blue sky and, together with all the colourful flowers, created a heart-warming vista. It seemed to me that those tending the graves, most of whom I imagined to be believers, were doing a wonderful job of creating a little bit of heaven for their loved ones.

We wandered down the neat footpaths amongst the tombs. Here was my great uncle Alexei - Дядя Лёша and his wife Ekaterina, in a resplendent joint marble grave, as befitted the patriarch of the Shliapnikoff family and a successful businessman. Nearby was his mother, Praskovia, known to the family as *'Babinka'*, the true matriarch and mother of eight. A photograph of her in her customary black garb and head scarf adorned her tombstone. Two of Alexei's sons were here too, Volodya and Victor, both taken at an early age. We also found Aunt Polya's grave and my favourite uncle, Vadim's, the one I knew as my 'American' uncle, for his

*The graves of Alexei and Ekaterina, and their sons Victor and Vladimir.*

family had settled there before arriving in Australia. This all came as something of a revelation to my British sons. They had no idea they had so many relatives and were curious to meet their generational counterparts, the descendents of all these aunts, uncles and cousins.

We also came across many of my parents' friends, people whom they had known from Shanghai. Their epitaphs, usually written in both Russian and English for the benefit of their descendents, often quoting their place of birth as Harbin, China. We stumbled across one Avenir Avenirovich,

known as Venya to his friends, whom we remembered fondly as a sprightly bachelor who had gained notoriety amongst the Russian community for his habit of frequenting naturist beaches. We had lost touch with him and here was the explanation lying at our feet. We smiled at his memory and were reminded that people are not truly gone while they live in the hearts and minds of others.

The day's task was not yet done until we had visited the grave of the unforgettable Maria Zinovyevna, John's mother. Since her death 20 years earlier John has loyally visited

*The cupola of the Orthodox monument, Sydney Necropolis.*

her grave several times a year, usually on the anniversary of her death, her birthday and Mother's day. Her grave, like the others, was meticulously maintained.

We also took a few moments to admire the attractive blue and gold cupola of the Orthodox monument, a symbol of the faith that was dedicated to the memory of the destroyed cathedral in Harbin. The memorials reads *'In memory of all Russian Orthodox people resting in peace throughout the world.'*

Julie is survived by three children, seven grandchildren and one great grandson. Her eldest daughter, Helen, born in Shanghai, was particularly close to her mother. They had endured many hard years together in China before her mother's eventual remarriage.

As the recipient of a traditional upbringing, my sister's generation were encouraged to marry early. Being a wartime baby and suffering early privations led her to seek security and 'settle' as quickly as possible. She did so and had two sons in quick succession. By the birth of her third son, however, her marriage had begun to flounder. The subsequent years were very difficult and in the end Helen was left on her own with three school age children to raise. To support herself and her sons, Helen immediately returned to work, fulfilling her mother's aspirations of becoming a successful secretary. She has held many responsible administrative positions, including that of Personal Assistant, where she quickly and competently adapted to using the latest computer technology. Only very recently has she reduced her hours in semi-retirement and now works in a call centre.

*Helen and nephew Daniel, 1981.*

Helen is close to her sons and is rightly very proud of how they have developed, considering she was solely responsible for their upbringing. She now focuses her time on them and their families as well as her job. An intelligent woman, she has a fantastic memory, reads prolifically and keeps fully abreast of current affairs. She also enjoys playing computer games, does crossword puzzles and avidly watches films. In fact, very much the same sort of activities that our mother also enjoyed in her latter years.

*Helen's eldest son, Rob, and his son James, 1995.*

*John on his wedding day.*

Helen's eldest son Rob has a son of his own and is living in a stable family environment, as does her second son, John. Suffering from severe lifelong diabetes, John has had to overcome enormous obstacles to lead a normal life. We witnessed him routinely performing manual kidney dialysis as though it was the most natural thing in the world. Since then John has undergone a pancreas and kidney transplant and demonstrated great courage and fortitude to live an independent and productive life. He has recently married and is very happy with his newly acquired large family.

Helen now lives with her youngest son Andrew. He has a good job and his greatest interest is his motor cycle track club, which numbers nearly 1,600 and meets periodically to race at tracks around Australia. Andrew loves the Australian outback and has travelled extensively across this vast and diverse continent, enjoying its nature and unique wildlife.

*Andrew.*

A few years ago Helen rediscovered her Aunt Elena (the sister of her biological father, Yura) after whom she was named. Yura returned to Russia from Shanghai in the 1940's, remarried and, like Julie, produced a son and daughter. Helen traced her half sister, Olga, now living in Kazakhstan and enjoyed a correspondence with her for many years.

*Helen visiting a Russian ship, berthed in Sydney Harbour.*

*Andrew with his motor bike club, Sydney Harbour (Andrew in centre, back).*

Michael, the only son of John and Julie, lives a happy and fulfilling life with his beautiful and vivacious wife Karen, an accomplished and popular nurse. They run a thriving company selling personal computers and office solutions, Michael having attained his goal of working for no one but himself. He devotes much of his free time studying and refining his computer skills in order to meet the demands of his customers. Michael is proud of his country and, when work permits, enjoys the great Australian outdoors. He loves fishing, camping, boating, even hunts on occasion, practising the shooting skills he learns at his gun club. He also successfully plays competitive squash and jogs, to offset those other popular Australian pastimes of drinking beer and having barbeques. Positive, outgoing and supremely optimistic, Michael is a brother of whom one can be proud. Karen is intensely social with an array of friends as well as grateful patients who often ask for her by name. An inspirational nurse, she has a genuine warm empathy with people. The couple are very neighbourly and will often hold parties on the front lawn, to which all and sundry are invited.

*Michael and Karen.*

*David.*

They have two delightful children. David John (DJ), the eldest, studies at a Sydney Grammar school and has ambitions to become an engineer, which he will undoubtedly achieve. David appears to have absorbed much of his grandfather John's earnestness and integrity, to which his devoted parents have, of course, also contributed a great deal. A charming, studious boy, he appears to have adopted the cultural legacy of his mother's family and studies German. He recently enjoyed a student exchange in that country and is keen to travel further afield.

Jack is an energetic and happy boy, full of fun and mischief. He played soccer as a little boy but has recently taken up rugby league, much to the dismay of his grandfather, who considers it to be dangerous. Jack can be determined however, and may

*Jack.*

well become a successful sportsman, though his current hobby is watching weather patterns and cloud formations. He also enjoys observing nature in his own backyard, especially spiders and insects, and helps his 'Deda' grow vegetables. A pumpkin that they cultivated to grow up a lemon tree was recently dubbed a *'Lemkin'* by Jack.

As for me, the family exile, who can rarely keep still, forever burning with a passion to see and to make sense of the world around me; I have led a mostly charmed life.

After leaving Cabramatta High, I gained a degree in History and Philosophy from the University of NSW. I subsequently went to work for an Australian bank, where I trained as a programmer before progressing to systems analyst. After several years in computing, in Sydney and London, I eventually left the industry following the birth of our first child. When our second started nursery school I decided to teach History and gained my teaching certificate from the University of Reading, close to our home in the very congenial atmosphere of semi-rural Berkshire, England, where I had taken 'root' as it were.

I pursue my love of history, which I also attempt to share with pupils, and travel as frequently as I can, to observe other cultures and to stay in touch with my extended family around the globe. When possible I continue to read and study the applications of my lifelong commitment to Liberty, a constant quest for understanding. Dance, literature, theatre and music are further interests I would like more time to enjoy. But whatever I do, I always have the support and encouragement of my husband Ken.

*Marina, Stefan and Daniel, Prague 2005.*

We share a love of the natural world enjoying walking in the beautiful British countryside, preferably beside rivers or canals. Our first home was a traditional narrow boat in which we spent an idyllic summer exploring the extensive canal system of England and Wales. A legacy of Britain's industrial past, today they gently meander through picturesque countryside, historic cities and lovely villages. A most enjoyable way to see the heart of Britain. Since then we have established a permanent home in the south which Ken maintains with the same characteristic dedication and precision he brings to all challenges, whether in his role as a computer consultant or at home. Whatever the problem, his logical and calm approach to life always finds a solution. A wonderful father and a thoughtful and considerate husband, he is a gem.

*Ken, 2006.*

Hailing from Northern, Mancunian stock, his warm and friendly family welcomed me with open arms. I shall never forget Ken's late mother, Lily, and her extraordinary generosity of spirit, very reminiscent of my grandmother Maria, whom she uncannily resembled. Lily and Ken Senior's two other sons and their families maintain the Brierley family links and I am grateful to be accepted into their culture, quite foreign to my own background. Thank you, Geoff, Barbara, Karen, David, Emma, Dave, Judith, Helen and Hannah.

*Daniel Ivan, 2004.*

Our son Daniel Ivan, graduated with a B.Sc.(Hons.) in Bio-medical Sciences and has embarked on a career in scientific research, based in London. He is involved in studying neuro-physiology, which concerns the structure and function of the brain, which he considers the final frontier of medical science. He likes living in the East end of the capital, an area noted for its cultural diversity. Daniel shares a house with friends, follows current affairs, relishes satirical humour and enjoys English pubs, clubs and music venues. Inspired by Gap year travels to Peru and South America, his second language is, alas, more likely to be

Spanish rather than Russian. A keen traveller, he remembers many happy childhood summers spent in Australia, which we left when he was one year old and talks of spending more time there as an adult if and when the opportunity arises.

*Stefan and his grandfather John.*

However, it is his British born younger brother, Stefan, who has actually done so. As part of his world wide travels he spent several months in Sydney working for a major bank and in the process re-established close ties with his grandfather, uncle, aunt and cousins. Stefan worked hard to accomplish his goal of travelling and visited America, Canada and New Zealand on his way to Australia, then South east Asia on his return, particularly relishing Laos and Cambodia. He works in web publishing in a management position and is valued by his colleagues for his dedication, excellent work ethic and communication skills. A popular and truly generous individual, Stefan aspires to a career in computing and music, with the aim of eventually running his own business. With his charm and energy he will surely succeed.

Both sons are fine young men with unbounded confidence, a multitude of friends and the capacity to enjoy life to the full. I do not expect them to be constrained to any one country any more than I was. The world is our home.

## The remaining Shalavins.

Our family history returns to the Shalavins, which for obvious reasons, I know most about. What had become of them in the intervening years?

John had moved into a new home with his son just over a year before Julie's sudden and untimely death. Thankfully John could seek solace in the company of Michael, Karen and their son David for, as a naturally gregarious person, he would have found solitary widowhood intolerable. After two years on his own, he fulfilled a longstanding ambition to visit his daughter in England. (Julie had been to the UK and Europe before but by the time I settled there she was too ill to travel.) John had a wonderful time visiting us, spending time with his grandsons and seeing as much of the country as we could fit into a hectic two month schedule. He saw not only the famed attractions of London, but much of the beautiful English countryside in the 'home counties' of Berkshire,

*John on the River Thames, Berkshire, 1997; a traditional narrowboat in the background.*

Hampshire and Oxfordshire. He enjoyed white water rafting in the lovely rivers of Wales, walked the rugged Pennines up North in Lancashire and marvelled at the historic sites of York and the wonders of the Yorkshire Dales. He returned to Australia grateful for the experience and with a better understanding of why his loving daughter had chosen to live so far from 'home'.

Still handsome, active and essentially a very joyful person, it is not surprising that John was in demand amongst the single females of his acquaintance. He coped reasonably well with widowhood though it was not the preferred state for someone who had been accustomed to a soul mate. After six years of being on his own, a chance meeting with some old Shanghai acquaintances led to a 'date' with Olga Pronin, another Russian widow. Was it all engineered by aunt Galina? We cannot say but the outcome has been a very fulfilling and happy relationship. In Olga he found a companion who mirrors his optimism, resilience and strength of character. They have no need of an all consuming marital tie, both relish

*John and Olga.*

their independence to pursue their own interests and devote time to their respective families. But weekends are spent together, walking hand in hand along Sydney's beaches or attending concerts, the Russian club or playing mahjong with friends. They bring only positive elements to their relationship and are both thoroughly deserving of their happiness. Long may it continue.

As to the remaining Shalavins. John's younger brother, Anatoly or Tony as he was known, was rather less responsible than his mother Maria would have liked, yet he was also full of *joie de vivre* when one met him socially. A self confessed alcoholic, he eventually died of Tuberculosis. Yet he was not inherently malicious, was capable of kindness, certainly jovial and by all accounts he was a competent mechanic.

Tony's first marriage to Ludmilla produced a son and daughter, Nicholas and Natasha. Following her parent's divorce, Natasha, who was still very young at the time, went to live with her mother and so we did not see much of her. However, Babushka, to her credit, maintained a very loving relationship with her granddaughter and was rewarded many years later when she was guest of honour at Natalie's wedding. I still remember Natalie weeping copiously at her funeral not long after. Natalie married a Ukrainian Australian, Vassili (Basil), and they have three sons. I believe they now live in the country in western NSW.

*Nick Shalavin.*

Nick also lives in the country with his partner. Nick and I had been childhood friends, our ages being closer than our siblings. His family had lived in our back garden for a few years, in the same 'garage' that had been our first home. Nick was an amiable companion in those days, but once they had moved to their own place, and as we grew, our lives drifted further apart. He had been a successful businessman in the city, running a lucrative toy store in a very prestigious downtown location. Later, he moved into the greengrocery business as a wholesaler before relocating to the country. Today he lives in contented seclusion in a remote property in northern NSW. I was delighted to resume contact with him recently and find that in his retirement he has returned to studying, gaining educational qualifications and moreover, has been studying Russian language as well as traditional cookery. Good for him!

Nick's younger brother George had been Michael's play friend in childhood and, living in the same city, they still keep in touch. A tall, dark, attractive man he has the same swarthy, Mediterranean appearance of his father and uncle. George married an English girl, Jacqueline, and they have three children. George served in the forces for a while, much to the pride of his mother, and now works in telecommunications in a successful managerial capacity.

*John and nephew George*
*at John's 80th birthday celebrations, 2007.*

*George and Jacqueline's children Mark, Courtney and Robert.*

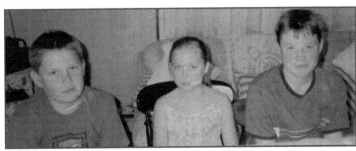

Nick and George's younger brother, Alex, tragically died in a freak accident in his teens. Tanya, his mother, bore this tragedy with strength and stoicism. A determined and capable woman, she is thriving in her own independent flat, attached to the Orthodox monastery in the western suburb of Campbelltown, Sydney. She recently enjoyed a surprise 70th birthday party arranged by her loving family. John continues to take a great interest in his brother's children, Tanya's sons and their children, to whom he is also, like an honorary grandfather. So, the Shalavins by and large, are flourishing in Australia and John has the comfort of knowing that at least six of the next generation bear his name.

# The Shliapnikoffs today.

The families of the second branch of the Shliapnikoff clan are scattered far and wide. Alexei and Ekaterina had become quite comfortable from his small goods factory and had lived long enough to enjoy their retirement and their 50th Wedding anniversary.

*The 50th Wedding anniversary party of Alexei and Ekaterina (seated). To their left, Olga and Volodya, Katya and George. To their right, Vadim and Vera, Valya and Victor.*

Alexei passed away in 1974, Ekaterina lived a further 16 years, initially living with her daughter Vera and her family before eventually moving to the Russian Old People's home in Cabramatta when she became too frail. It had been a long journey from that momentous decision back in 1930 when Alexei was barely 28, to leave his troubled motherland and start afresh in an unknown land. Little did they know then that they would end up so far away, in a sun bleached country, so foreign to their own familiar climate.

The three sons continued to work the factory but control passed to the eldest son George (Yura). The business continued to prosper and George and his wife Katya lived a luxurious lifestyle amongst Sydney's elite society. They had a spectacular home overlooking the breathtaking harbour and the time to enjoy leisure and cultural pursuits. They were musical, George played the dombra, a haunting string instrument not dissimilar to the more famous balalaika, in the Sydney Dombra Ensemble. Katya plays the piano, still does as far as I know, and took pride in performing publicly, occasionally on television. A woman of great beauty, with similarities to Elizabeth Taylor, she was one of the glamorous faces of the family. Her husband was the last of the three sons to pass away. They had one son, Nicholas, who was at university at about the same time as me but our paths never crossed. I believe he married and moved to America.

The second son, Volodya (Walter) and his wife Olga had two children, Tania and Michael who are thriving in Sydney. Tania graduated in Russian and Psychology and works as a Coordinator for Russian Old People's homes. Widowed early, Olga worked for a number of Russian charities and helped administer the St. Sergius Russian convalescent home in Cabramatta, where my mother had for a long time also enjoyed working. She is a very attractive woman who keeps active and busy and whom I last met at my mother's funeral.

The strongest memories I have of Alexei's three sons are of his youngest, Victor. He was a boisterous, larger than life character, who liked his vodka, especially at social gatherings when he was the life and soul of the party. Married twice, his first wife, Dawn, an Australian, died tragically young, leaving two young children, Tony and Nina. Tony married Cathy and they have six children, Kyle, Jade, Josie, Amore (Amy), Dane and Kate. Tony is also 'Deda' to Taeya and Chelsea (Kyle's daughters), Makaylah, Aysha and Kaleb (Jade's children) and Layla (Amy's daughter). Following the birth of Kyle, they settled in the cool temperate, southern island state of Tasmania, where they grow blueberries. Daughter Josie has left the island to work as an Environmental scientist in Western Australia.

*Tony and his family (plus grandmother Ekaterina, centre, Vera and Vovie Mihailoff on the right) c. 1988.*

Tony's sister Nina also lives in Tasmania, with her partner Geoff. Their son Jock and his partner Nardia have just had a baby boy Liam, Nina's first grandchild. Nina's daughter Rowena is a lawyer, living in the state capital, Hobart. It was a pleasure to recently discover that the 'Tassie' branch of the family are flourishing.

*Vera and Vadim, California 1950's.*

Alexei and Ekaterina's remaining child is their daughter Vera, who is also my godmother. A very intelligent, sensitive woman, she is a devout practising Christian who finds solace in the teachings of the Orthodox faith. She married Vadim, now sadly no longer with us; he was an ambitious engineer who gained his degree in California, where they had settled after leaving China and where their three sons, Victor, Vad and Volodya were born.

When the boys were still young they decided to join the rest of the family in Australia. I can still recall meeting them for the first time and having the usual arguments about how to pronounce things, they with their American accents and we with our Australian ones. (How could anyone make *'aloomanum'* out of *'aluminium'?*) The parents had particularly intriguing accents. Like most of that generation they spoke with distinct Russian overtones, but whereas we were used to hearing Russian Australian from our elders, they spoke in a very gentle Russian American.

Vadim continued to practice engineering in Sydney and two of his three sons followed in his footsteps. Vad graduated from the University of NSW and works in various engineering capacities all over the country. He also likes to travel and has frequently returned to his country of birth, America. Volodya or Vovie as he is known (pictured with Tony's family on the previous page), has also travelled extensively, including Vietnam and other parts of Asia where he has worked. Their eldest son, Victor, developed a love for religion and attended a seminary in America for several years, with the aim of becoming an Orthodox monk. It did not eventuate for various reasons and he returned to Australia, where he is now semi-retired through illness and pursuing a new career in writing. A very interesting family who I am pleased to call friends as well as kin.

*Victor in Jerusalem.*

*Vad, Sydney 2008.*

*Vera in her home in Carlingford, Sydney.*

Some members of the family succeeded in reaching the promised land of America, which so many had dreamt of back in China. Obtaining visas for the USA was very difficult and so the third branch of the clan, Peter and Tania Bakaldin, like many others, initially evacuated to Tubabao in the Philippines before migrating to Australia. However, after five years they succeeded in obtaining the necessary documents for American immigration and relocated to California. Tania and Peter went on to live

*Peter and Tania Bakaldin and son Nick, San Francisco.*

long, happy productive lives in the USA. Their route to the 'American Dream' had been an arduous one, from Russia to Shanghai, the Philippines to Sydney and finally to San Francisco. In California they had at last found their 'home', where they lived for the rest of their lives, 33 and 37 years respectively. They had lived to see both their children establish themselves in their adopted country and go on to become successful in their chosen fields.

What of their children Olga and Nicholas? Nikolai, the 'mischievous' toddler whose demands for water within earshot of the patrolling guards on the Soviet-Manchurian border had nearly cost the family its chance of escaping the USSR, was always ambitious. He had entered Australia on a student's visa and went on to gain his degree and become a successful engineer. He also relocated to California when he had the opportunity and married Natasha, another Russian expatriate and a qualified teacher. They have three adult children, Anna, Michael and Nina, all graduates of American universities and practising professionals in their respective fields. Nicholas and Natasha are active in the Russian community in San Francisco, teaching in the Russian school there, based like most Russian schools around the world, within the Orthodox church. They now live in comfortable retirement in their beautiful San Francisco home and are no doubt thoroughly enjoying being grandparents.

Unlike most other first generation Australians or Americans of my era, this branch of the family appeared to marry within the Russian community. Their eldest daughter Nina married Dimitri, and they have two children, Elih and Alena. Michael married Katya and they have three children, John, Larissa and Natasha. It sounds like Anna has broken with tradition by marrying Robert, but this is conjecture on my part. I am delighted to report the addition of two more sons to the clan, Gabe and little Daniel.

Nicholas' sister Olga has had a most rewarding and interesting career. After the war she went to nursing school, presumably still in China. Growing up during wartime had obviously made a deep impression upon this very serious and sensitive woman. Having married during this time, she and her husband Anatoly, chose to go to Argentina in July 1948, where there was also a small Russian community. She relates that life was not easy in Buenos Aires and the wages were low. She learned Spanish and slowly adjusted to life there, but naturally missed the rest of her family. Their eldest daughter, Irene was born in Argentina. After two and a half years they decided to move to Australia where her parents were still living at that time. She lived in Sydney for three years, where her second daughter, Helen was born. Following the break-up of her marriage in 1954 she obtained permission to go to the USA with her two daughters, where she could be reunited with her parents and brother, who incidentally had been conscripted to fight in the Korean War. Having obtained her American nursing qualifications, Olga worked as an operating theatre nursing sister at a general hospital in San Francisco for many years until her retirement. Her career had given her both fulfilment and financial security. An astute business-woman, as well as a genuinely caring person, she succeeded in buying not only her own flat, but the entire block, which she oversees as a careful landlady. Having finally settled in the country of her choice, she is happy to be able to live quietly in peace, she claims, and only regrets the death of her beloved parents, whom she still misses.

*Olga in front of cable car, San Francisco.*

Olga's life has been a wonderful example of strength and resilience in the face of adversity. She was able to forge a career as a dedicated and professional nursing sister whilst bringing up two attractive daughters, largely as a single mother. To combine a successful career and motherhood is difficult at the best of times, but to do it on your own whilst circumstances oblige you to travel from country to country shows a remarkable strength of character, determination and flexibility. She now lives in comfortable retirement in San Francisco and pursues her passion for travel whenever she can. She has travelled extensively within the USA but also to Europe and on more than one occasion to her land of origin, Russia, where she makes a point of giving assistance – food, gifts and monetary aid to the relatives who remained behind and their

*Olga's granddaughter, Sasha Jouk from San Francisco, visiting her great aunt Lara in Russia.*

descendants. All the Russian relatives I have spoken to are united in praising Olga's consistent help and generosity. Olga's daughters, Irene and Helen are themselves married with four daughters between them – Lisa and Sasha (Elizabeth and Alexandra), Gina and Jessica. Gina is herself married with three sons and Olga takes great pride in being a great grandmother. This branch of the family still all live in California and to their credit, continue the family tradition of keeping strong ties with their extended families.

*The American branch of the family, San Francisco, 2006.*
*From left - Tom, Jessica, Sasha, Helen, Irene,Olga, Nick, Elih, Misha, little Natasha in front, Rob, holding Gabe, Nina, Dima, Alena, Natasha, John, Nick, kneeling in front.*

So what of Polya's descendants, the fourth branch of our family? Of the two children that survived into adulthood, Vera returned to Russia and Dima Pravosudov recently passed away, in his eighties. He had lived to a ripe old age in Sydney, despite suffering from throat cancer. He was one of the few Russians of that generation to marry outside the culture. His wife, Jo, was a warm and affectionate New Zealander who had been welcomed into the family fold. She had been friends with my mother and they both died suddenly within a few months of each other. Dima and Jo are survived by a son, Peter, who calls himself Peter Prava I believe. He is a tall, strapping, handsome man who I had the pleasure of meeting only at my mother's funeral. He was congenial, easy going and thoroughly Australian. Peter lives in the country, where he was establishing a trout farm if I recall correctly. He has two children, Belinda and Dylan. Do they know of their heritage I wonder?

Elena, the fifth Shliapnikoff sibling died tragically young in China of Tuberculosis. She was succeeded by two children, Galina, still sprightly and as active as ever though not far off 80, and Alexander, who went to live in Canada when his father obtained a deacon's post there. Alexander's branch of the family is thriving in Canada. He has six children, Boris, Fred, Alexander, Natalie, Olga and Paul, three of whom have children of their own.

Galina (my aunt Galia) and her devoted husband Leo recently celebrated their 60th wedding anniversary (pictured below).

*Leo enjoys fishing in Australia's Snowy Mountains.*

They still live in the very house they bought soon after arriving from their tempestuous time in Tubabao in the Philippines.

Though retired now, they still live productive and creative lives. Leo paints very proficiently, Galina also creates interesting tapestries and embroiders. Both competent linguists, Galina continues to study and teach French, a legacy of her school years in *Ecole Remi* in Shanghai.

Of all our relatives, they probably embraced Australian culture most enthusiastically, working with youth groups as Scoutmasters, in Parents and Citizen's Associations and other worthy local groups. They have thoroughly immersed themselves in their communities and are truly grateful for the opportunities Australia presented them.

Yet their lives have been blighted by the untimely deaths of their three sons, for which there is no rational explanation. A cruel fate took each son in the prime of his life and one cannot begin to comprehend how painful that must be for any parent. Nonetheless, each son had children of their own and Galina and Leo have the consolation of not just grand-children, but great grandchildren.

Their youngest son Theodore, or Teddy as he was known, fathered Daniel, who like my Daniel is also coincidentally a biologist, though specialising in microbiology, as his proud grandfather informed me. Dan, like his grandfather, also enjoys fishing.

Teddy's daughter, Eliza, remains in touch with her grandparents and they delight in her children, their great grandchildren.

*Dan Ivanoff with a successful catch.*

*John, Louise (Leo's sister-in-law). Galina and Leo. Olga, Olga
Pronin and Irene Kounitsky.*

Finally there is the youngest son
Nicholas, only 16 when he embarked on
that perilous flight through the
Manchurian wilderness in 1930. He was
to grow up in China and marry his first
wife Falia there, though she was to die
tragically young of TB, I believe.
Nicholas left China in the late 1940's,
bound for the shores of the USA and the
fulfilment of the American dream. He
married another Russian American,
became a businessman and lived to the
ripe old age of 91. The last of the original
Shliapnikoff siblings of our story, he
passed away in 2004.

He had a daughter, Tania, by his first wife
and a son, Alexander, by the second of
his three wives. Tania married Rouben
Chakalian and they had five daughters,

*Tania and her father Nicholas.*

Angela, Annette, Nina, Victoria and Rosa. Tania and Rouben lived a
comfortable life in California, having travelled around the world. They
lived for a time in Switzerland I believe and it is possible that some of the

girls may have been born there. I was delighted to recently receive some interesting information from them that had been published in their local newspaper to celebrate their 50th Wedding Anniversary. I was aware that Tania and Rouben had been acquaintances during their childhoods in Shanghai, after all the Shliapnikoffs and Chakalians had been neighbours so it was not surprising that their children knew one another. It transpires, however, that following their respective families move to California, Tania and Rouben had met again at a school dance in San Francisco. Love blossomed and when they graduated in 1956, Tania from High School and Rouben from University, they married that same year. Rouben continued to study, earning his Master's degree whilst serving as an officer in the army. He pursued an illustrious career in business, reaching senior executive positions with major U.S. corporations and spent many years working in Europe. Following his retirement he was a frequent guest speaker on international business at various universities, was a Knight of Columbus and an American Legionnaire. He found time to relax too, enjoying American and international soccer. It is with great regret, however, that I must report that he suddenly passed away in late 2007.

Tania is active in her local parish, enjoys bowling and swimming and undoubtedly takes pride in having raised five daughters who in turn have ten children between them. All the daughters and their families reside in the San Francisco bay area, an apparently close extended family and indeed, extending further I believe. May they all enjoy long life and happiness.

The Shalavins and Shliapnikoffs are indeed scattered far and wide. Their close family bonds and mutual support, forged in the face of shared hardships in Russia, China and the new countries, now all but a fading memory. As each passing year claims yet more witnesses to those tumultuous times, there is a risk that their heritage will be lost forever.

Therefore, I offer this story to all Russians abroad, wherever in the world Russians have fled, but particularly to the descendents of our brave emigré families. The flight from their homeland should not be forgotten, nor the reason for the diaspora undervalued. To this end, I respectfully dedicate this family history to the countless number of people whose personal freedoms are still denied. The search for freedom is our forebears' legacy and our right. Let it also be our conscious goal.

# Shliapnikoff Family Trees

*(Overleaf)*

Part 1: the eldest four of Artemy & Praskovia's eight children.

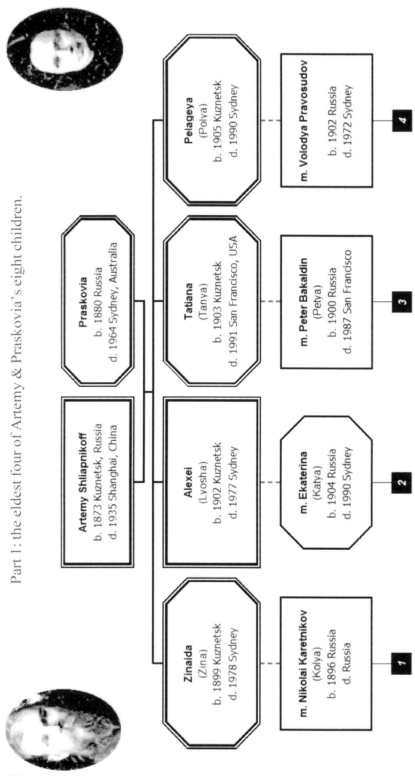

**Artemy Shliapnikoff**
b. 1873 Kuznetsk, Russia
d. 1935 Shanghai, China

**Praskovia**
b. 1880 Russia
d. 1964 Sydney, Australia

**Zinaida**
(Zina)
b. 1899 Kuznetsk
d. 1978 Sydney

m. Nikolai Karetnikov
(Kolya)
b. 1896 Russia
d. Russia

**1**

**Alexei**
(Lyosha)
b. 1902 Kuznetsk
d. 1977 Sydney

m. Ekaterina
(Katya)
b. 1904 Russia
d. 1990 Sydney

**2**

**Tatiana**
(Tanya)
b. 1903 Kuznetsk
d. 1991 San Francisco, USA

m. Peter Bakaldin
(Petya)
b. 1900 Russia
d. 1987 San Francisco

**3**

**Pelageya**
(Polya)
b. 1905 Kuznetsk
d. 1990 Sydney

m. Volodya Pravosudov
b. 1902 Russia
d. 1972 Sydney

**4**

Part 2: the youngest four of **Artemy** & **Praskovia**'s eight children.

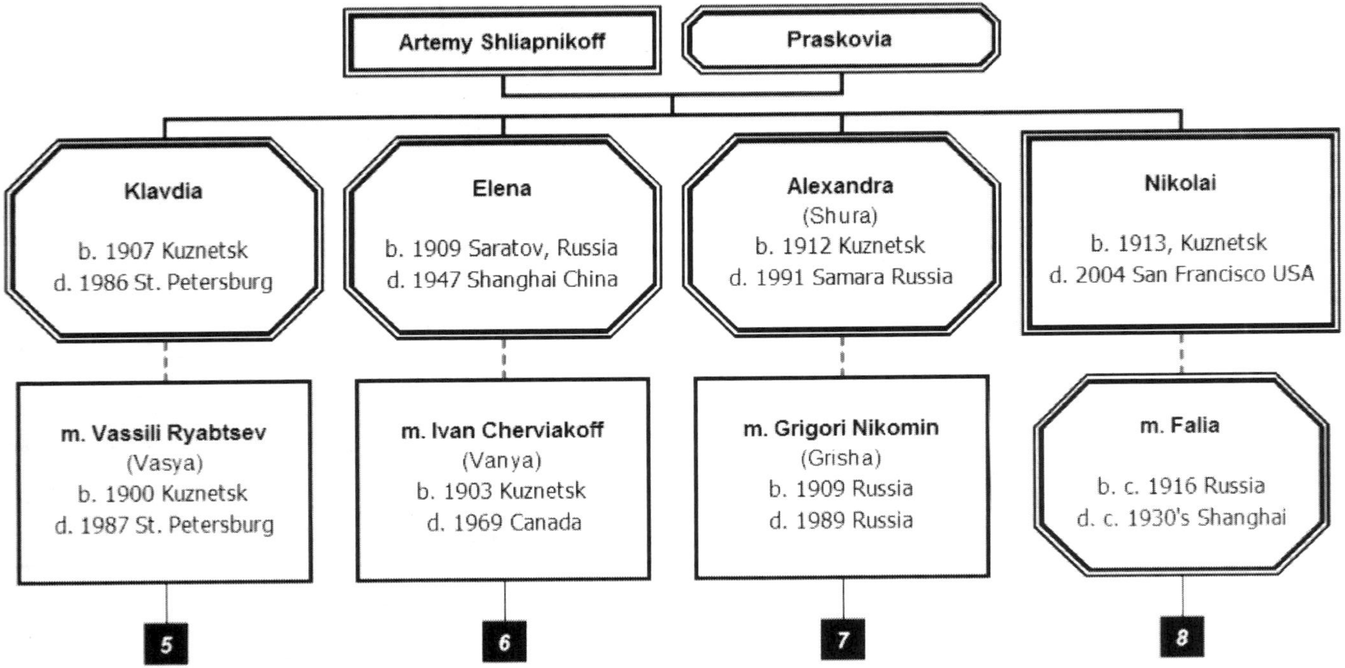

**Artemy Shliapnikoff**

**Praskovia**

**Klavdia**
b. 1907 Kuznetsk
d. 1986 St. Petersburg

**Elena**
b. 1909 Saratov, Russia
d. 1947 Shanghai China

**Alexandra**
(Shura)
b. 1912 Kuznetsk
d. 1991 Samara Russia

**Nikolai**
b. 1913, Kuznetsk
d. 2004 San Francisco USA

**m. Vassili Ryabtsev**
(Vasya)
b. 1900 Kuznetsk
d. 1987 St. Petersburg

**m. Ivan Cherviakoff**
(Vanya)
b. 1903 Kuznetsk
d. 1969 Canada

**m. Grigori Nikomin**
(Grisha)
b. 1909 Russia
d. 1989 Russia

**m. Falia**
b. c. 1916 Russia
d. c. 1930's Shanghai

5

6

7

8

**1** Zinaida & Nikolai's children

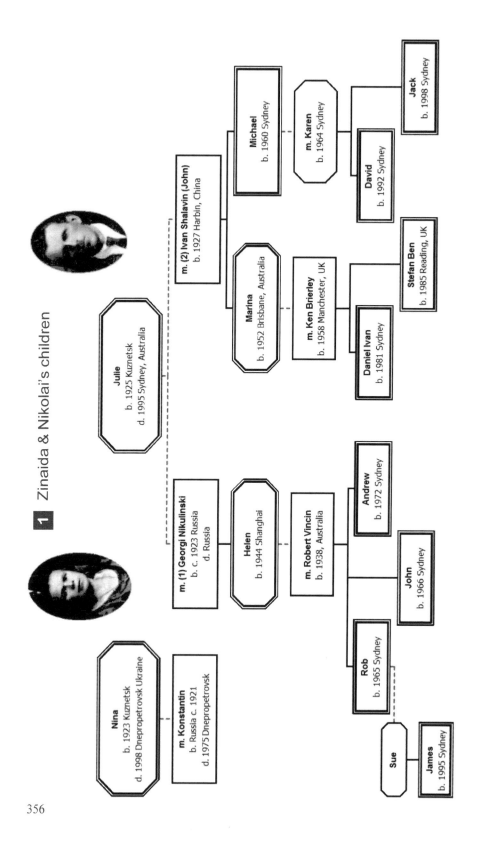

Nina
b. 1923 Kuznetsk
d. 1998 Dnepropetrovsk Ukraine

m. Konstantin
b. Russia c. 1921
d. 1975 Dnepropetrovsk

Julie
b. 1925 Kuznetsk
d. 1995 Sydney, Australia

m. (1) Georgi Nikulinski
b. c. 1923 Russia
d. Russia

Helen
b. 1944 Shanghai

m. Robert Vincin
b. 1938, Australia

Rob
b. 1965 Sydney

John
b. 1966 Sydney

Andrew
b. 1972 Sydney

Sue

James
b. 1995 Sydney

m. (2) Ivan Shalavin (John)
b. 1927 Harbin, China

Marina
b. 1952 Brisbane, Australia

m. Ken Brierley
b. 1958 Manchester, UK

Daniel Ivan
b. 1981 Sydney

Stefan Ben
b. 1985 Reading, UK

Michael
b. 1960 Sydney

m. Karen
b. 1964 Sydney

David
b. 1992 Sydney

Jack
b. 1998 Sydney

2 Alexei & Ekaterina's children (part 1)

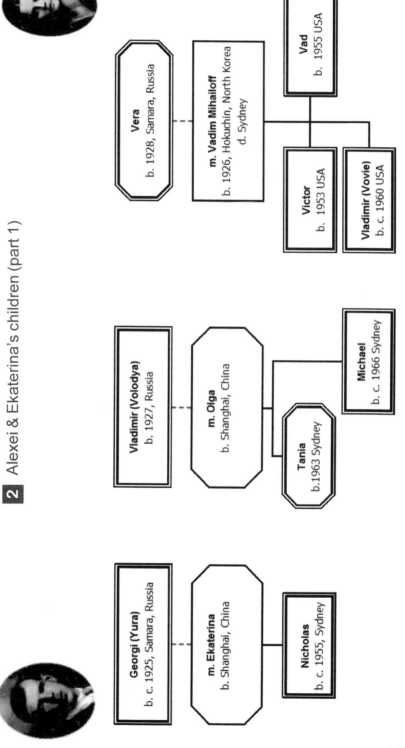

**Georgi (Yura)**
b. c. 1925, Samara, Russia

m. **Ekaterina**
b. Shanghai, China

**Nicholas**
b. c. 1955, Sydney

**Vladimir (Volodya)**
b. 1927, Russia

m. **Olga**
b. Shanghai, China

**Tania**
b.1963 Sydney

**Michael**
b. c. 1966 Sydney

**Vera**
b. 1928, Samara, Russia

m. **Vadim Mihailoff**
b. 1926, Hokuchin, North Korea
d. Sydney

**Vad**
b. 1955 USA

**Victor**
b. 1953 USA

**Vladimir (Vovie)**
b. c. 1960 USA

357

# 2 Alexei & Ekaterina's children (part 2)

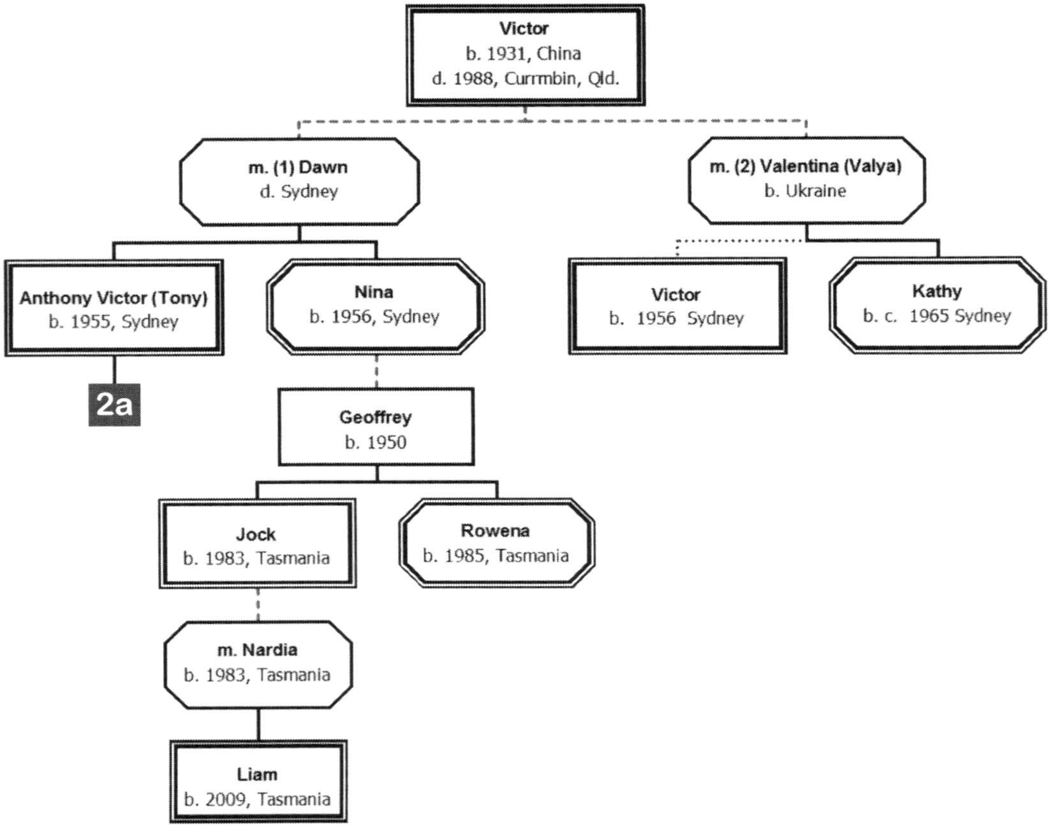

**Victor**
b. 1931, China
d. 1988, Currmbin, Qld.

**m. (1) Dawn**
d. Sydney

**m. (2) Valentina (Valya)**
b. Ukraine

**Victor**
b. 1956 Sydney

**Kathy**
b. c. 1965 Sydney

**Anthony Victor (Tony)**
b. 1955, Sydney

**2a**

**Nina**
b. 1956, Sydney

**Geoffrey**
b. 1950

**Jock**
b. 1983, Tasmania

**m. Nardia**
b. 1983, Tasmania

**Rowena**
b. 1985, Tasmania

**Liam**
b. 2009, Tasmania

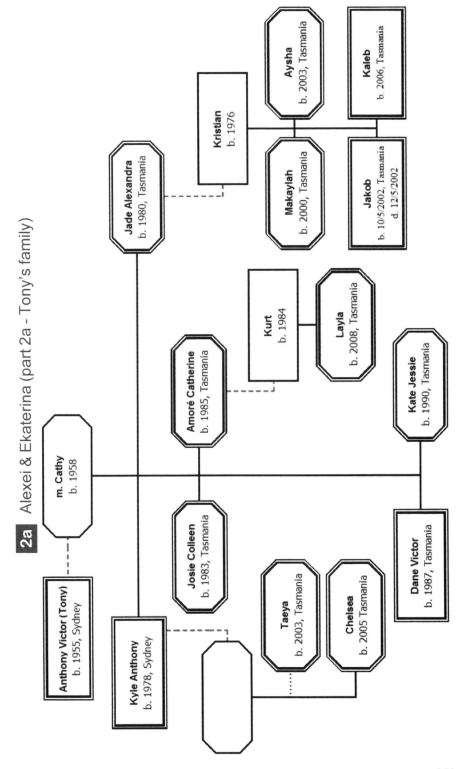

**2a** Alexei & Ekaterina (part 2a - Tony's family)

Anthony Victor (Tony)
b. 1955, Sydney

m. Cathy
b. 1958

Kyle Anthony
b. 1978, Sydney

Josie Colleen
b. 1983, Tasmania

Amoré Catherine
b. 1985, Tasmania

Jade Alexandra
b. 1980, Tasmania

Kristian
b. 1976

Taeya
b. 2003, Tasmania

Chelsea
b. 2005 Tasmania

Dane Victor
b. 1987, Tasmania

Kate Jessie
b. 1990, Tasmania

Kurt
b. 1984

Layla
b. 2008, Tasmania

Makaylah
b. 2000, Tasmania

Jakob
b. 10/5/2002, Tasmania
d. 12/5/2002

Aysha
b. 2003, Tasmania

Kaleb
b. 2006, Tasmania

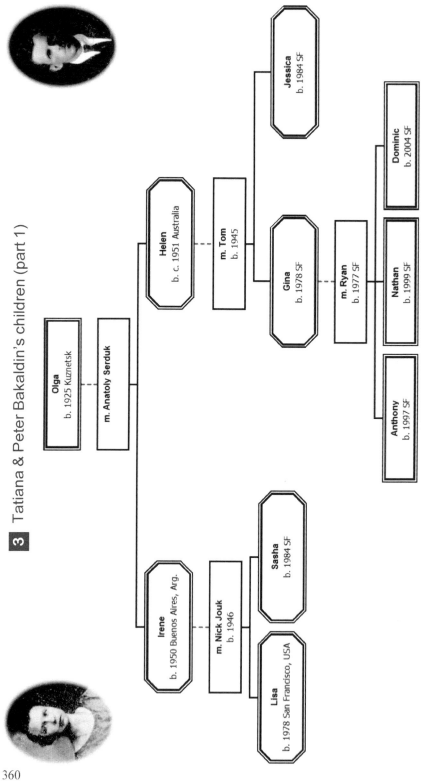

**3** Tatiana & Peter Bakaldin's children (part 1)

Olga
b. 1925 Kuznetsk

m. Anatoly Serduk

Irene
b. 1950 Buenos Aires, Arg.

m. Nick Jouk
b. 1946

Lisa
b. 1978 San Francisco, USA

Sasha
b. 1984 SF

Helen
b. c. 1951 Australia

m. Tom
b. 1945

Jessica
b. 1984 SF

Gina
b. 1978 SF

m. Ryan
b. 1977 SF

Anthony
b. 1997 SF

Nathan
b. 1999 SF

Dominic
b. 2004 SF

**3** Tatiana & Peter Bakaldin's children (part 2)

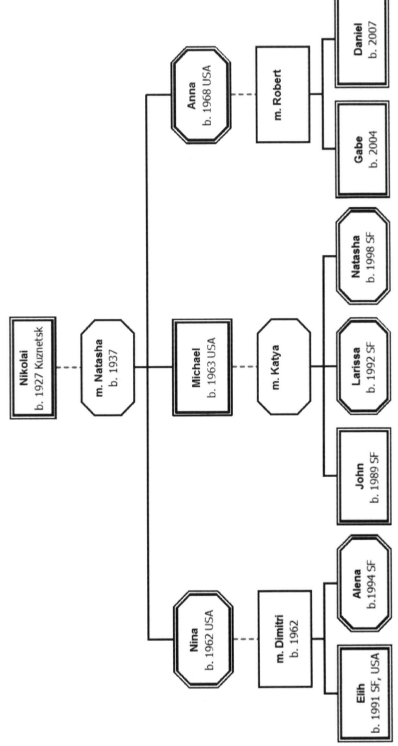

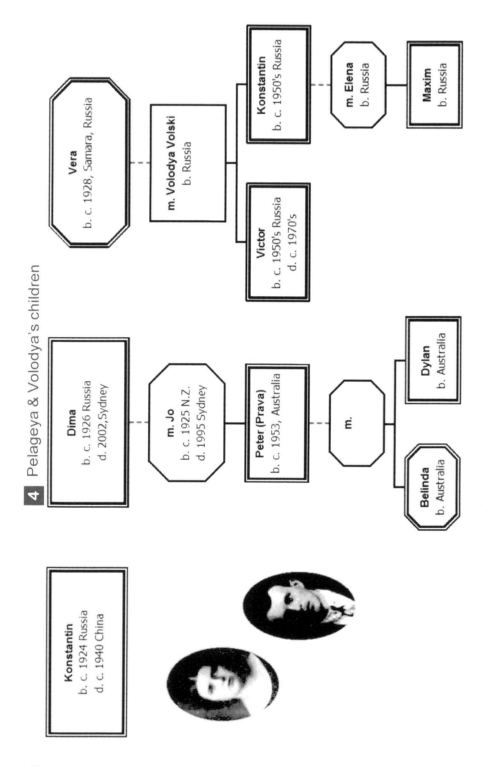

4 Pelageya & Volodya's children

**Konstantin**
b. c. 1924 Russia
d. c. 1940 China

**Dima**
b. c. 1926 Russia
d. 2002, Sydney

m. **Jo**
b. c. 1925 N.Z.
d. 1995 Sydney

**Peter (Prava)**
b. c. 1953, Australia

m.

**Belinda**
b. Australia

**Dylan**
b. Australia

**Vera**
b. c. 1928, Samara, Russia

m. **Volodya Volski**
b. Russia

**Victor**
b. c. 1950's Russia
d. c. 1970's

**Konstantin**
b. c. 1950's Russia

m. **Elena**
b. Russia

**Maxim**
b. Russia

# 5 Klavdia & Vassili's children

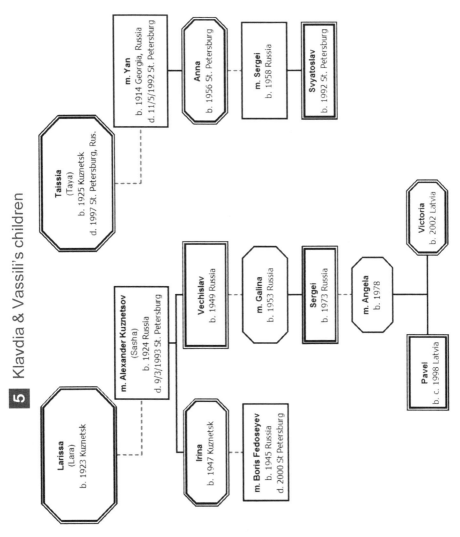

**Larissa**
(Lara)
b. 1923 Kuznetsk

**m. Alexander Kuznetsov**
(Sasha)
b. 1924 Russia
d. 9/3/1993 St. Petersburg

**Taissia**
(Taya)
b. 1925 Kuznetsk
d. 1997 St. Petersburg, Rus.

**m. Yan**
b. 1914 Georgia, Russia
d. 11/5/1992 St. Petersburg

**Anna**
b. 1956 St. Petersburg

**m. Sergei**
b. 1958 Russia

**Svyatoslav**
b. 1992 St. Petersburg

**Vechislav**
b. 1949 Russia

**m. Galina**
b. 1953 Russia

**Sergei**
b. 1973 Russia

**m. Angela**
b. 1978

**Victoria**
b. 2002 Latvia

**Pavel**
b. c. 1998 Latvia

**Irina**
b. 1947 Kuznetsk

**m. Boris Fedoseyev**
b. 1945 Russia
d. 2000 St Petersburg

363

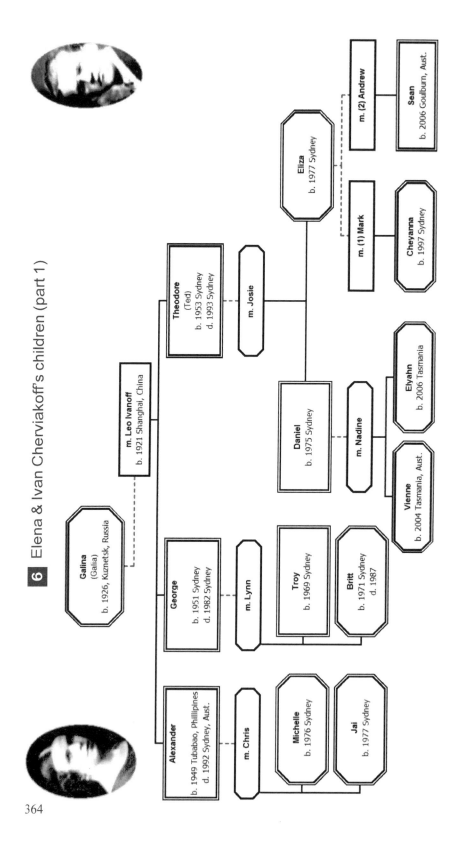

**6** Elena & Ivan Cherviakoff's children (part 1)

**Galina**
(Galia)
b. 1926, Kuznetsk, Russia

**m. Leo Ivanoff**
b. 1921 Shanghai, China

**Alexander**
b. 1949 Tubabao, Phillipines
d. 1992 Sydney, Aust.

m. Chris

**Michelle**
b. 1976 Sydney

**Jai**
b. 1977 Sydney

**George**
b. 1951 Sydney
d. 1982 Sydney

m. Lynn

**Troy**
b. 1969 Sydney

**Britt**
b. 1971 Sydney
d. 1987

**Theodore**
(Ted)
b. 1953 Sydney
d. 1993 Sydney

m. Josie

**Daniel**
b. 1975 Sydney

m. Nadine

**Vienne**
b. 2004 Tasmania, Aust.

**Elyahn**
b. 2006 Tasmania

**Eliza**
b. 1977 Sydney

**m. (1) Mark**

**Cheyanna**
b. 1997 Sydney

**m. (2) Andrew**

**Sean**
b. 2006 Goulburn, Aust.

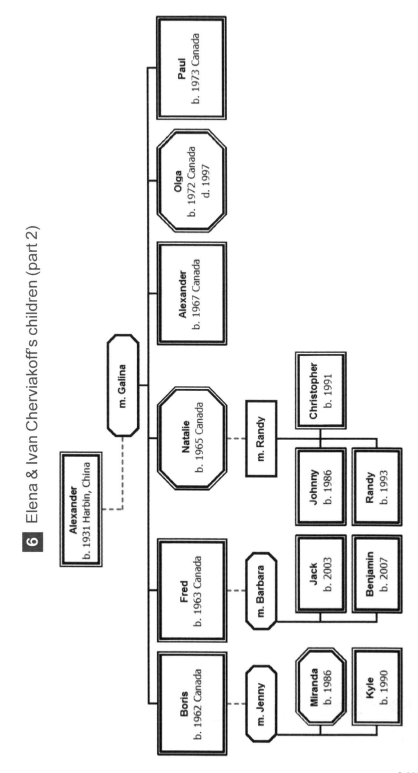

**6** Elena & Ivan Cherviakoff's children (part 2)

# 7 Alexandra & Grigori Nikomin's children

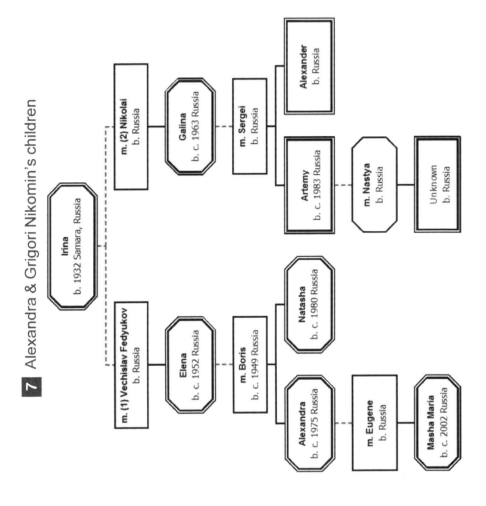

**Irina**
b. 1932 Samara, Russia

**m. (1) Vechislav Fedyukov**
b. Russia

**m. (2) Nikolai**
b. Russia

**Elena**
b. c. 1952 Russia

**Galina**
b. c. 1963 Russia

**m. Boris**
b. c. 1949 Russia

**m. Sergei**
b. Russia

**Natasha**
b. c. 1980 Russia

**Alexandra**
b. c. 1975 Russia

**Artemy**
b. c. 1983 Russia

**Alexander**
b. Russia

**m. Eugene**
b. Russia

**m. Nastya**
b. Russia

**Masha Maria**
b. c. 2002 Russia

Unknown
b. Russia

366

**8** Nikolai's children

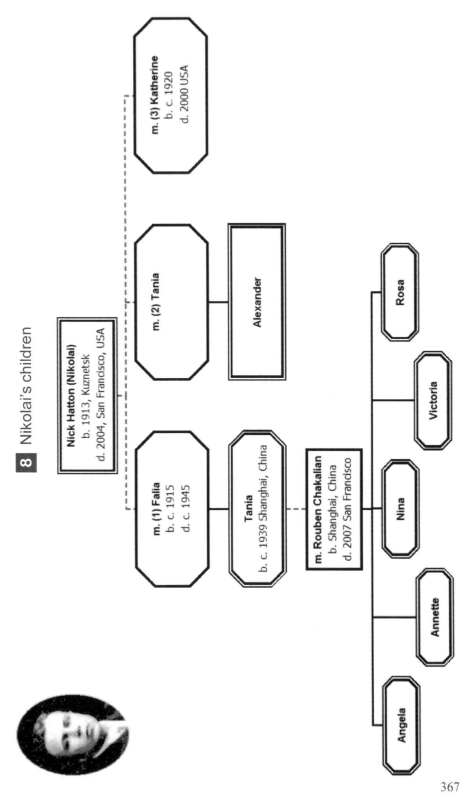

**Nick Hatton (Nikolai)**
b. 1913, Kuznetsk
d. 2004, San Francisco, USA

**m. (1) Falia**
b. c. 1915
d. c. 1945

**m. (2) Tania**

**m. (3) Katherine**
b. c. 1920
d. 2000 USA

**Alexander**

**Tania**
b. c. 1939 Shanghai, China

**m. Rouben Chakalian**
b. Shanghai, China
d. 2007 San Francisco

Angela

Annette

Nina

Victoria

Rosa

# Shalavin family tree.

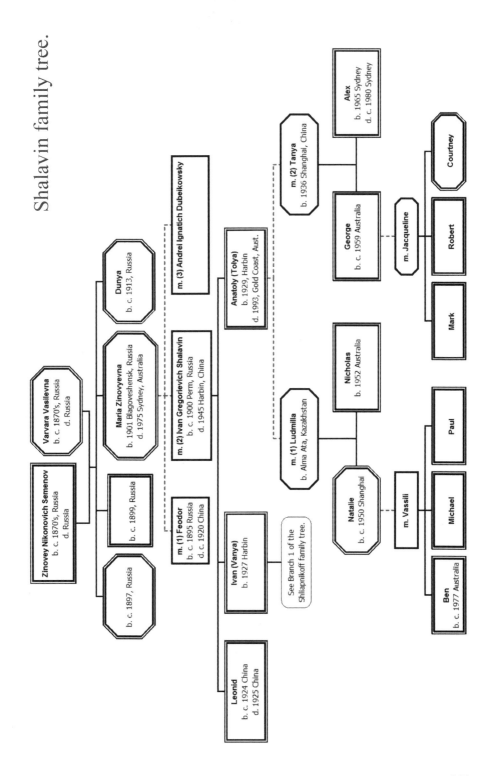

# Cyrillic alphabet

| *Alphabet* | | *Equivalent English sound.* |
|---|---|---|
| А | а | a, as in f*a*ther |
| Б | б | b |
| В | в | v |
| Г | г | g |
| Д | д | d |
| Е | е | e, as in y*e*t |
| Ё | ё | yo, as in ***you***r |
| Ж | ж | zh, as in vi*s*ion |
| З | з | z |
| И | и | I |
| Й | й | y, as in ma*y* |
| К | к | k |
| Л | л | l |
| М | м | m |
| Н | н | n |
| О | о | o |
| П | п | p |
| Р | р | r |
| С | с | s |
| Т | т | t |
| У | у | oo, as in b*oo*k |
| Ф | ф | f |
| Х | х | h |
| Ц | ц | ts, as in ma*ts* |

| Alphabet | | Equivalent English sound. |
|---|---|---|
| Ч | ч | ch |
| Ш | ш | sh |
| Щ | щ | shi, as in *she* |
| Ъ | ъ | hard sign |
| Ы | ы | indeterminate vowel, as in *a*bout |
| Ь | ь | soft sign, softens preceding consonant, as in *t*ulip |
| Э | э | open 'e' as in *a*ny |
| Ю | ю | yoo, as in *u*nite |
| Я | я | ya, as in *y*ard |

# References

## Chapter 1
### Setting the scene, a brief history of Russia.

1.      Wallace, R. 'Rise of Russia.'

2.      Kirchner, W. 'History of Russia'

3       Wallace, op. cit.

4       Brooman, 'Russia in war and revolution'.

5       Author's note:

*During the 1980's these countries, amongst others, had Communist regimes for varying lengths of time or were supported by them:*

USSR: Russia and 14 other republics, that have since gained their independence: Estonia, Latvia, Lithuania, Ukraine, Georgia, Uzbekistan, Tajikistan, Kirgizstan, Belarus, Kazakhstan, Turkmenistan, Azerbaijan, Armenia, Moldavia.

| | | |
|---|---|---|
| Afghanistan, | Albania, | Angola |
| Biafra, | Bulgaria, | China, |
| Costa Rica, | Cuba, | Czechoslovakia, |
| East Germany, | East Timor, | El Salvador, |
| Ethiopia, | Grenada, | Guatemala, |
| Hungary, | Kenya, | Libya, |
| Mongolia, | Mozambique, | North Korea, |
| Poland, | Romania, | Vietnam, |
| Western Sahara, | Yugoslavia | |

*It seems to be a phase that countries emerging from colonialism had to pass through, rather like the maturing phase of an individual. As the famous maxim declares*, 'If a man is not a Communist at 20 he has no heart, if he is still one at 40 he has no brain'.

6       *England in the late 18th century had developed a climate of enterprise which allowed a small handful of men to make revolutionary technical advances, first in textiles, which led to*

the birth of the factory system, then in iron making and other industries. Whole village populations of peasant farmers moved to factory work in order to benefit from the higher wages and greater security offered by it. In the process, a new middle class emerged. Factory owners, industrialists, traders, craftspeople, engineers, shopkeepers and a host of others, many of them drawn from the ranks of the workers themselves. The process was spontaneous, driven by individuals and entirely voluntary, fuelled by the laws of supply and demand, which Adam Smith so eloquently spelt out in 'The Wealth of Nations'. The key to his insight is division of labour, where each worker does what he is best suited to and buys his other necessities from those who also do the same, each engaging in commerce for mutual benefit. Thus, each person pursuing his own self interest would result in optimum economic growth for society at large, as if guided by an 'invisible hand'. "It is not from the benevolence of the butcher, the brewer, or the baker that we expect our dinner, but from their regard to their own interest. We address ourselves, not to their humanity but to their self-love, and never talk to them of our own necessities but of their advantages. Nobody but a beggar chooses to depend chiefly upon the benevolence of his fellow citizens." Indeed not.

7    Ashton, T.S. 'The Industrial Revolution 1760-1830'.

8    www.spartacus.schoolnet.co.uk

9    Warnes, D, 'Russia: A modern History'.

10   Radway, R. 'Russia and the USSR'.

11   Ignatieff, M. 'The Russian Album'.

12   Brooman, op. cit.

13   Warnes, op. cit.

14   Radway, op. cit.

15   Brooman, op. cit.

16   Oakley, J. 'Rasputin'.

17   Note on Gregorian and Julian calendars:
     The Russian calendar was based on the Roman Julian calendar (named after Julius Caesar) whereas the majority of the world had, by the time of the Russian Revolution, adopted the

*Gregorian calendar (named after Pope Gregory who introduced it in the 7th century). The Julian calendar falls behind the Gregorian calendar by one day every hundred years. By the 20th century it was 13 days behind, hence the February revolution took place in March by the Gregorian calendar and the October revolution in November. When the Soviet Union subsequently adopted the Gregorian calendar, in line with the rest of the world, the Orthodox Church and many exiled Russians refused to recognise the change, it being a 'Communist' action. To this day they still celebrate Christmas on the 7th of January.*

18  Warnes, op. cit.

19  Ibid

20  Radway, op. cit.

21  Time-watch (History program on British TV)

22  Reed, J. 'Ten days that shook the world'.
*An American journalist's account of the Russian Revolution. Reed was present in Russia at the time. He was sympathetic to Communism and the Soviets made much play of this, even composing a song on his behalf, 'John Reed walks in Petrograd', regularly churned out by the Red Army choir. He died a broken man in Russia, sickly and disillusioned but the song in his honour endured for many more decades. Warren Beatty movingly portrayed his story in the film 'Reds'.*

## Chapter 2
## The emergence of the Union of Soviet Socialist Republics.

1.  Radway, R. 'Russia and the USSR'.

2.  Ibid

3   Ibid

4   Kluge, K. 'Konstantin Kluge'.

5   Brooman, J. 'Russia in war and revolution'.

6   Radway, R. op. cit.

7   Brooman, J. op. cit.

8    *By 1992 at least some of the mystery had been solved. Bones discovered in a pit in Ekaterinburg were taken to Britain for forensic analysis. The new technology of DNA matching linked these bones with the DNA of the current Duke of Edinburgh, Prince Philip, who is a great nephew of the Tsarina. The analysis confirmed that the bones did indeed belong to the Tsarina, four other members of her family and four unrelated individuals, according to the British newspaper 'The Independent' (quoted in Radway). The others were presumably the family's doctor and three servants. Two bodies could not be accounted for, Alexei and one of his sisters, possibly Anastasia or Maria. The remains of the rest of the family and their retinue were interred in St Petersburg's St Peter and Paul Cathedral, exactly 80 years after their execution.*
*23rd August 2007: a Russian archaeologist discovers the burned, partial skeletons of a boy between the age of 10-13 and a young woman between 18-23, near Ekaterinburg.*
*30th April 2008: Russian forensic scientists announced that DNA testing proves that the remains discovered in 2007 are those of Tsarevich Alexei and one of his sisters.*

9    Radway, R. op. cit.

10    Warnes, D. 'Russia: A modern history'.

11    Ibid

12    Homburger, quoted in Reed, J. '10 days that shook the world'.

13    Nove, A. quoted in Warnes, D. op. cit.

14    Radway, R. op. cit.

15    Warnes, D. op. cit.

16    Brooman, J. 'Stalin and the Soviet Union'.

17    Chamberlain, W. in 'Russian Review',
      quoted in Warnes, D. op. cit.

18    Kravchenko, V. 'I Chose Freedom', quoted in Parsons, H. 'Russia and the USSR, 1905-1964'.

19    Muggeridge, M. From R. Conquest's 'Harvest of Sorrow', quoted in Parsons, H. op. cit.

20    Radway, R. op. cit.

21    Chamberlain, W. op. cit.

## Chapter 3
## **Exodus from Russia.**

1    Warnes, D, 'Russia: A modern History'.

## Chapter 4
## **China and life in Harbin.**

1.   Brooman, J. 'Imperial China'.

2    Ibid

3    Ibid

4    Macdonald, J. 'Modern China'.

5    Ibid

6    Brooman, J. op. cit.

7    Polytechnic Journal, published by former Harbin residents, Sydney, Australia.

8    Behr, E. 'The Last Emperor'.
     (See also the excellent film of the same name.)

9    Macdonald, J. op. cit.

10   Ibid

11   Ibid

12   Ibid.

## Chapter 5
## **Shanghai, city of wonder.**

1    Jiganoff, Capt. V. D. 'Russians in Shanghai'.

2    Kuhn, I.C. 'Shanghai – the vintage years', article in 'Gourmet', 1986; supplied by members of Russian Historical Association, Sydney.

3    Fortune magazine, January 1935.

4    Jiganoff, V. op. cit.

## Chapter 6
## Tubabao, Philippines - a tropical interlude.

1    Bologoff, Colonel quoted in 'Tubabao - Russian Refugee camp, Philippines, 1949-1951', published by the Russian Historical Association, Sydney, 1999.

2    Ibid

3    Kluge, Konstantin in 'Tubabao' op. cit.

4    Miram, Oleg  op. cit.

5    'Manila Times' op. cit.

6    Tatarinoff, Kyra op. Cit.

7    Miram, O. op. cit.

8    Ivanoff, Galina 'The Ivanoff story' (privately published).

9    Sokoloff, V. op. cit.

10    *In addition to the single cross bar of the familiar Latin crucifix, the Orthodox cross has a smaller top bar and diagonal lower bar, the precise meaning of which is subject to debate. The top bar is generally accepted to represent the plaque nailed to Jesus' cross bearing the inscription Iesus Nazarenus Rex Iudaeorum (meaning Jesus the Nazorean, King of the Jews).*

*The lower bar is a little more contentious but the most widely accepted interpretation is that it represents the incorporation of the cross of St. Andrew, the patron saint of Russia, who was martyred on an X-shaped cross for preaching Christianity. He is reputed to have requested an X-shaped cross because he did not believe himself worthy of dying on the same shaped cross as Jesus.*

*Other interpretations are that it represents the step onto which Jesus' feet were nailed or the fate of the two criminals crucified along with Jesus. The side pointing up represents St. Dismas, who, having shown remorse and asked for Christ's forgiveness, ascended to heaven. The other side points down to hell, the fate that awaited the other, unrepentant criminal.*

11    Sokoloff, V. op. cit.

# Chapter 7
## Australia, the promised land.

1    *A term of abuse by Australians to those English people who complained that Australia did not live up to their expectations. Some say 'Poms' originated from the pomegranates English sailors were told to eat in the 18th century to ward off scurvy. This discovery was credited to the great English seaman and explorer Captain James Cook, the 'discoverer' of Australia. (Americans call English 'limies' as they ate limes for the same reason). Others claim POM stood for Prisoners of Mother (England).*

2    *The Petrovs were a Russian 'diplomat' and his wife who were working in Australia for the USSR, as genuine Soviet spies. In 1954 they decided to defect, asking Australia for political asylum. However, KGB agents (the Russian secret service) tried to force them to return. They were literally being manhandled onto the plane when the Australian authorities intervened at the last minute. The KGB agents returned empty handed.*

3    *Ayn Rand is a Russian born philosopher who fled St. Petersburg in the 1920's to find success and fame as a novelist in America. Passionately anti-Communist she is one of the very few 20th century philosophers to offer a genuine and comprehensive alternative to that doctrine. Her major works are listed in the Bibliography.*


# Chapter 8
## World War II and its aftermath, the people left behind.

1    Brooman, J. 'China since 1900'.

2    Ibid

3    Macdonald, C. 'China since 1900'.

4    Ibid

5    Ibid

6    Ibid

7    Ibid

8    Ibid

9    Ibid

10   Brooman, J. op. cit.

11   Parsons, H. 'Russia and the USSR, 1905-1964'.

12   Brooman, J. 'Stalin and the Soviet Union'.

13   Ibid

14   *North Korea is one of the last remaining Communist states (in 2007) and considerably poorer than South Korea. According to several sources (including CNN.com) its GDP is 21 billion (of which it spends 5 on arms) versus the South's GDP of 853 billion (of which it spends 15.5 on arms).*

15   Fisher, P. 'The Great Power Conflict after 1945'.

16   Ibid

17   www.Budapest-life.com/budapest/1956-hungarian-uprising
     *Sources before 1989 claim the numbers killed by the Soviets were 30,000 (e.g. Fisher) but since the fall of the USSR new documents give the numbers ranging from 2,500 up to 4,000.*

## Chapter 9
### Coming full circle - happy reunions.

1    Fisher, P. 'The Great Power Conflict after 1945'.

2    Radway, R. 'Russia and the USSR'.

3    Ibid.

## Chapter 10
### Russia and China moving into the 21st century.

1    Brierley, M. 'Good news from Russia',
     Personal Perspectives No. 14, published by the Libertarian Alliance (www.libertarian.co.uk).

2. *One final note on 'Capitalism' in general. Many readers may have assumed by my simplistic usage of the term that 'Western' nations I have referred to, particularly, USA, Britain but also Australia, Canada and indeed Western Europe, are exponents of this system. They are not. They are mere approximations only. All of these countries as well as Eastern nations that profess to have free enterprise systems, such as Singapore, Japan, South Korea, Taiwan, Malaysia amongst many others, actually have 'mixed economies' with varying proportions of state control.*

*We must be careful not to look at such economies with their myriad examples of tariffs, price control, subsidised industries, direct, indirect taxes, VAT, 'social security' and so on and then condemn 'private enterprise' for the resulting dislocations and inefficiencies. If one is genuinely concerned with the plight of the world's poor, then genuine capitalism, the solution to poverty is worth studying in more detail. The 'Economic notes' in the web site quoted in point 1 above is a good a place to start. The 'General' section of the following Bibliography is also recommended.*

Chapter 11

## Next generation, the families today.

1. *The Economist,* November 19th 1998.
'Life in the Russian army'.

# Bibliography/Further reading

## Russia

Brooman, J.          **Russia in war and revolution** *Longman, 1986*
                     **Stalin and the Soviet Union** *Longman, 1988*

Dostoevsky, F.       **The Idiot** *Penguin, 1955*

Fisher, P.           **The Great Power Conflict**
                     *Stanley Thornes, 1998*

Gogol,N.             **Dead Souls** *Everyman's Library, 2004*

Ignatieff, M.        **The Russian Album** *Vintage, 1997*

Kirchner, W.         **History of Russia** *Barnes and Noble, 1964*

Lermontov, M.        **A hero of our time**
                     *Foreign Language Publishing House*

Parsons, H.          **Russia and the USSR, 1905-1964**
                     *Thomas Nelson and sons, 1994*

Pushkin, A.          **Eugene Onegin** *Penguin, 1977*
                     **Dubrovsky**
                     *Foreign languages Publishing House, 1955*

Radway, R.           **Russia and the USSR** *Stanley Thornes, 1996*

Reed, J.             **10 days that shook the world** *Sutton, 1997*

Simkin, J.           **The Russian Revolution**
                     *Spartacus International, 1986*

Solzhenitsyn, A.     **Gulag Archipelago** *Harper Perennial, 2007*

Tolstoy, N.          **Resurrection** *Penguin, 1966*

Volkogonov, D.       **Lenin, Life and Legacy** *Harper Collins, 1995*

Wallace, R.          **Rise of Russia. (Time-Life books)**
                     *Time Inc. 1967*

Warnes, D.           **Russia: A Modern History**
                     *University Tutorial Press, 1984*

| Westwood, J. | **Endurance and Endeavour,**<br>**Russian history 1812 -1980**<br>*Oxford University Press, 1973* |
|---|---|

# China

| Behr, E. | **The Last Emperor** *Macdonald, 1987* |
|---|---|
| Brooman, J. | **Imperial China** *Longman, 1991*<br>**China since 1900** *Longman, 1998* |
| Macdonald, C.K. | **Modern China** *Basil Blackwell, 1985* |

# General

*For those readers interested in studying the principles of liberty and how and why they should be upheld.*

Rand, Ayn

**We the Living** *Penguin, 1936*

*A love story set in Russia in the 1920's, passionate and persuasive. An eyewitness account of Lenin's Russia.*

**Capitalism, the unknown ideal**
*New American Library, 1967*

*The name says it all. A much maligned system that meets man's material and moral needs.*

**Atlas Shrugged** *Penguin, 1959*

*Rand's Magnum Opus – a brilliant philosophical novel that upholds individual freedom, by demonstrating what happens when the giants of industry who move the world go on strike. Set in a futuristic America.*

**The Virtues of Selfishness**
*New American Library, 1961*

*A collection of essays that shows how a rational concern with 'self' is the necessary condition for social progress.*

| Smith, A. | **Wealth of Nations** *Penguin, 1982 (Orig. 1776)* |
| | *Considered the 'Father of Economics', he is the first thinker to explain why some nations are richer than others.* |
| Hazlitt, H. | **Economics in one lesson** *Ernest Benn, 1947* |
| | *A very readable and enlightening explanation of general economic principles, bringing Adam Smith's ideas into the modern age.* |
| Hayek, F. A. | **Road to Serfdom** *Routledge and Kegan Paul, 1944* |
| | *A convincing and powerful argument depicting the dangers of creeping socialism.* |
| Friedman, M. and R. | **Free to Choose** *Harvest, 1990* |
| | *Milton is a Nobel Prize winner for Economics. In this book he and his wife Rose explore the connection between political and economic freedom. Through a series of powerful essays they describe the negative consequences of government interference in the economy. Well meaning laws are always counterproductive. Wonderful reading.* |
| Friedman, D. | **Machinery of Freedom** *Open Court, 1989* |
| | *A fascinating collection of articles that demonstrate how the principles of economic freedom can be applied in practice, without relying on the state. David goes further than his distinguished father Milton, in upholding the ideas of what is often described as anarcho-capitalism.* |

## Internet references

www.libertarian.co.uk